FORGOT TO
DRAW
KENSHIN'S
SWORD!

NO
FOLLOW
THRU

THE COVER'S DONE FOR THE

SOUTH COUNTY

Volume
Cover

...THAT NEEDS TAKING CARE OF,
AND I DIDN'T WANT TO BOTHER
... SO ... DOING THE
... IT WAS FUN, ACTUALLY; I
... THE FUTURE, I'D
... MUCH OF IT AS I
CAN ... ... 'S WHAT I
... ENOUGH ... BEEN DOING ALL
ALONG ... DOES THAT MAKE ME A
BAD PERSON...?

Rurouni Kenshin, which has found
fans not only in Japan but around
the world, first made its appearance
in 1992, as an original short story in
Weekly Shonen Jump Special. Later
rewritten and published as a regular,
continuing ***Jump*** series in 1994,
Rurouni Kenshin ended serialization
in 1999 but continued in popularity,
as evidenced by the 2000 publica-
tion of ***Yahiko no Sakabatô***
("Yahiko's Reversed-Edge Sword")
in ***Weekly Shonen Jump***. His most
current work, ***Busô Renkin***
("Armored Alchemist"), began publi-
cation in June 2003, also in ***Jump***.

RUROUNI KENSHIN
VOL. 7: IN THE 11TH YEAR OF MEIJI, MAY 14TH
SHONEN JUMP Manga Edition

STORY AND ART BY
NOBUHIRO WATSUKI

English Adaptation/Gerard Jones
Translation/Kenichiro Yagi
Touch-Up Art & Lettering/Steve Dutro
Graphics, Cover Design & Layout/Sean Lee
Editor/Avery Gotoh

VP, Production/Alvin Lu
VP, Sales & Product Marketing/Gonzalo Ferreyra
VP, Creative/Linda Espinosa
Publisher/Hyoe Narita

Printed in the U.S.A.

Published by VIZ, LLC
P.O. Box 77010 • San Francisco, CA 94107

10 9 8 7 6 5 4 3 2
First printing, September 2004
Second printing, July 2009

www.viz.com

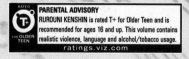

PARENTAL ADVISORY
RUROUNI KENSHIN is rated T+ for Older Teen and is recommended for ages 16 and up. This volume contains realistic violence, language and alcohol/tobacco usage.
ratings.viz.com

Rurouni Kenshin

MEIJI SWORDSMAN ROMANTIC STORY

Vol. 7: IN THE 11TH YEAR OF MEIJI, MAY 14TH

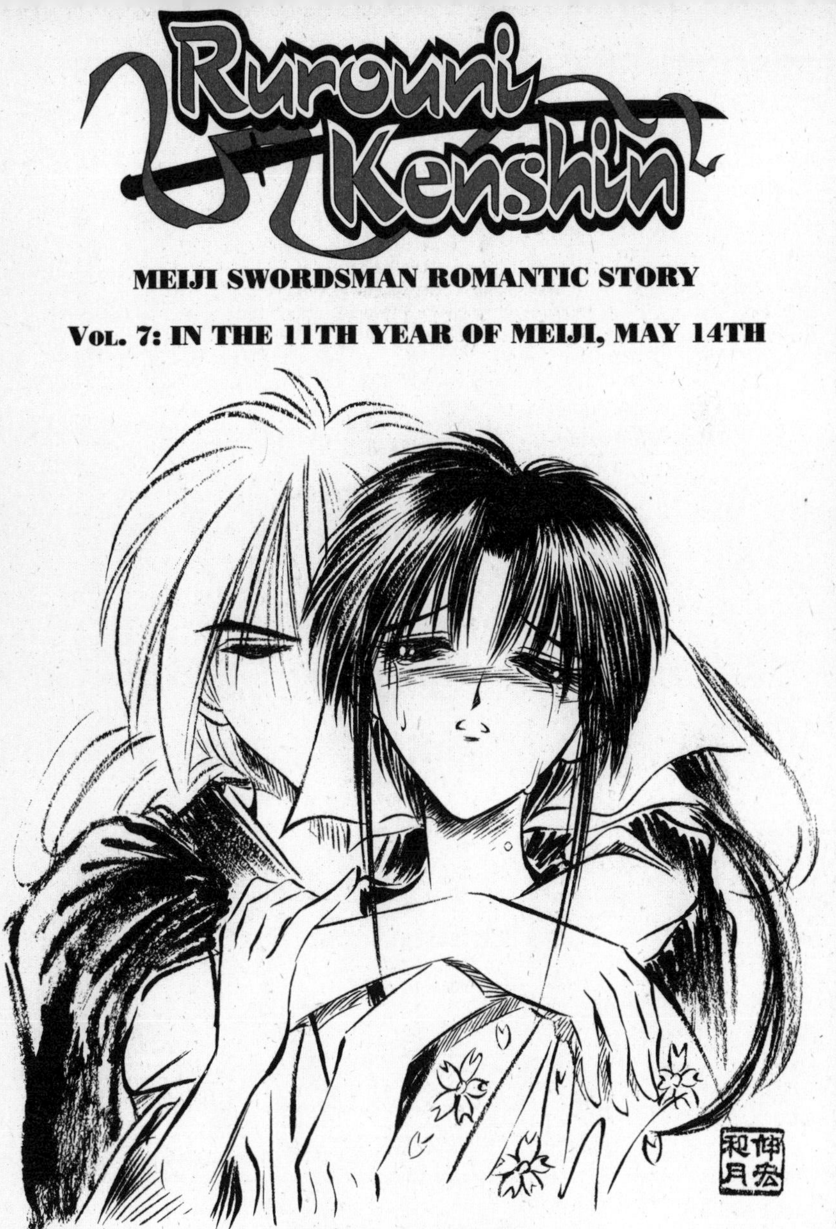

STORY AND ART BY

NOBUHIRO WATSUKI

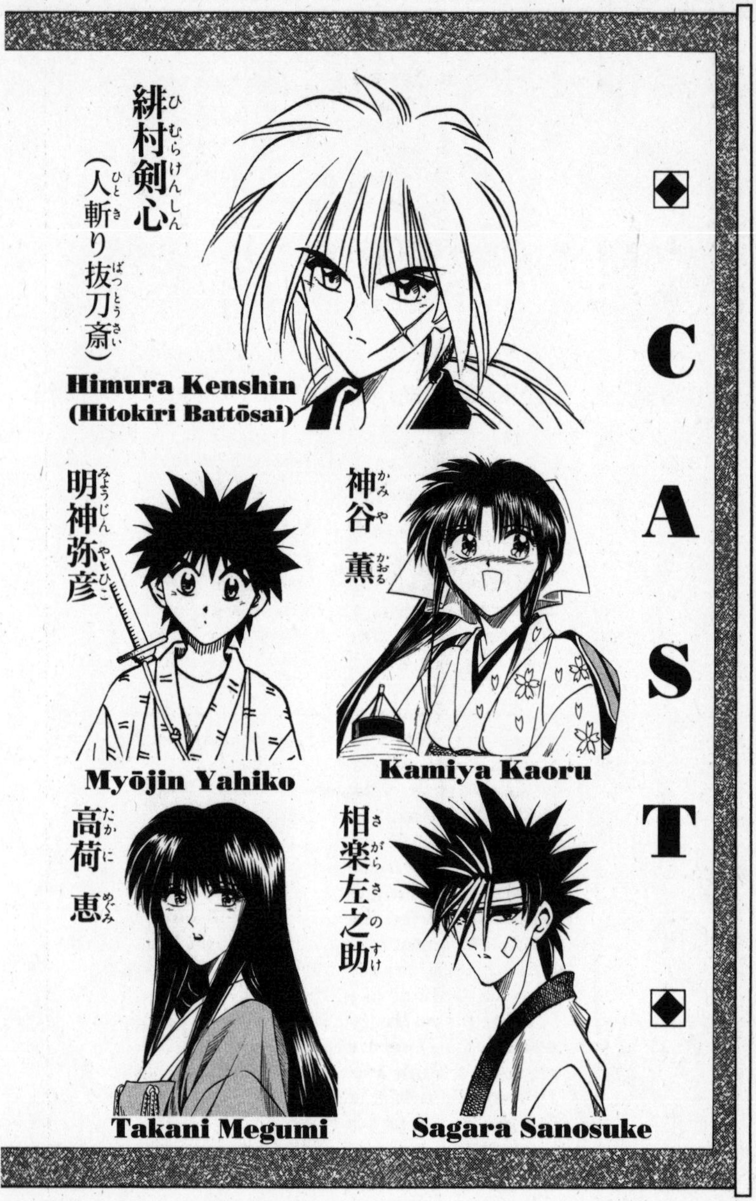
CAST
緋村剣心
(人斬り抜刀斎)
Himura Kenshin
(Hitokiri Battōsai)
神谷 薫
Kamiya Kaoru
明神弥彦
Myōjin Yahiko
相楽左之助
Sagara Sanosuke
高荷 恵
Takani Megumi

るろうに剣心

Akamatsu Arundo

赤末有人（あかまつあるんど）

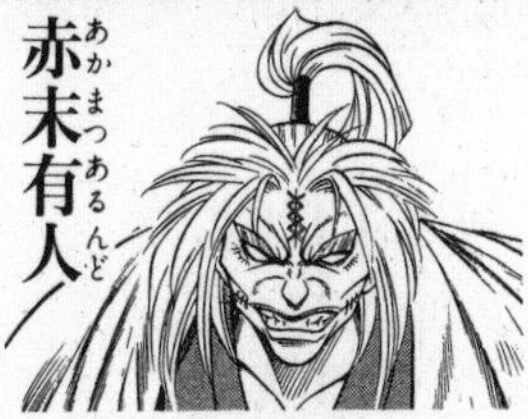

斎藤一（さいとうはじめ）

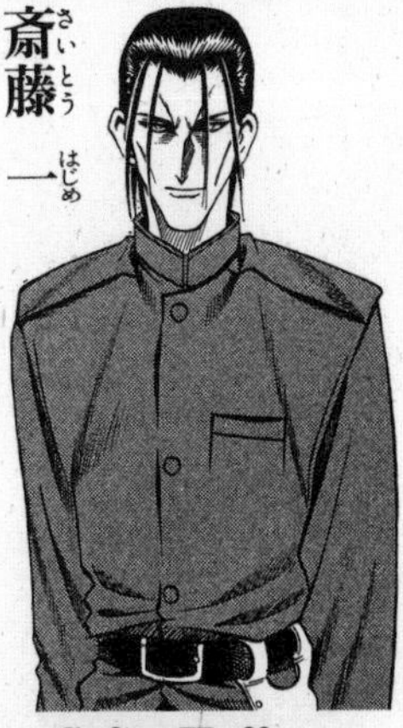

Saitō Hajime

大久保利通（おおくぼとしみち）

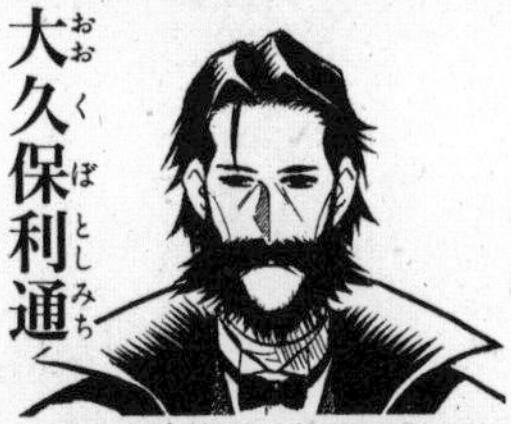

Ōkubo Toshimichi

THUS FAR

Himura Kenshin, the man who carries a *sakabatō* to prohibit himself from killing people. Once he was known as *hitokiri*—the assassin Himura Battōsai, a legend of incomparable awe among the pro-Imperialist *Ishin Shishi* patriots who fought for the new era—but, since the end of the civil war, he has been *rurouni*. After solving the case of the "fake Battōsai," Kenshin has remained at the Kamiya dojo, where Kamiya Kaoru is the acting instructor. Soon after, Myōjin Yahiko—a young man Kenshin saved from the yakuza—joined the dojo, which had lost all its students. Sagara Sanosuke, who gave up being a "fight merchant" after meeting Kenshin, goes in and out of the dojo frequently, making it a far more lively place than when Kaoru used to live there alone. Changing the assassin's blade into a weapon that cannot kill, *rurouni* Kenshin freely continues to defend the people. His next adventure is....

CONTENTS

RUROUNI KENSHIN
Meiji Swordsman Romantic Story
BOOK SEVEN: IN THE 11th YEAR OF MEIJI, MAY 14th

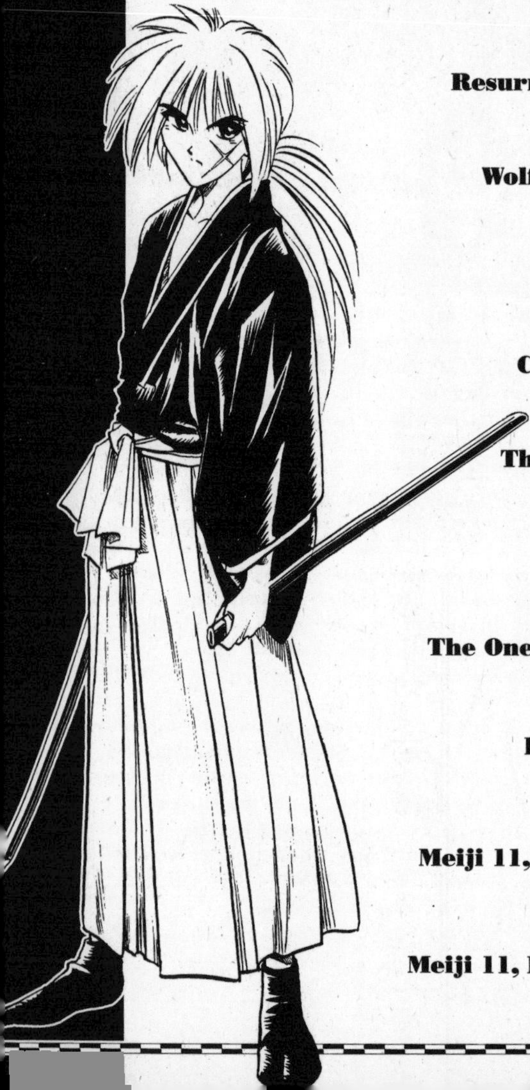

Act 48—Resurrection of the Wolf

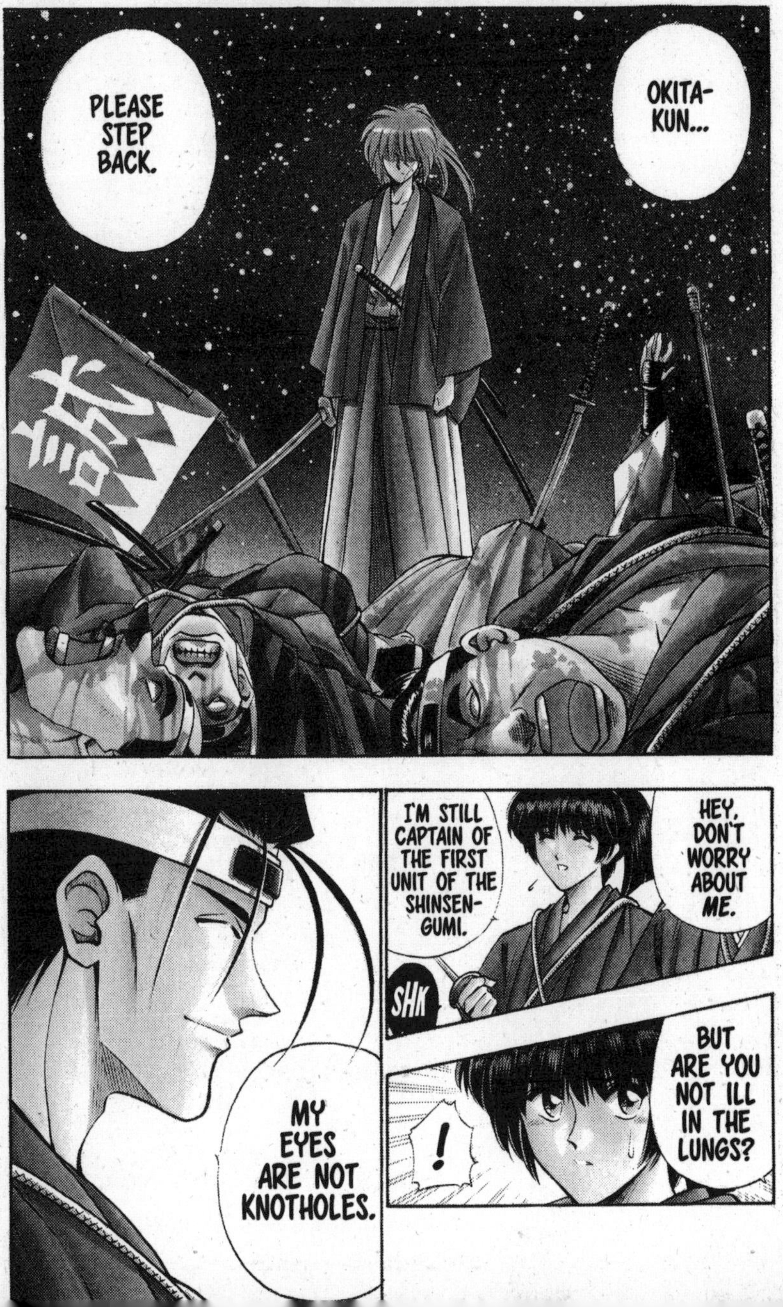
OKITA-KUN...
PLEASE STEP BACK.
HEY, DON'T WORRY ABOUT ME.
I'M STILL CAPTAIN OF THE FIRST UNIT OF THE SHINSEN-GUMI.
SHK
BUT ARE YOU NOT ILL IN THE LUNGS?
!
MY EYES ARE NOT KNOTHOLES.

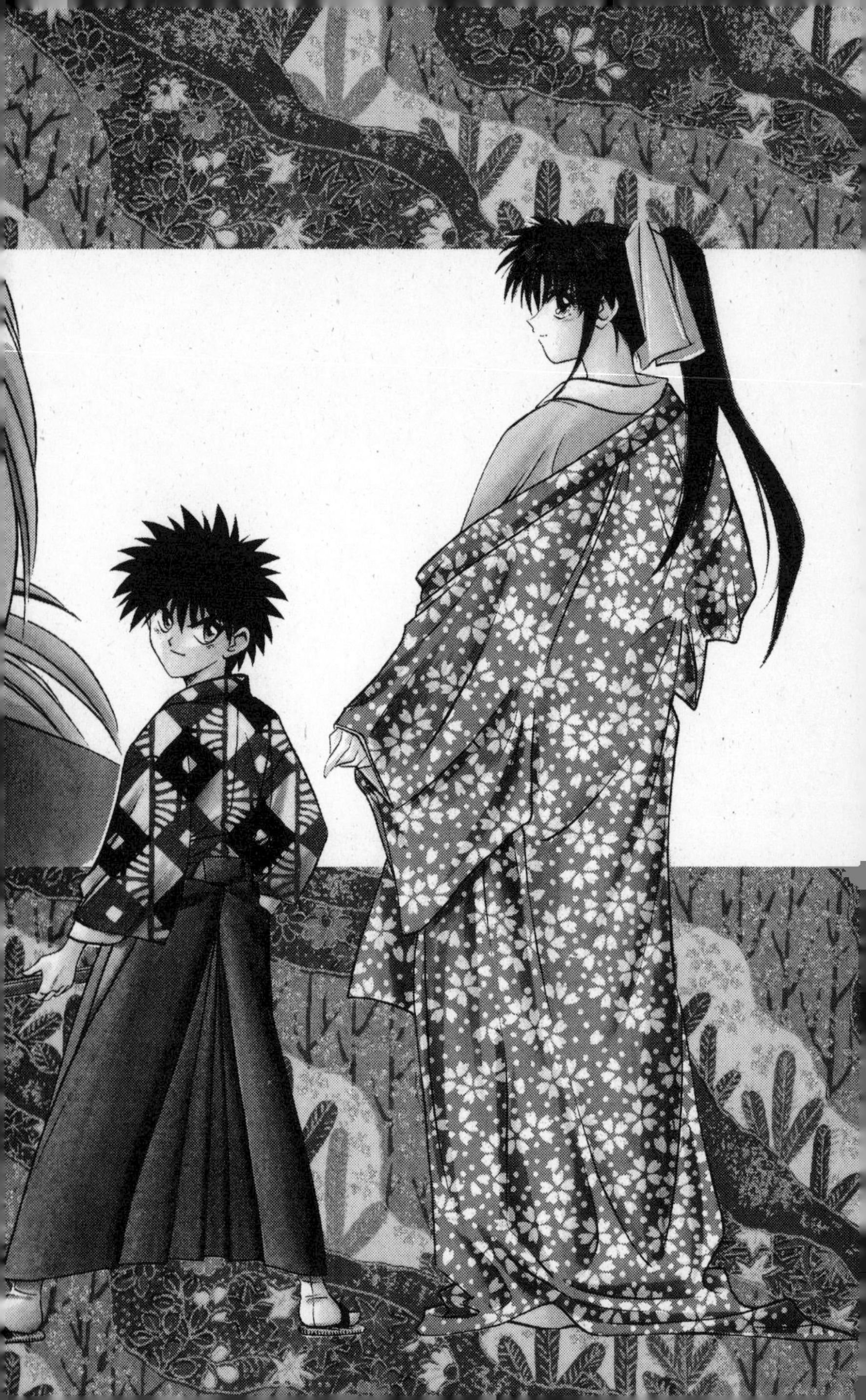

Act 48
Resurrection of the Wolf

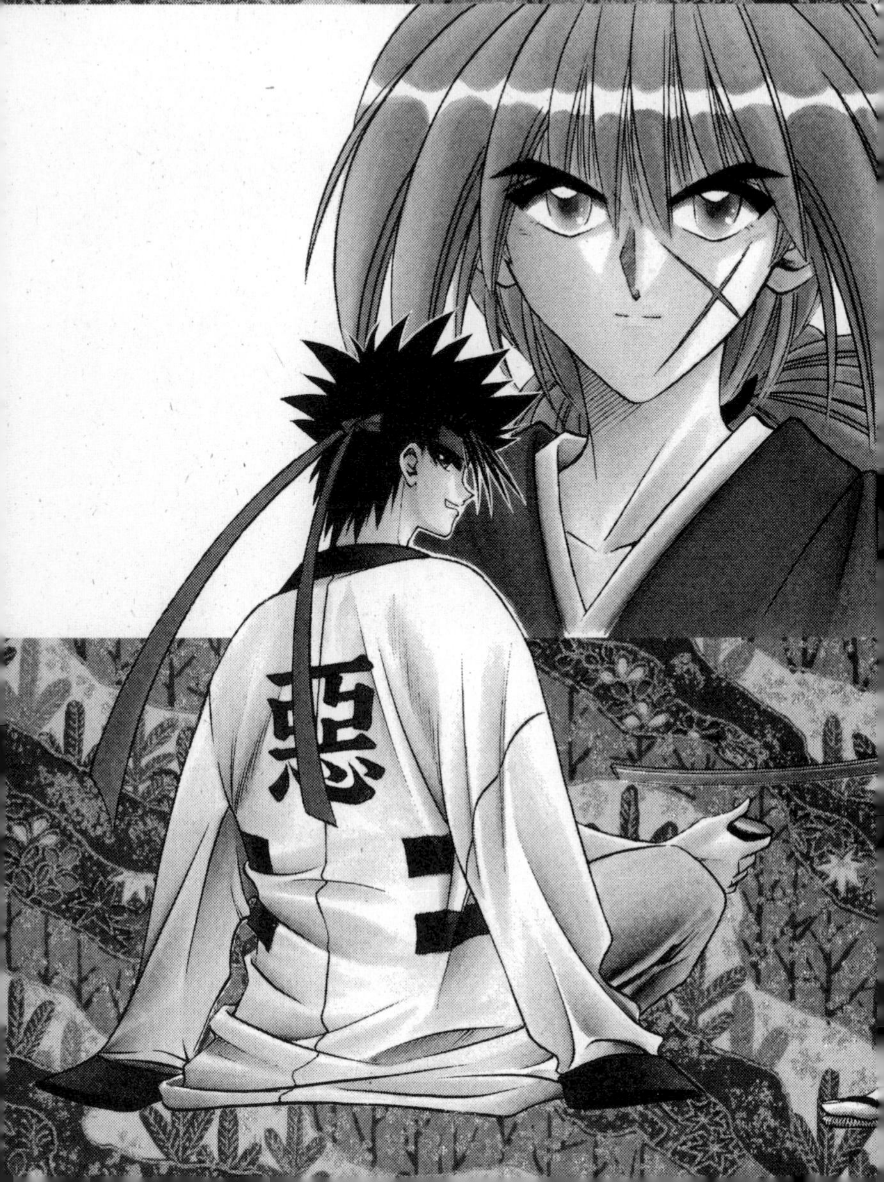
悪

READ THIS WAY

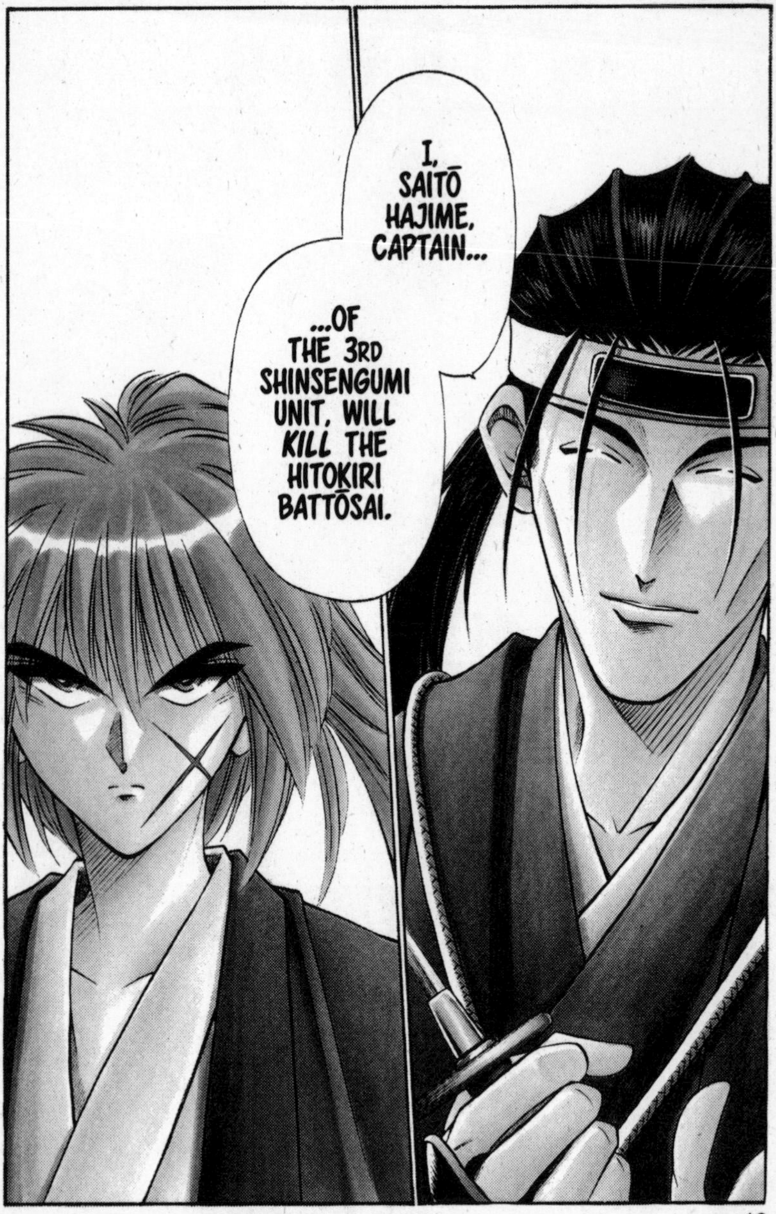
I, SAITŌ HAJIME, CAPTAIN...
...OF THE 3RD SHINSENGUMI UNIT, WILL *KILL* THE HITOKIRI BATTŌSAI.

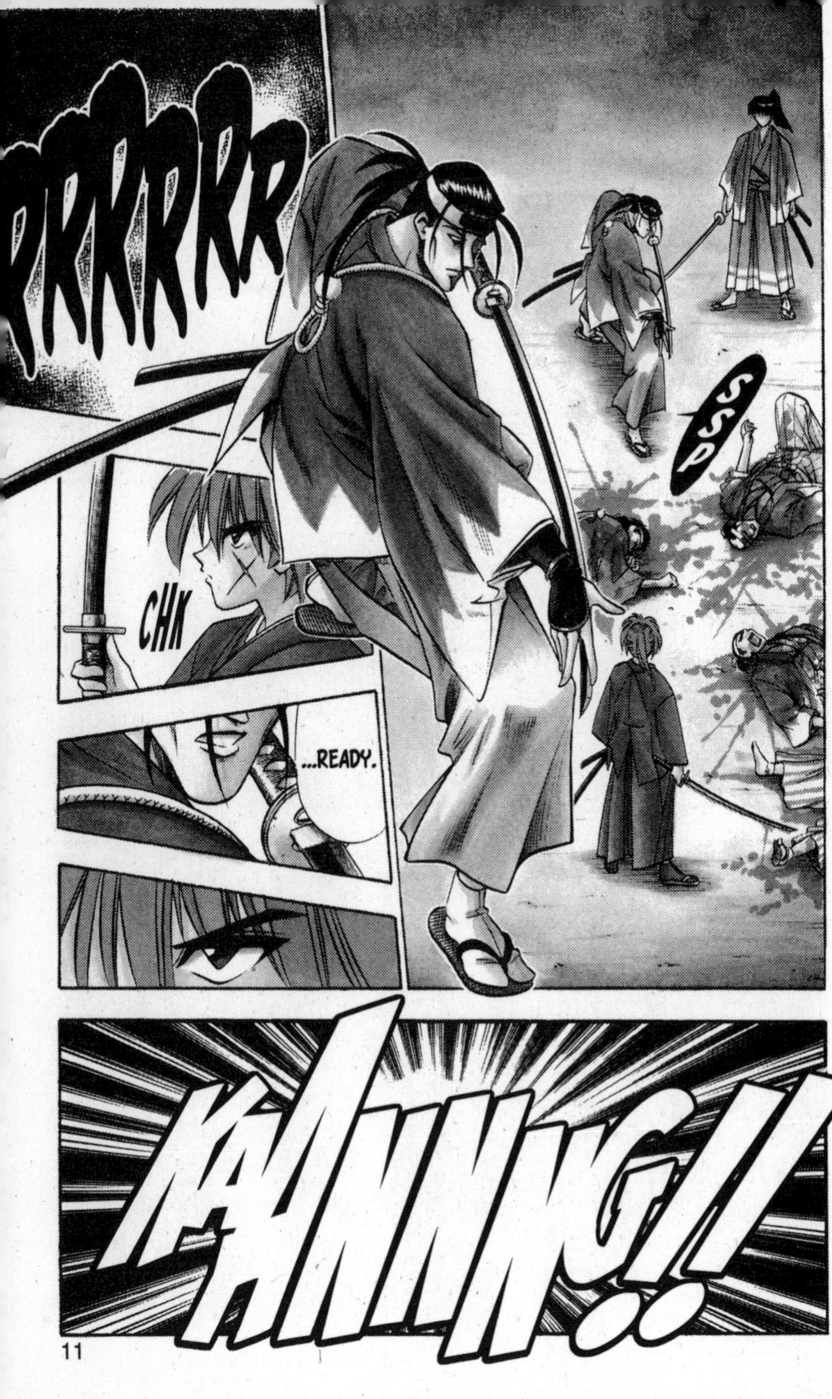
SSP
RRRRRRR
CHK
...READY.
KANNG!!

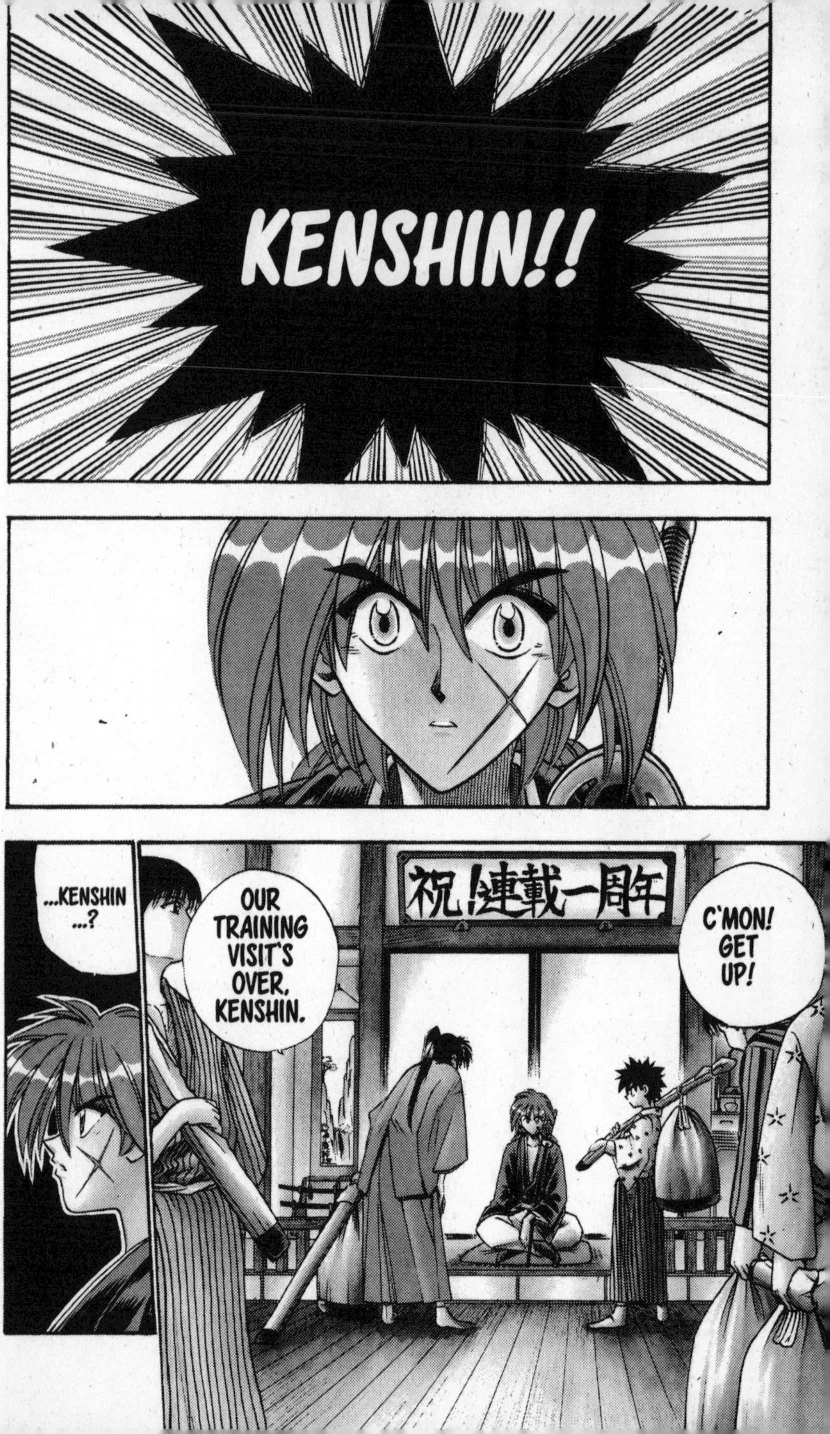
KENSHIN!!
C'MON! GET UP!
祝!連載一周年
OUR TRAINING VISIT'S OVER, KENSHIN.
...KENSHIN ...?

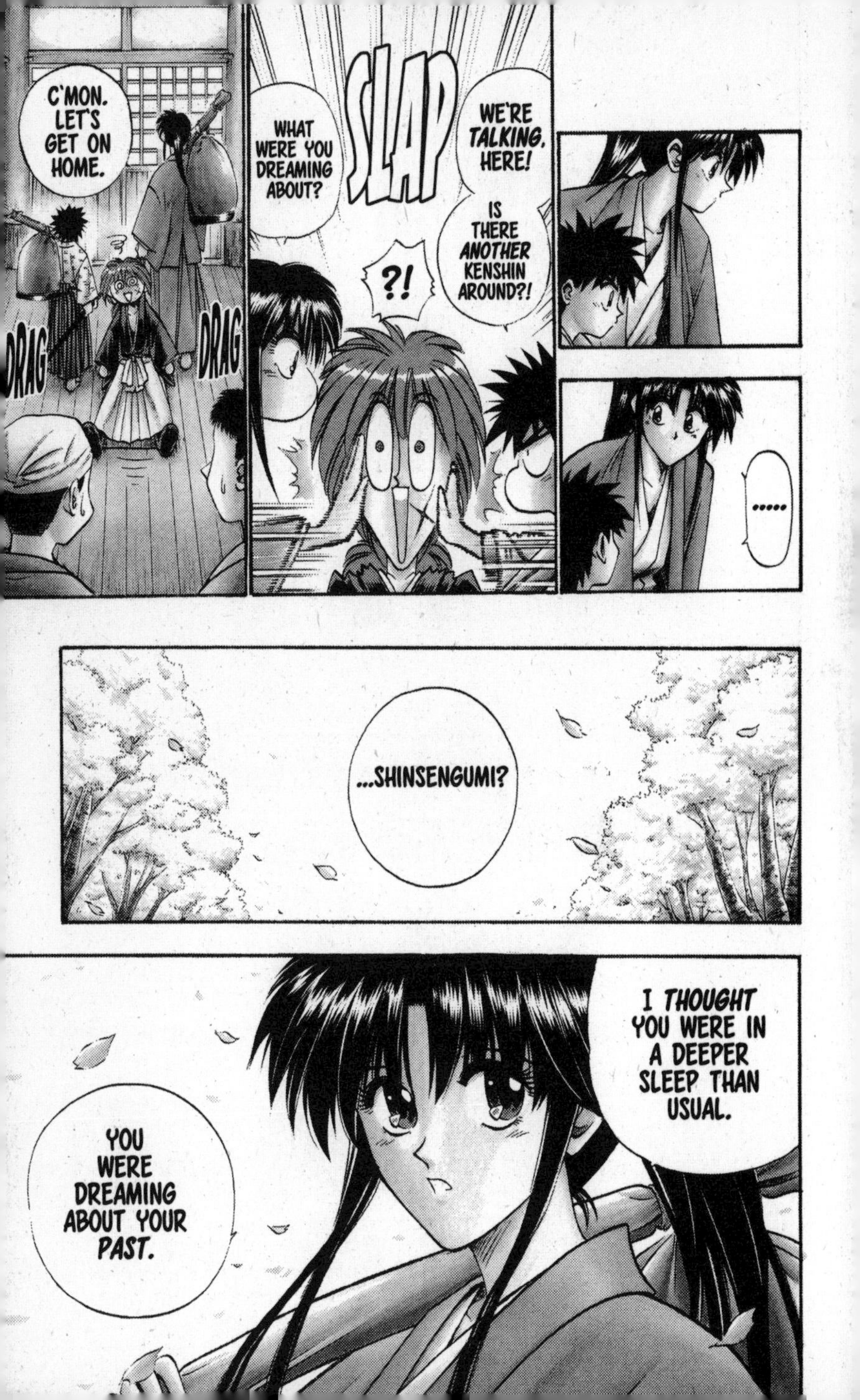
......
WE'RE TALKING, HERE!
IS THERE ANOTHER KENSHIN AROUND?!
SLAP
WHAT WERE YOU DREAMING ABOUT?
?!
C'MON. LET'S GET ON HOME.
DRAG
DRAG
...SHINSENGUMI?
I THOUGHT YOU WERE IN A DEEPER SLEEP THAN USUAL.
YOU WERE DREAMING ABOUT YOUR PAST.

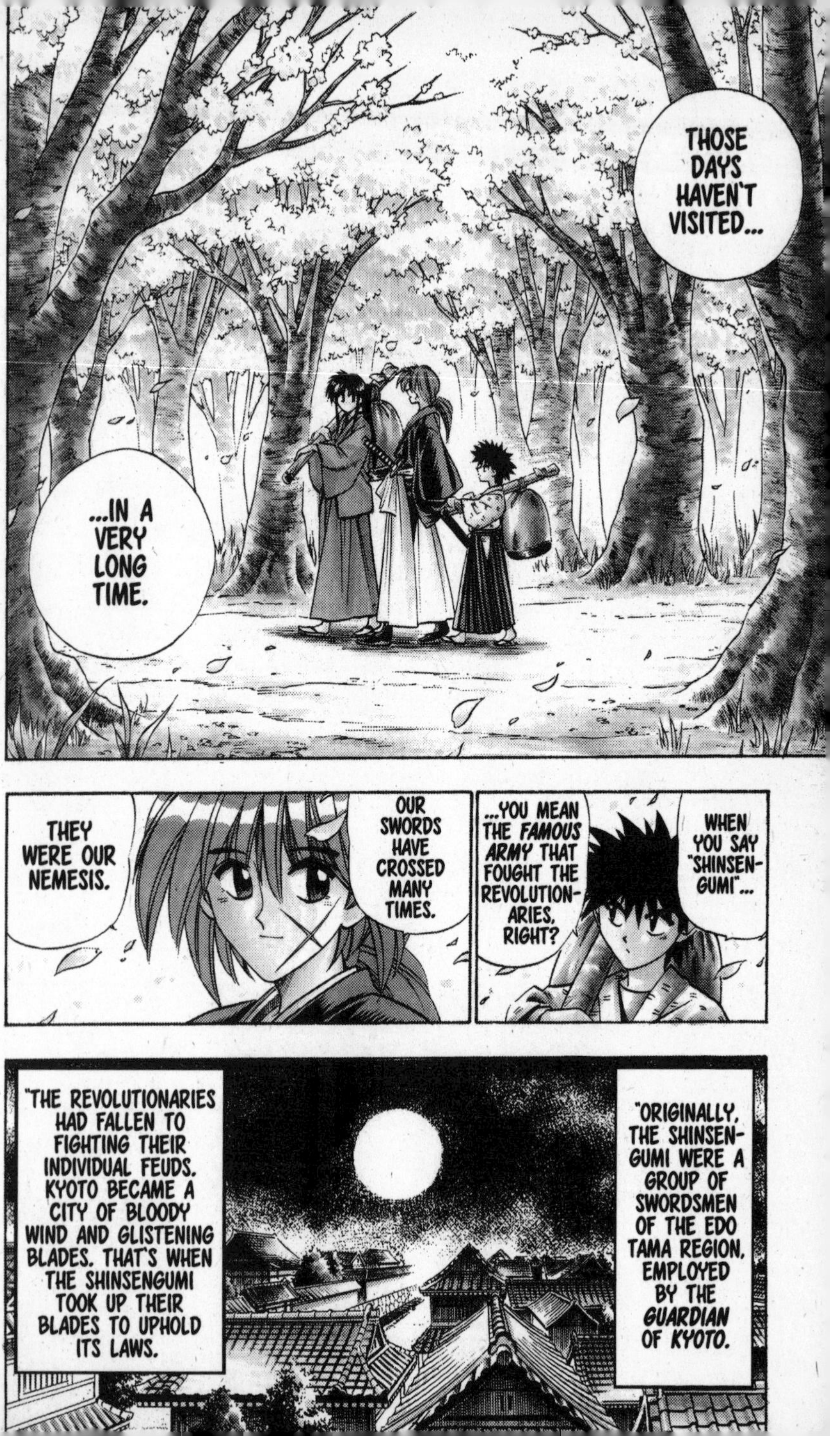
THOSE DAYS HAVEN'T VISITED...
...IN A VERY LONG TIME.
WHEN YOU SAY "SHINSEN-GUMI"...
...YOU MEAN THE *FAMOUS ARMY* THAT FOUGHT THE REVOLUTION-ARIES, RIGHT?
OUR SWORDS HAVE CROSSED MANY TIMES.
THEY WERE OUR NEMESIS.
"ORIGINALLY, THE SHINSEN-GUMI WERE A GROUP OF SWORDSMEN OF THE EDO TAMA REGION, EMPLOYED BY THE *GUARDIAN OF KYOTO*.
"THE REVOLUTIONARIES HAD FALLEN TO FIGHTING THEIR INDIVIDUAL FEUDS. KYOTO BECAME A CITY OF BLOODY WIND AND GLISTENING BLADES. THAT'S WHEN THE SHINSENGUMI TOOK UP THEIR BLADES TO UPHOLD ITS LAWS.

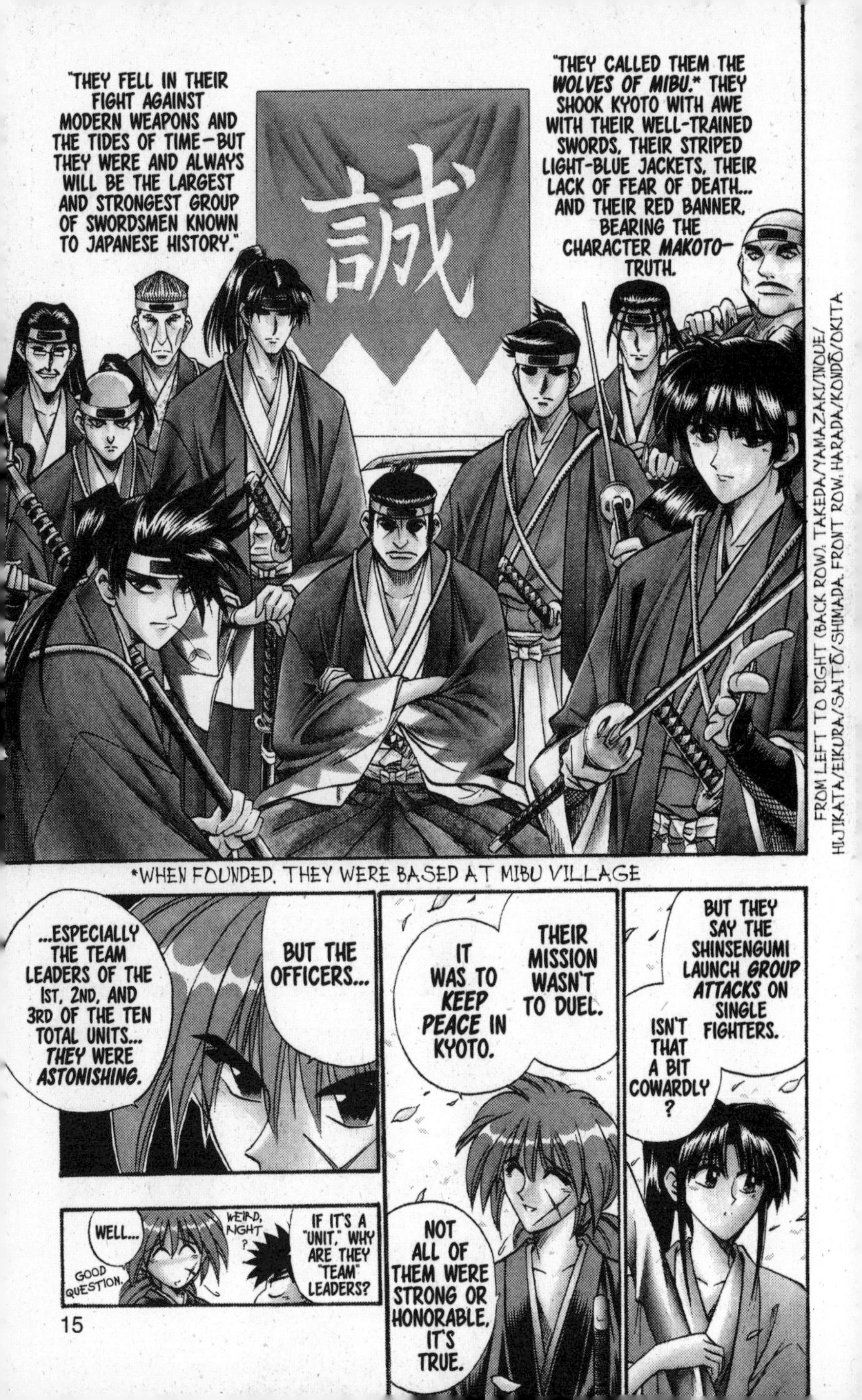
"THEY CALLED THEM THE *WOLVES OF MIBU.** THEY SHOOK KYOTO WITH AWE WITH THEIR WELL-TRAINED SWORDS, THEIR STRIPED LIGHT-BLUE JACKETS, THEIR LACK OF FEAR OF DEATH... AND THEIR RED BANNER, BEARING THE CHARACTER *MAKOTO*—TRUTH.
"THEY FELL IN THEIR FIGHT AGAINST MODERN WEAPONS AND THE TIDES OF TIME—BUT THEY WERE AND ALWAYS WILL BE THE LARGEST AND STRONGEST GROUP OF SWORDSMEN KNOWN TO JAPANESE HISTORY."
誠
FROM LEFT TO RIGHT (BACK ROW): TAKEDA/YAMAZAKI/INOUE/HIJIKATA/EIKURA/SAITŌ/SHIMADA. FRONT ROW: HARADA/KONDŌ/OKITA
*WHEN FOUNDED, THEY WERE BASED AT MIBU VILLAGE
BUT THEY SAY THE SHINSENGUMI LAUNCH *GROUP ATTACKS* ON SINGLE FIGHTERS.
ISN'T THAT A BIT COWARDLY?
THEIR MISSION WASN'T TO DUEL.
IT WAS TO *KEEP PEACE* IN KYOTO.
NOT ALL OF THEM WERE STRONG OR HONORABLE, IT'S TRUE.
BUT THE OFFICERS...
...ESPECIALLY THE TEAM LEADERS OF THE 1ST, 2ND, AND 3RD OF THE TEN TOTAL UNITS... *THEY WERE ASTONISHING.*
IF IT'S A "UNIT," WHY ARE THEY "TEAM" LEADERS?
WEIRD, RIGHT?
WELL...
GOOD QUESTION.

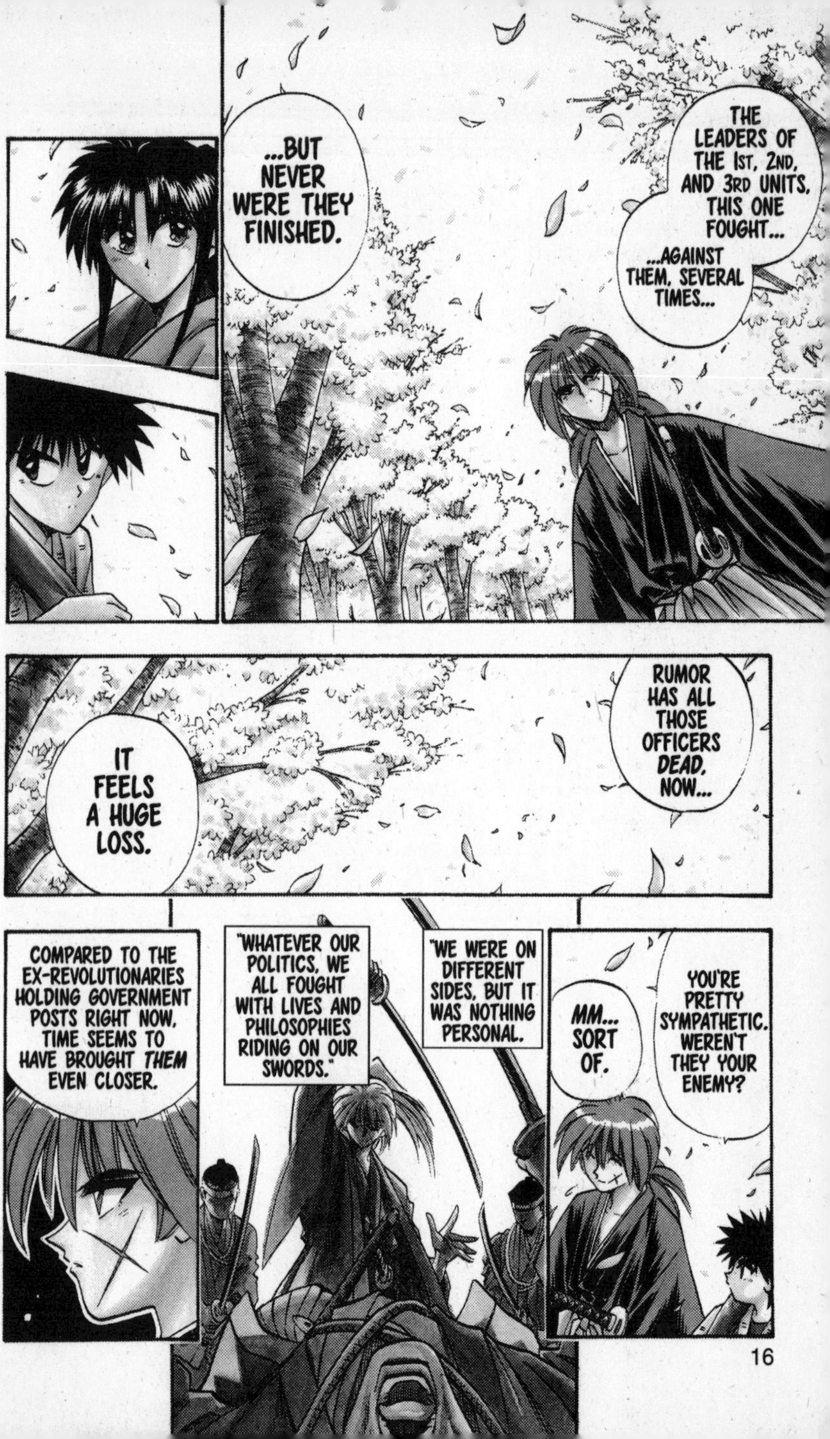
THE LEADERS OF THE 1st, 2nd, AND 3rd UNITS, THIS ONE FOUGHT...
...AGAINST THEM, SEVERAL TIMES...
...BUT NEVER WERE THEY FINISHED.
RUMOR HAS ALL THOSE OFFICERS *DEAD*, NOW...
IT FEELS A HUGE LOSS.
YOU'RE PRETTY SYMPATHETIC. WEREN'T THEY YOUR ENEMY?
MM... SORT OF.
"WE WERE ON DIFFERENT SIDES, BUT IT WAS NOTHING PERSONAL.
"WHATEVER OUR POLITICS, WE ALL FOUGHT WITH LIVES AND PHILOSOPHIES RIDING ON OUR SWORDS."
COMPARED TO THE EX-REVOLUTIONARIES HOLDING GOVERNMENT POSTS RIGHT NOW, TIME SEEMS TO HAVE BROUGHT *THEM* EVEN CLOSER.

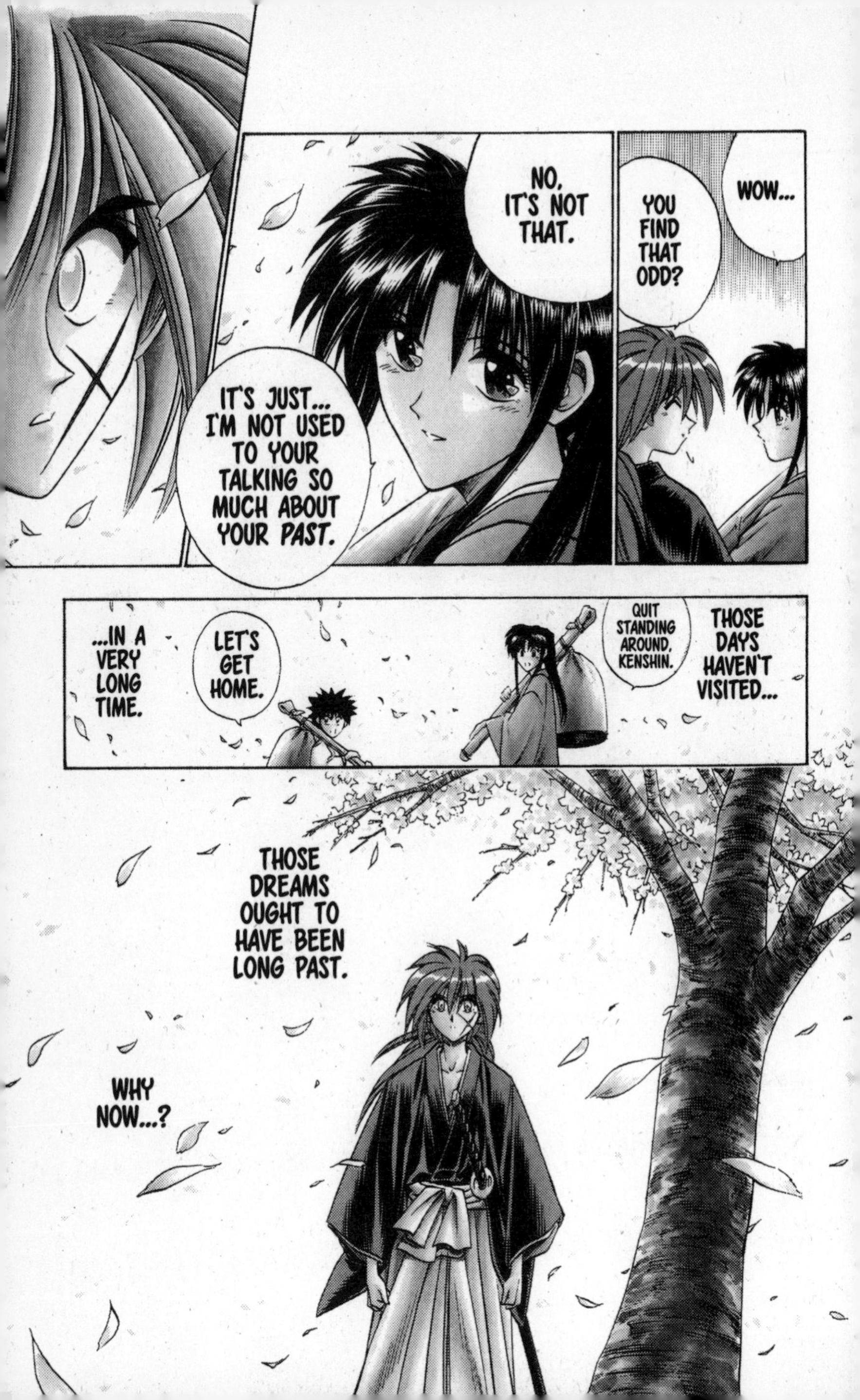
WOW...
YOU FIND THAT ODD?
NO, IT'S NOT THAT.
IT'S JUST... I'M NOT USED TO YOUR TALKING SO MUCH ABOUT YOUR PAST.
THOSE DAYS HAVEN'T VISITED...
QUIT STANDING AROUND, KENSHIN.
LET'S GET HOME.
...IN A VERY LONG TIME.
THOSE DREAMS OUGHT TO HAVE BEEN LONG PAST.
WHY NOW...?

READ THIS WAY

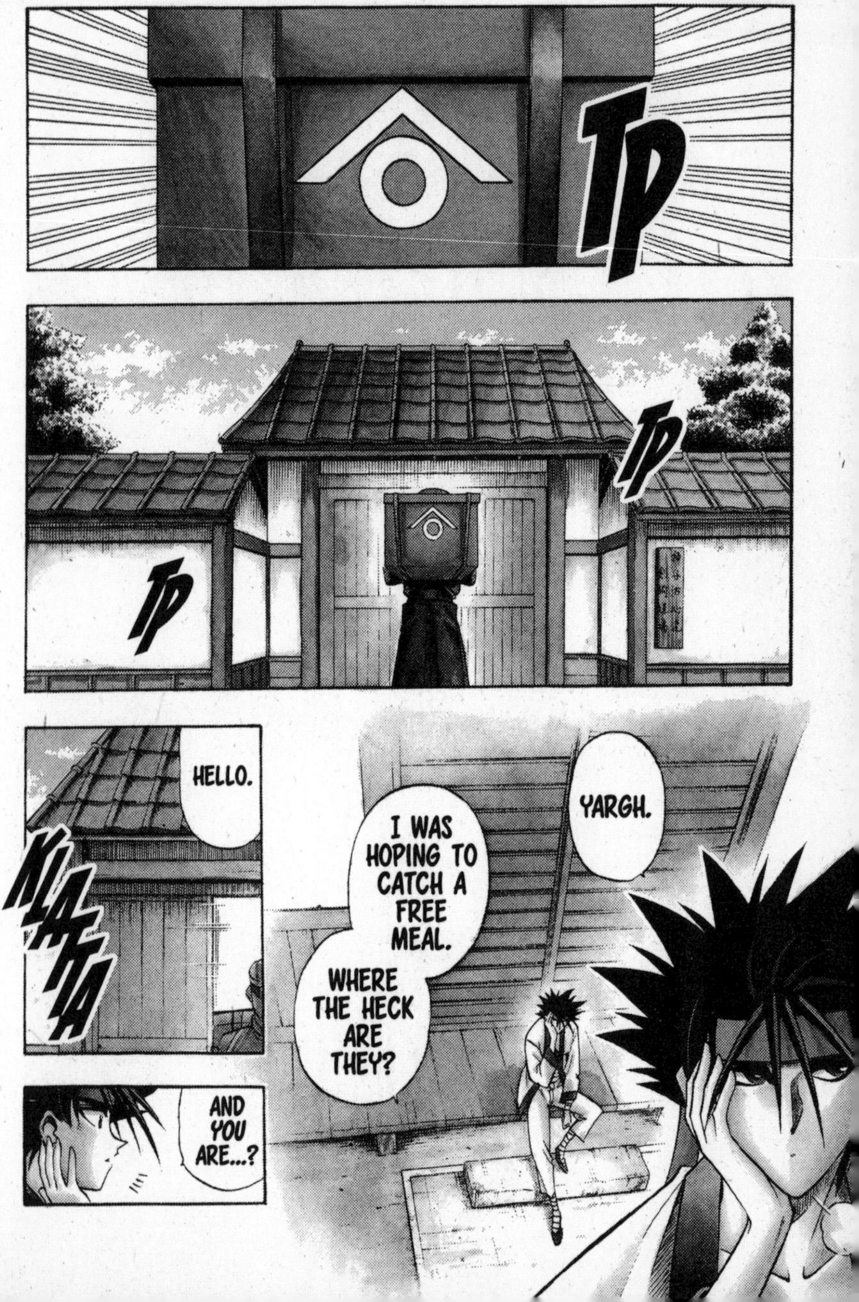
TP
TP
TP
YARGH.
I WAS HOPING TO CATCH A FREE MEAL.
WHERE THE HECK ARE THEY?
HELLO.
KLATTA
AND YOU ARE...?

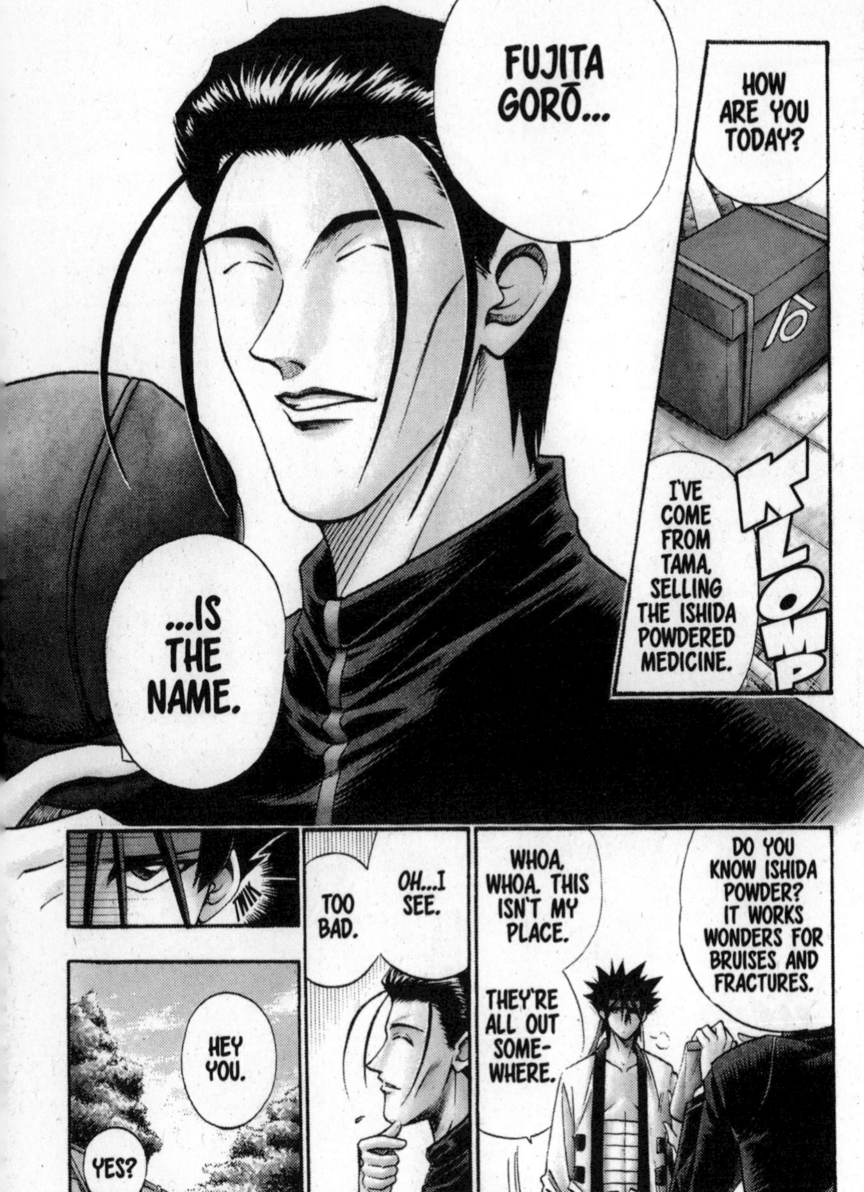

HOW ARE YOU TODAY?
I'VE COME FROM TAMA, SELLING THE ISHIDA POWDERED MEDICINE.
KLOMP
FUJITA GORŌ...
...IS THE NAME.
DO YOU KNOW ISHIDA POWDER? IT WORKS WONDERS FOR BRUISES AND FRACTURES.
WHOA, WHOA. THIS ISN'T MY PLACE.
THEY'RE ALL OUT SOME-WHERE.
OH...I SEE.
TOO BAD.
TWIK
HEY YOU.
YES?

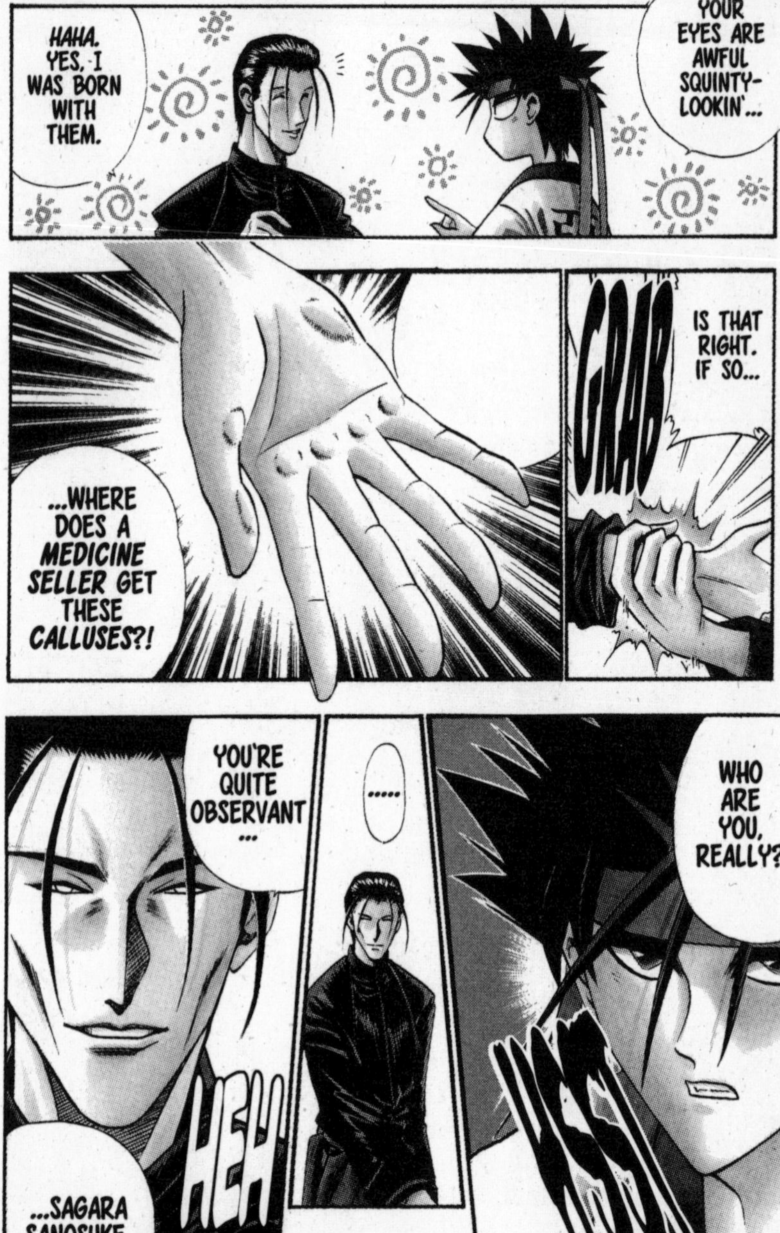
YOUR EYES ARE AWFUL SQUINTY-LOOKIN'...
HAHA. YES, I WAS BORN WITH THEM.
IS THAT RIGHT. IF SO...
GRAB
...WHERE DOES A MEDICINE SELLER GET THESE CALLUSES?!
WHO ARE YOU, REALLY?
......
YOU'RE QUITE OBSERVANT...
HEH
...SAGARA SANOSUKE.

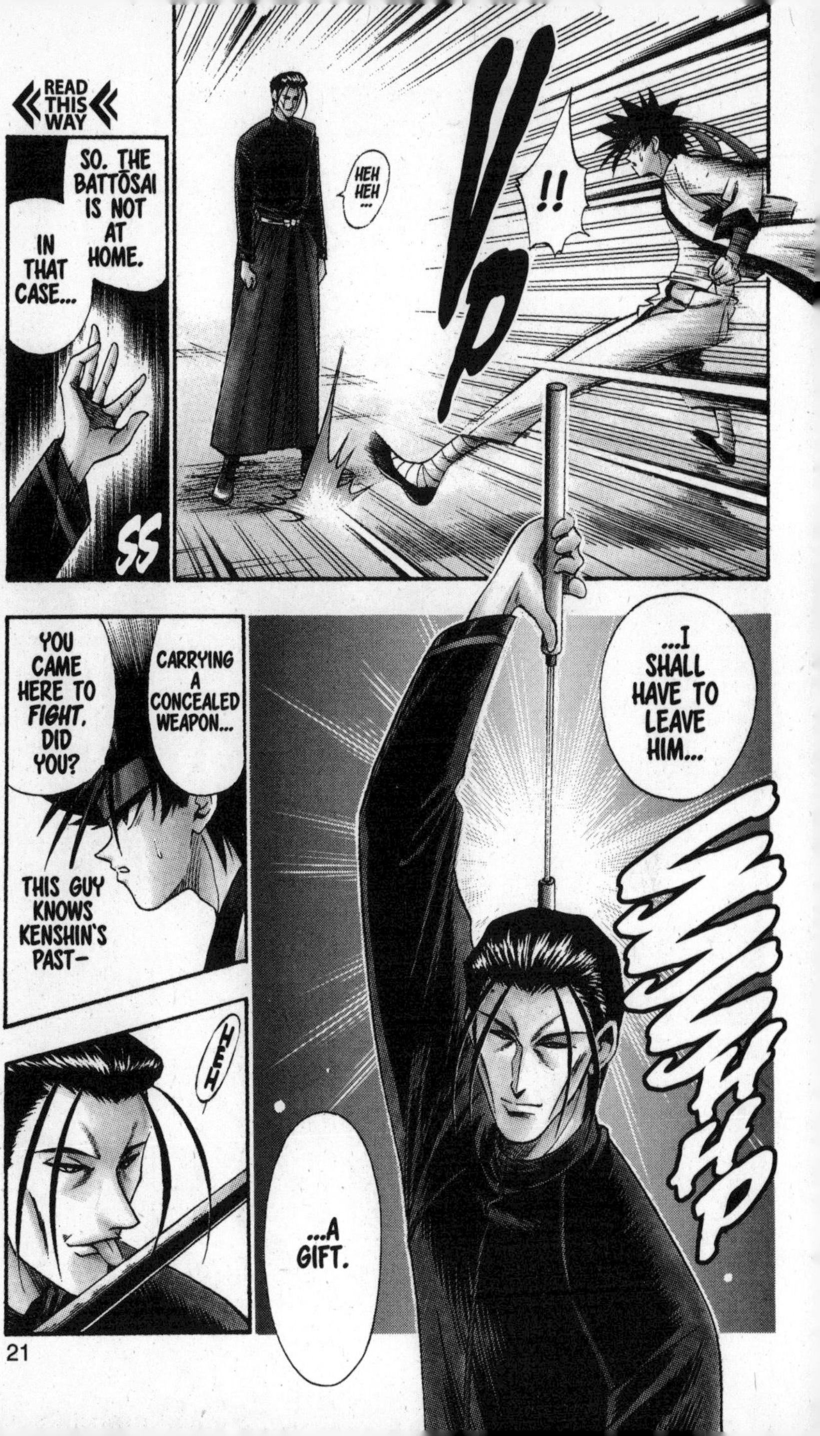
READ THIS WAY
HEH HEH...
!!
SO. THE BATTŌSAI IS NOT AT HOME.
IN THAT CASE...
SS
...I SHALL HAVE TO LEAVE HIM...
...A GIFT.
CARRYING A CONCEALED WEAPON...
YOU CAME HERE TO FIGHT, DID YOU?
THIS GUY KNOWS KENSHIN'S PAST–
HEH

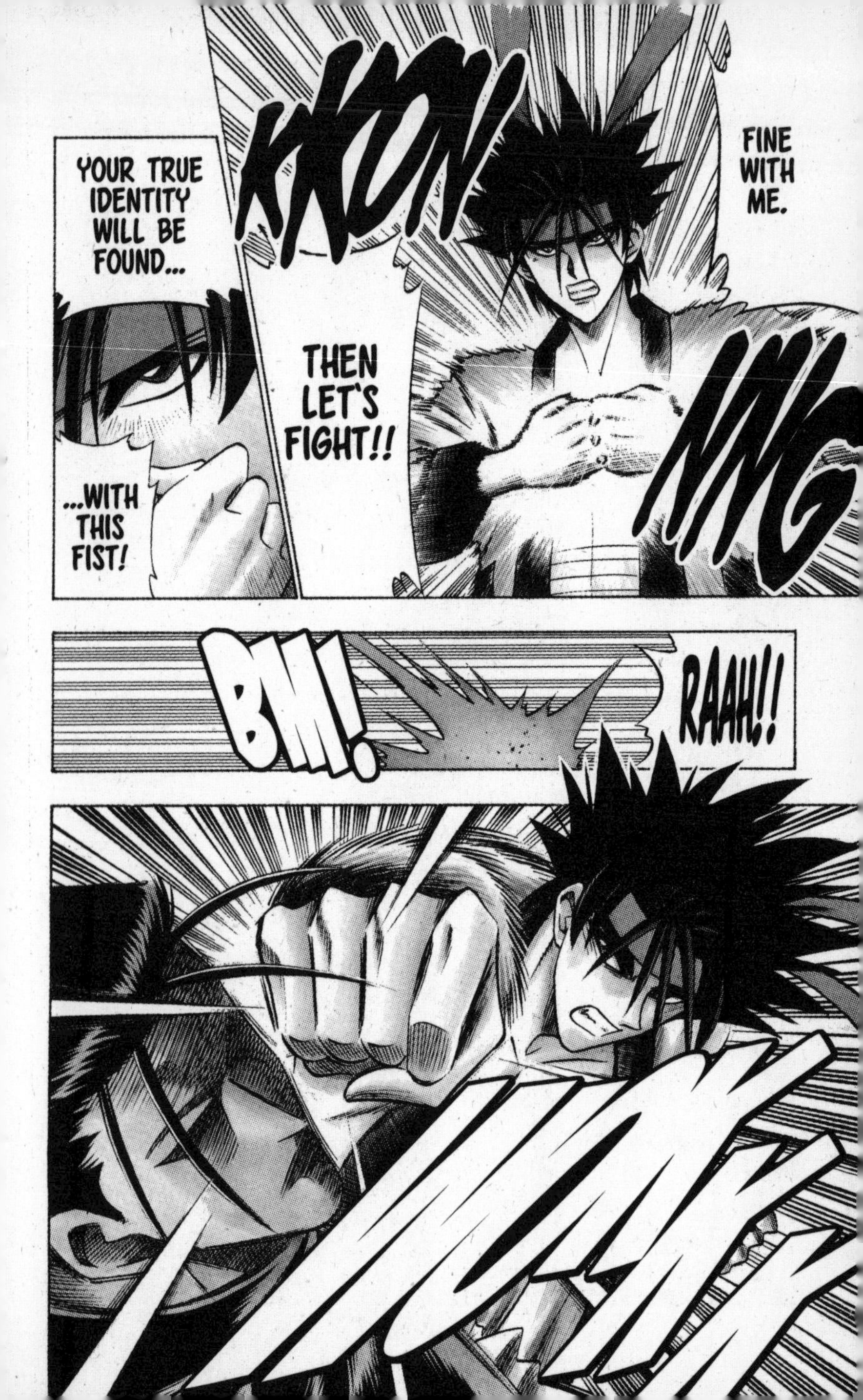
FINE WITH ME.
KYON
NNG
THEN LET'S FIGHT!!
YOUR TRUE IDENTITY WILL BE FOUND...
...WITH THIS FIST!
RAAH!!
BM!

READ THIS WAY

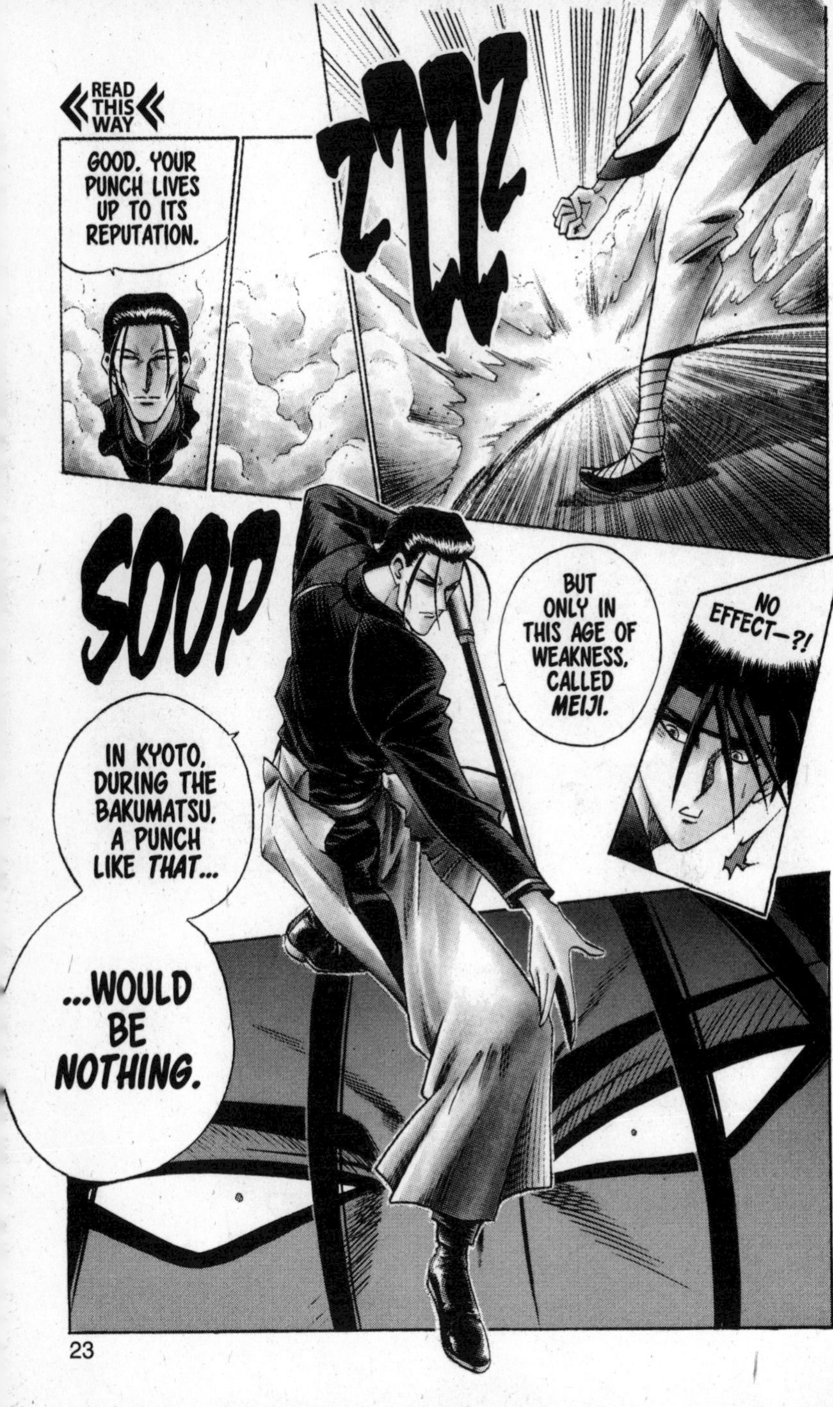
ZZZZ
GOOD. YOUR PUNCH LIVES UP TO ITS REPUTATION.
NO EFFECT—?!
BUT ONLY IN THIS AGE OF WEAKNESS, CALLED *MEIJI*.
SOOP
IN KYOTO, DURING THE BAKUMATSU, A PUNCH LIKE *THAT*...
...WOULD BE NOTHING.

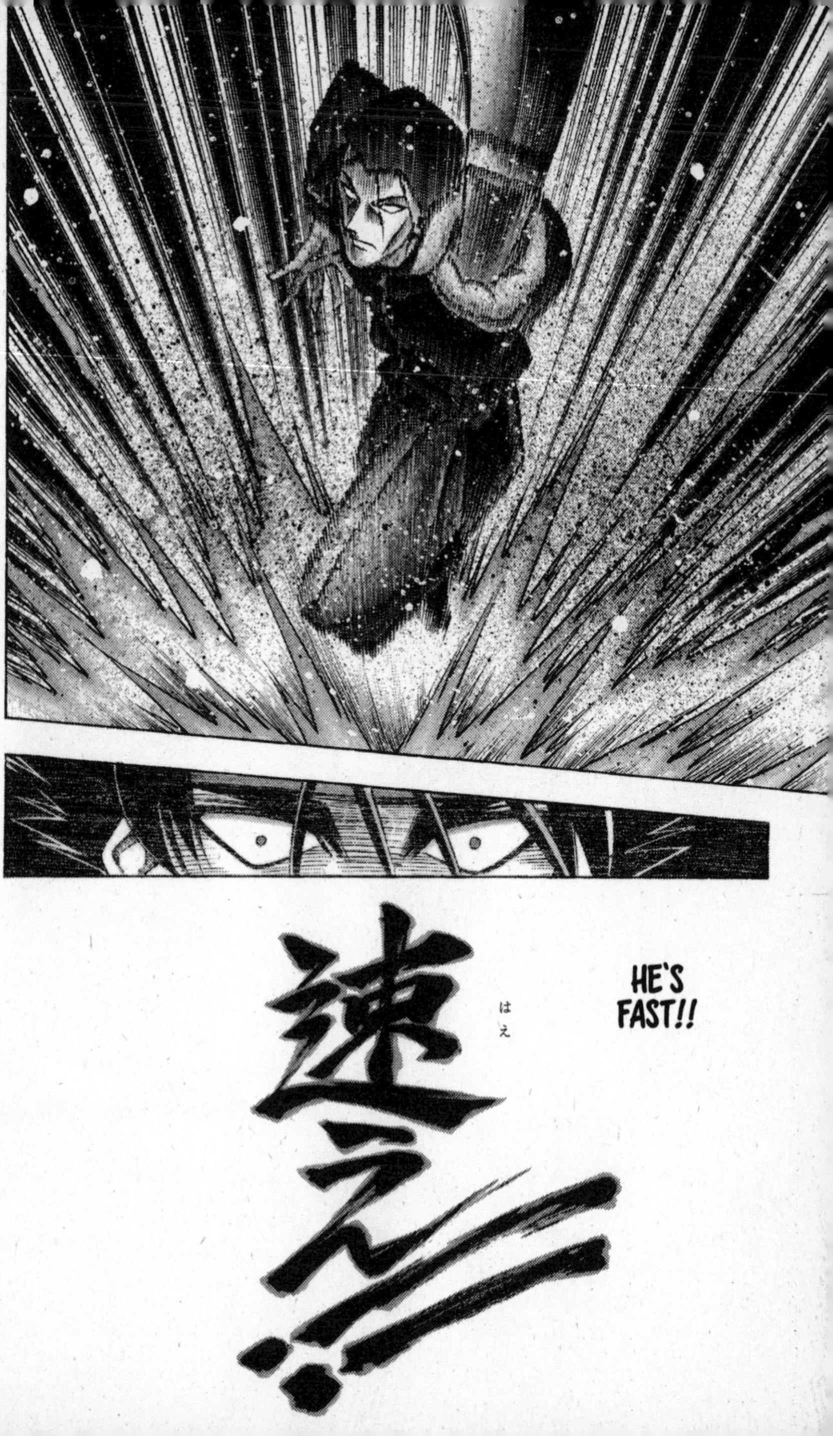
HE'S FAST!!
速え!!

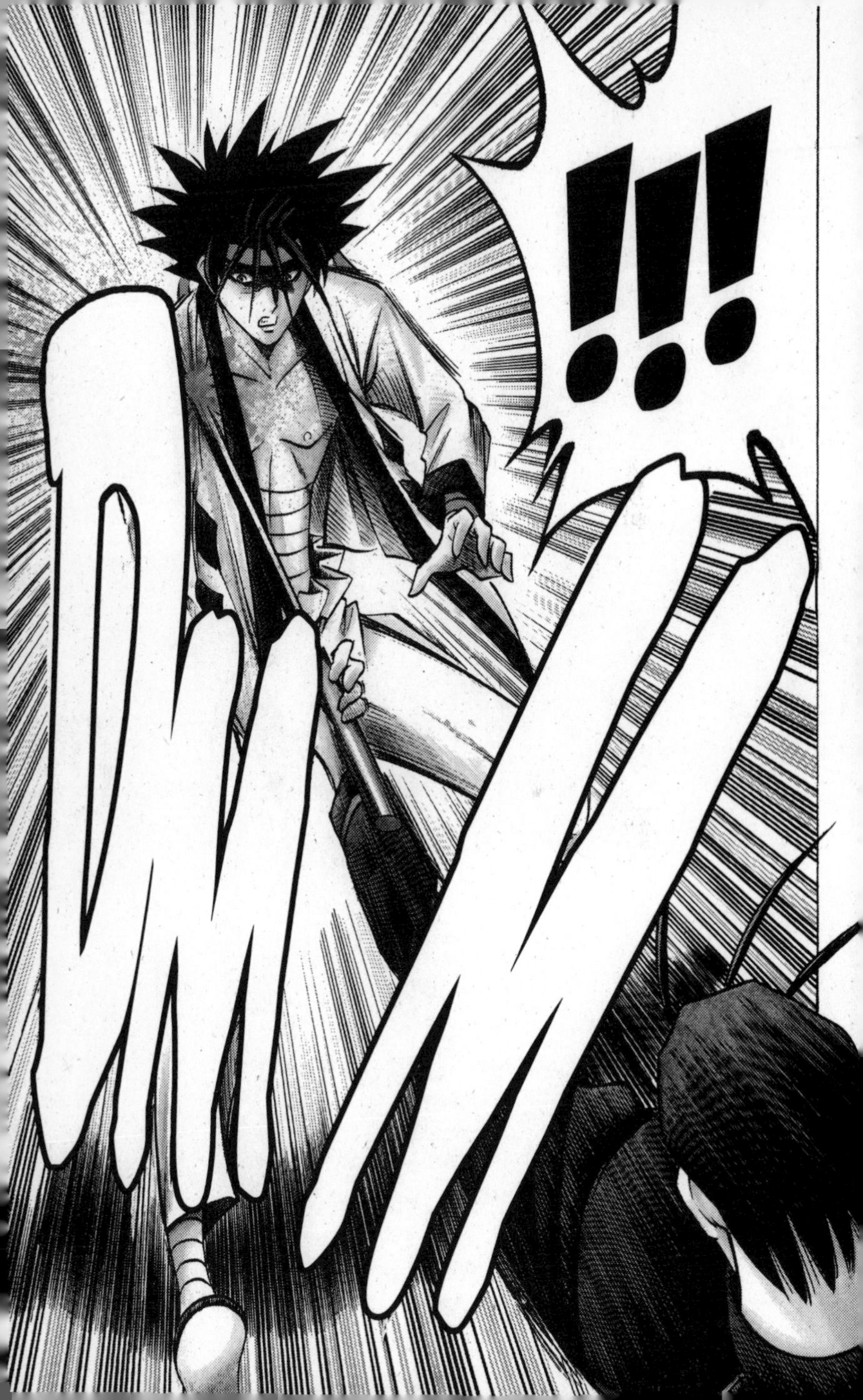
!!!

Rurouni Kenshin

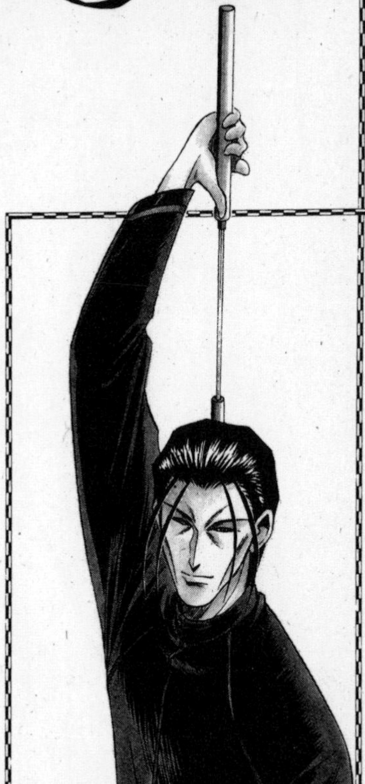

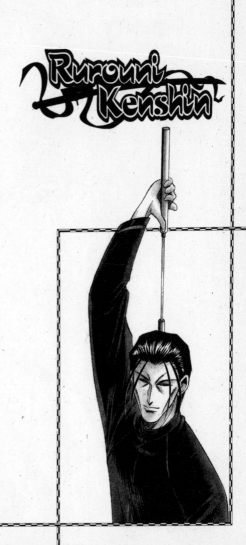

READ THIS WAY

Act 49
Wolf Without Mercy

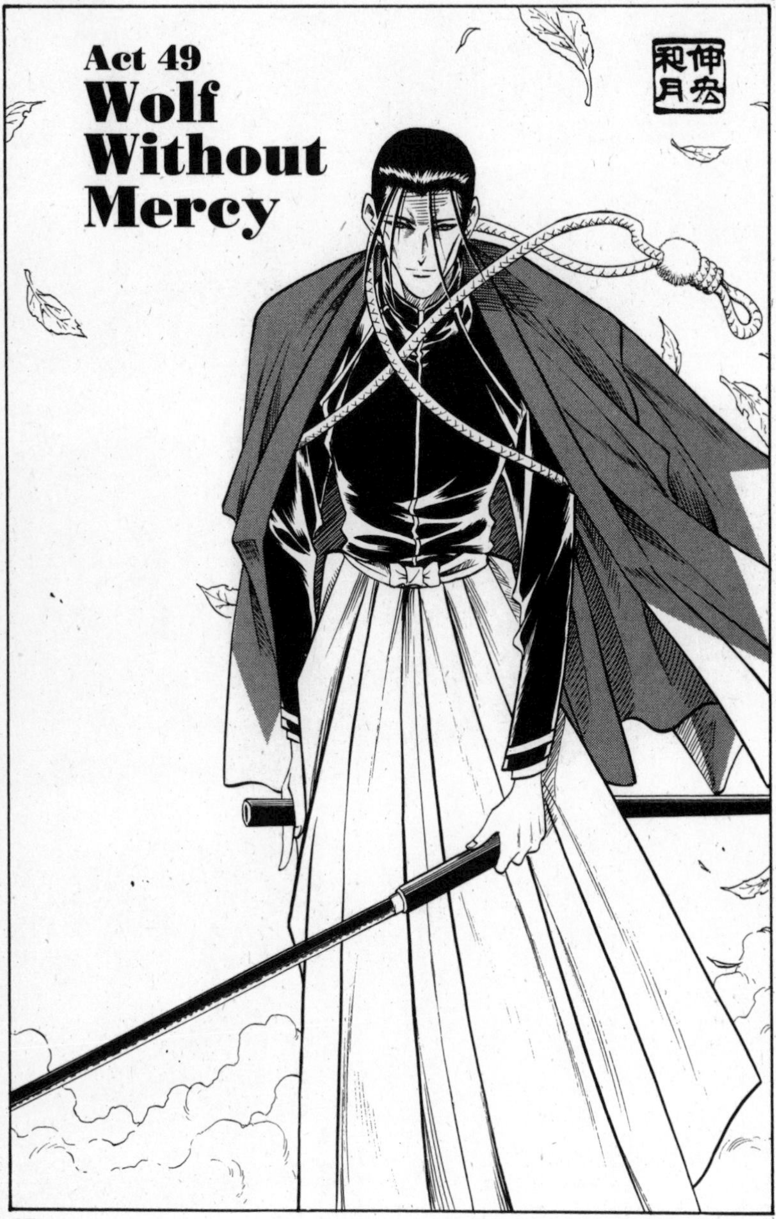

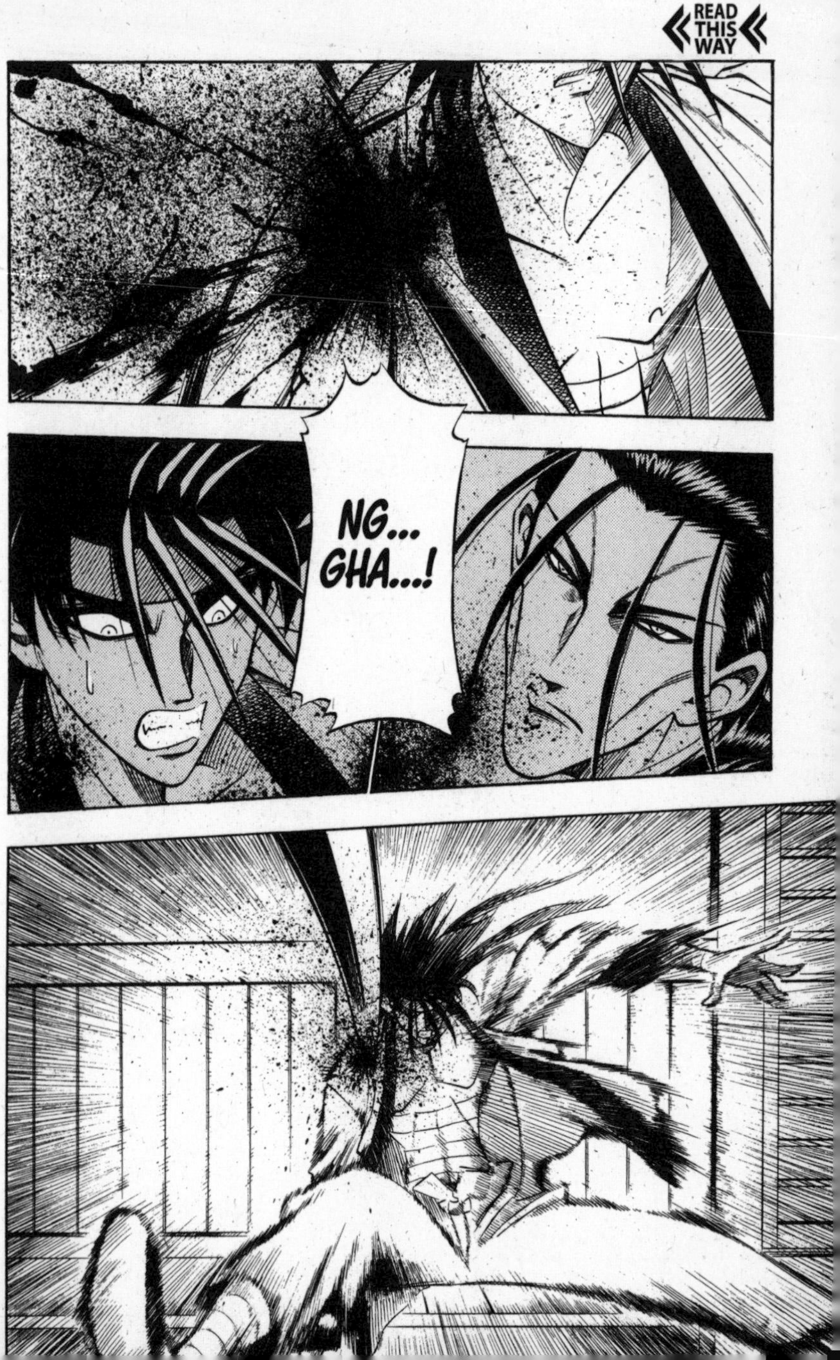
READ THIS WAY
NG... GHA...!

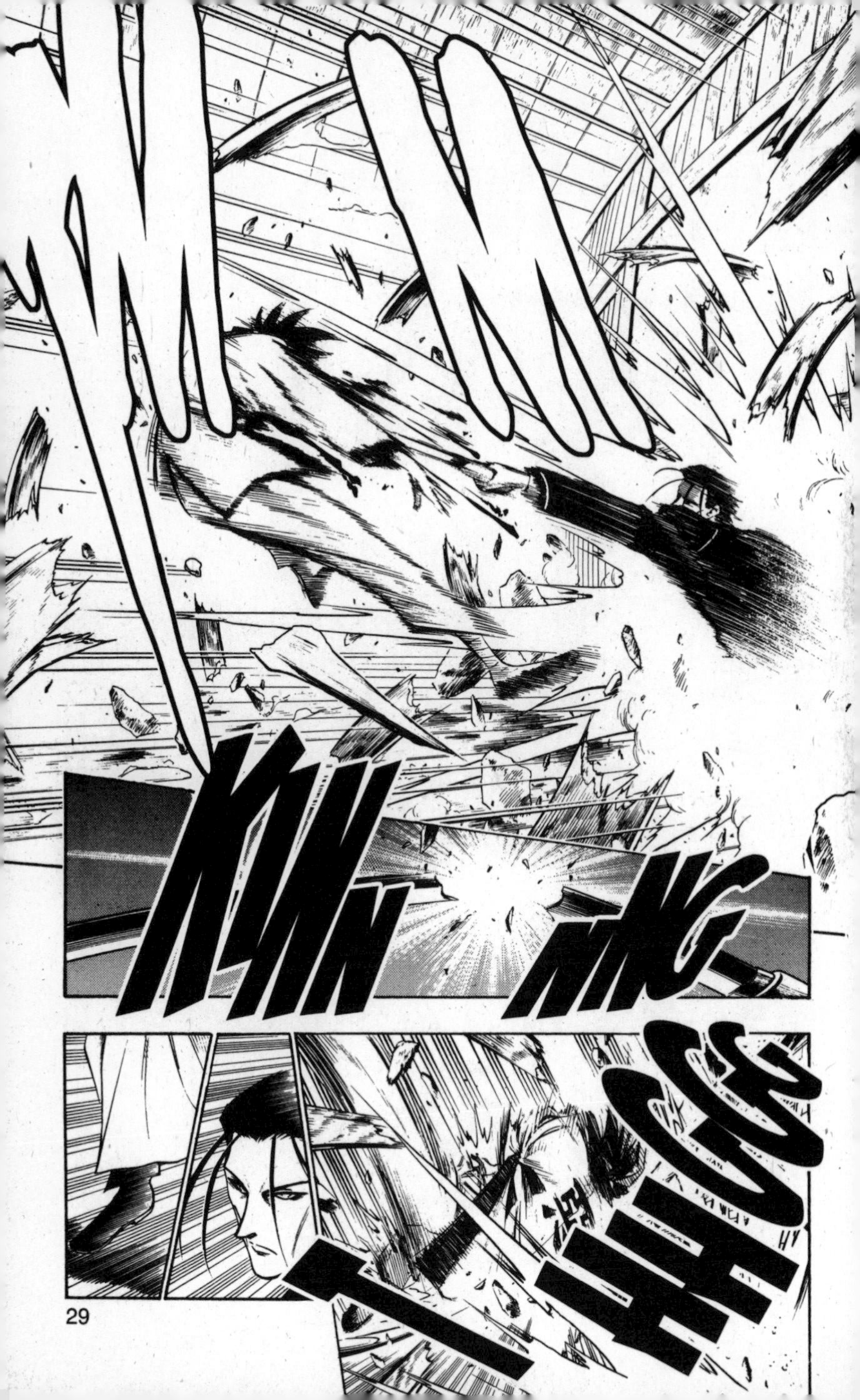

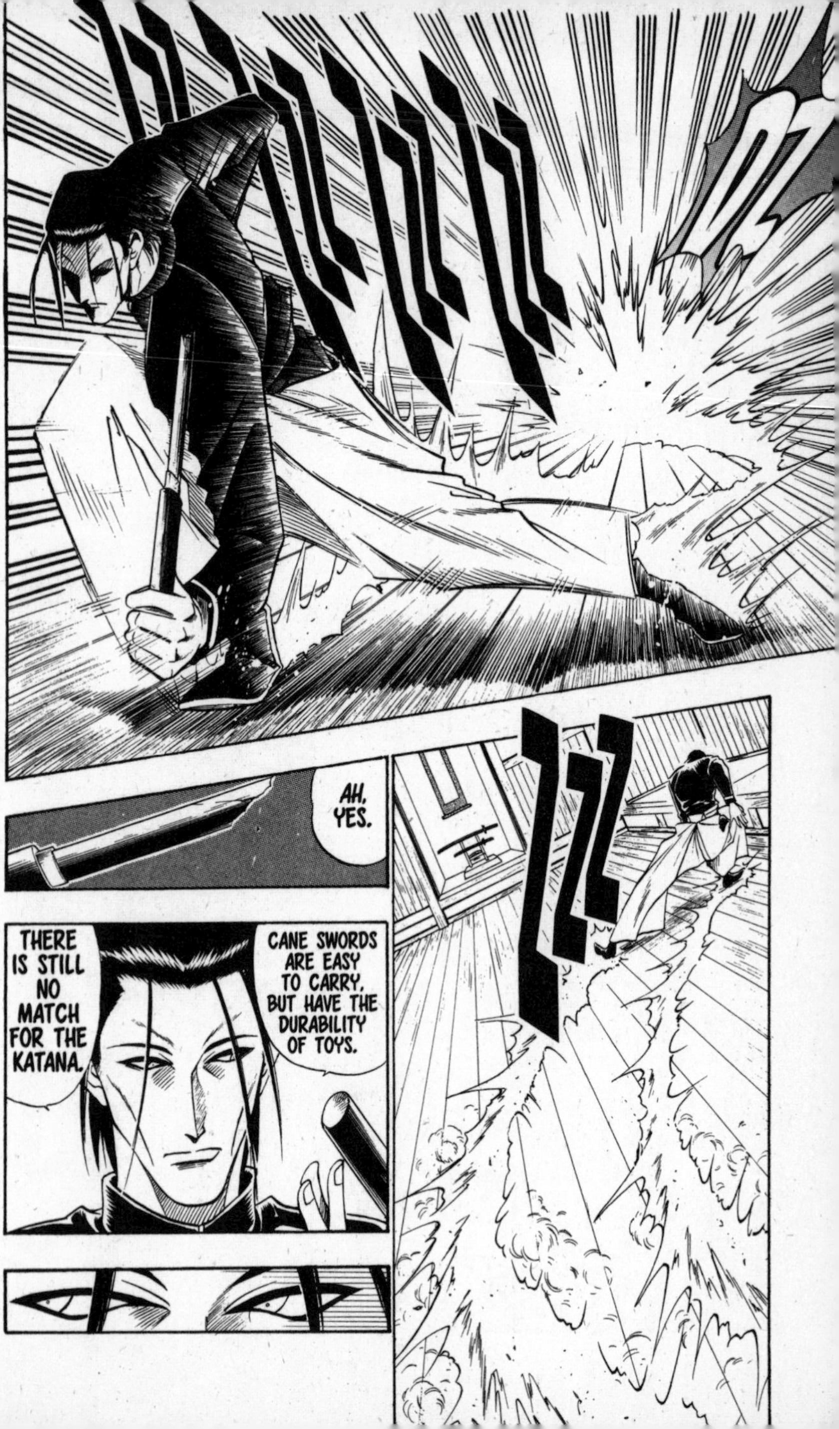
AH, YES.
CANE SWORDS ARE EASY TO CARRY, BUT HAVE THE DURABILITY OF TOYS.
THERE IS STILL NO MATCH FOR THE KATANA.

READ THIS WAY

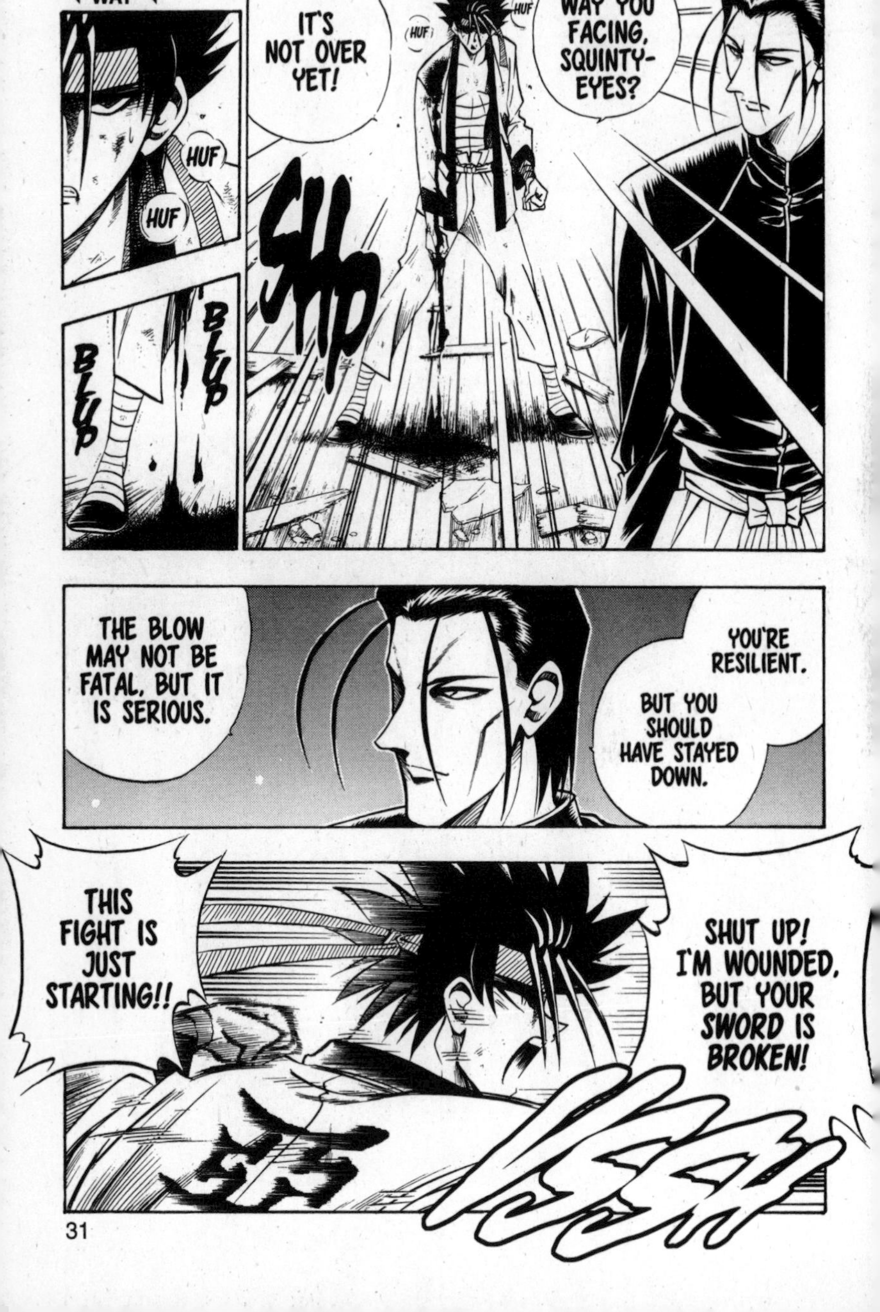
WHICH WAY YOU FACING, SQUINTY-EYES?
HUF
HUF
IT'S NOT OVER YET!
SHP
HUF
HUF
BLUP
BLUP
YOU'RE RESILIENT.
BUT YOU SHOULD HAVE STAYED DOWN.
THE BLOW MAY NOT BE FATAL, BUT IT IS SERIOUS.
SHUT UP! I'M WOUNDED, BUT YOUR SWORD IS BROKEN!
THIS FIGHT IS JUST STARTING!!

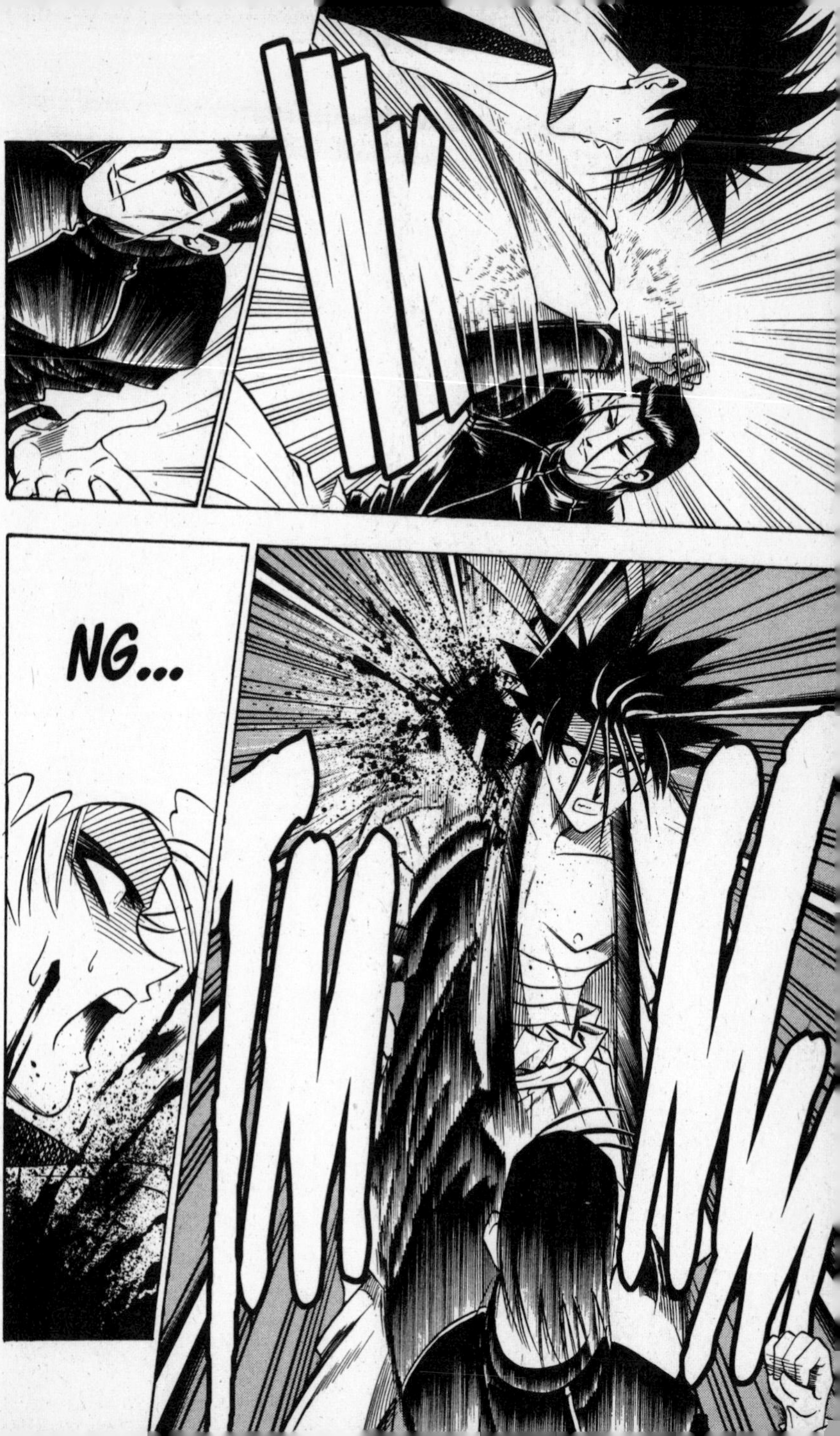
NG...

READ THIS WAY

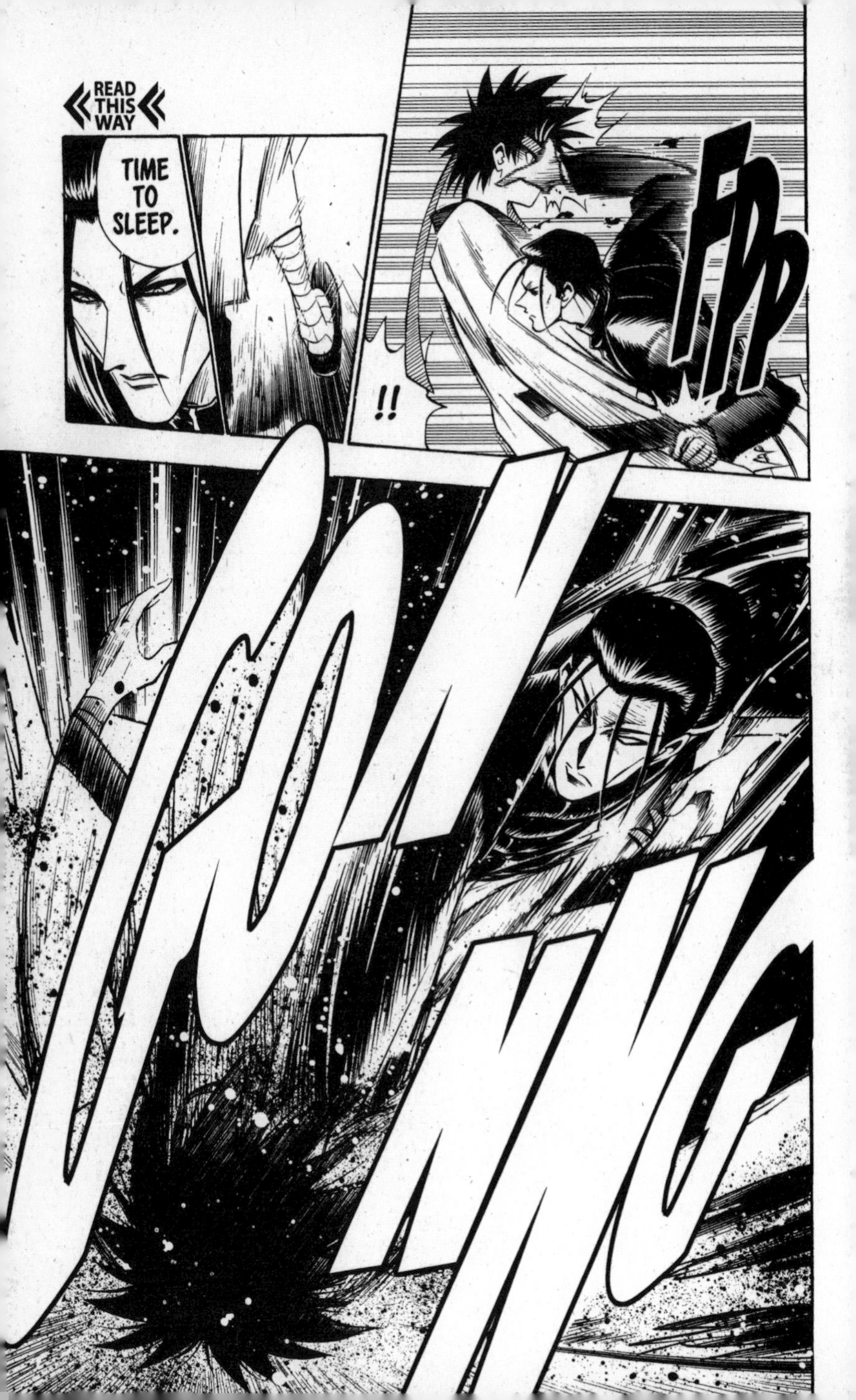

FP
!!
TIME TO SLEEP.

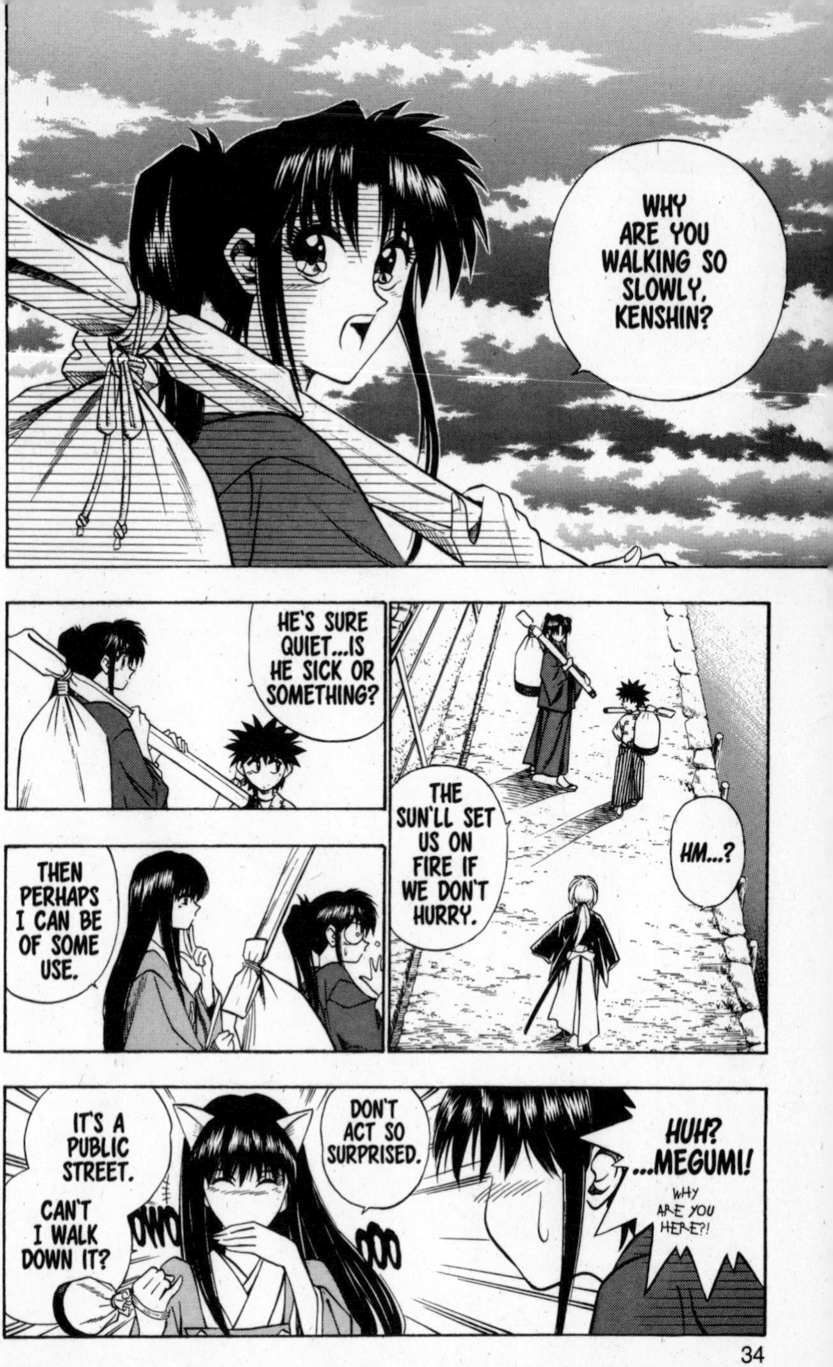
WHY ARE YOU WALKING SO SLOWLY, KENSHIN?
THE SUN'LL SET US ON FIRE IF WE DON'T HURRY.
HM...?
HE'S SURE QUIET...IS HE SICK OR SOMETHING?
THEN PERHAPS I CAN BE OF SOME USE.
HUH? ...MEGUMI!
WHY ARE YOU HERE?!
DON'T ACT SO SURPRISED.
IT'S A PUBLIC STREET.
CAN'T I WALK DOWN IT?

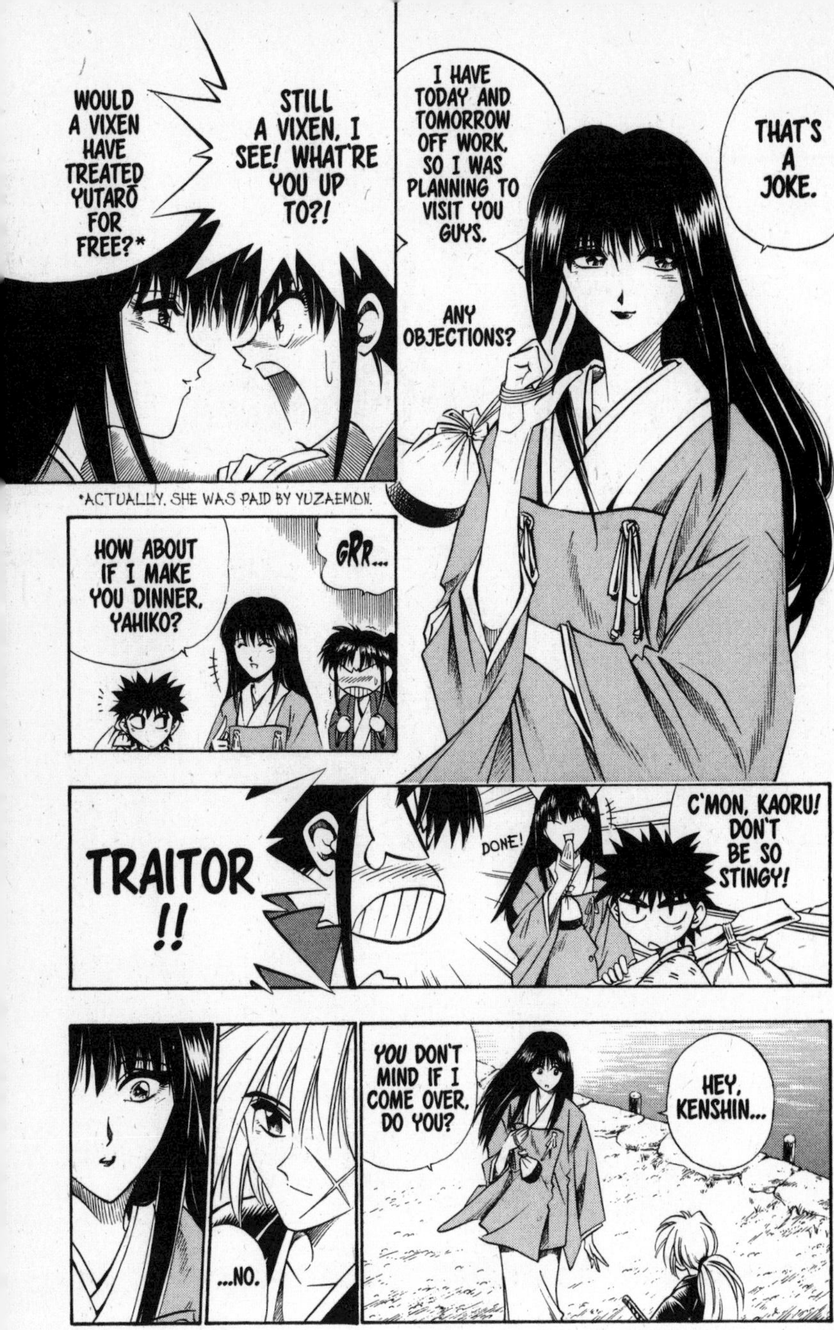
THAT'S A JOKE.
I HAVE TODAY AND TOMORROW OFF WORK, SO I WAS PLANNING TO VISIT YOU GUYS.
ANY OBJECTIONS?
STILL A VIXEN, I SEE! WHAT'RE YOU UP TO?!
WOULD A VIXEN HAVE TREATED YUTARŌ FOR FREE?*
*ACTUALLY, SHE WAS PAID BY YUZAEMON.
GRR...
HOW ABOUT IF I MAKE YOU DINNER, YAHIKO?
C'MON, KAORU! DON'T BE SO STINGY!
DONE!
TRAITOR!!
HEY, KENSHIN...
YOU DON'T MIND IF I COME OVER, DO YOU?
...NO.

READ THIS WAY

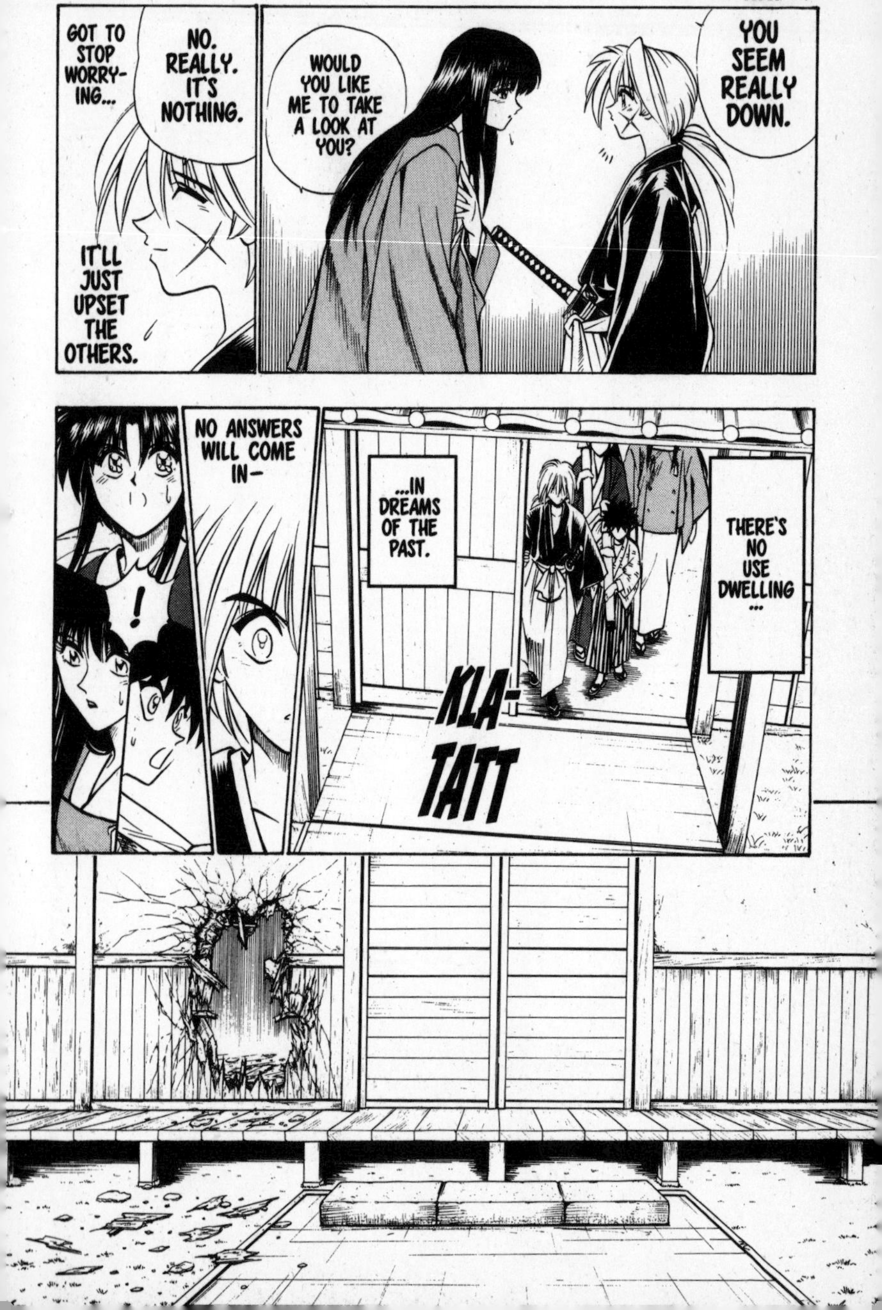
YOU SEEM REALLY DOWN.
WOULD YOU LIKE ME TO TAKE A LOOK AT YOU?
NO. REALLY. IT'S NOTHING.
GOT TO STOP WORRYING...
IT'LL JUST UPSET THE OTHERS.
THERE'S NO USE DWELLING ...
...IN DREAMS OF THE PAST.
KLA-TATT
NO ANSWERS WILL COME IN-
!

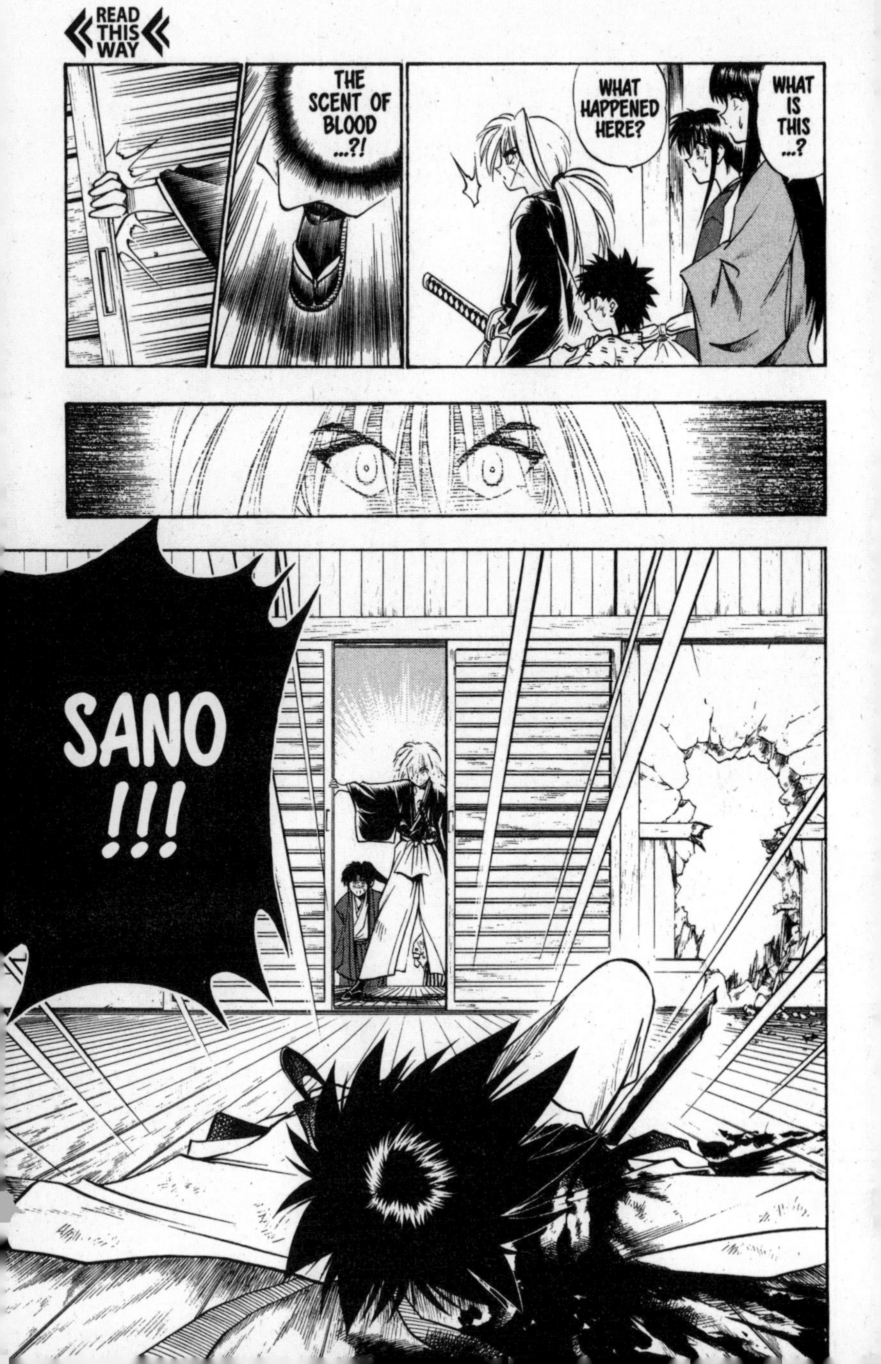
READ THIS WAY
WHAT IS THIS ...?
WHAT HAPPENED HERE?
THE SCENT OF BLOOD ...?!
SANO !!!

READ THIS WAY

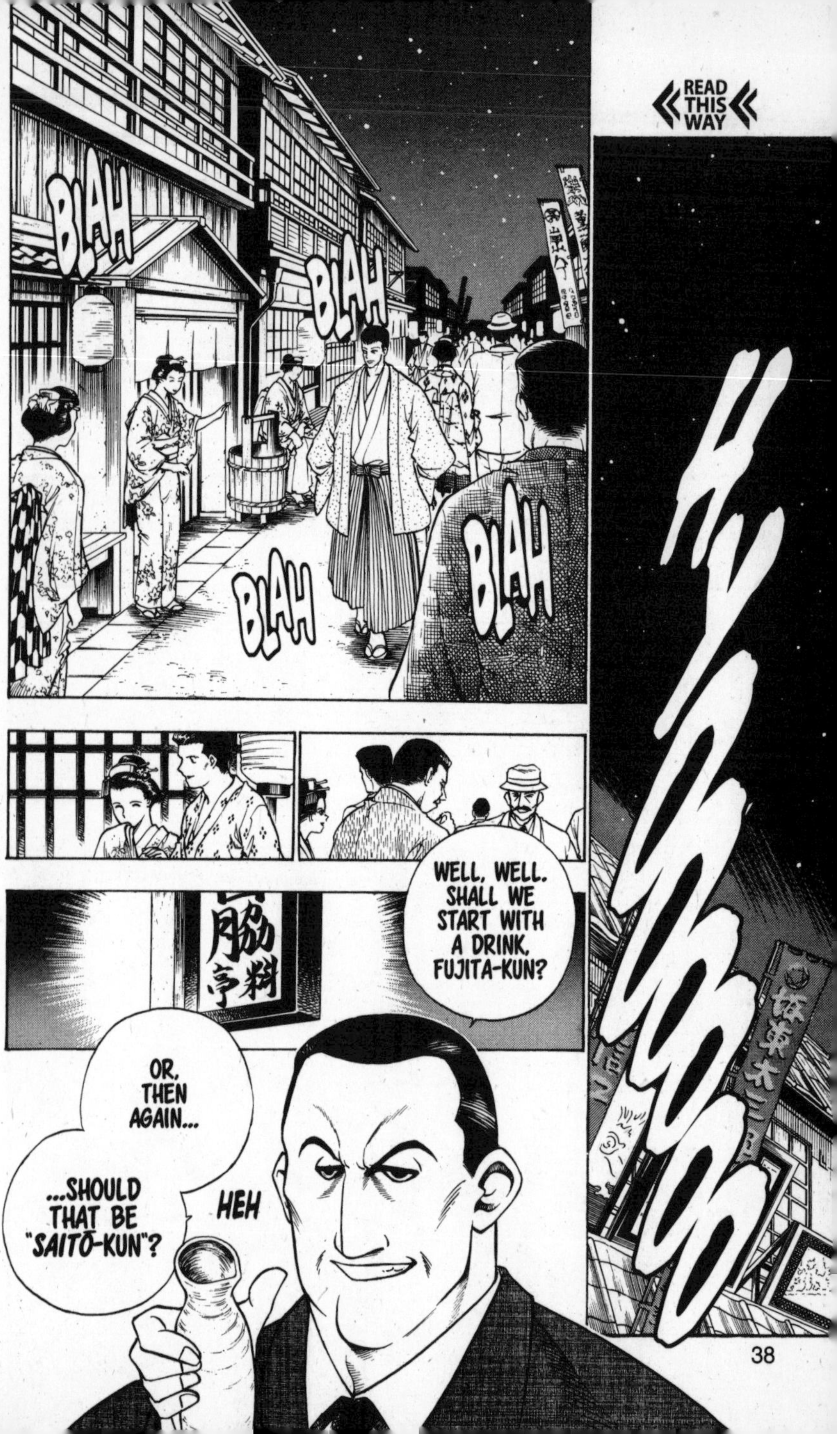

HYUUOOOOO
BLAH
BLAH
BLAH
BLAH
BLAH
WELL, WELL. SHALL WE START WITH A DRINK, FUJITA-KUN?
OR, THEN AGAIN...
...SHOULD THAT BE "SAITŌ-KUN"?
HEH

READ THIS WAY

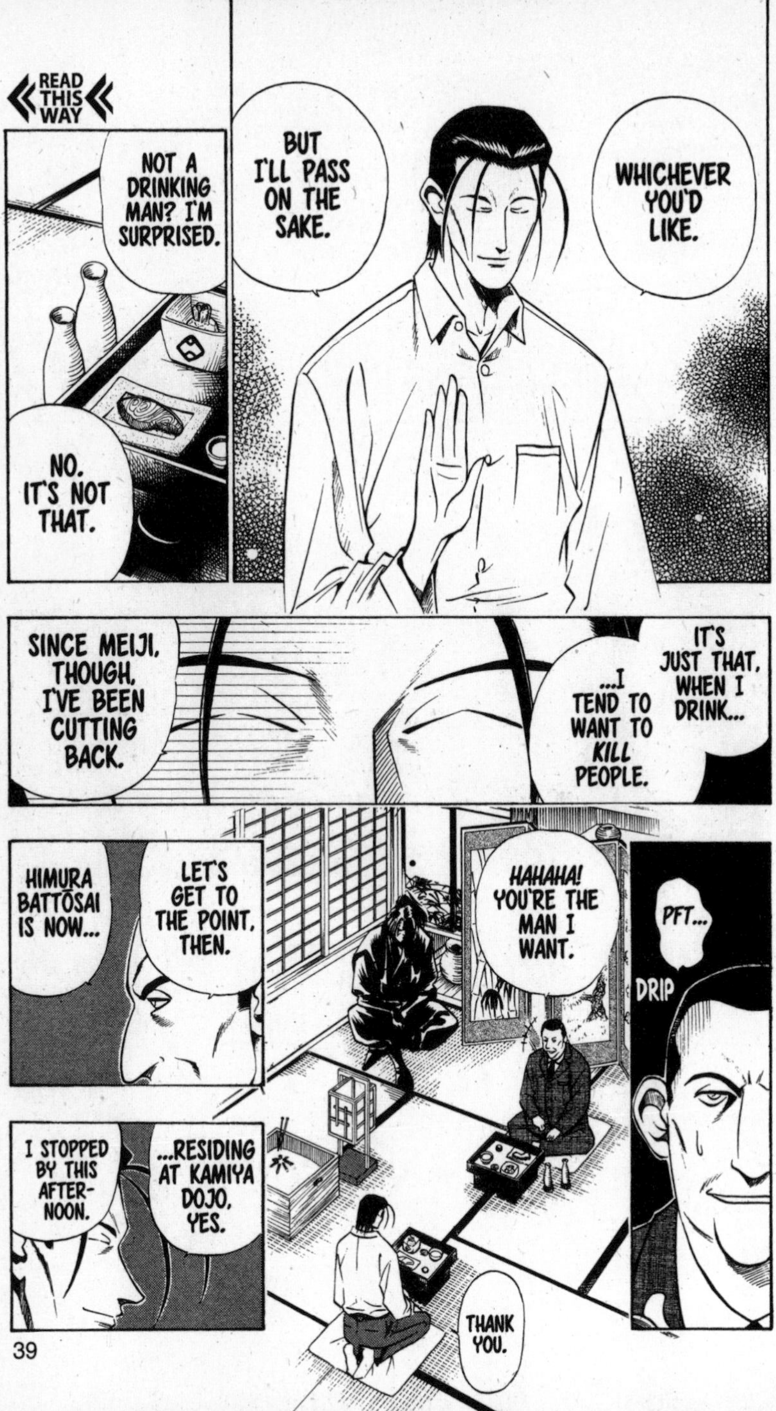
WHICHEVER YOU'D LIKE.
BUT I'LL PASS ON THE SAKE.
NOT A DRINKING MAN? I'M SURPRISED.
NO. IT'S NOT THAT.
IT'S JUST THAT, WHEN I DRINK...
...I TEND TO WANT TO *KILL* PEOPLE.
SINCE MEIJI, THOUGH, I'VE BEEN CUTTING BACK.
PFT...
DRIP
HAHAHA! YOU'RE THE MAN I WANT.
THANK YOU.
LET'S GET TO THE POINT, THEN.
HIMURA BATTŌSAI IS NOW...
...RESIDING AT KAMIYA DOJO, YES.
I STOPPED BY THIS AFTER-NOON.

READ THIS WAY

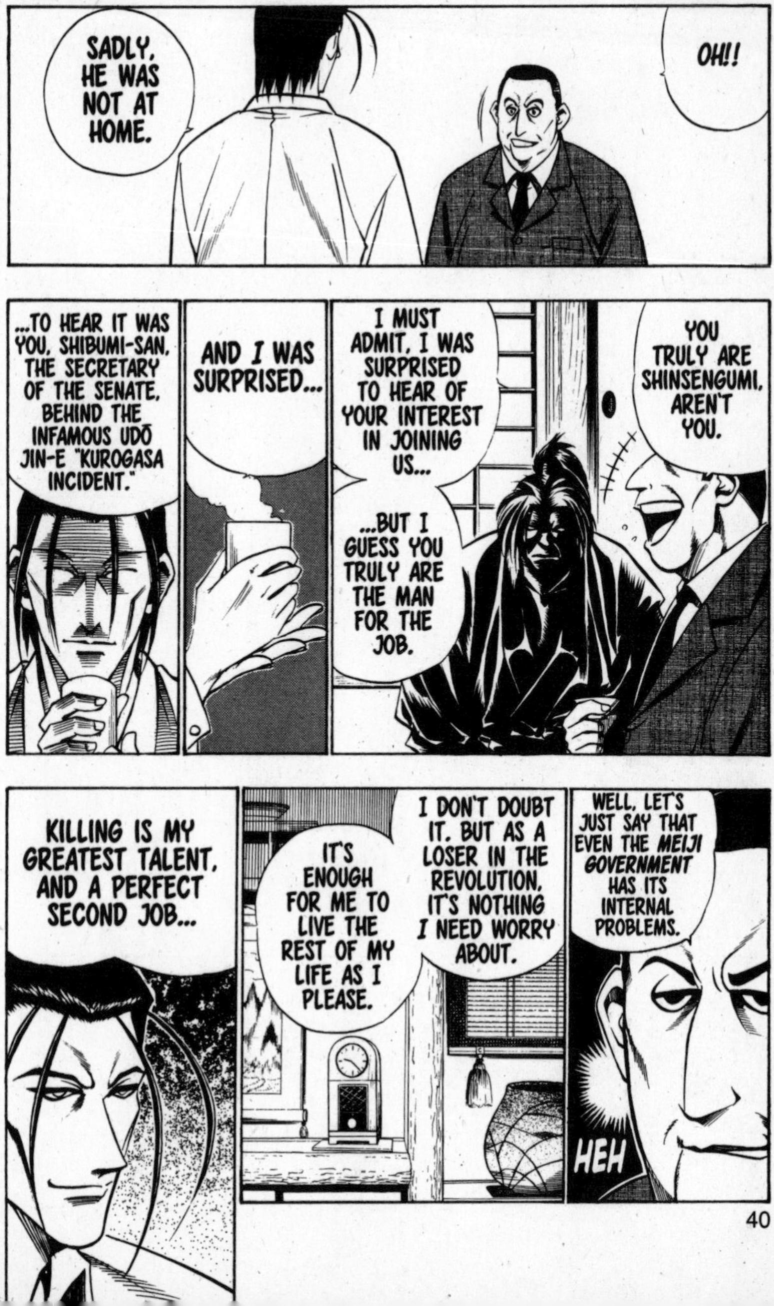
OH!!
SADLY, HE WAS NOT AT HOME.
YOU TRULY ARE SHINSENGUMI, AREN'T YOU.
I MUST ADMIT, I WAS SURPRISED TO HEAR OF YOUR INTEREST IN JOINING US...
...BUT I GUESS YOU TRULY ARE THE MAN FOR THE JOB.
AND *I* WAS SURPRISED...
...TO HEAR IT WAS YOU, SHIBUMI-SAN, THE SECRETARY OF THE SENATE, BEHIND THE INFAMOUS UDŌ JIN-E "KUROGASA INCIDENT."
WELL, LET'S JUST SAY THAT EVEN THE *MEIJI GOVERNMENT* HAS ITS INTERNAL PROBLEMS.
HEH
I DON'T DOUBT IT. BUT AS A LOSER IN THE REVOLUTION, IT'S NOTHING *I* NEED WORRY ABOUT.
IT'S ENOUGH FOR ME TO LIVE THE REST OF MY LIFE AS I PLEASE.
KILLING IS MY GREATEST TALENT, AND A PERFECT SECOND JOB...

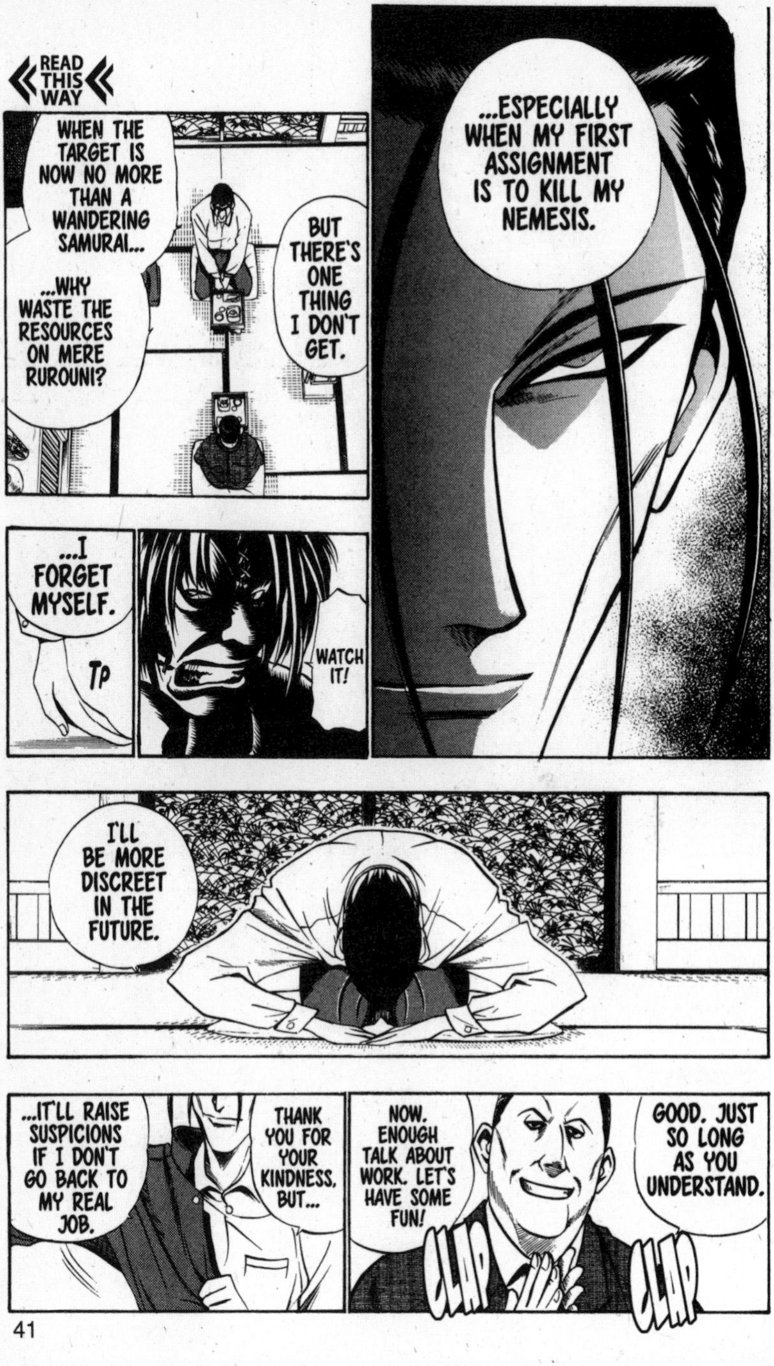
READ THIS WAY
...ESPECIALLY WHEN MY FIRST ASSIGNMENT IS TO KILL MY NEMESIS.
BUT THERE'S ONE THING I DON'T GET.
WHEN THE TARGET IS NOW NO MORE THAN A WANDERING SAMURAI...
...WHY WASTE THE RESOURCES ON MERE RUROUNI?
WATCH IT!
...I FORGET MYSELF.
TP
I'LL BE MORE DISCREET IN THE FUTURE.
GOOD. JUST SO LONG AS YOU UNDERSTAND.
NOW. ENOUGH TALK ABOUT WORK. LET'S HAVE SOME FUN!
CLAP
CLAP
THANK YOU FOR YOUR KINDNESS. BUT...
...IT'LL RAISE SUSPICIONS IF I DON'T GO BACK TO MY REAL JOB.

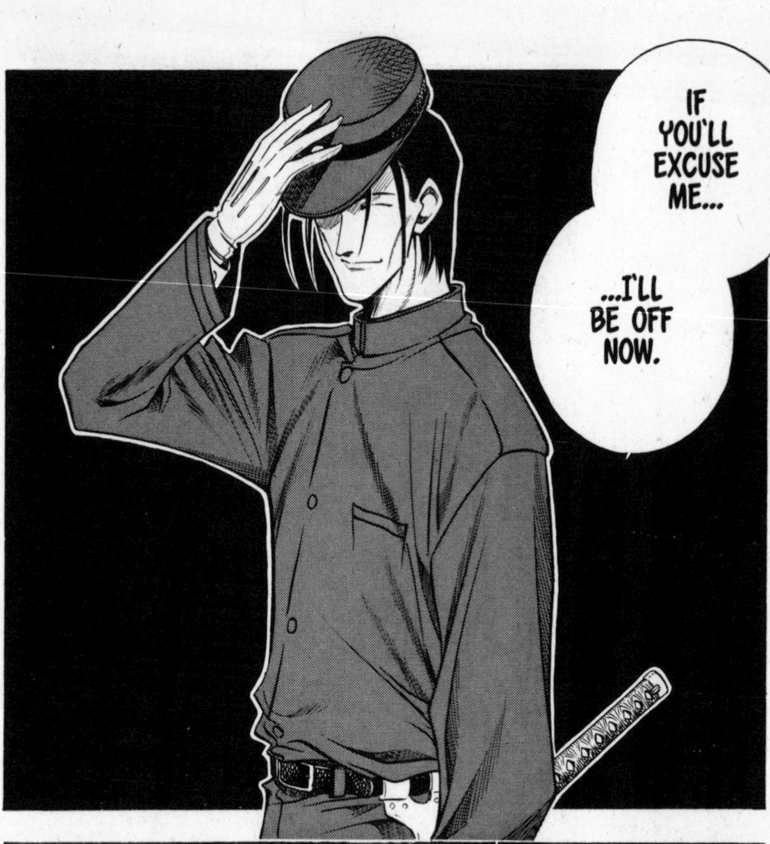
IF YOU'LL EXCUSE ME...
...I'LL BE OFF NOW.

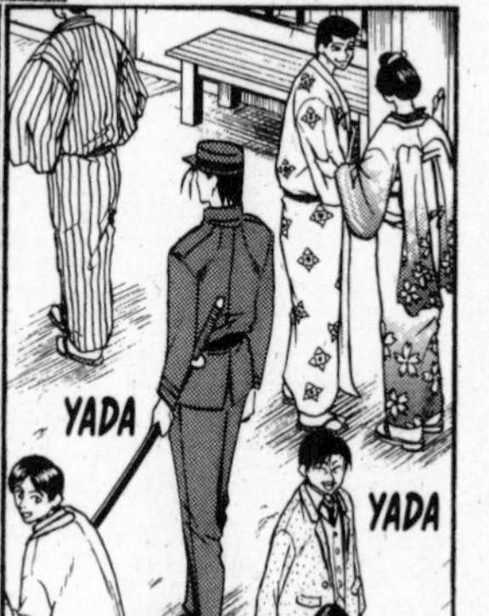
YADA
YADA

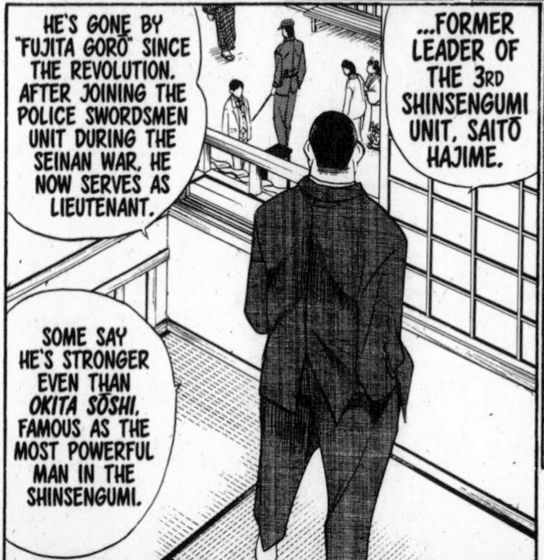
...FORMER LEADER OF THE 3RD SHINSENGUMI UNIT, SAITŌ HAJIME.
HE'S GONE BY "FUJITA GORŌ" SINCE THE REVOLUTION. AFTER JOINING THE POLICE SWORDSMEN UNIT DURING THE SEINAN WAR, HE NOW SERVES AS LIEUTENANT.
SOME SAY HE'S STRONGER EVEN THAN OKITA SŌSHI, FAMOUS AS THE MOST POWERFUL MAN IN THE SHINSENGUMI.

READ THIS WAY

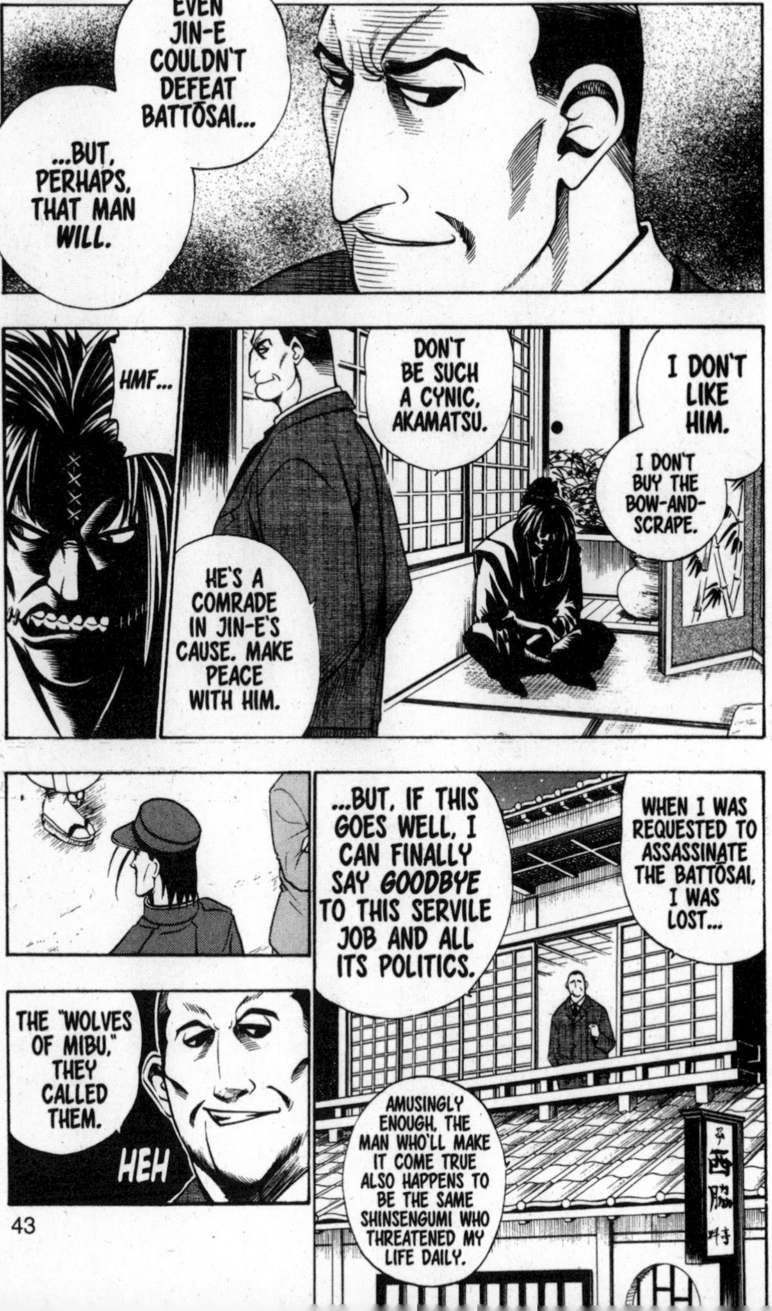

EVEN JIN-E COULDN'T DEFEAT BATTŌSAI...
...BUT, PERHAPS, THAT MAN *WILL.*
I DON'T LIKE HIM.
I DON'T BUY THE BOW-AND-SCRAPE.
DON'T BE SUCH A CYNIC, AKAMATSU.
HE'S A COMRADE IN JIN-E'S CAUSE. MAKE PEACE WITH HIM.
HMF...
WHEN I WAS REQUESTED TO ASSASSINATE THE BATTŌSAI, I WAS LOST...
...BUT, IF THIS GOES WELL, I CAN FINALLY SAY *GOODBYE* TO THIS SERVILE JOB AND ALL ITS POLITICS.
AMUSINGLY ENOUGH, THE MAN WHO'LL MAKE IT COME TRUE ALSO HAPPENS TO BE THE SAME SHINSENGUMI WHO THREATENED MY LIFE DAILY.
THE "WOLVES OF MIBU," THEY CALLED THEM.
HEH

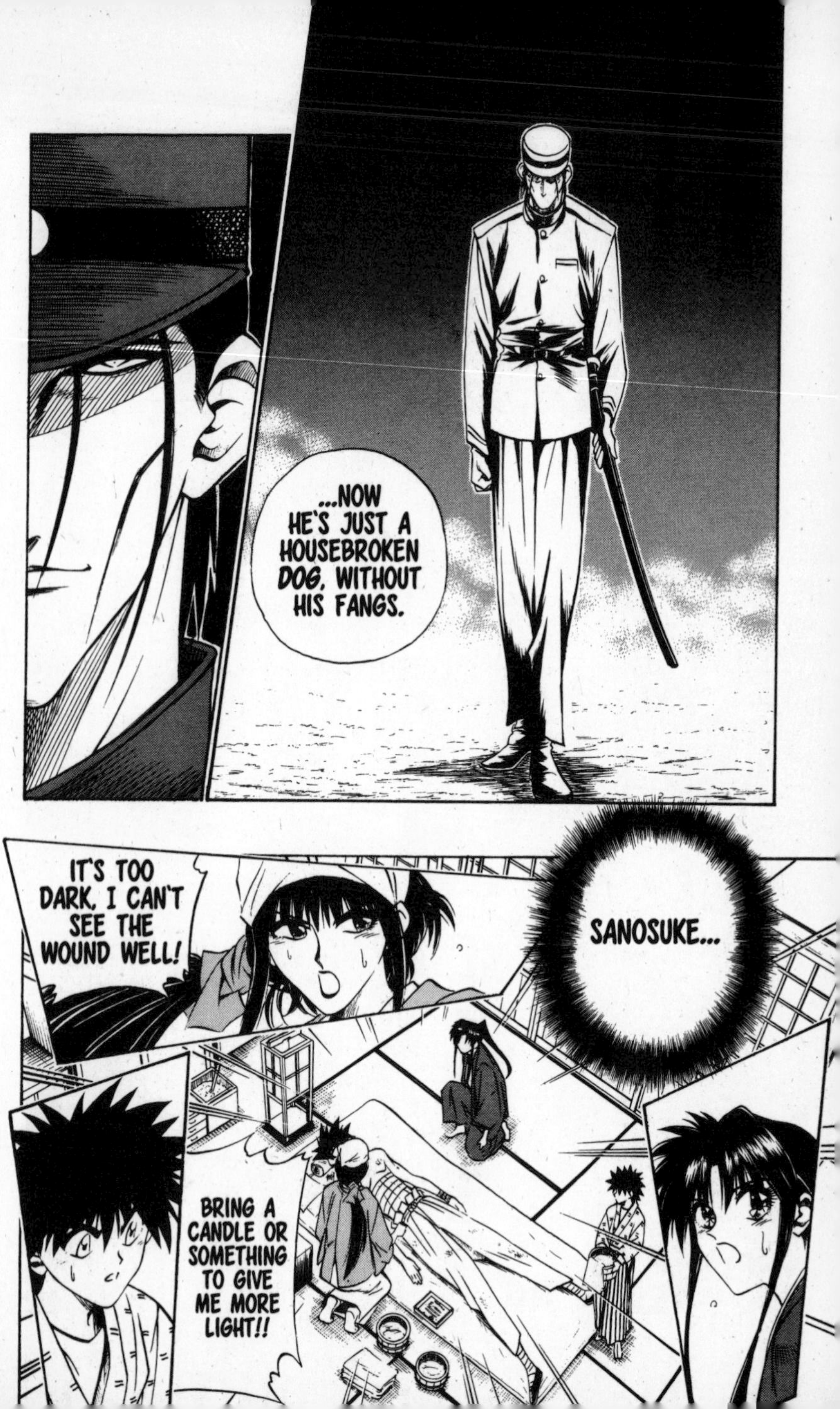
...NOW HE'S JUST A HOUSEBROKEN DOG, WITHOUT HIS FANGS.
SANOSUKE...
IT'S TOO DARK, I CAN'T SEE THE WOUND WELL!
BRING A CANDLE OR SOMETHING TO GIVE ME MORE LIGHT!!

READ THIS WAY

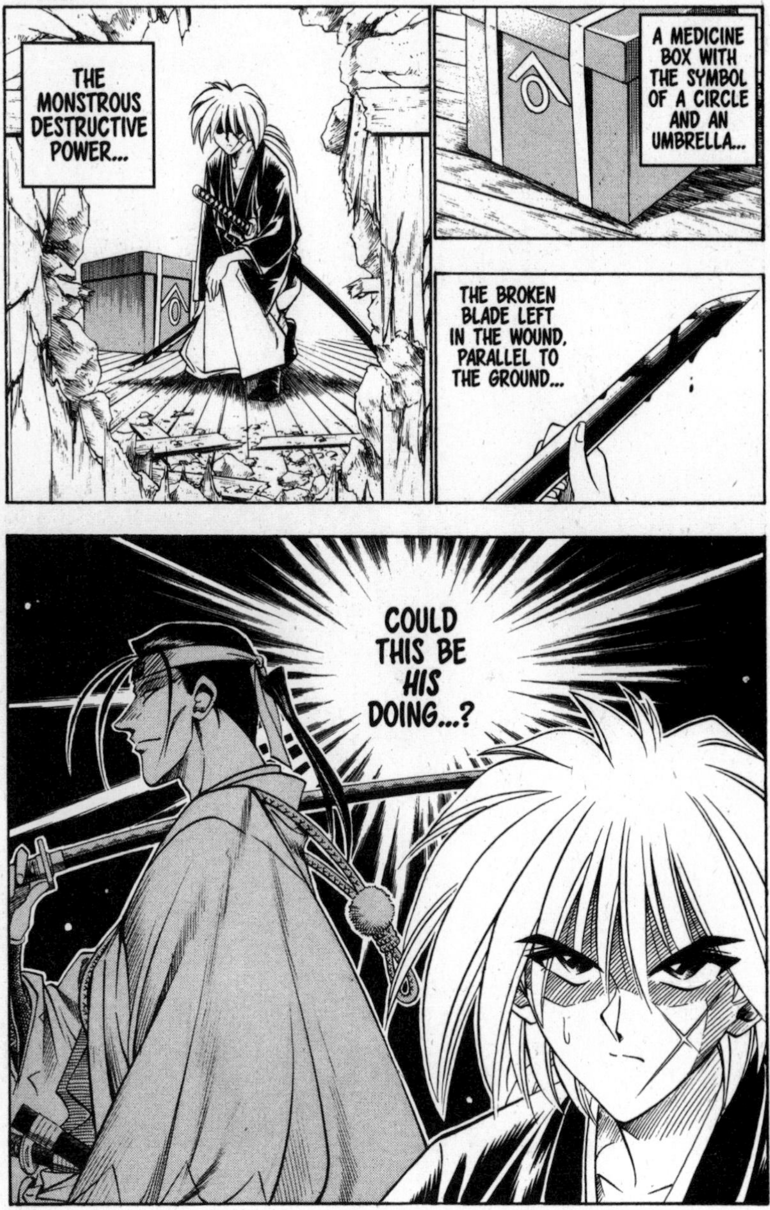
A MEDICINE BOX WITH THE SYMBOL OF A CIRCLE AND AN UMBRELLA...
THE BROKEN BLADE LEFT IN THE WOUND, PARALLEL TO THE GROUND...
THE MONSTROUS DESTRUCTIVE POWER...
COULD THIS BE *HIS* DOING...?

Rurouni Kenshin

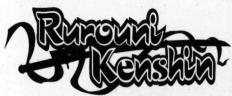

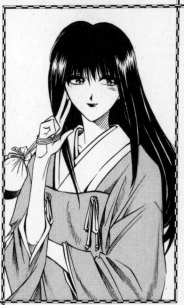

READ THIS WAY

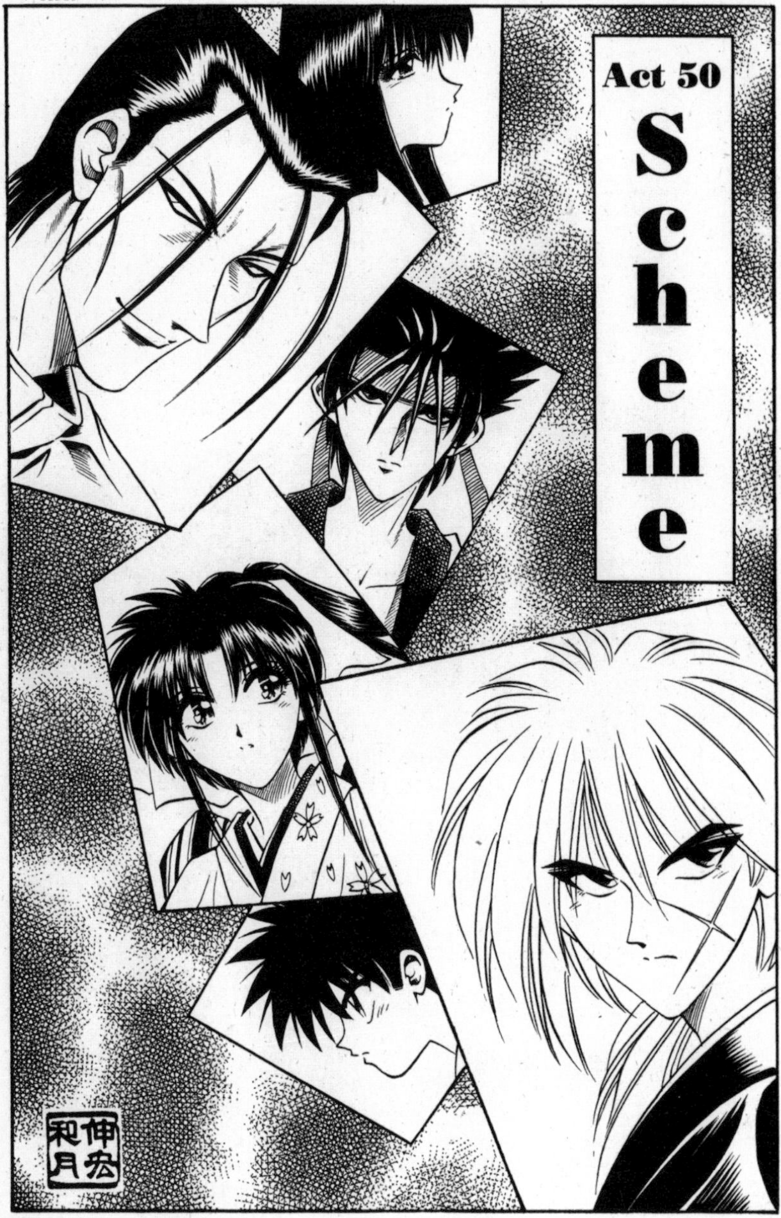
Act 50
Scheme
伸宏
和月

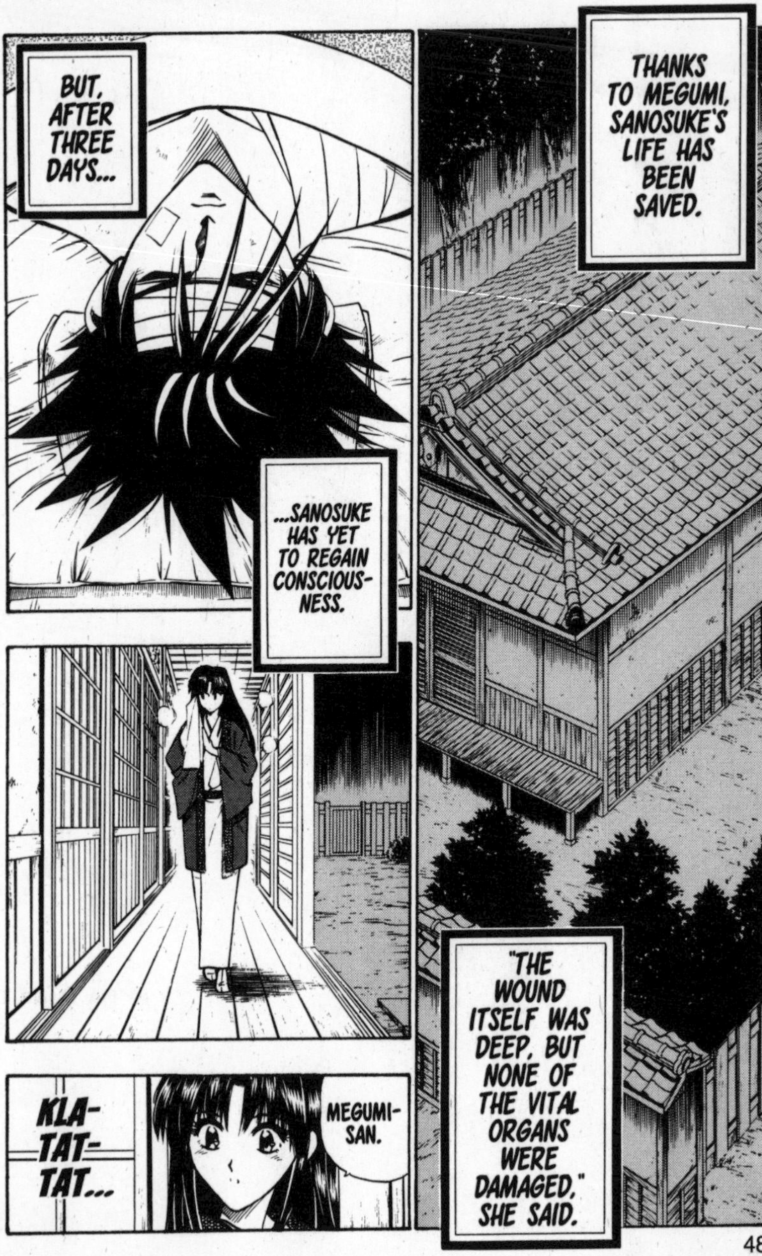
THANKS TO MEGUMI, SANOSUKE'S LIFE HAS BEEN SAVED.
"THE WOUND ITSELF WAS DEEP, BUT NONE OF THE VITAL ORGANS WERE DAMAGED," SHE SAID.
BUT, AFTER THREE DAYS...
...SANOSUKE HAS YET TO REGAIN CONSCIOUS-NESS.
MEGUMI-SAN.
KLA-TAT-TAT...

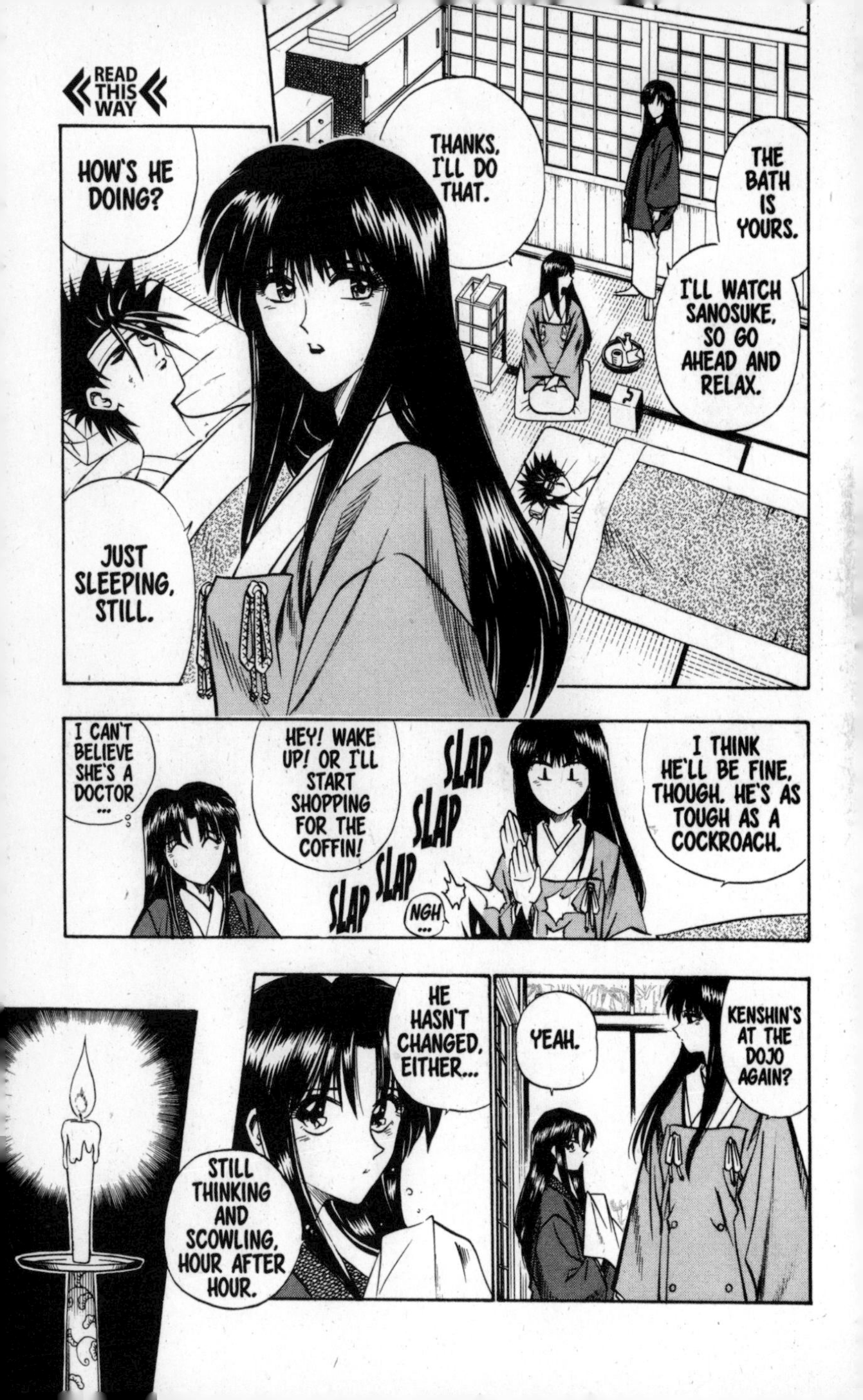
READ THIS WAY
THE BATH IS YOURS.
I'LL WATCH SANOSUKE, SO GO AHEAD AND RELAX.
THANKS, I'LL DO THAT.
HOW'S HE DOING?
JUST SLEEPING, STILL.
I THINK HE'LL BE FINE, THOUGH. HE'S AS TOUGH AS A COCKROACH.
SLAP
SLAP
SLAP
SLAP
NGH...
HEY! WAKE UP! OR I'LL START SHOPPING FOR THE COFFIN!
I CAN'T BELIEVE SHE'S A DOCTOR...
KENSHIN'S AT THE DOJO AGAIN?
YEAH.
HE HASN'T CHANGED, EITHER...
STILL THINKING AND SCOWLING, HOUR AFTER HOUR.

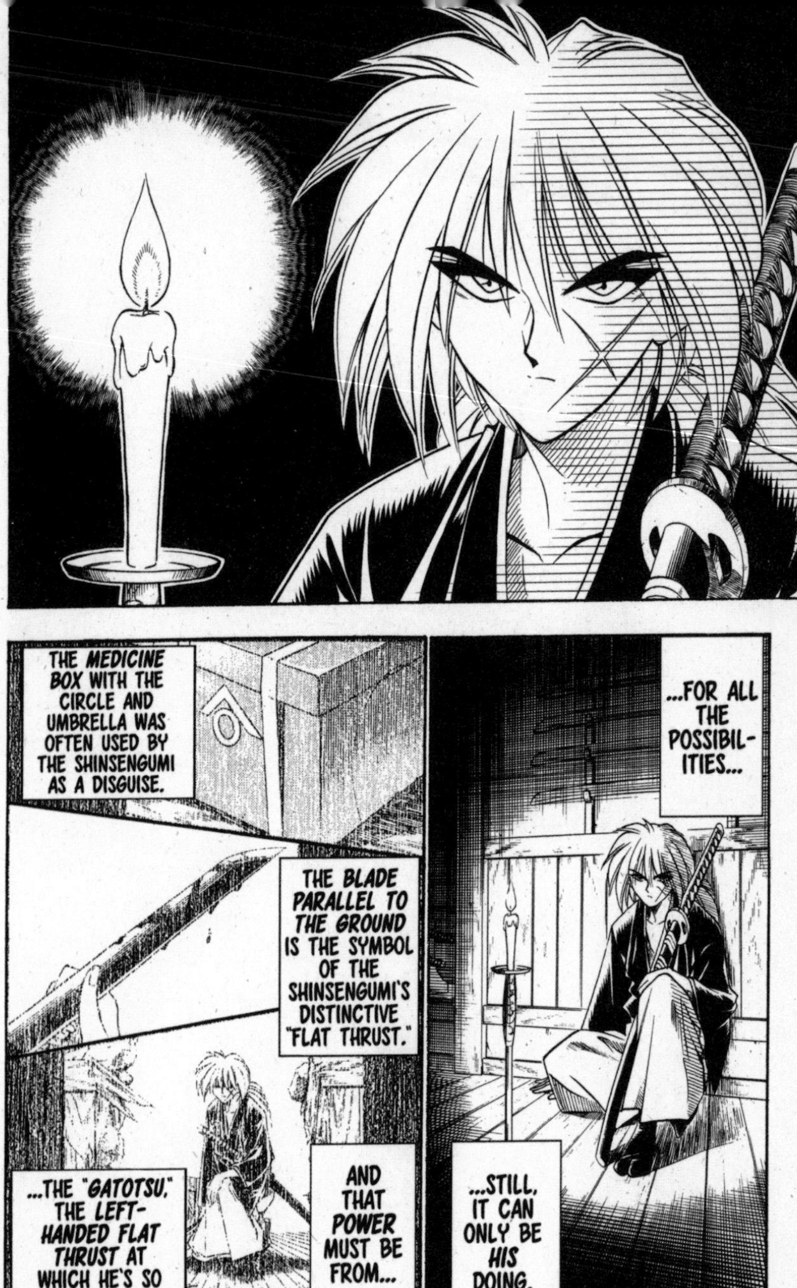
...FOR ALL THE POSSIBIL-ITIES...
...STILL, IT CAN ONLY BE HIS DOING.
THE MEDICINE BOX WITH THE CIRCLE AND UMBRELLA WAS OFTEN USED BY THE SHINSENGUMI AS A DISGUISE.
THE BLADE PARALLEL TO THE GROUND IS THE SYMBOL OF THE SHINSENGUMI'S DISTINCTIVE "FLAT THRUST."
AND THAT POWER MUST BE FROM...
...THE "GATOTSU," THE LEFT-HANDED FLAT THRUST AT WHICH HE'S SO PROFICIENT.

READ THIS WAY

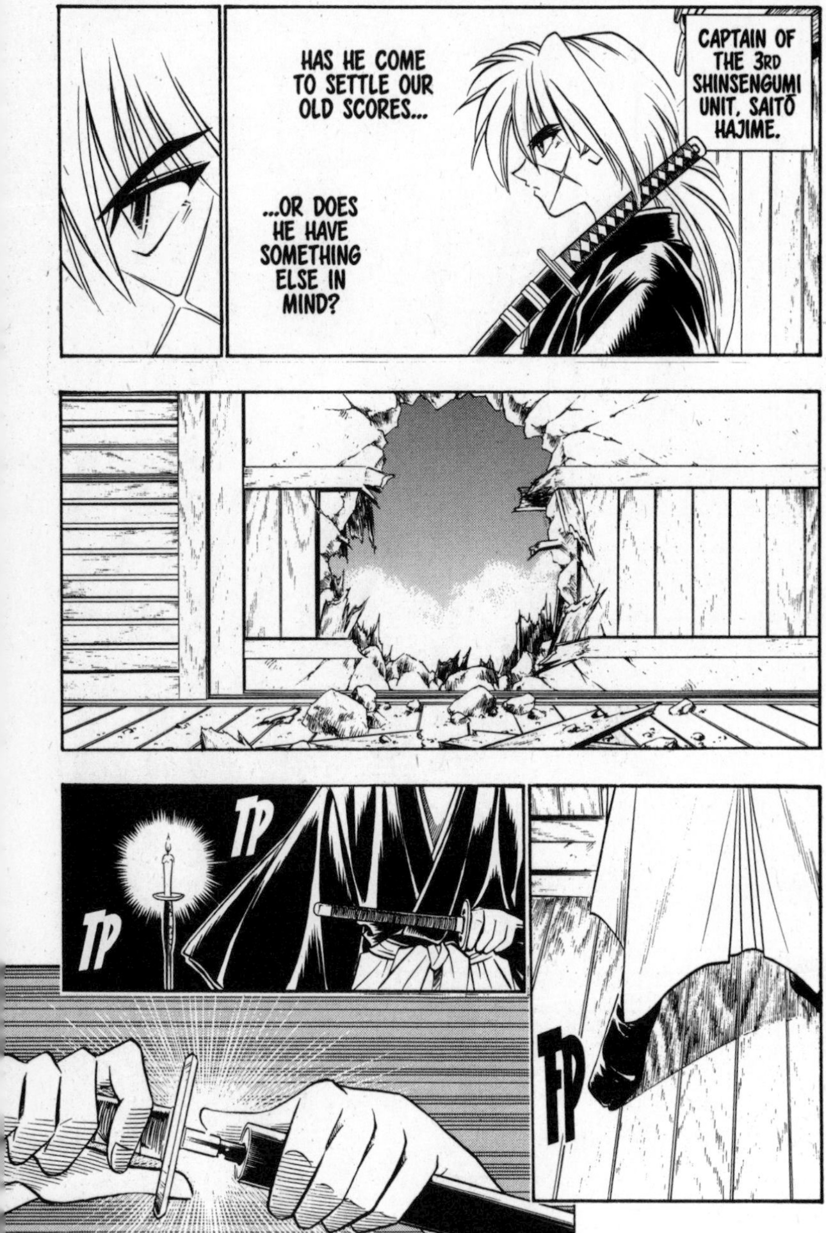
CAPTAIN OF THE 3RD SHINSENGUMI UNIT, SAITŌ HAJIME.
HAS HE COME TO SETTLE OUR OLD SCORES...
...OR DOES HE HAVE SOMETHING ELSE IN MIND?
TP
TP
TP

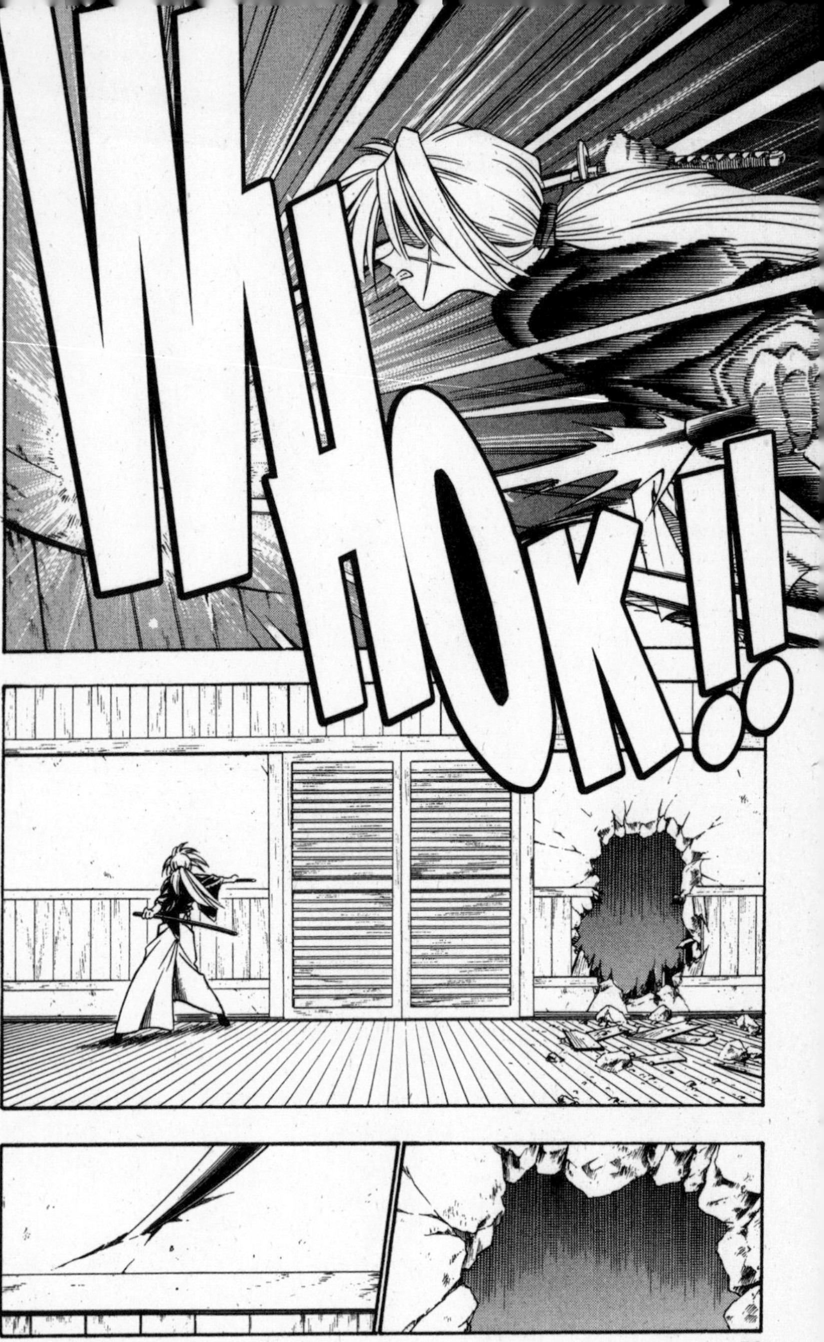
WHOK!!

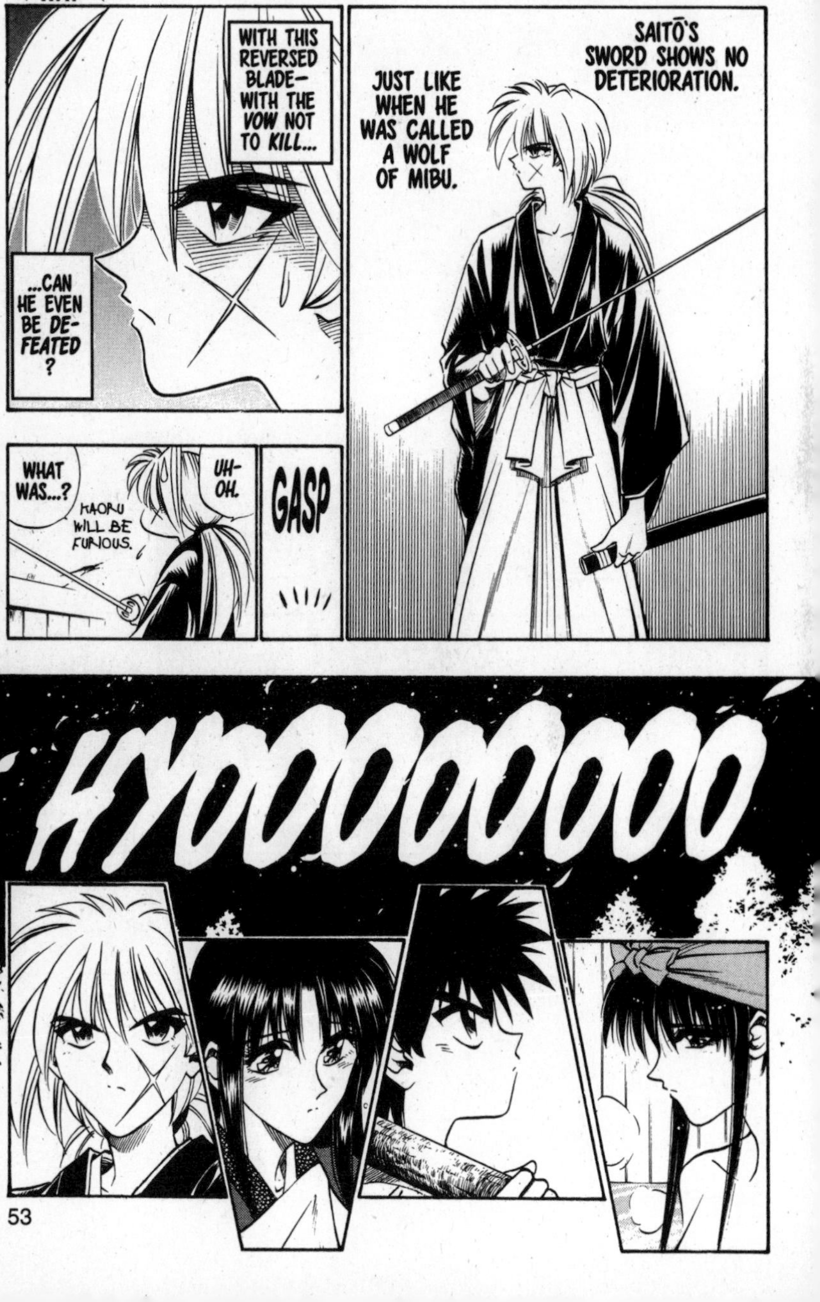
SAITŌ'S SWORD SHOWS NO DETERIORATION.
JUST LIKE WHEN HE WAS CALLED A WOLF OF MIBU.
WITH THIS REVERSED BLADE— WITH THE VOW NOT TO KILL...
...CAN HE EVEN BE DE- FEATED ?
GASP
UH- OH.
WHAT WAS...?
KAORU WILL BE FURIOUS.
HYOOOOOOOO

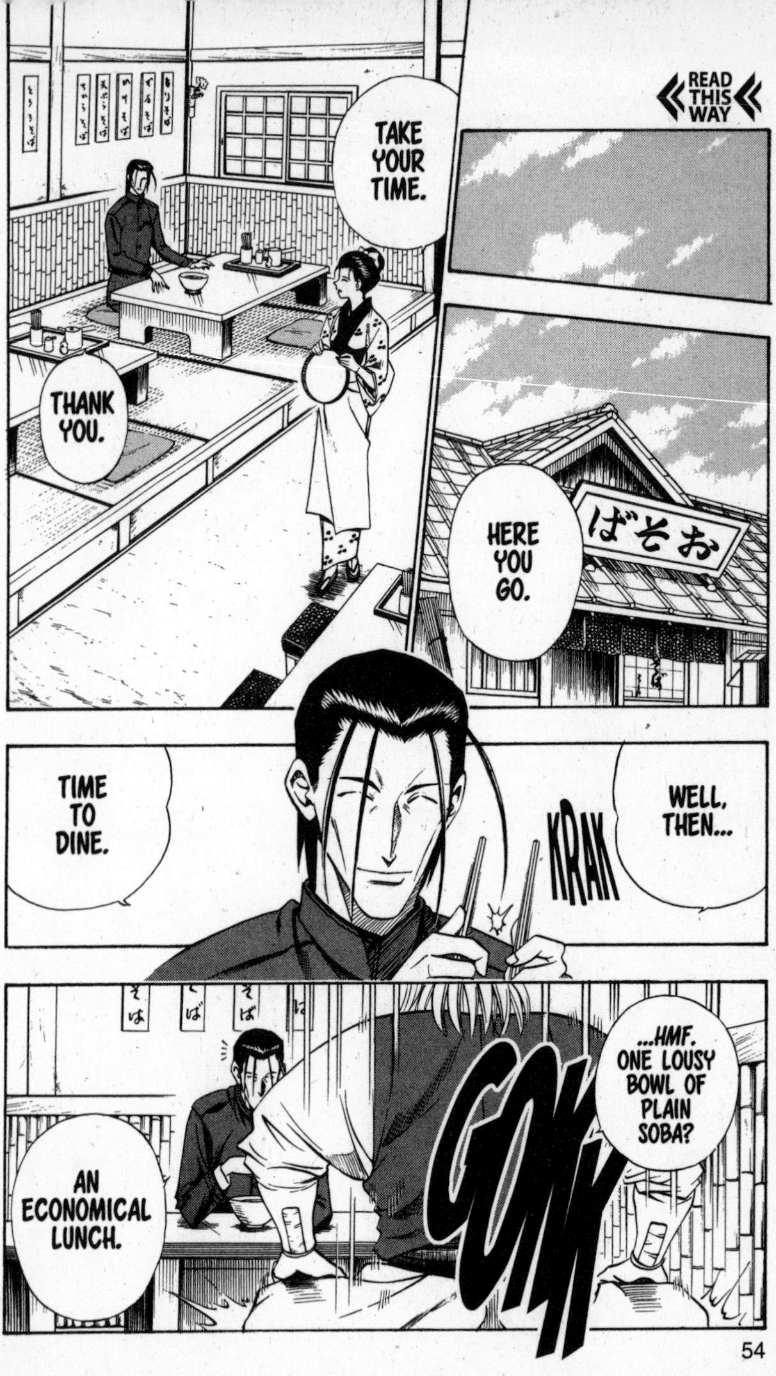
READ THIS WAY
HERE YOU GO.
おそば
TAKE YOUR TIME.
THANK YOU.
WELL, THEN...
KRAK
TIME TO DINE.
...HMF. ONE LOUSY BOWL OF PLAIN SOBA?
GONK
AN ECONOMICAL LUNCH.

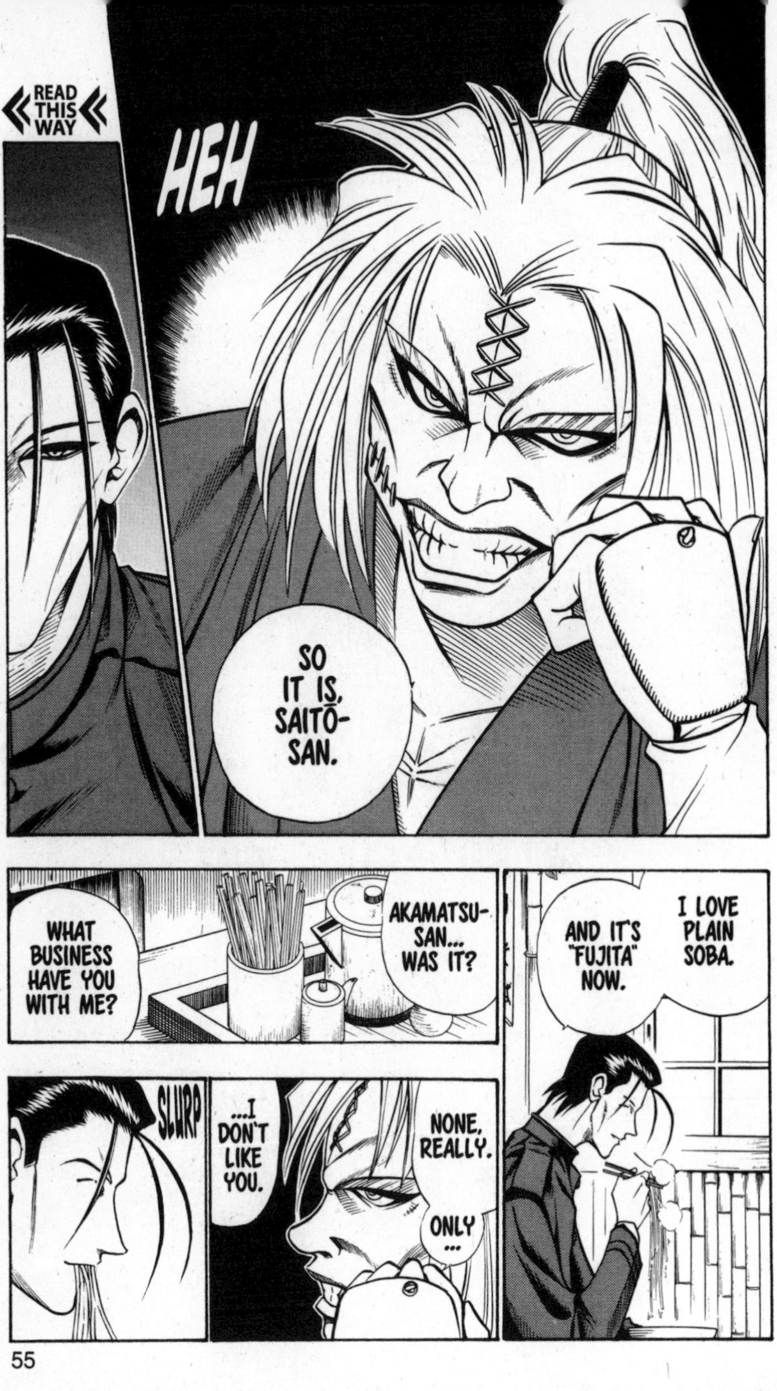
READ THIS WAY
HEH
SO IT IS, SAITŌ-SAN.
I LOVE PLAIN SOBA.
AND IT'S "FUJITA" NOW.
AKAMATSU-SAN... WAS IT?
WHAT BUSINESS HAVE YOU WITH ME?
NONE, REALLY.
ONLY ...
...I DON'T LIKE YOU.
SLURP

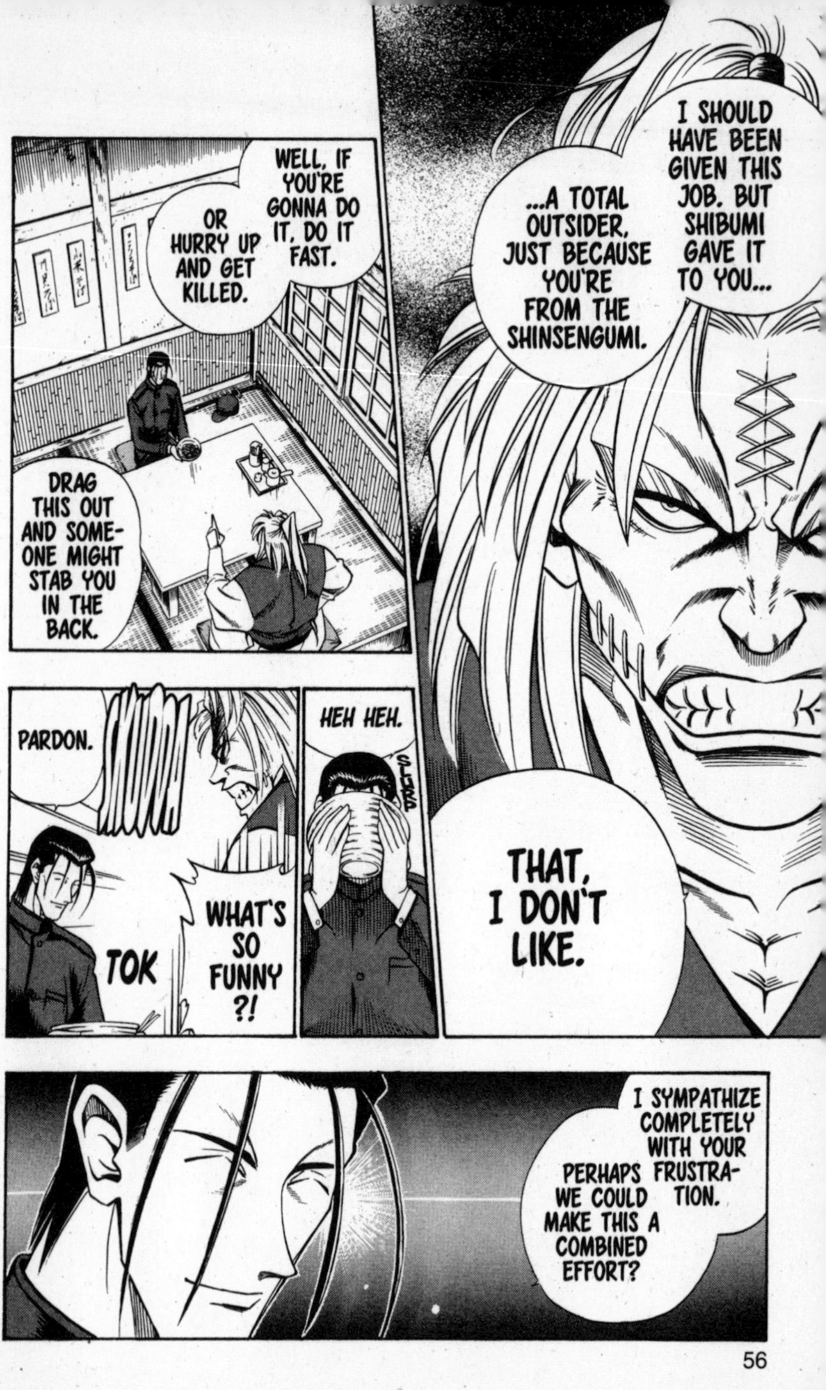
I SHOULD HAVE BEEN GIVEN THIS JOB. BUT SHIBUMI GAVE IT TO YOU...
...A TOTAL OUTSIDER, JUST BECAUSE YOU'RE FROM THE SHINSENGUMI.
THAT, I DON'T LIKE.
WELL, IF YOU'RE GONNA DO IT, DO IT FAST.
OR HURRY UP AND GET KILLED.
DRAG THIS OUT AND SOME-ONE MIGHT STAB YOU IN THE BACK.
HEH HEH.
SLURP
PARDON.
WHAT'S SO FUNNY ?!
TOK
I SYMPATHIZE COMPLETELY WITH YOUR FRUSTRA-TION.
PERHAPS WE COULD MAKE THIS A COMBINED EFFORT?

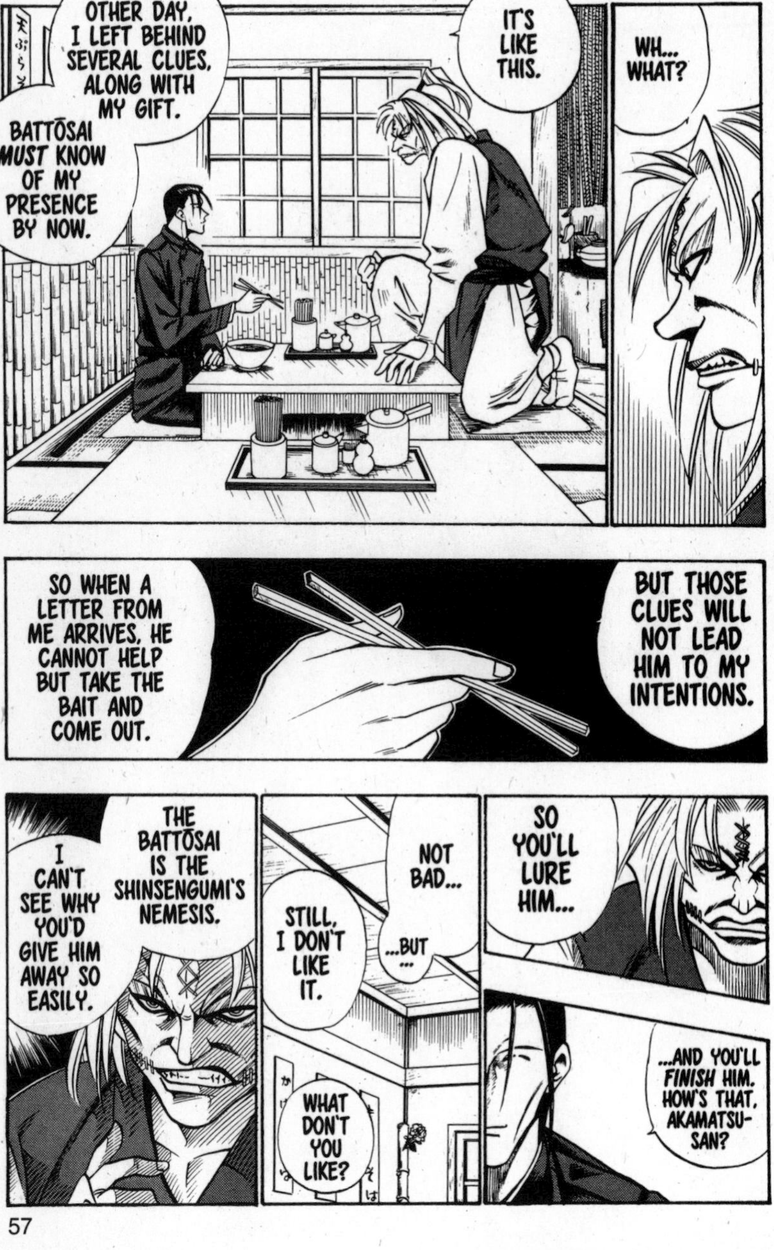
WH... WHAT?
IT'S LIKE THIS.
THE OTHER DAY, I LEFT BEHIND SEVERAL CLUES, ALONG WITH MY GIFT.
BATTŌSAI *MUST* KNOW OF MY PRESENCE BY NOW.
BUT THOSE CLUES WILL NOT LEAD HIM TO MY INTENTIONS.
SO WHEN A LETTER FROM ME ARRIVES, HE CANNOT HELP BUT TAKE THE BAIT AND COME OUT.
SO YOU'LL LURE HIM...
...AND YOU'LL *FINISH* HIM. HOW'S THAT, AKAMATSU-SAN?
NOT BAD...
...BUT ...
STILL, I DON'T LIKE IT.
WHAT DON'T YOU LIKE?
THE BATTŌSAI IS THE SHINSENGUMI'S NEMESIS.
I CAN'T SEE WHY YOU'D GIVE HIM AWAY SO EASILY.

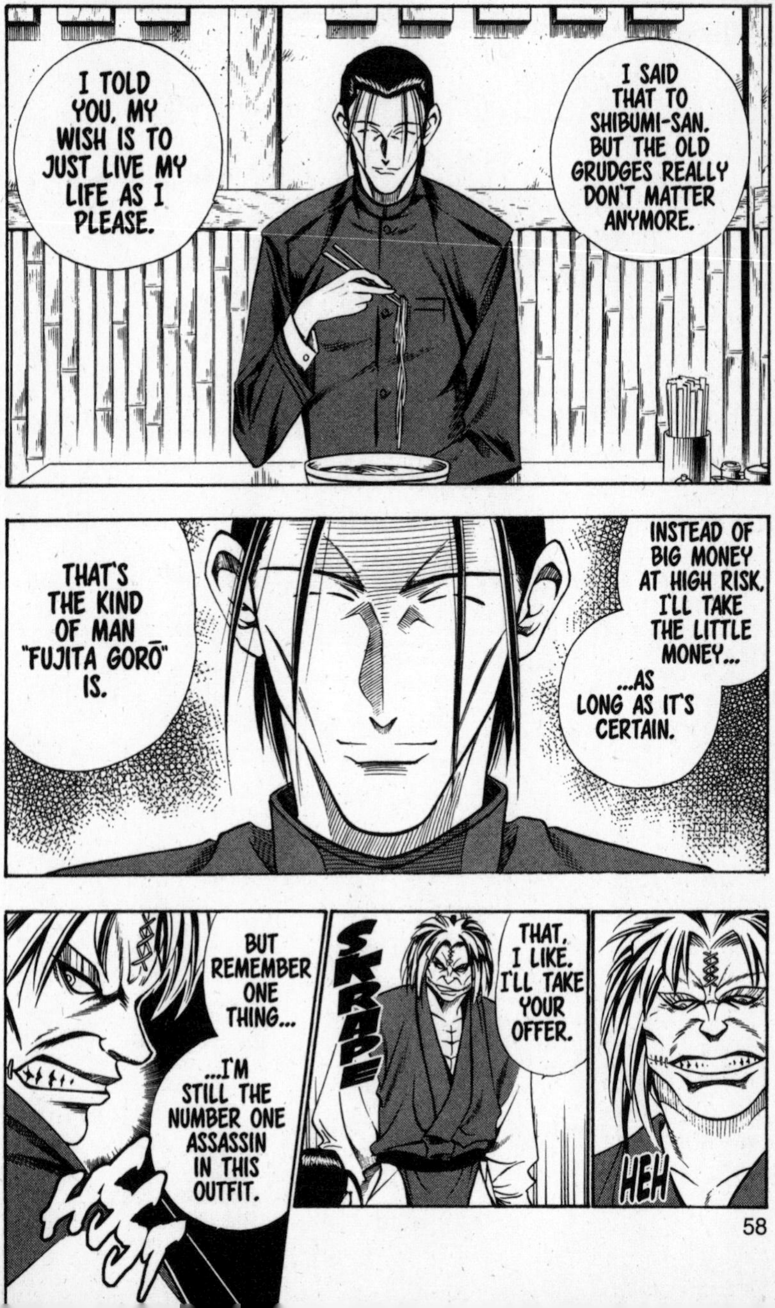
I SAID THAT TO SHIBUMI-SAN. BUT THE OLD GRUDGES REALLY DON'T MATTER ANYMORE.
I TOLD YOU, MY WISH IS TO JUST LIVE MY LIFE AS I PLEASE.
INSTEAD OF BIG MONEY AT HIGH RISK, I'LL TAKE THE LITTLE MONEY...
...AS LONG AS IT'S CERTAIN.
THAT'S THE KIND OF MAN "FUJITA GORŌ" IS.
HEH
THAT, I LIKE. I'LL TAKE YOUR OFFER.
SKRAPE
BUT REMEMBER ONE THING...
...I'M STILL THE NUMBER ONE ASSASSIN IN THIS OUTFIT.

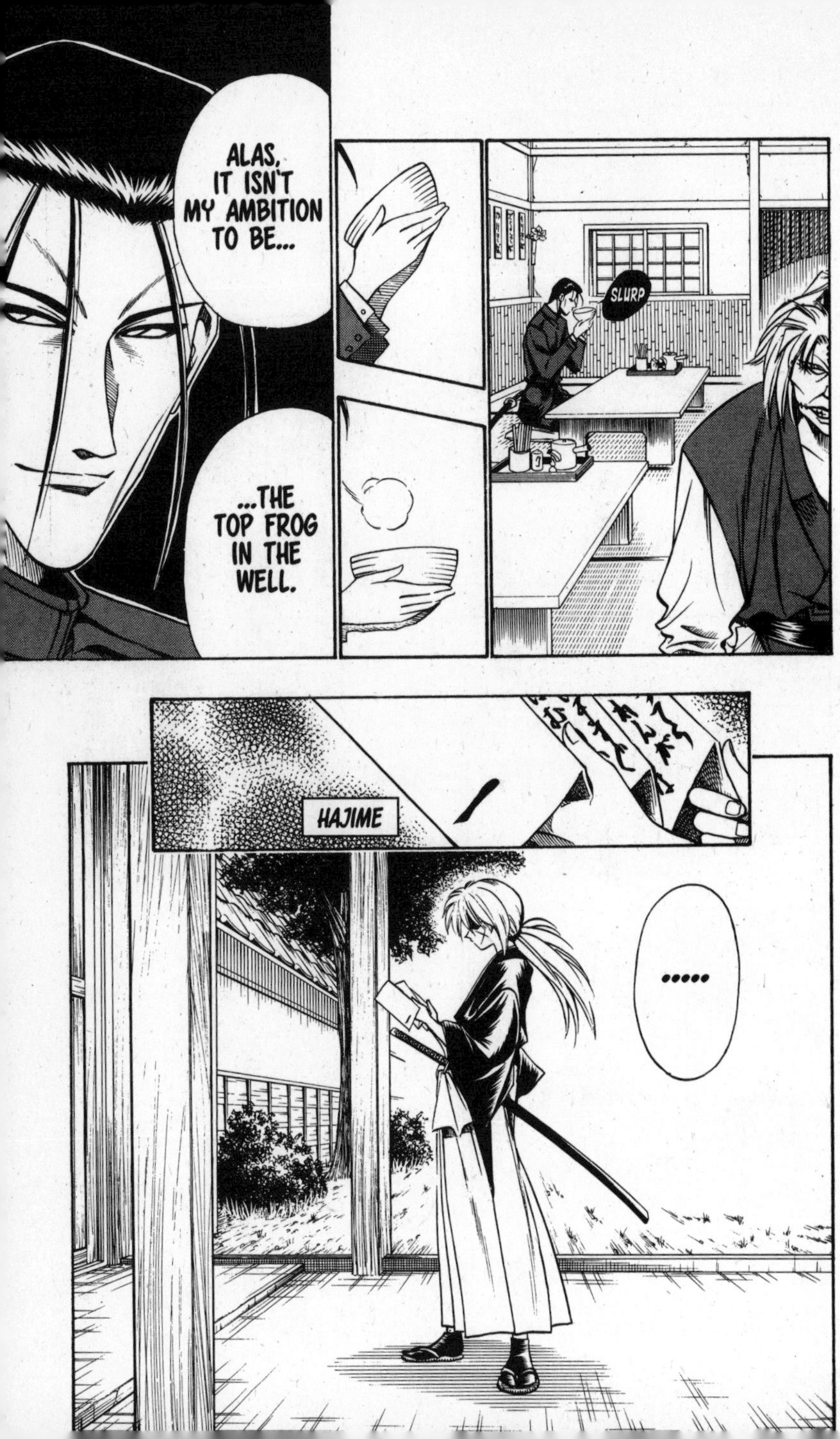
SLURP
ALAS, IT ISN'T MY AMBITION TO BE...
...THE TOP FROG IN THE WELL.
HAJIME
.....

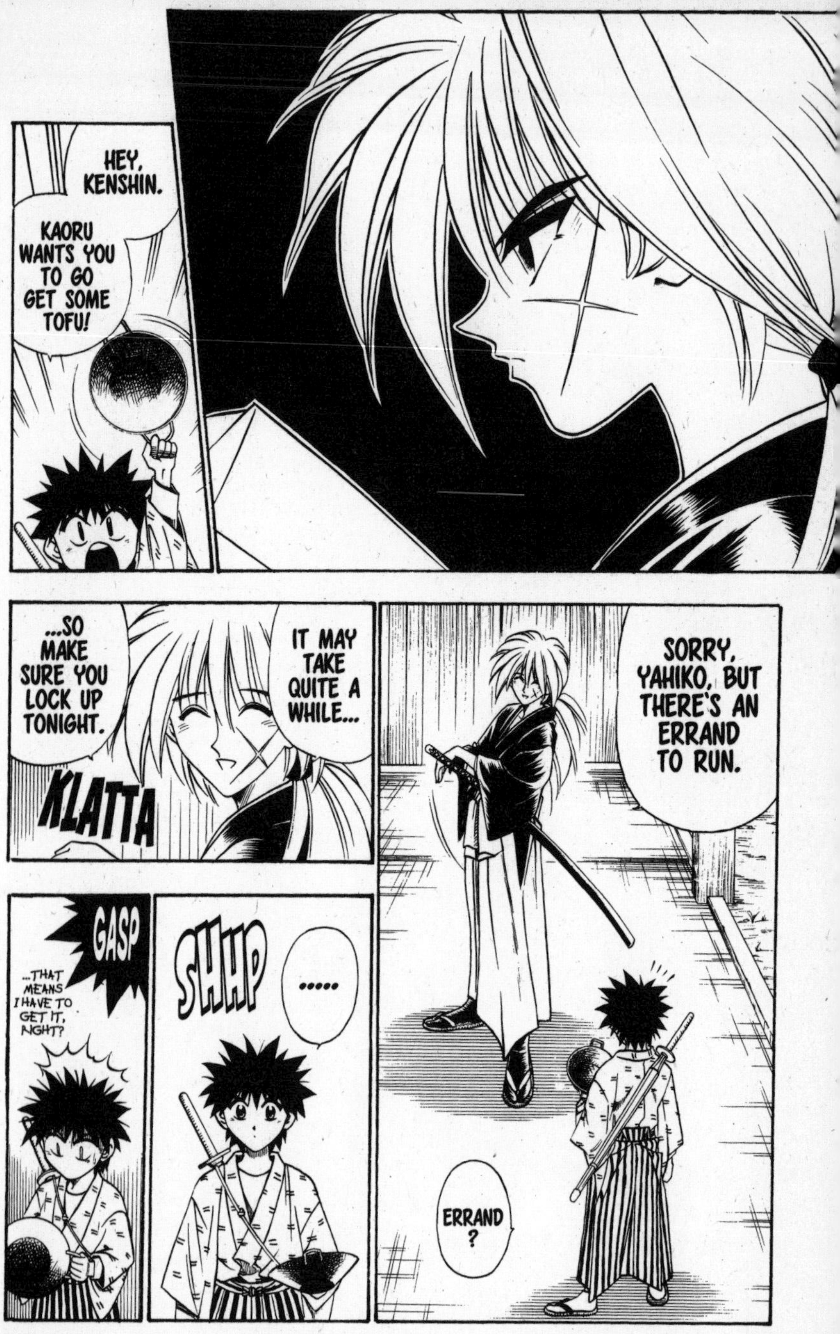
HEY, KENSHIN.
KAORU WANTS YOU TO GO GET SOME TOFU!
SORRY, YAHIKO, BUT THERE'S AN ERRAND TO RUN.
ERRAND?
IT MAY TAKE QUITE A WHILE...
...SO MAKE SURE YOU LOCK UP TONIGHT.
KLATTA
SHHP
......
GASP
...THAT MEANS I HAVE TO GET IT, RIGHT?

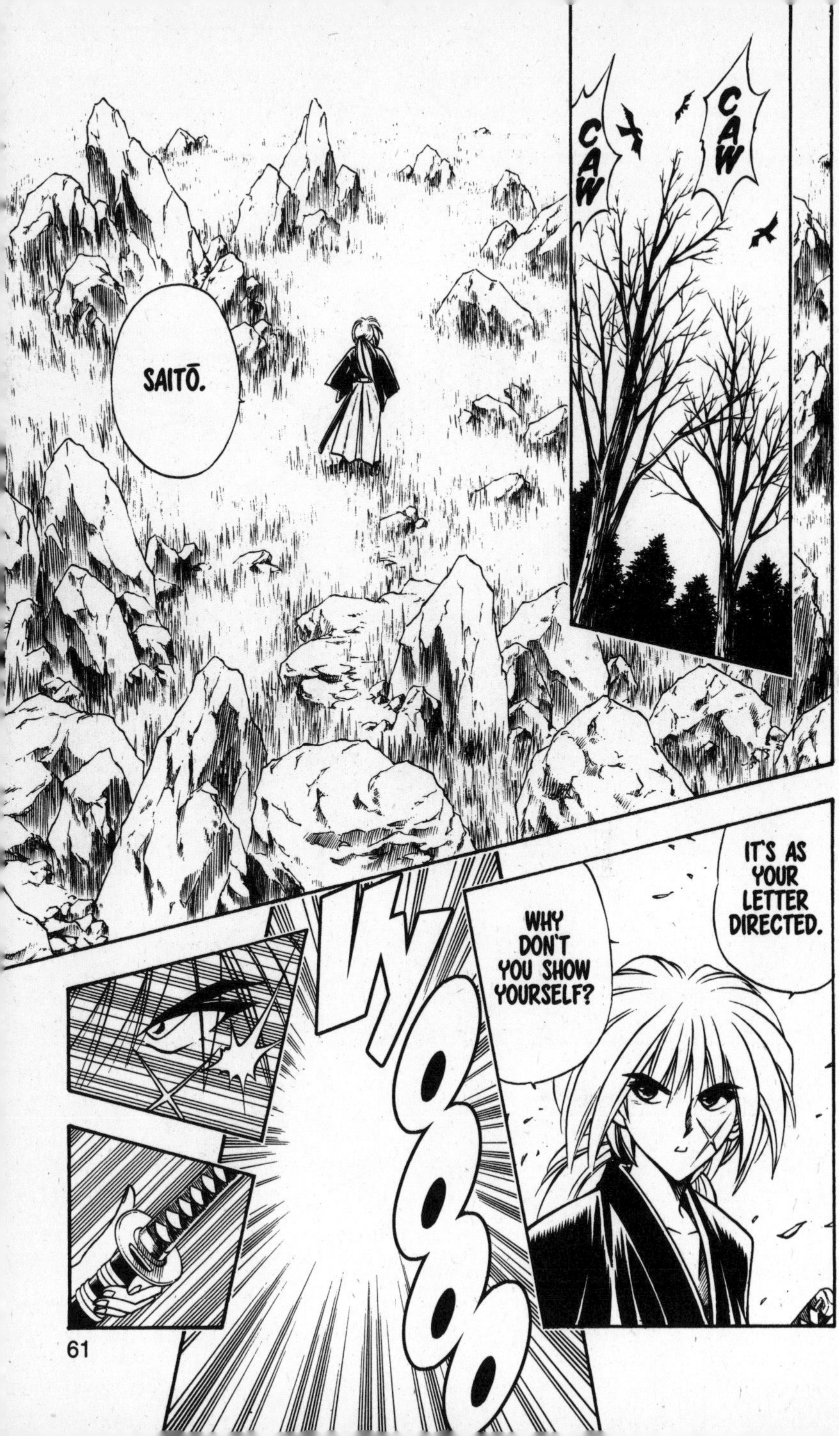
CAW
CAW
SAITŌ.
IT'S AS YOUR LETTER DIRECTED.
WHY DON'T YOU SHOW YOURSELF?
WOOOO

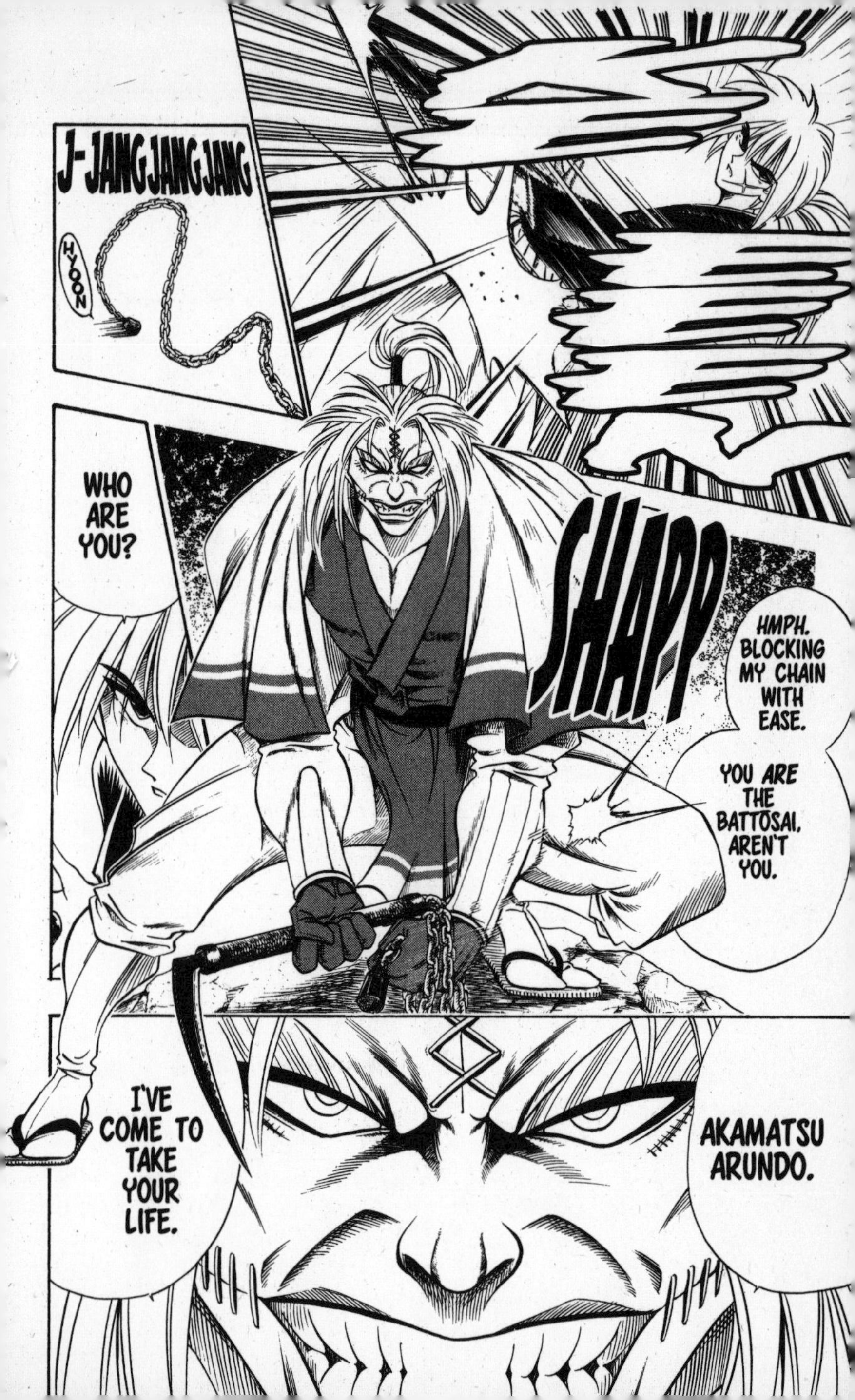
J- JANG JANG JANG
HYOON
SHAPP
HMPH. BLOCKING MY CHAIN WITH EASE.
YOU ARE THE BATTOSAI, AREN'T YOU.
WHO ARE YOU?
AKAMATSU ARUNDO.
I'VE COME TO TAKE YOUR LIFE.

READ THIS WAY

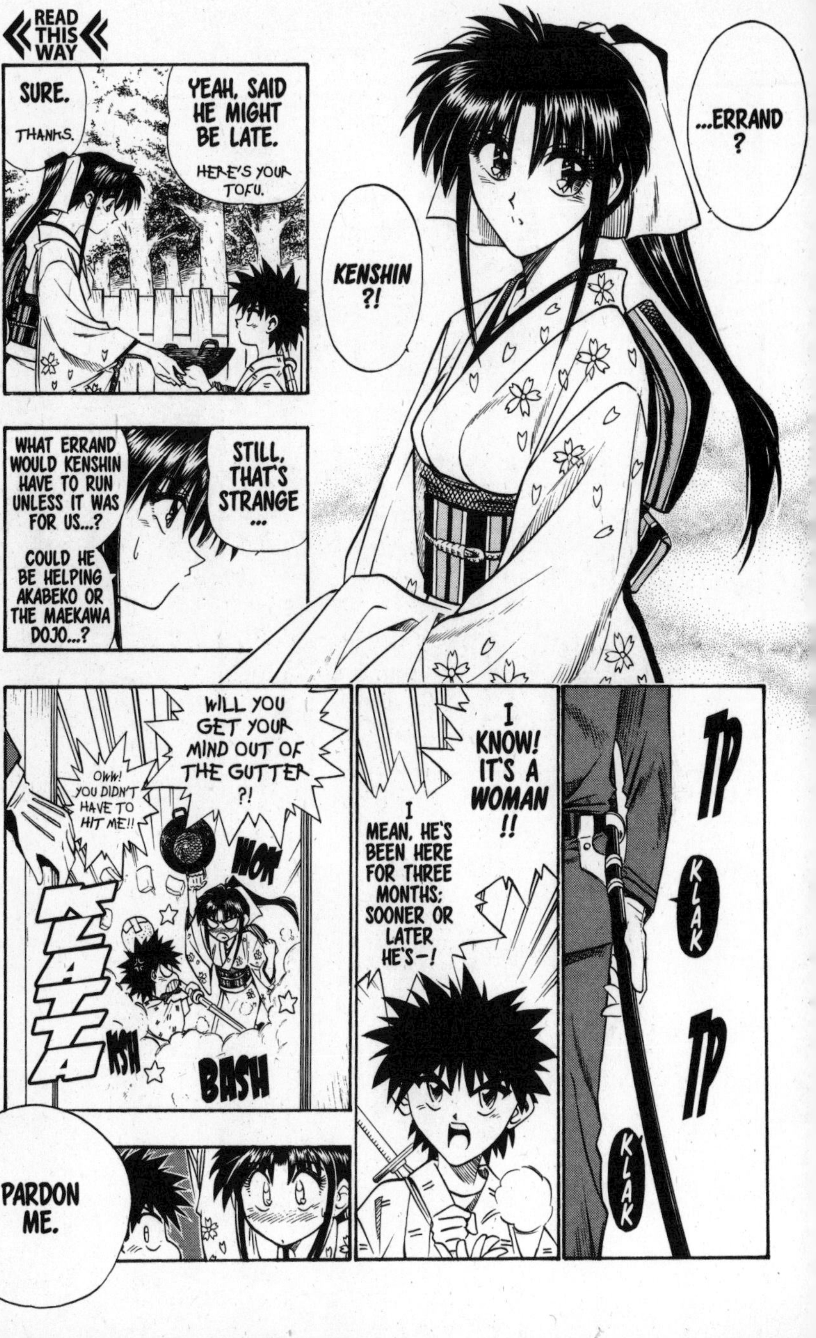
...ERRAND?
KENSHIN?!
YEAH, SAID HE MIGHT BE LATE.
HERE'S YOUR TOFU.
SURE.
THANKS.
STILL, THAT'S STRANGE...
WHAT ERRAND WOULD KENSHIN HAVE TO RUN UNLESS IT WAS FOR US...?
COULD HE BE HELPING AKABEKO OR THE MAEKAWA DOJO...?
TP
KLAK
TP
KLAK
I KNOW! IT'S A WOMAN!!
I MEAN, HE'S BEEN HERE FOR THREE MONTHS; SOONER OR LATER HE'S—!
WILL YOU GET YOUR MIND OUT OF THE GUTTER?!
OWW! YOU DIDN'T HAVE TO HIT ME!!
WOK
KLATTA
KSH
BASH
PARDON ME.

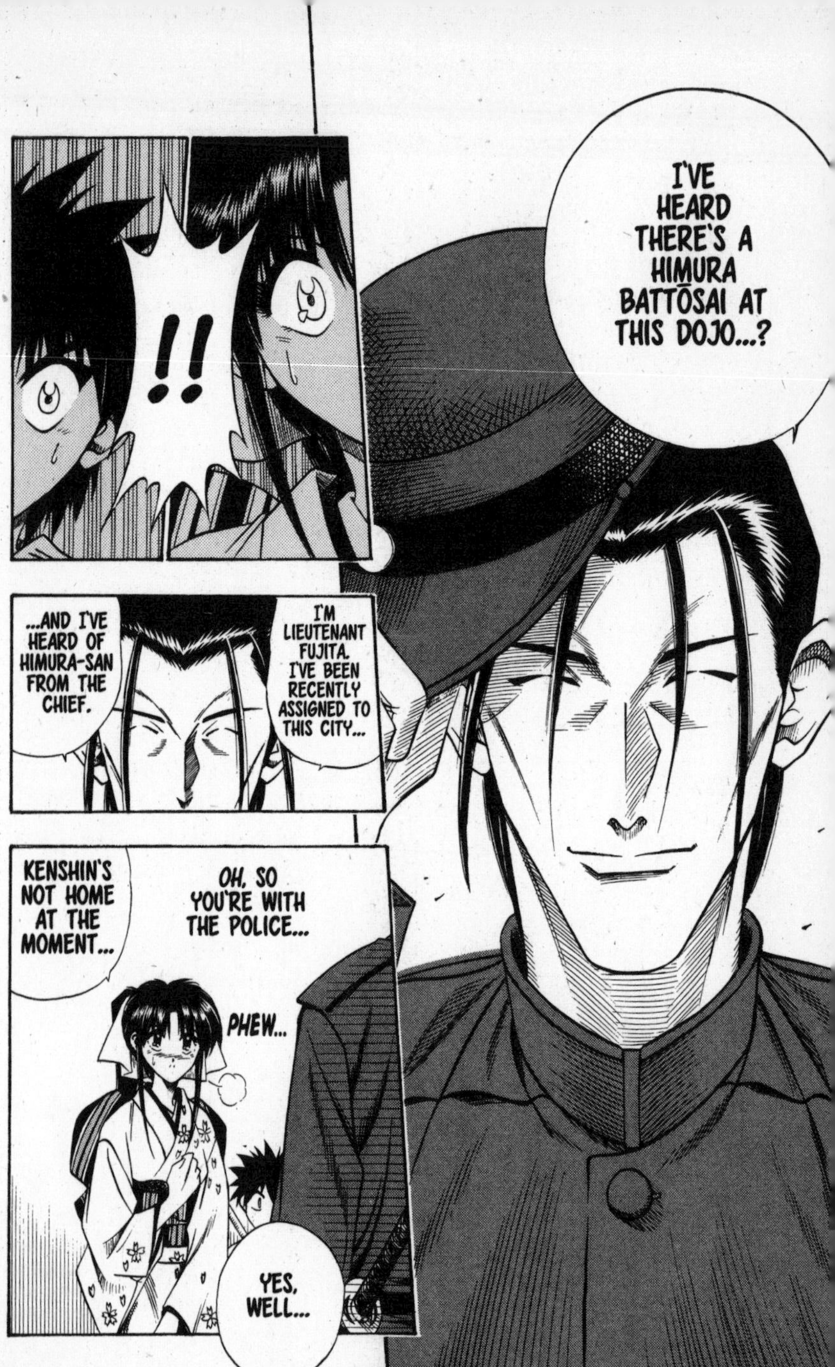
I'VE HEARD THERE'S A HIMURA BATTŌSAI AT THIS DOJO...?
!!
I'M LIEUTENANT FUJITA. I'VE BEEN RECENTLY ASSIGNED TO THIS CITY...
...AND I'VE HEARD OF HIMURA-SAN FROM THE CHIEF.
OH, SO YOU'RE WITH THE POLICE...
KENSHIN'S NOT HOME AT THE MOMENT...
PHEW...
YES, WELL...

READ THIS WAY

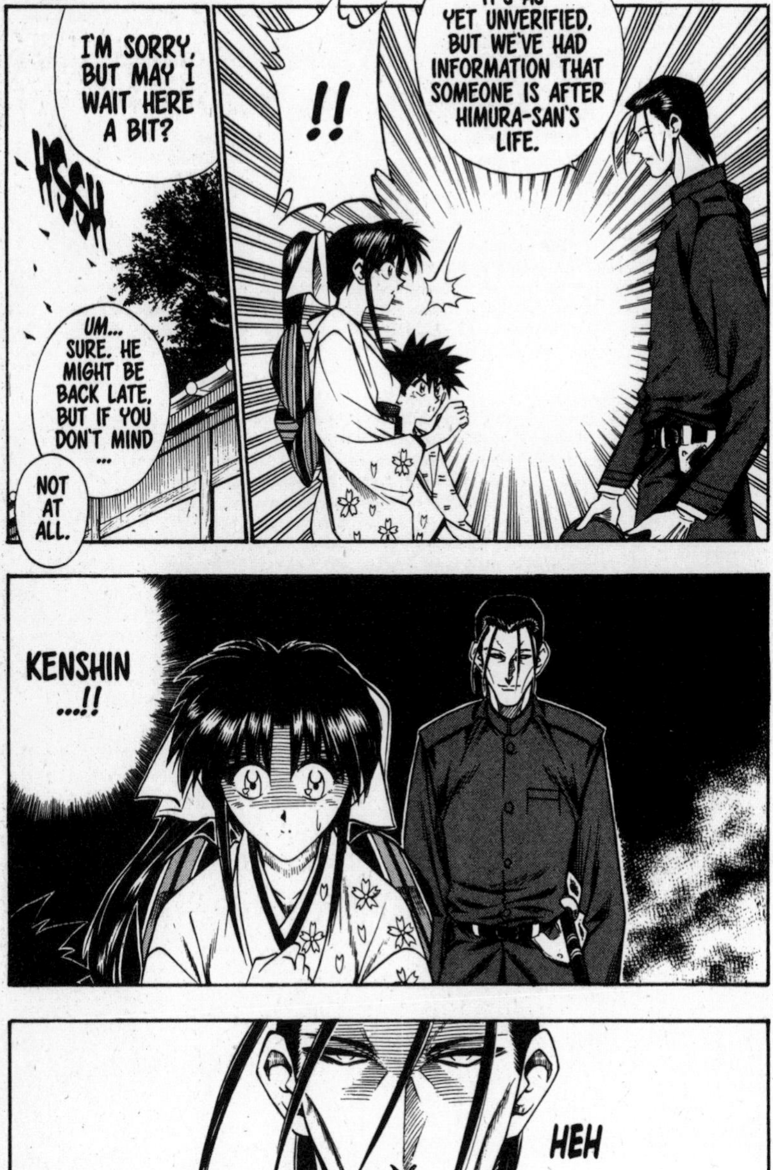
IT'S AS YET UNVERIFIED, BUT WE'VE HAD INFORMATION THAT SOMEONE IS AFTER HIMURA-SAN'S LIFE.
!!
I'M SORRY, BUT MAY I WAIT HERE A BIT?
HSSH
UM... SURE. HE MIGHT BE BACK LATE, BUT IF YOU DON'T MIND ...
NOT AT ALL.
KENSHIN ...!!
HEH

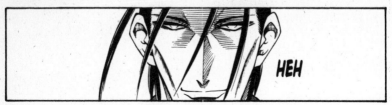

The Secret Life of Characters (20)

—Akamatsu Arundo—

***This character's here only to get beat up.**
(Just thought I'd get that out of the way.)*

As a character created to aid in story development during the "Saitō Hajime" arc, not much personality found its way in here. (He did get arrogance—my favorite "villain" trait—though.) One thing I was particular about with Akamatsu was the chain-scythe, but despite all the effort I put into drawing it, I never could catch the look of real chains. That makes me a little sad.

In terms of design, many of you have probably already guessed—he's the superhuman soldier from a "certain American comic" (the "Akamatsu Arundo" name is similar to his). I tell myself sometimes that I should stop fooling around, but being stuck in a hectic situation as I am and never being allowed to have any fun...well, Watsuki ends up having to make his own fun, you know? "*RuroKen*" has been a series for a year now. I am going to try and be better... but, if I happen to slip now and again, tell yourself "Watsuki must be really tired and busy," will you? Thanks.

On an unrelated note, the toy-line I touched upon in Volume 2 (the palm-sized figures) finally numbers over 80—only four more to complete the collection! ...Wait, what am I doing?! I turned 25 this year. Time to grow up...right??

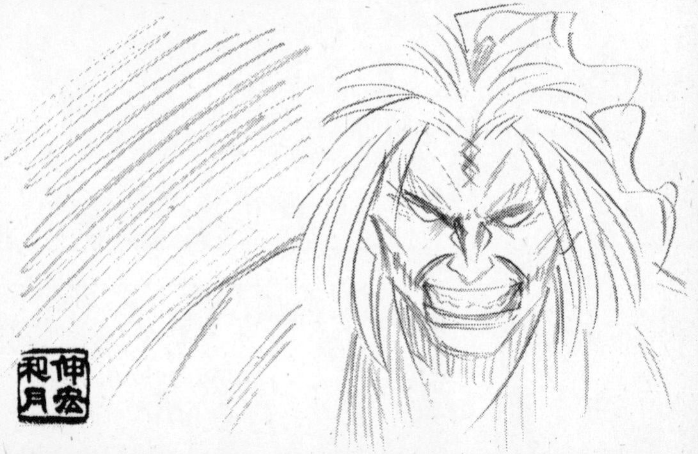
伸宏
和月

Act 51—Confrontation

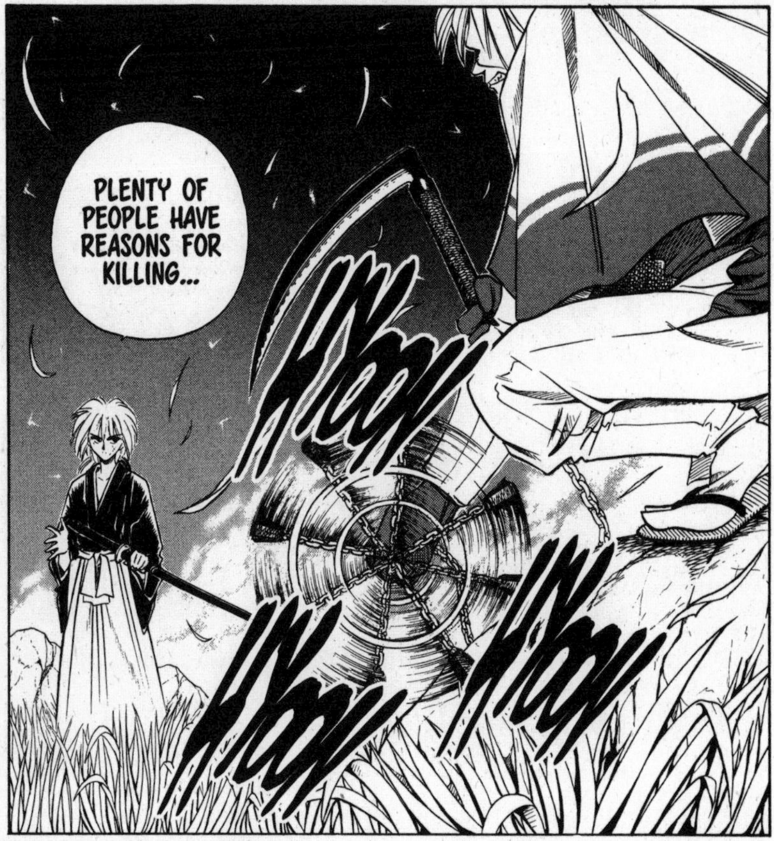
PLENTY OF PEOPLE HAVE REASONS FOR KILLING...

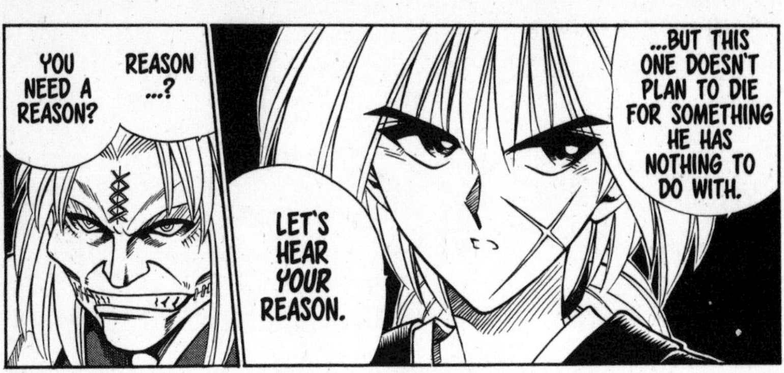
...BUT THIS ONE DOESN'T PLAN TO DIE FOR SOMETHING HE HAS NOTHING TO DO WITH.
LET'S HEAR YOUR REASON.
REASON ...?
YOU NEED A REASON?

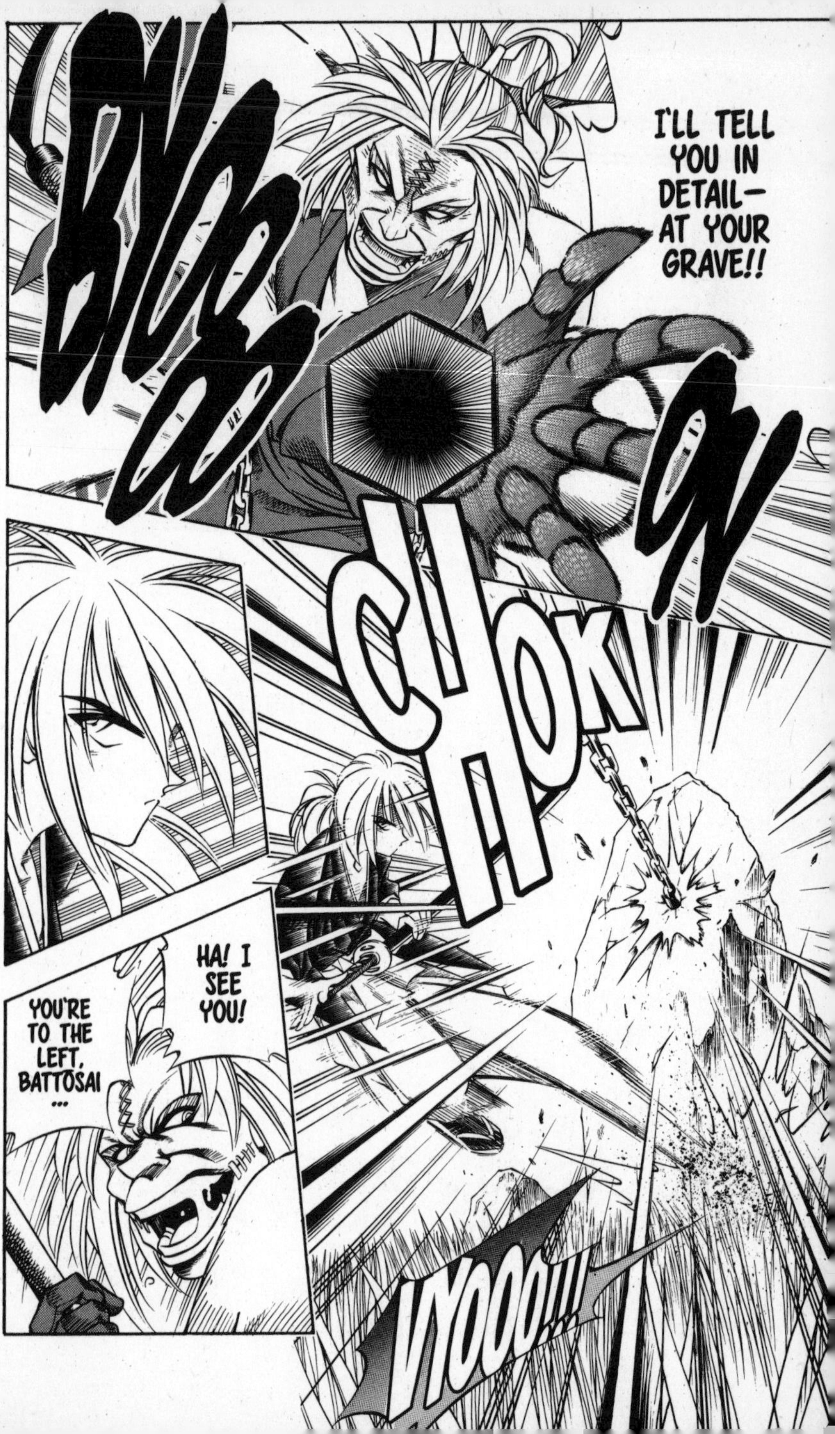
I'LL TELL YOU IN DETAIL— AT YOUR GRAVE!!
HA! I SEE YOU!
YOU'RE TO THE LEFT, BATTOSAI ...

READ THIS WAY

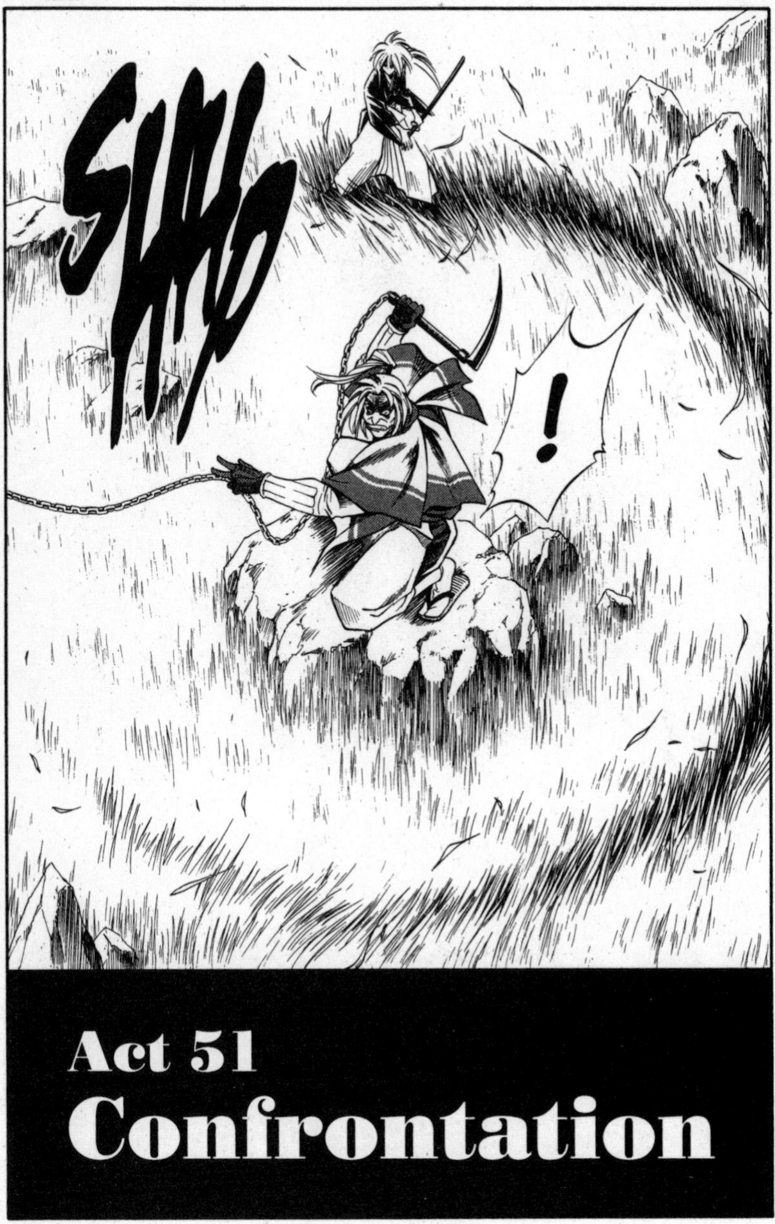
SHAAD
!

Act 51
Confrontation

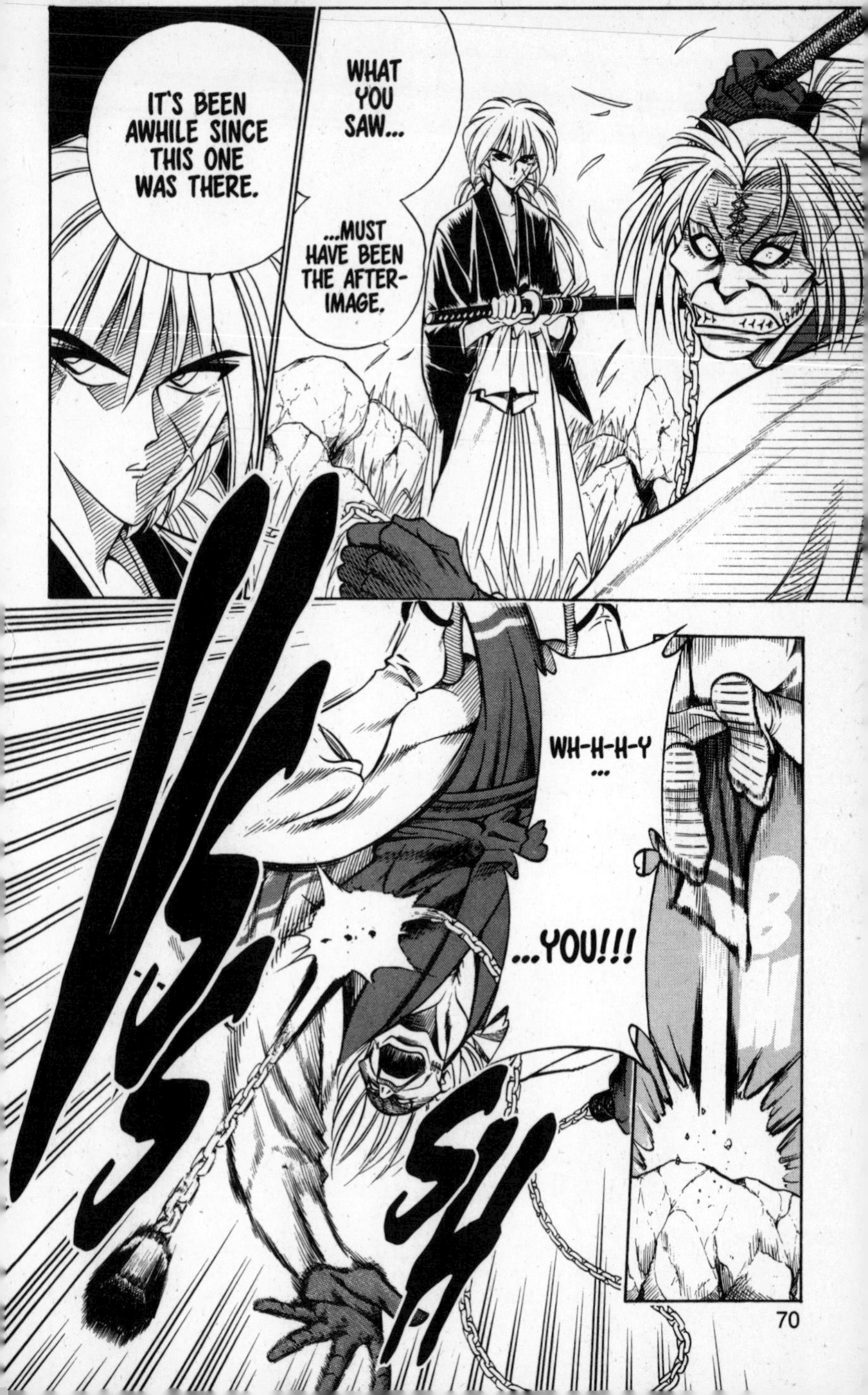
WHAT YOU SAW...
...MUST HAVE BEEN THE AFTER-IMAGE.
IT'S BEEN AWHILE SINCE THIS ONE WAS THERE.
WH-H-H-Y ...
...YOU!!!

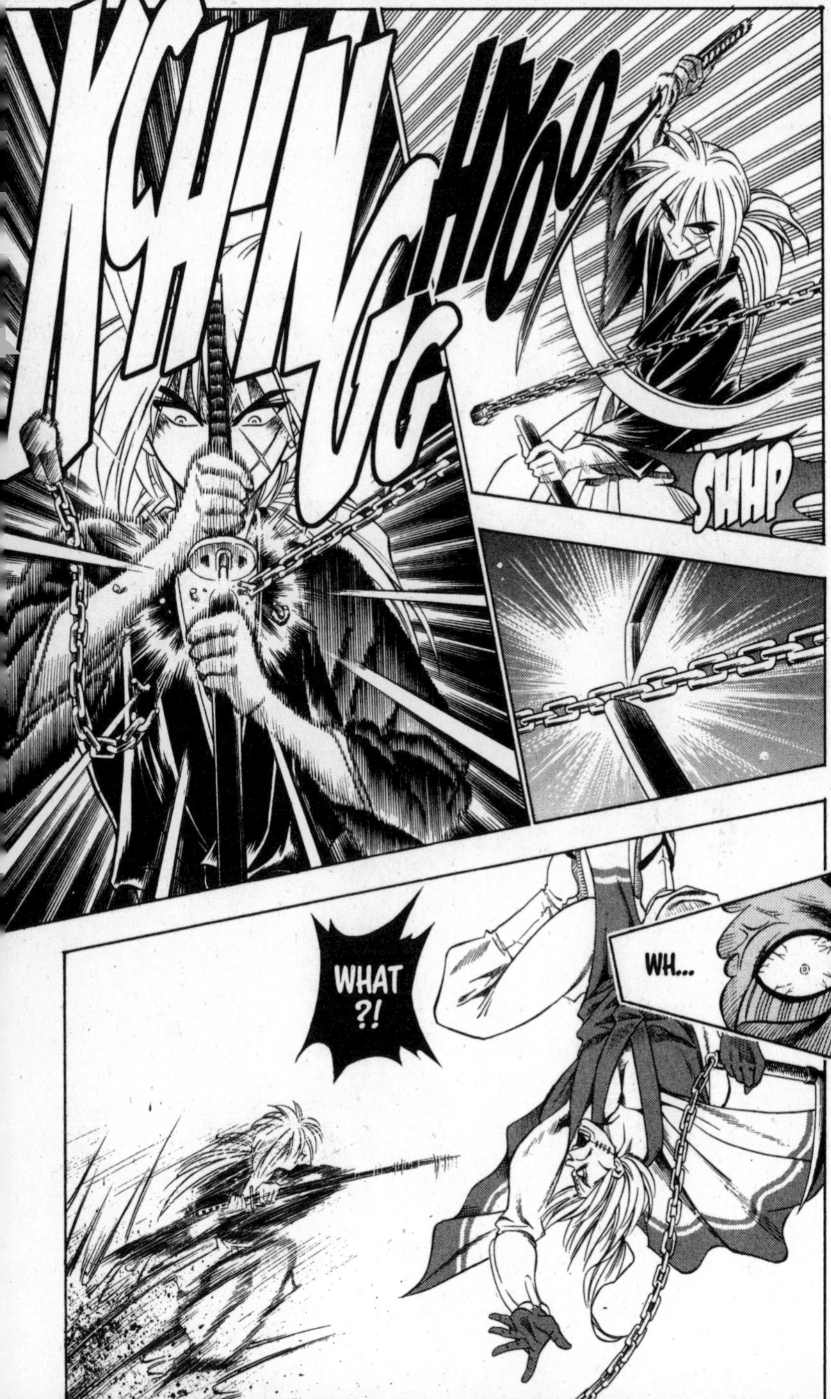
CHOO
SHHP
KCHIN
UG
WH...
WHAT ?!

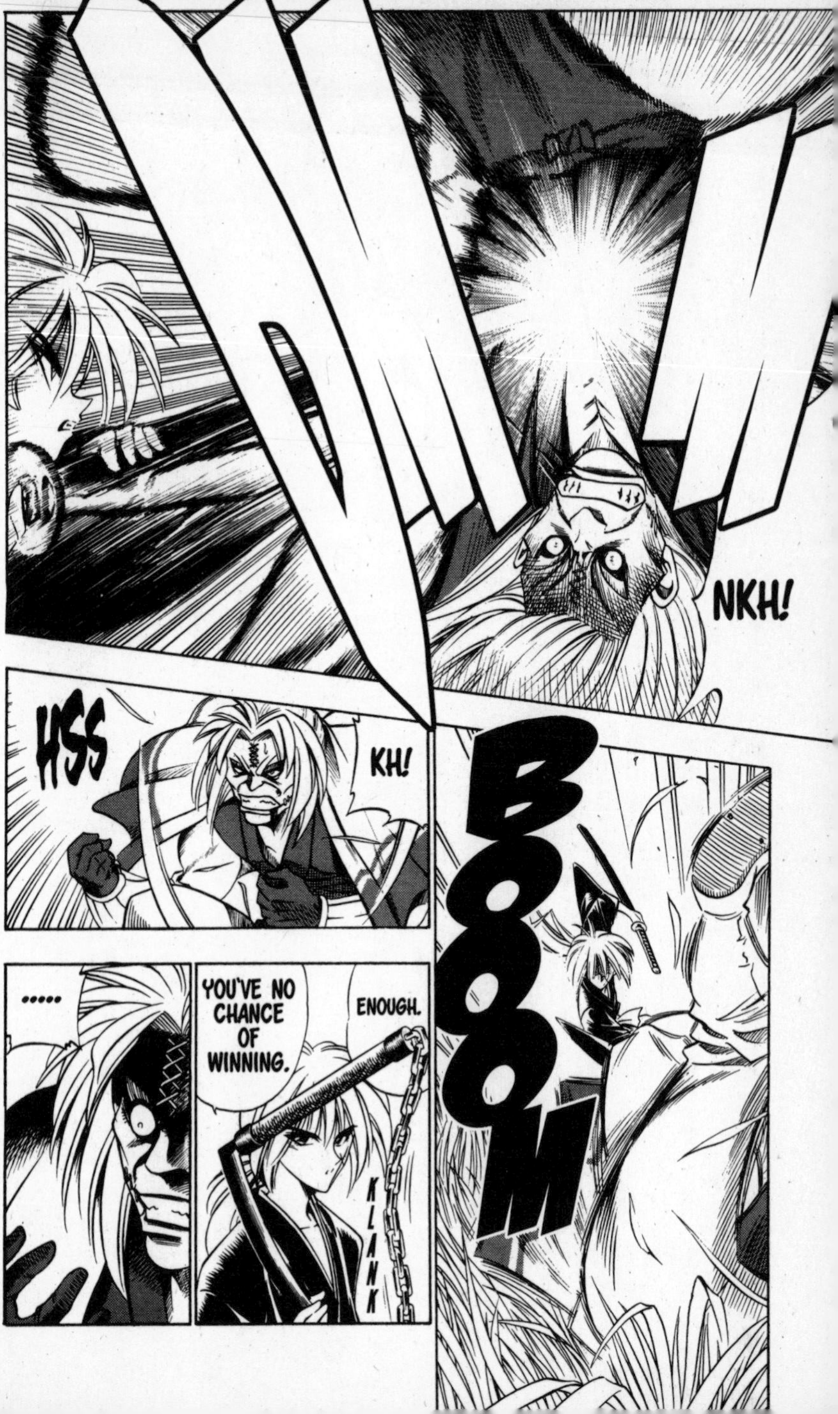
NKH!
BOOOM
KH!
HSS
ENOUGH.
YOU'VE NO CHANCE OF WINNING.
KLANK
.....

READ THIS WAY

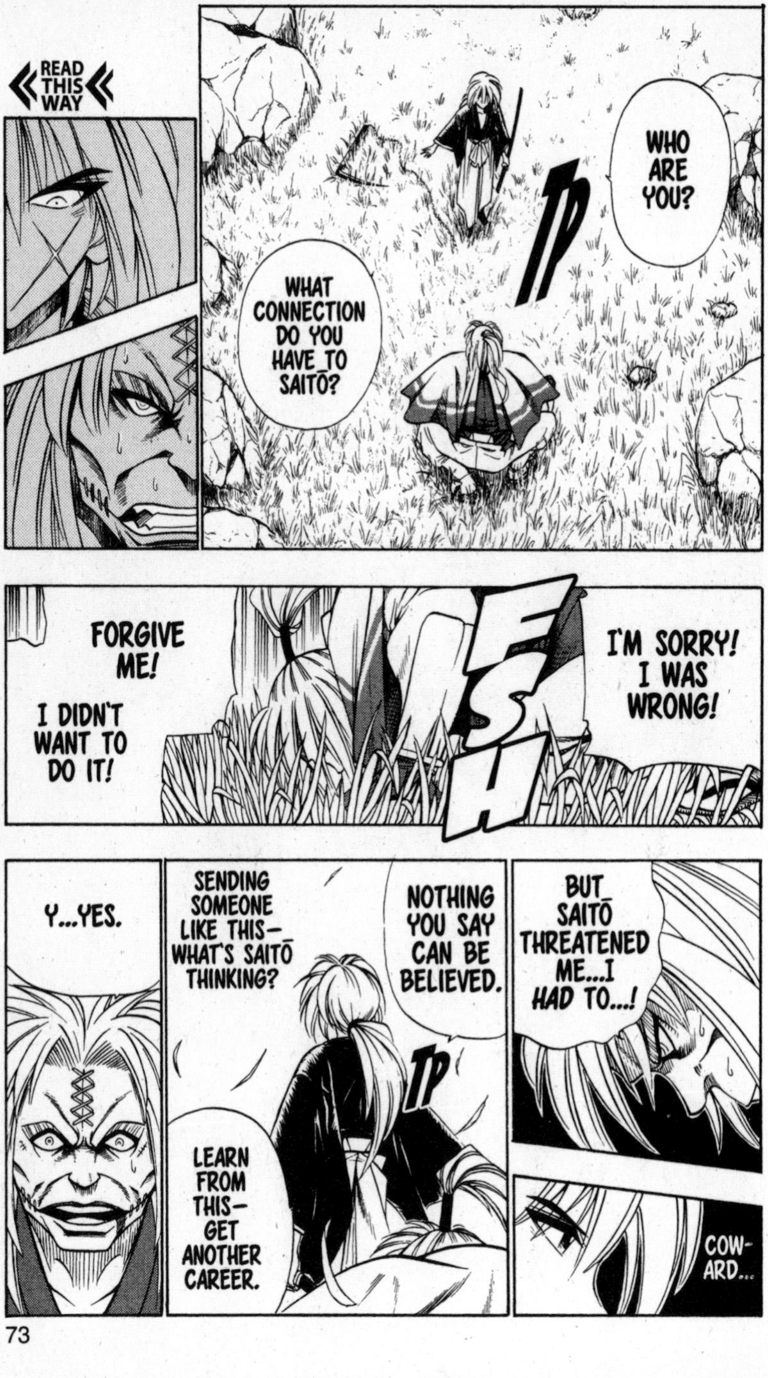

WHO ARE YOU?
TP
WHAT CONNECTION DO YOU HAVE TO SAITŌ?
I'M SORRY! I WAS WRONG!
FSH
FORGIVE ME!
I DIDN'T WANT TO DO IT!
BUT SAITŌ THREATENED ME...I HAD TO...!
COW-ARD...
NOTHING YOU SAY CAN BE BELIEVED.
TP
SENDING SOMEONE LIKE THIS— WHAT'S SAITŌ THINKING?
LEARN FROM THIS— GET ANOTHER CAREER.
Y...YES.

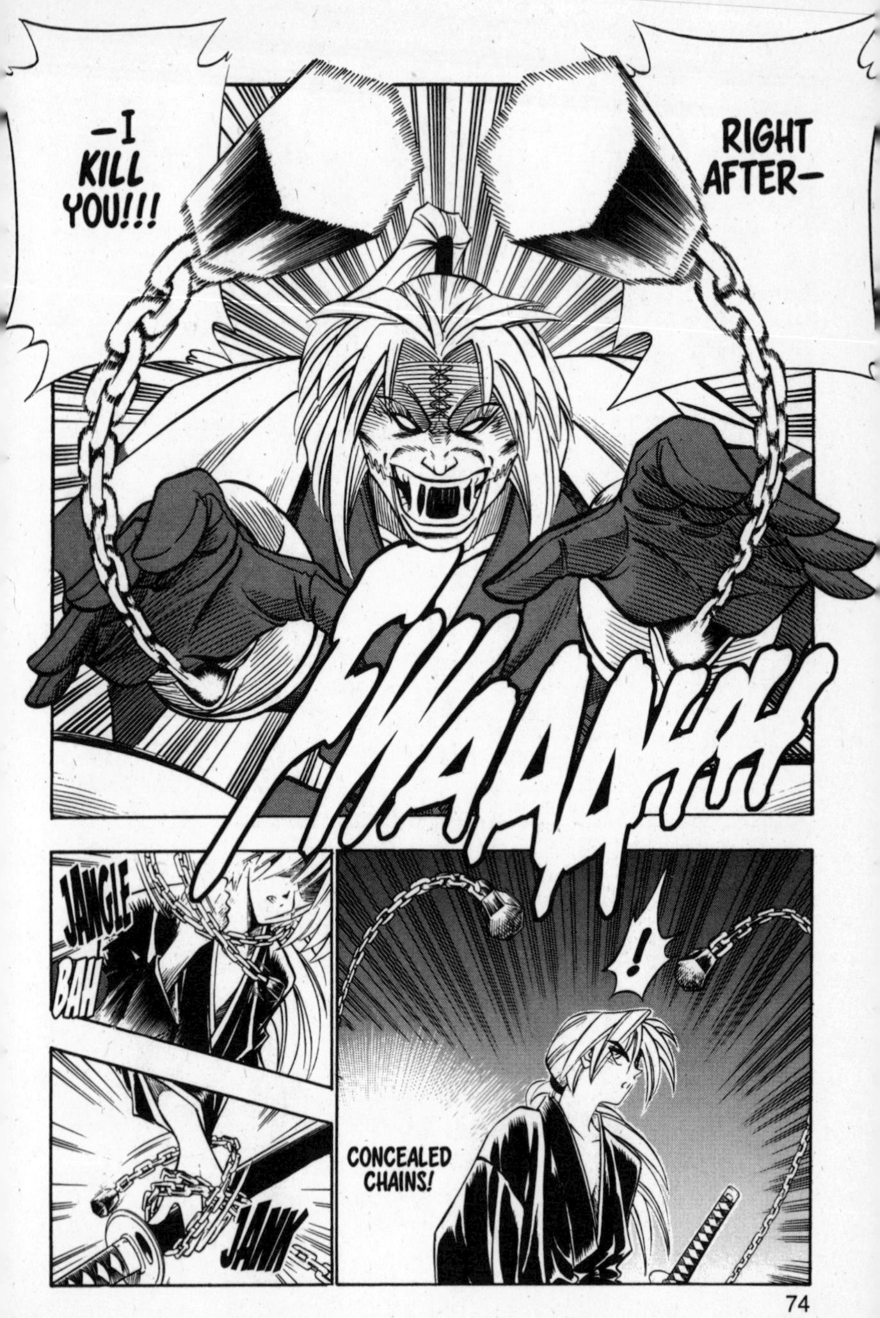
RIGHT AFTER—
—I KILL YOU!!!
WAAAHH
!
CONCEALED CHAINS!
JANGLE
BAH
JANK

READ THIS WAY

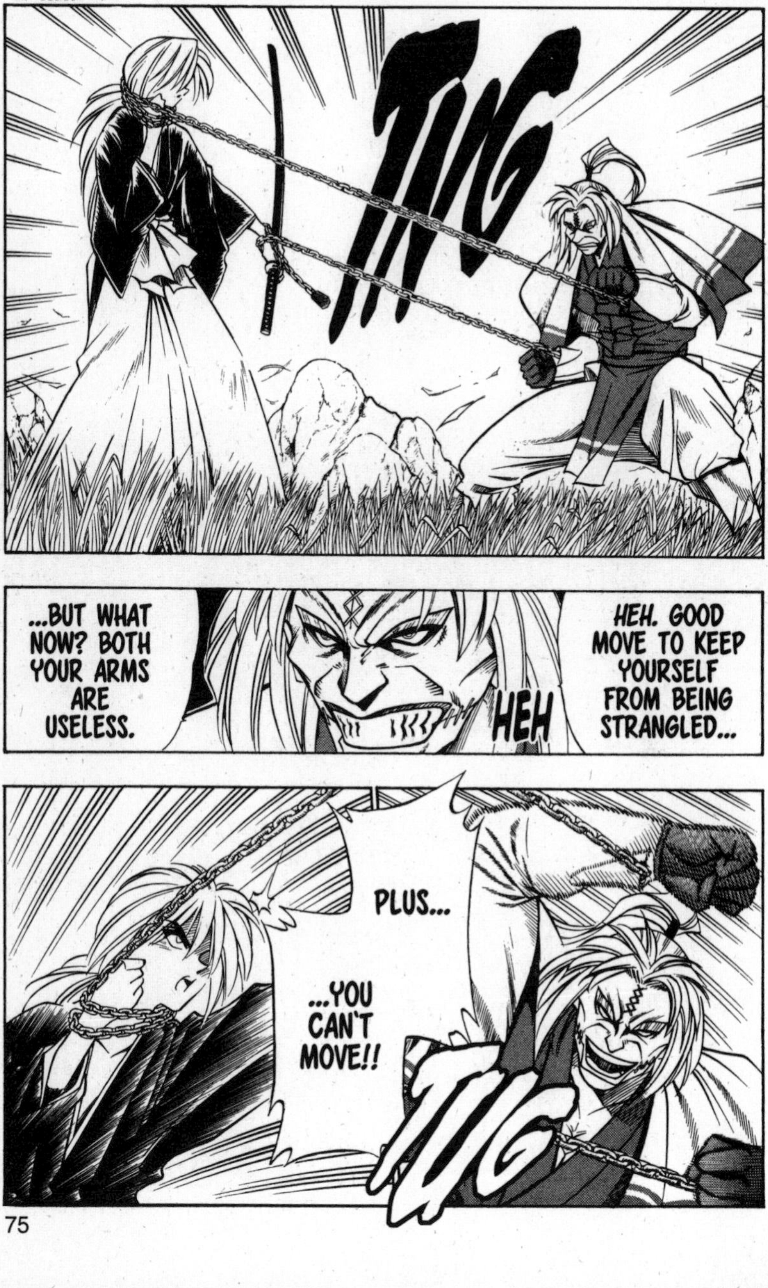

TUG
HEH. GOOD MOVE TO KEEP YOURSELF FROM BEING STRANGLED...
HEH
...BUT WHAT NOW? BOTH YOUR ARMS ARE USELESS.
PLUS...
...YOU CAN'T MOVE!!
TUG

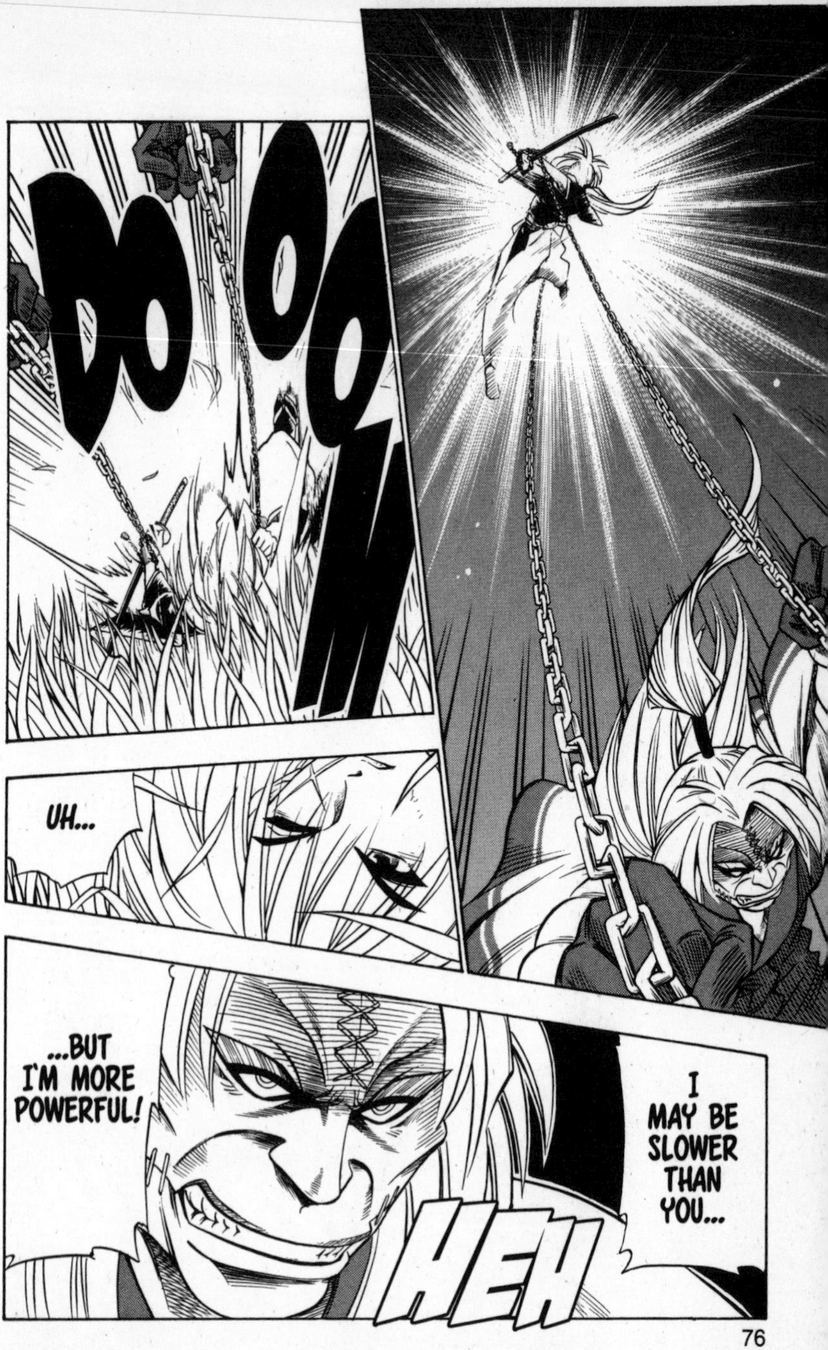
DOOOM
UH...
I MAY BE SLOWER THAN YOU...
...BUT I'M MORE POWERFUL!
HEH

READ THIS WAY

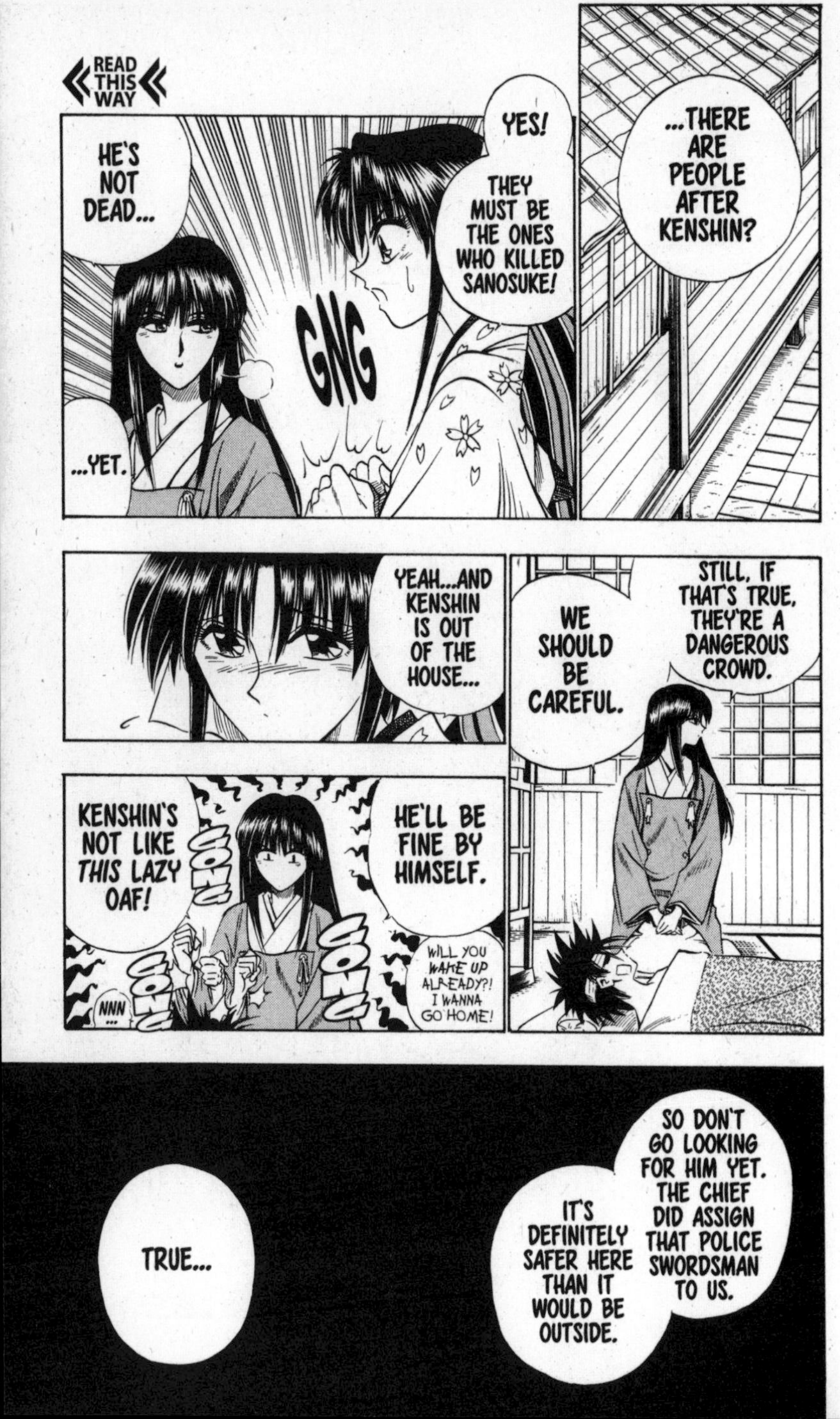
...THERE ARE PEOPLE AFTER KENSHIN?
YES!
THEY MUST BE THE ONES WHO KILLED SANOSUKE!
HE'S NOT DEAD...
GNG
...YET.
STILL, IF THAT'S TRUE, THEY'RE A DANGEROUS CROWD.
WE SHOULD BE CAREFUL.
YEAH...AND KENSHIN IS OUT OF THE HOUSE...
HE'LL BE FINE BY HIMSELF.
KENSHIN'S NOT LIKE THIS LAZY OAF!
GONG
GONG
GONG
WILL YOU WAKE UP ALREADY?! I WANNA GO HOME!
NNN...
SO DON'T GO LOOKING FOR HIM YET. THE CHIEF DID ASSIGN THAT POLICE SWORDSMAN TO US.
IT'S DEFINITELY SAFER HERE THAN IT WOULD BE OUTSIDE.
TRUE...

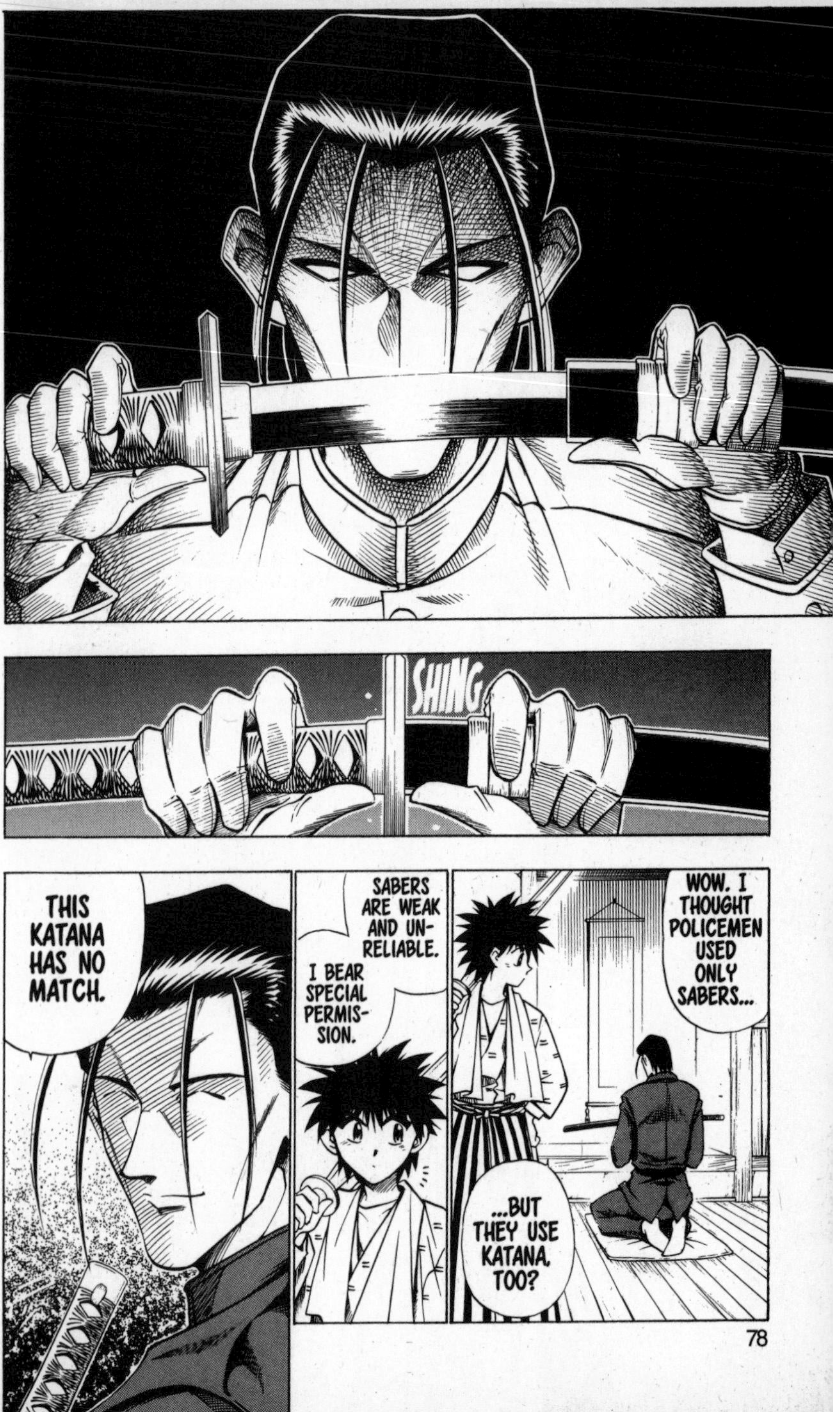
SHING
WOW. I THOUGHT POLICEMEN USED ONLY SABERS...
...BUT THEY USE KATANA, TOO?
SABERS ARE WEAK AND UN-RELIABLE.
I BEAR SPECIAL PERMIS-SION.
THIS KATANA HAS NO MATCH.

READ THIS WAY

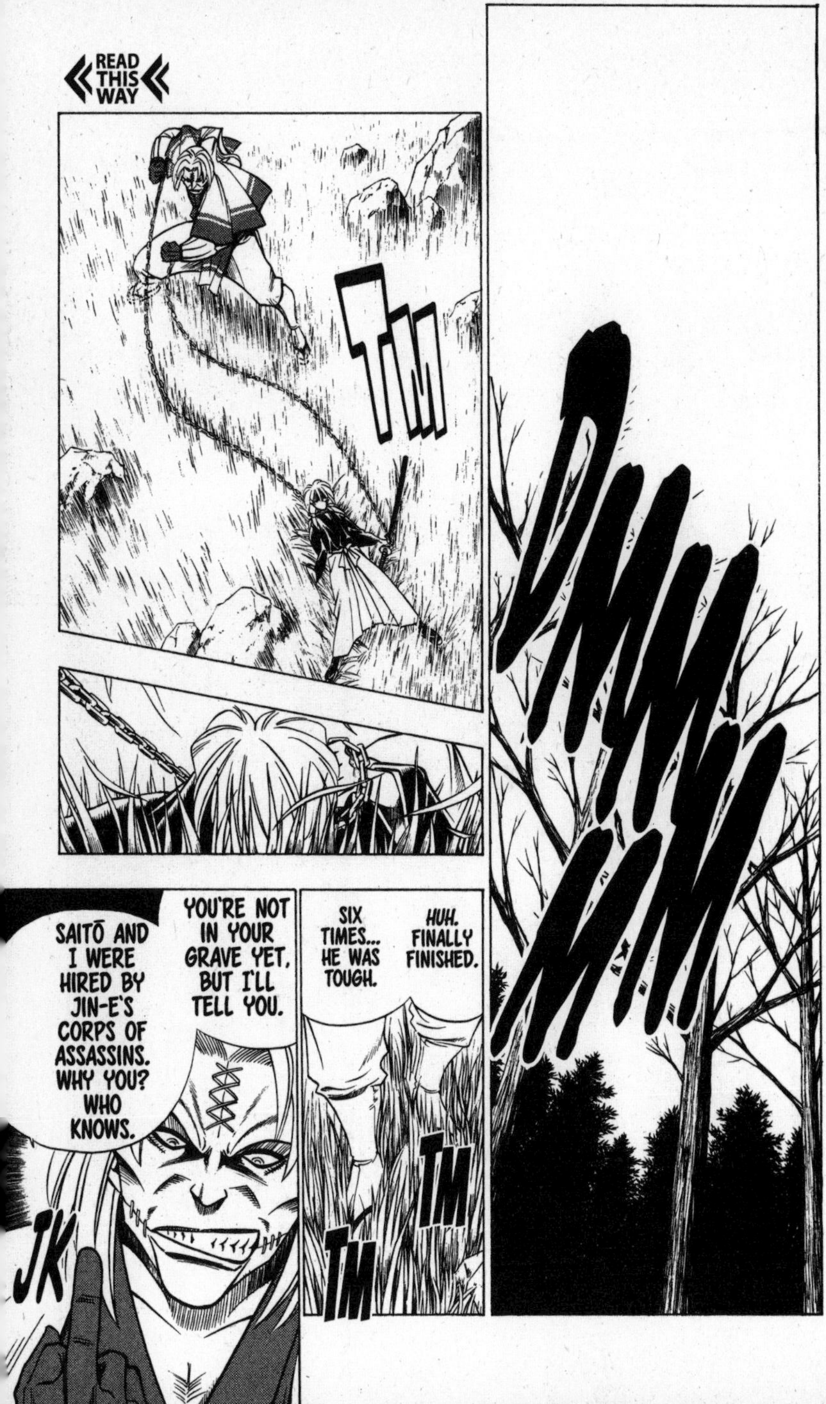
TM
HUH. FINALLY FINISHED.
SIX TIMES... HE WAS TOUGH.
TM
TM
YOU'RE NOT IN YOUR GRAVE YET, BUT I'LL TELL YOU.
SAITŌ AND I WERE HIRED BY JIN-E'S CORPS OF ASSASSINS. WHY YOU? WHO KNOWS.
JK

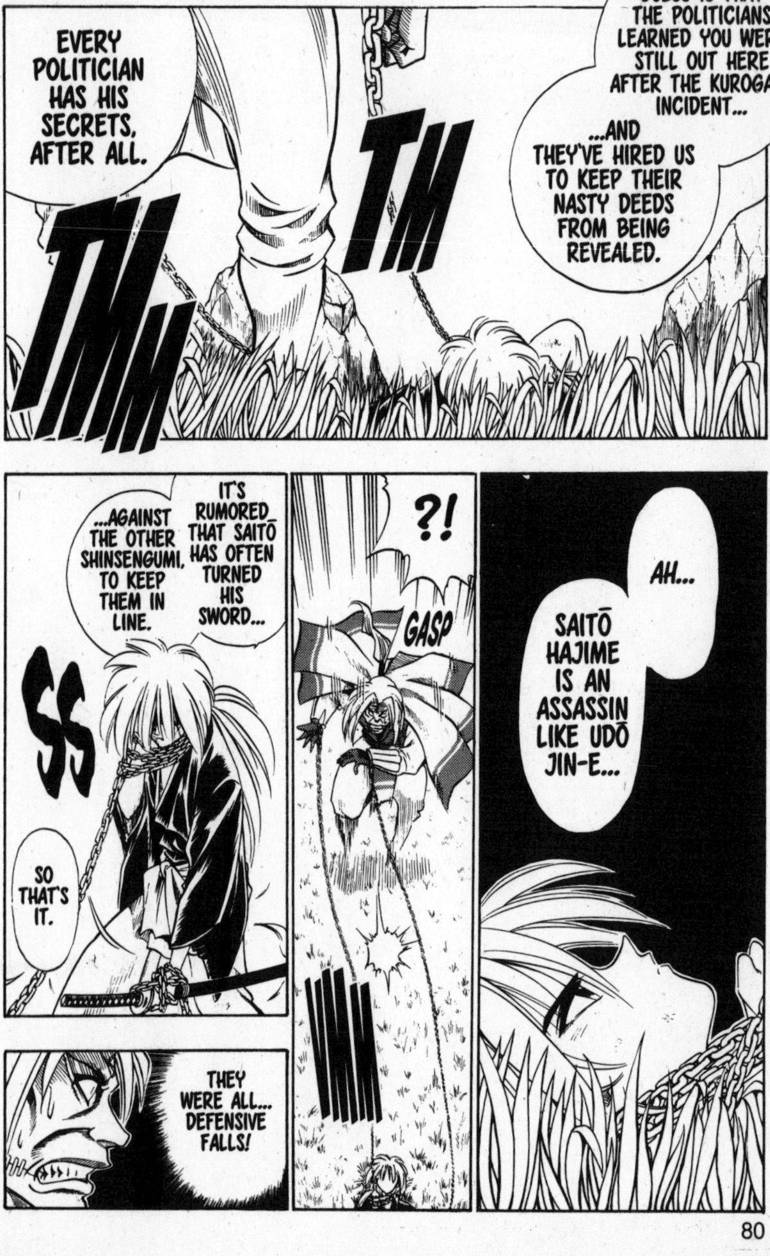
MY GUESS IS THAT THE POLITICIANS LEARNED YOU WERE STILL OUT HERE AFTER THE KUROGASA INCIDENT...
...AND THEY'VE HIRED US TO KEEP THEIR NASTY DEEDS FROM BEING REVEALED.
TM
EVERY POLITICIAN HAS HIS SECRETS, AFTER ALL.
TMM
AH...
SAITŌ HAJIME IS AN ASSASSIN LIKE UDŌ JIN-E...
?!
GASP
IT'S RUMORED THAT SAITŌ HAS OFTEN TURNED HIS SWORD...
...AGAINST THE OTHER SHINSENGUMI, TO KEEP THEM IN LINE.
SS
SO THAT'S IT.
THEY WERE ALL... DEFENSIVE FALLS!

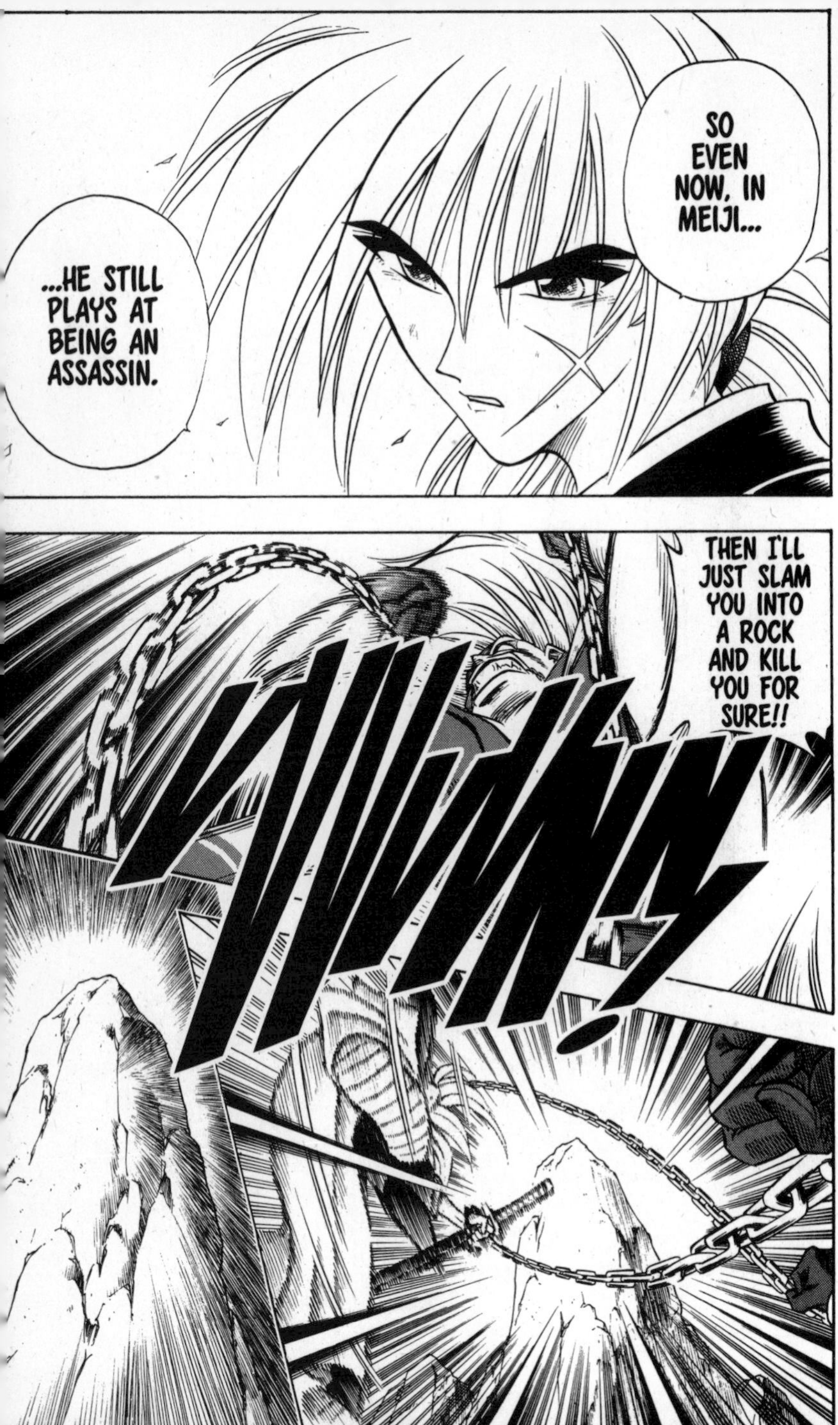
SO EVEN NOW, IN MEIJI...
...HE STILL PLAYS AT BEING AN ASSASSIN.
THEN I'LL JUST SLAM YOU INTO A ROCK AND KILL YOU FOR SURE!!

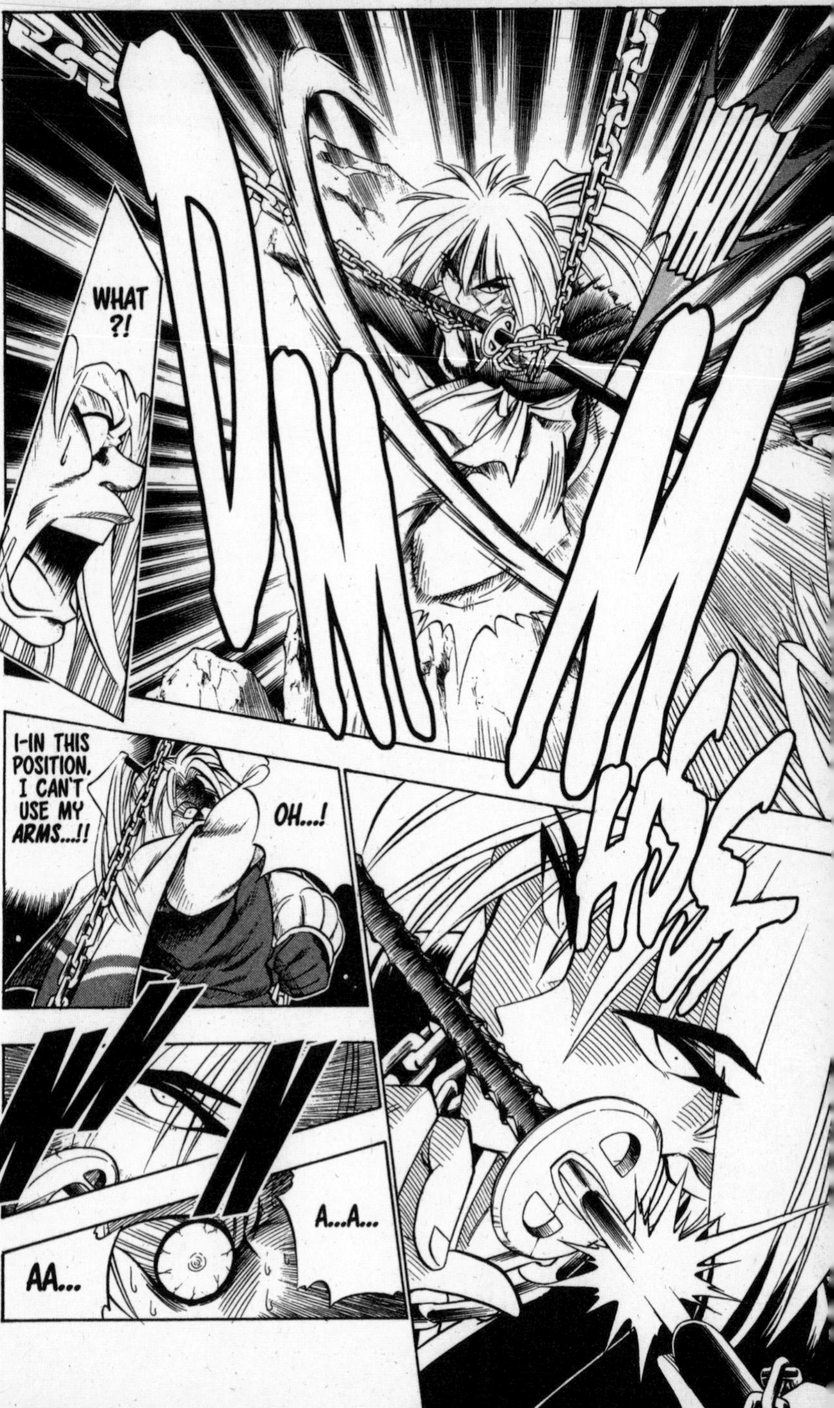
WHAT ?!
OH...!
I-IN THIS POSITION, I CAN'T USE MY *ARMS*...!!
A...A...
AA...

READ THIS WAY

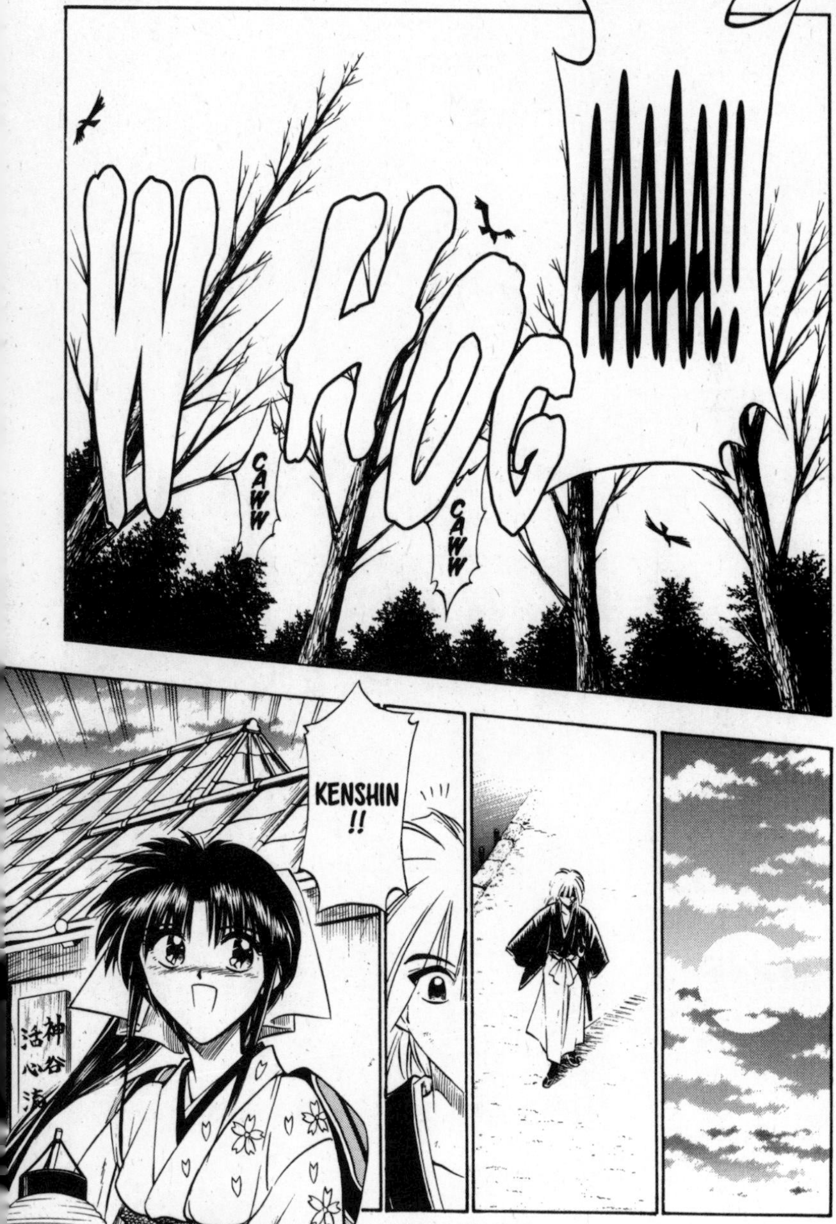
AAAAA!!
WHOG
CAWW
CAWW
KENSHIN!!
← WAITING AT THE GATE.

READ THIS WAY

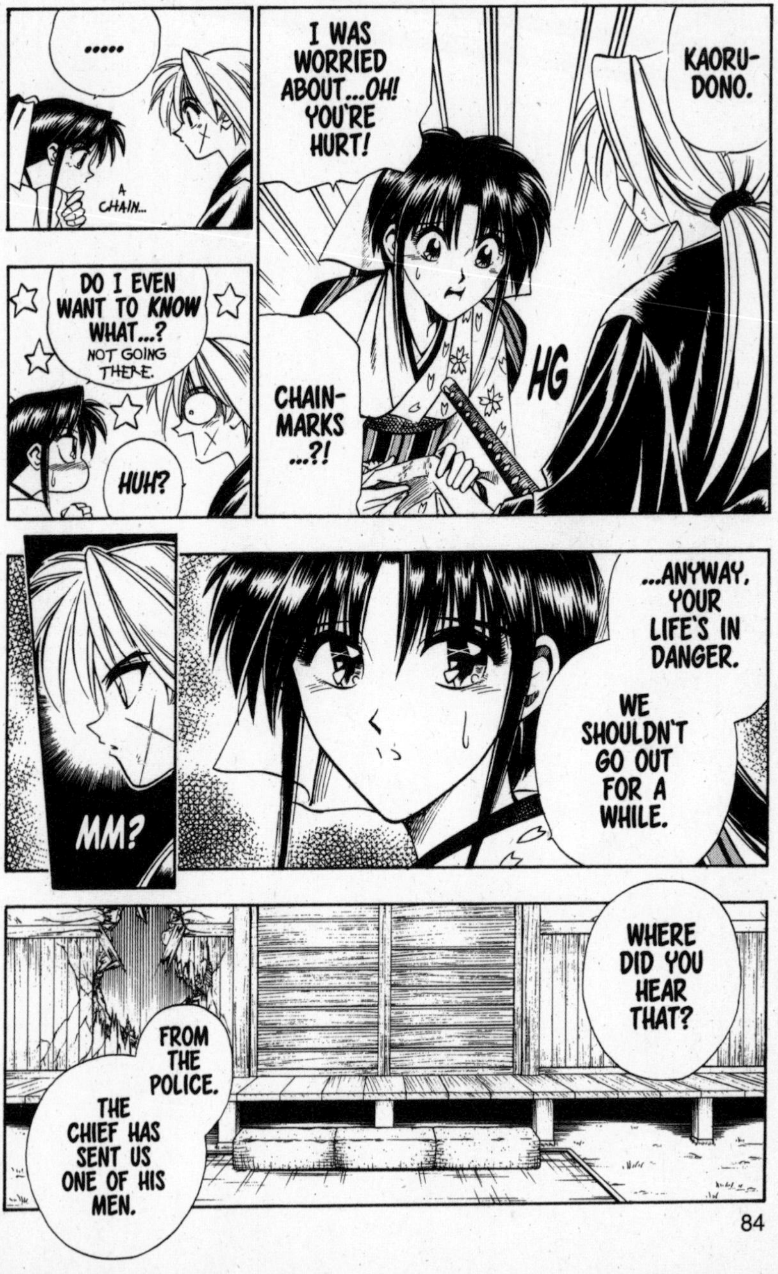
KAORU-DONO.
I WAS WORRIED ABOUT...OH! YOU'RE HURT!
HG
CHAIN-MARKS ...?!
......
A CHAIN...
DO I EVEN WANT TO KNOW WHAT...? NOT GOING THERE.
HUH?
...ANYWAY, YOUR LIFE'S IN DANGER.
WE SHOULDN'T GO OUT FOR A WHILE.
MM?
WHERE DID YOU HEAR THAT?
FROM THE POLICE.
THE CHIEF HAS SENT US ONE OF HIS MEN.

READ THIS WAY

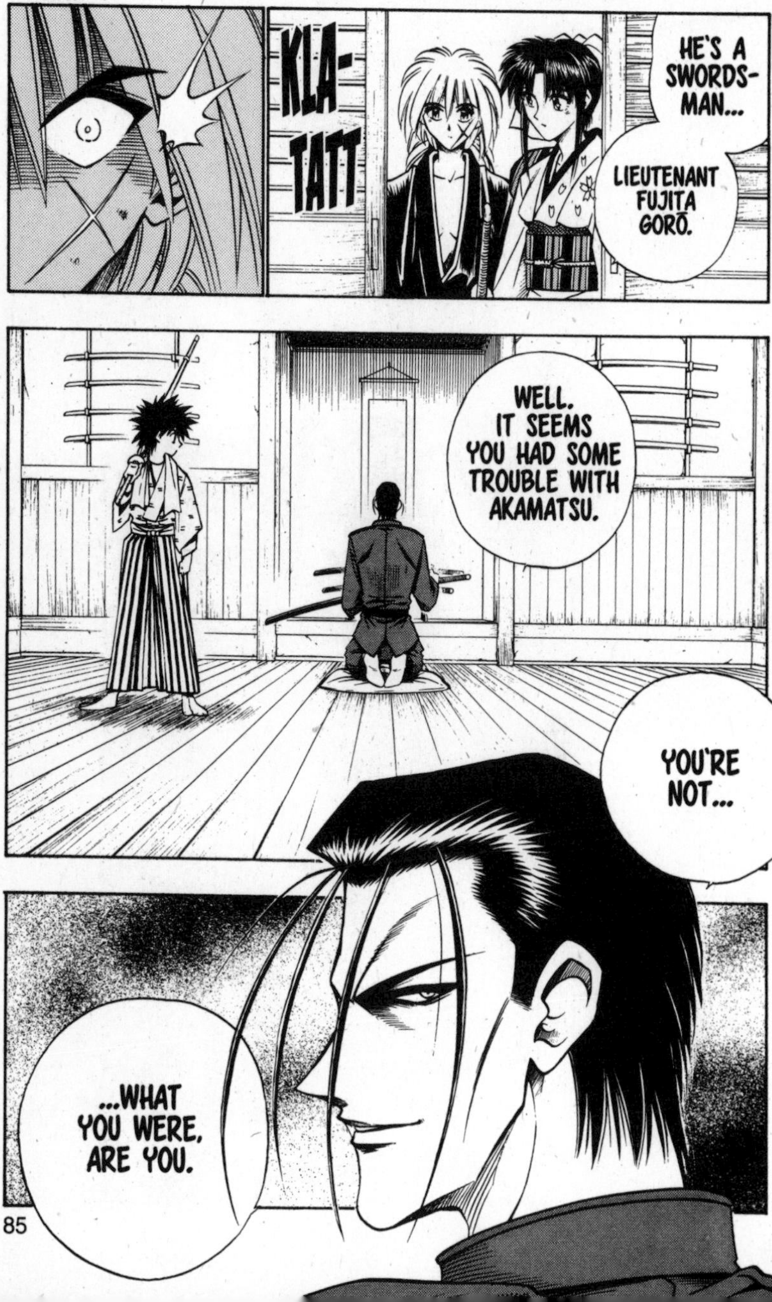
KLA-TATT
HE'S A SWORDS-MAN...
LIEUTENANT FUJITA GORŌ.
WELL. IT SEEMS YOU HAD SOME TROUBLE WITH AKAMATSU.
YOU'RE NOT...
...WHAT YOU WERE, ARE YOU.

Rurouni Kenshin

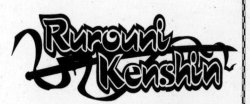

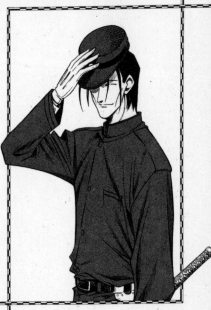

Act 52—The Wolf's Fangs

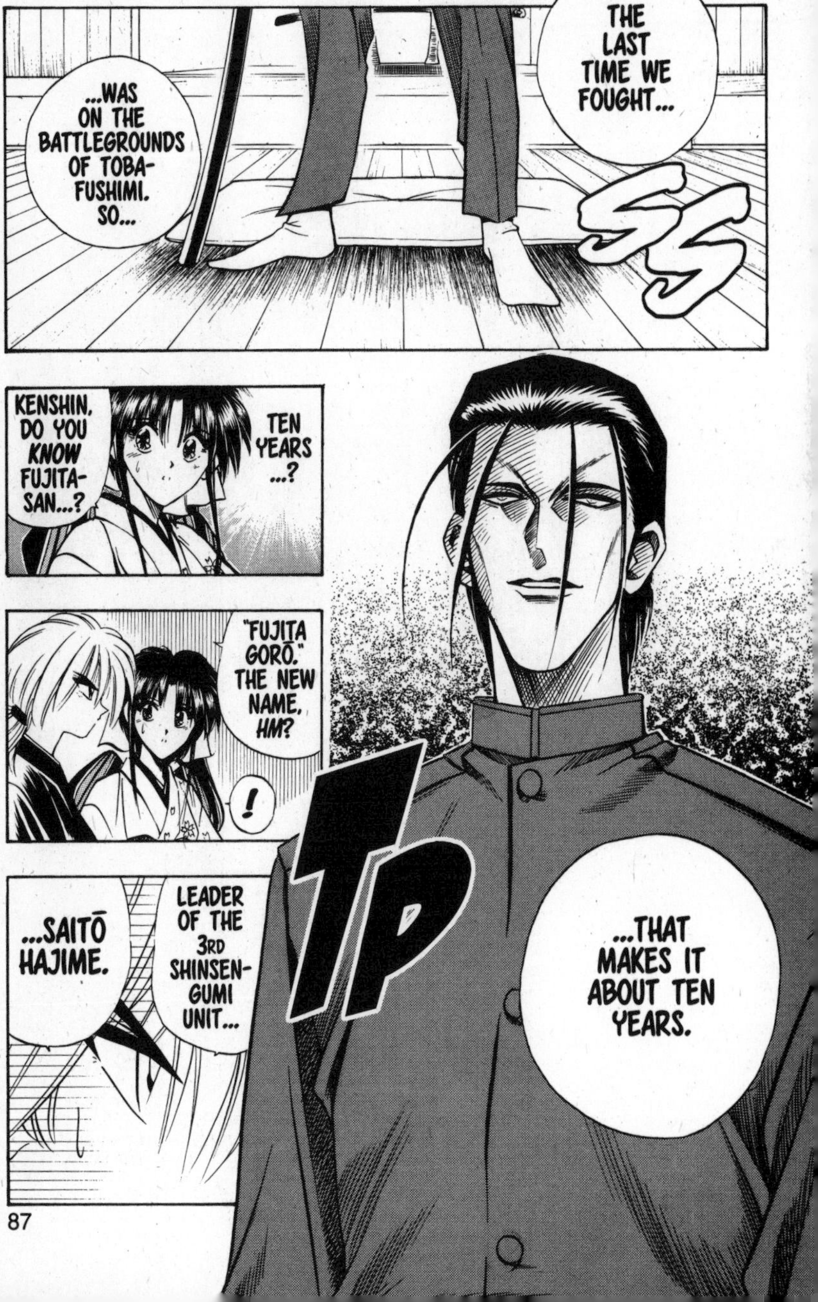
THE LAST TIME WE FOUGHT...
...WAS ON THE BATTLEGROUNDS OF TOBA-FUSHIMI. SO...
SS
TP
...THAT MAKES IT ABOUT TEN YEARS.
TEN YEARS ...?
KENSHIN, DO YOU KNOW FUJITA-SAN...?
"FUJITA GORŌ." THE NEW NAME, HM?
!
LEADER OF THE 3RD SHINSEN-GUMI UNIT...
...SAITŌ HAJIME.

READ THIS WAY

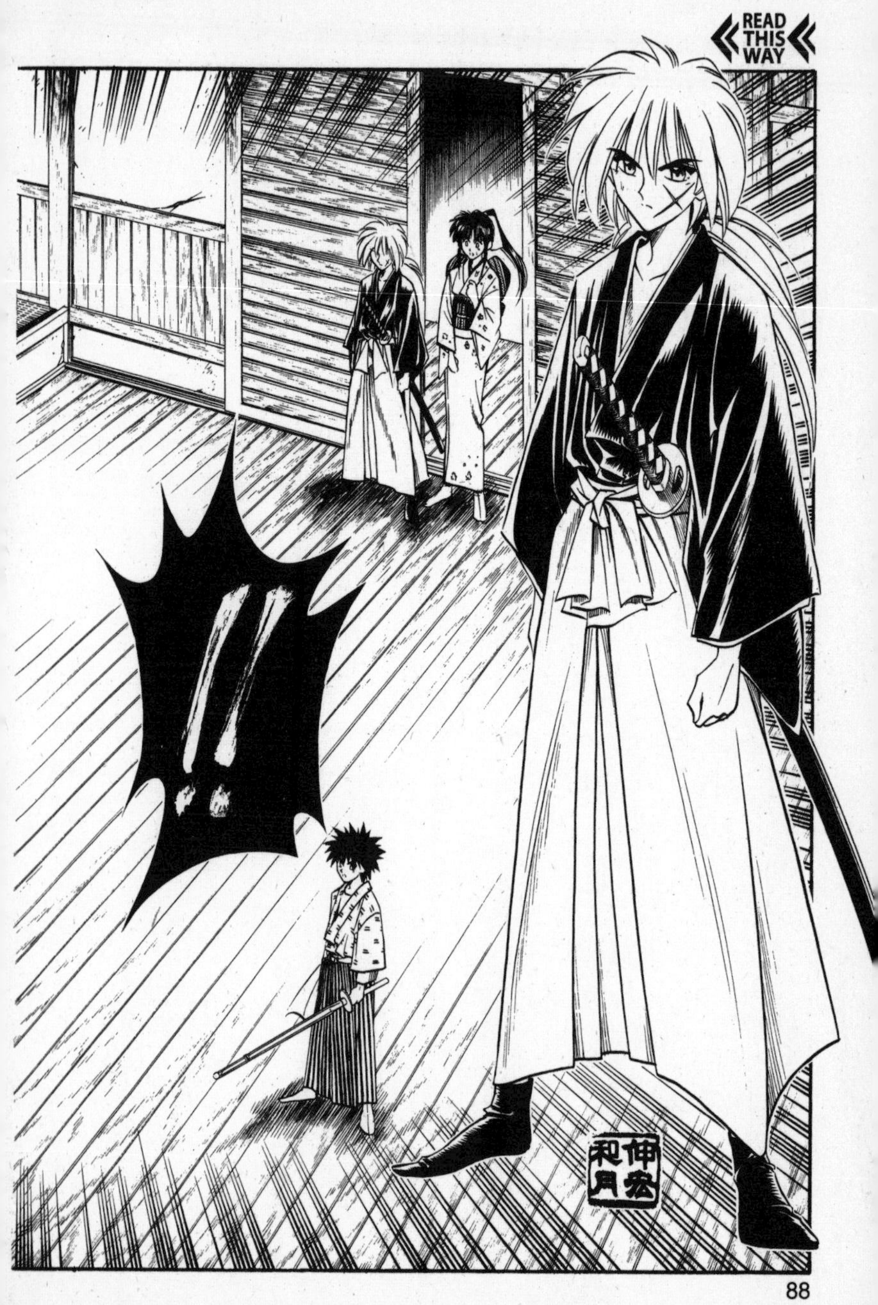
!!
伸宏和月

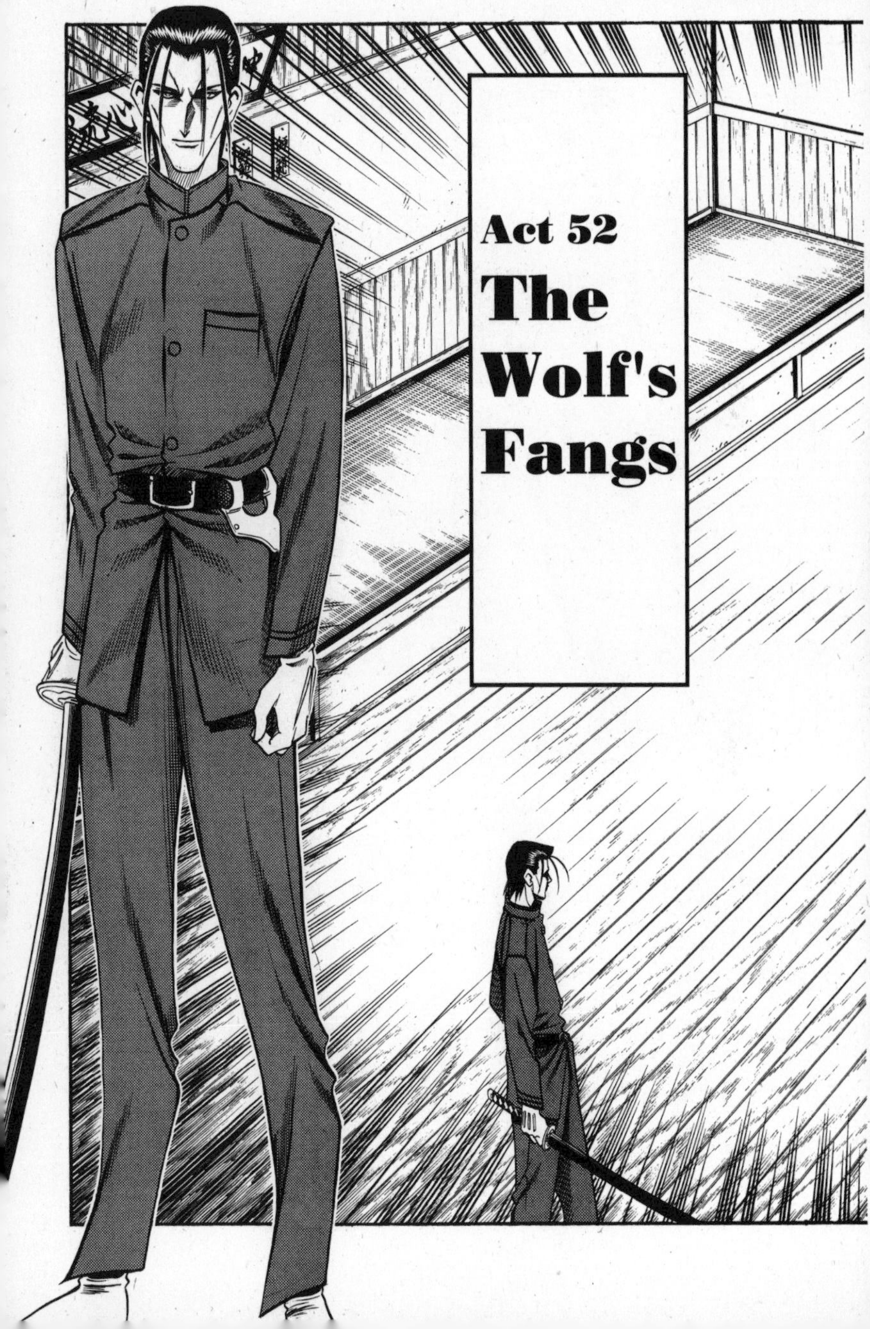
Act 52
The Wolf's Fangs

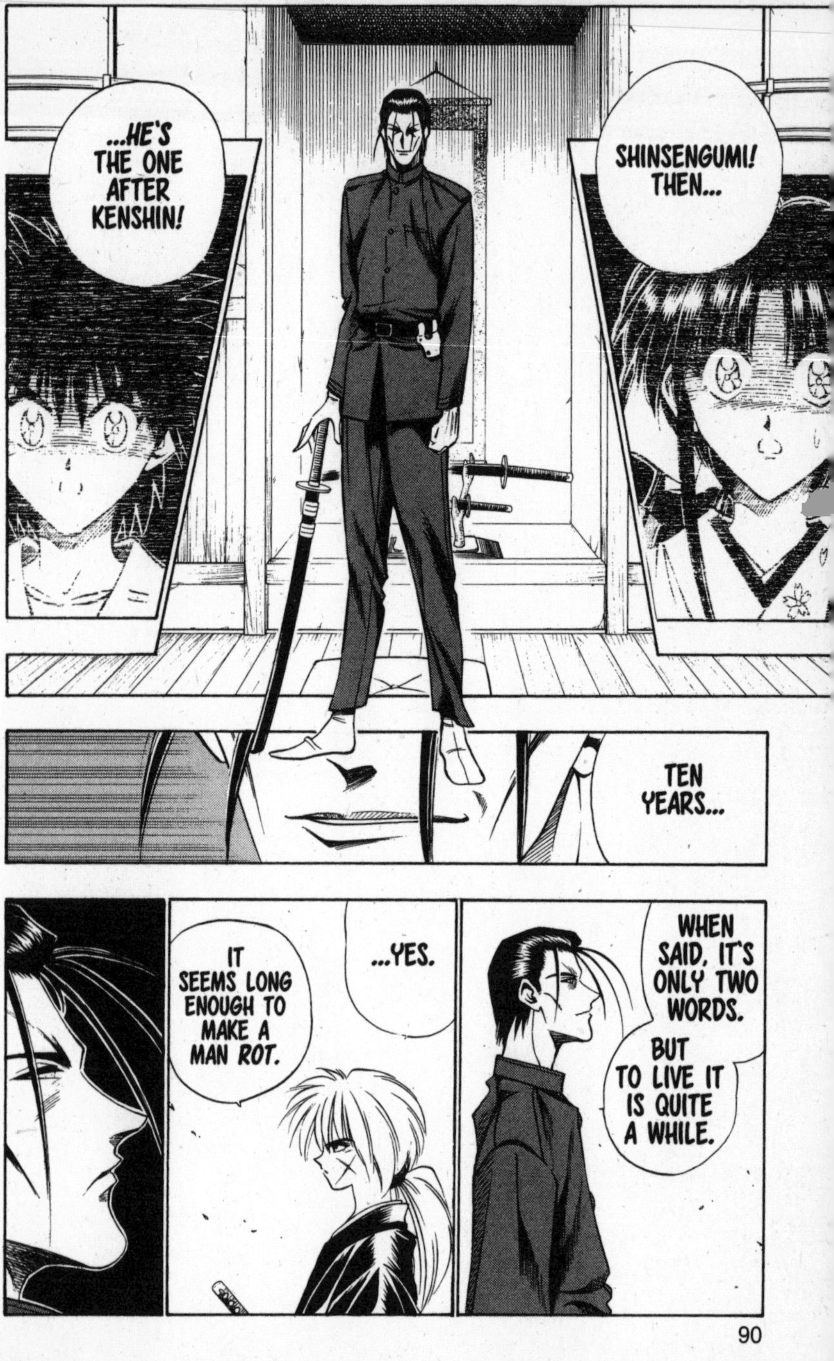
SHINSENGUMI! THEN...
...HE'S THE ONE AFTER KENSHIN!
TEN YEARS...
WHEN SAID, IT'S ONLY TWO WORDS.
BUT TO LIVE IT IS QUITE A WHILE.
...YES.
IT SEEMS LONG ENOUGH TO MAKE A MAN ROT.

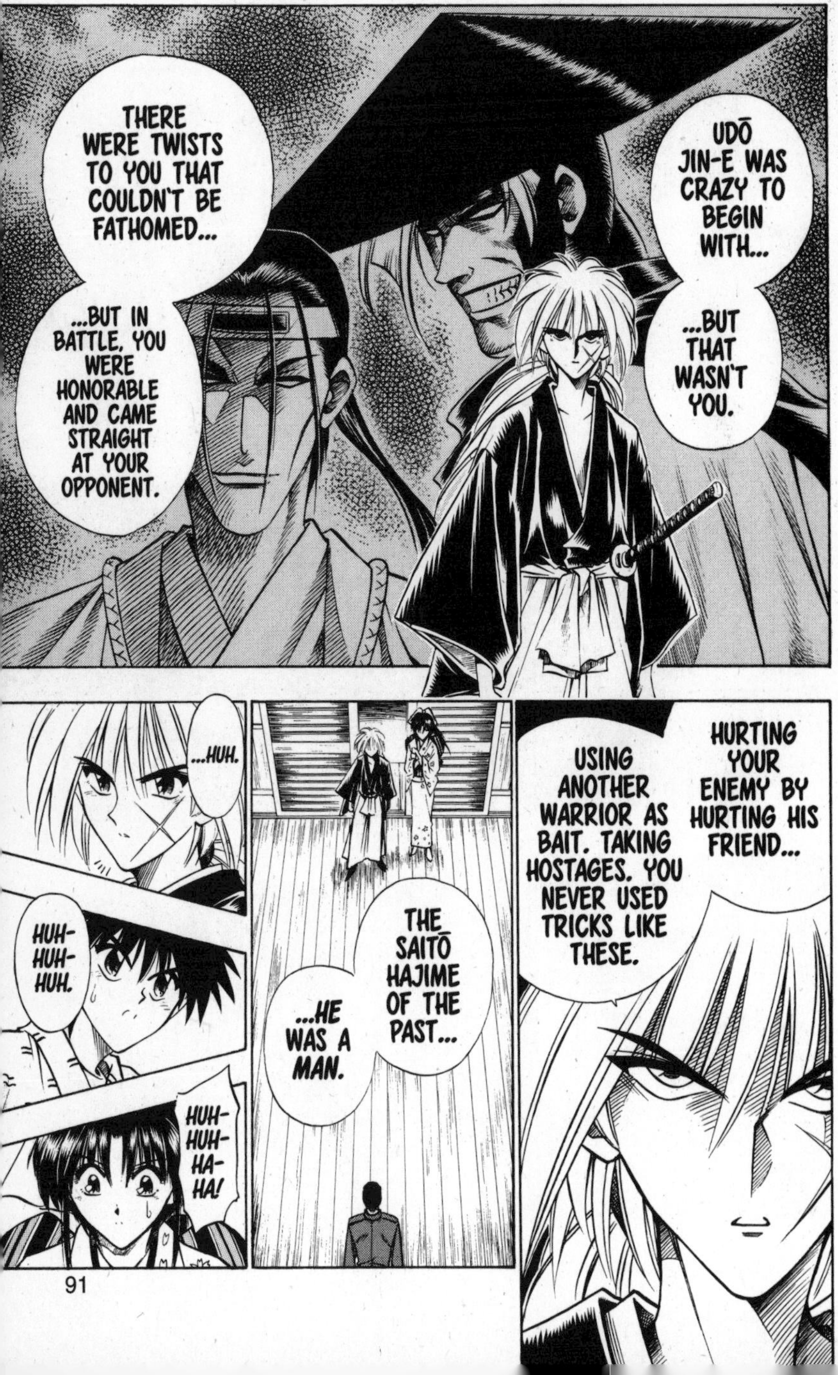
UDŌ JIN-E WAS CRAZY TO BEGIN WITH...
...BUT THAT WASN'T YOU.
THERE WERE TWISTS TO YOU THAT COULDN'T BE FATHOMED...
...BUT IN BATTLE, YOU WERE HONORABLE AND CAME STRAIGHT AT YOUR OPPONENT.
HURTING YOUR ENEMY BY HURTING HIS FRIEND...
USING ANOTHER WARRIOR AS BAIT. TAKING HOSTAGES. YOU NEVER USED TRICKS LIKE THESE.
THE SAITŌ HAJIME OF THE PAST...
...HE WAS A MAN.
...HUH.
HUH-HUH-HUH.
HUH-HUH-HA-HA!

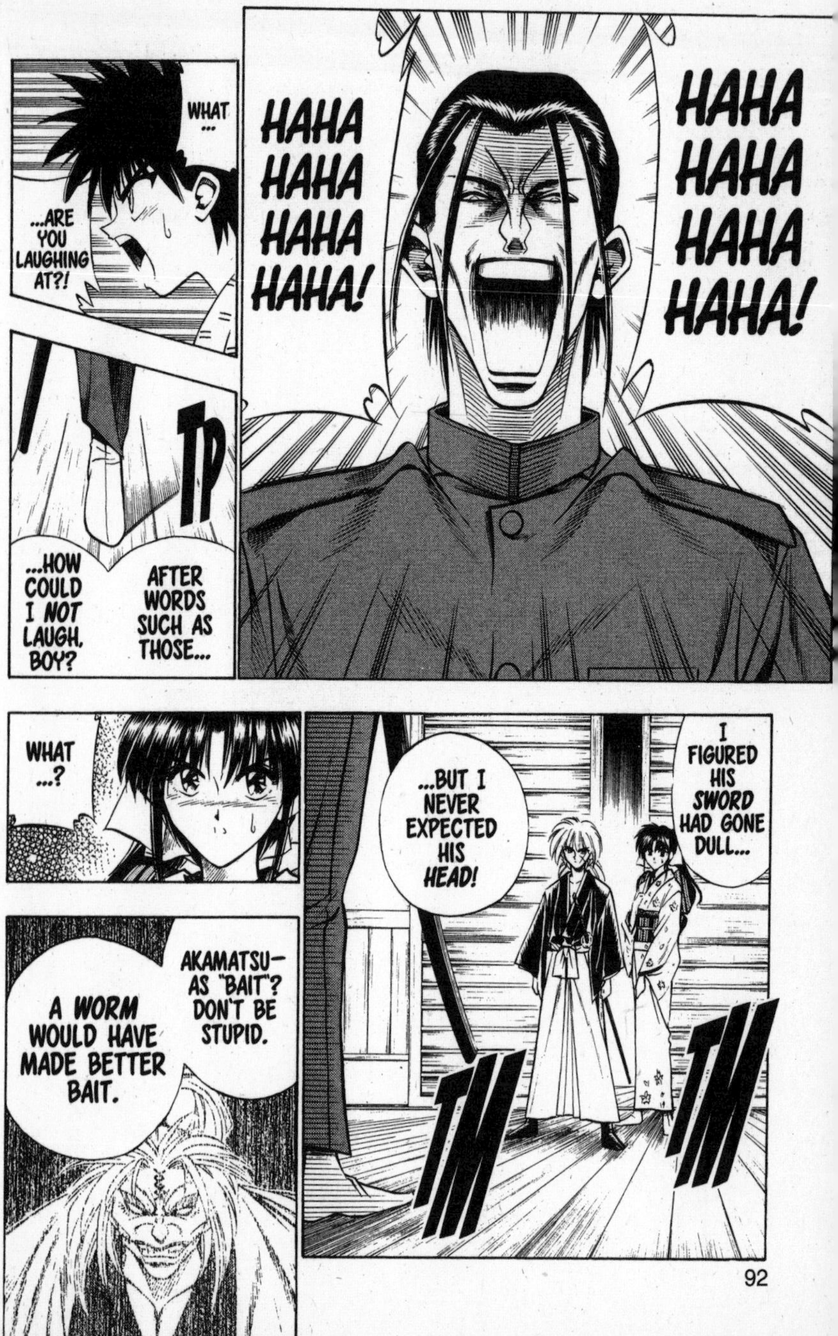
HAHA HAHA HAHA HAHA!
HAHA HAHA HAHA HAHA!
WHAT...
...ARE YOU LAUGHING AT?!
TP
AFTER WORDS SUCH AS THOSE...
...HOW COULD I NOT LAUGH, BOY?
I FIGURED HIS SWORD HAD GONE DULL...
...BUT I NEVER EXPECTED HIS HEAD!
TM
TM
WHAT ...?
AKAMATSU— AS "BAIT"? DON'T BE STUPID.
A WORM WOULD HAVE MADE BETTER BAIT.

READ THIS WAY

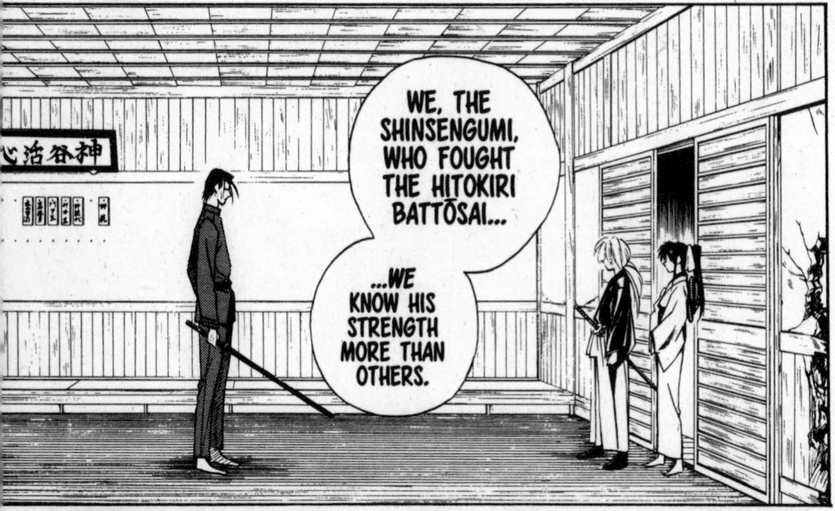
神谷活心
WE, THE SHINSENGUMI, WHO FOUGHT THE HITOKIRI BATTŌSAI...
...WE KNOW HIS STRENGTH MORE THAN OTHERS.

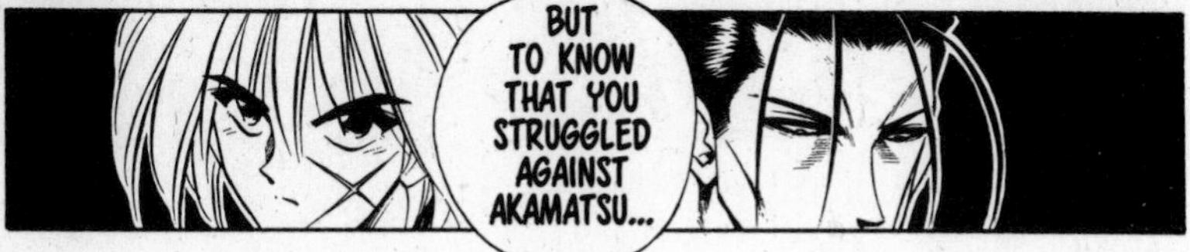
BUT TO KNOW THAT YOU STRUGGLED AGAINST AKAMATSU...

Long time no see. Watsuki here. This 52nd chapter was really tough. I had to go to Aomori for the J.S.A.T., but the schedule never seemed to get straightened out, and so I had to bring the work with me. Since I was unable to spend as much time on polish as I would have liked, there's maybe too much of my raw knowledge of and passion for the Shinsengumi in it, which maybe makes it harder to understand—it seems I just can't write good manga without that extra time. I've been hoping that a better-planned schedule would avoid this kind of thing, but then I ended up having to do a rough draft during a trip to my home town anyway. The 52nd chapter was written in spring, this comment was written in mid-summer, and the volume comes out [in Japan] in fall...no wonder manga artists lose track of their seasons...

伸宏和月

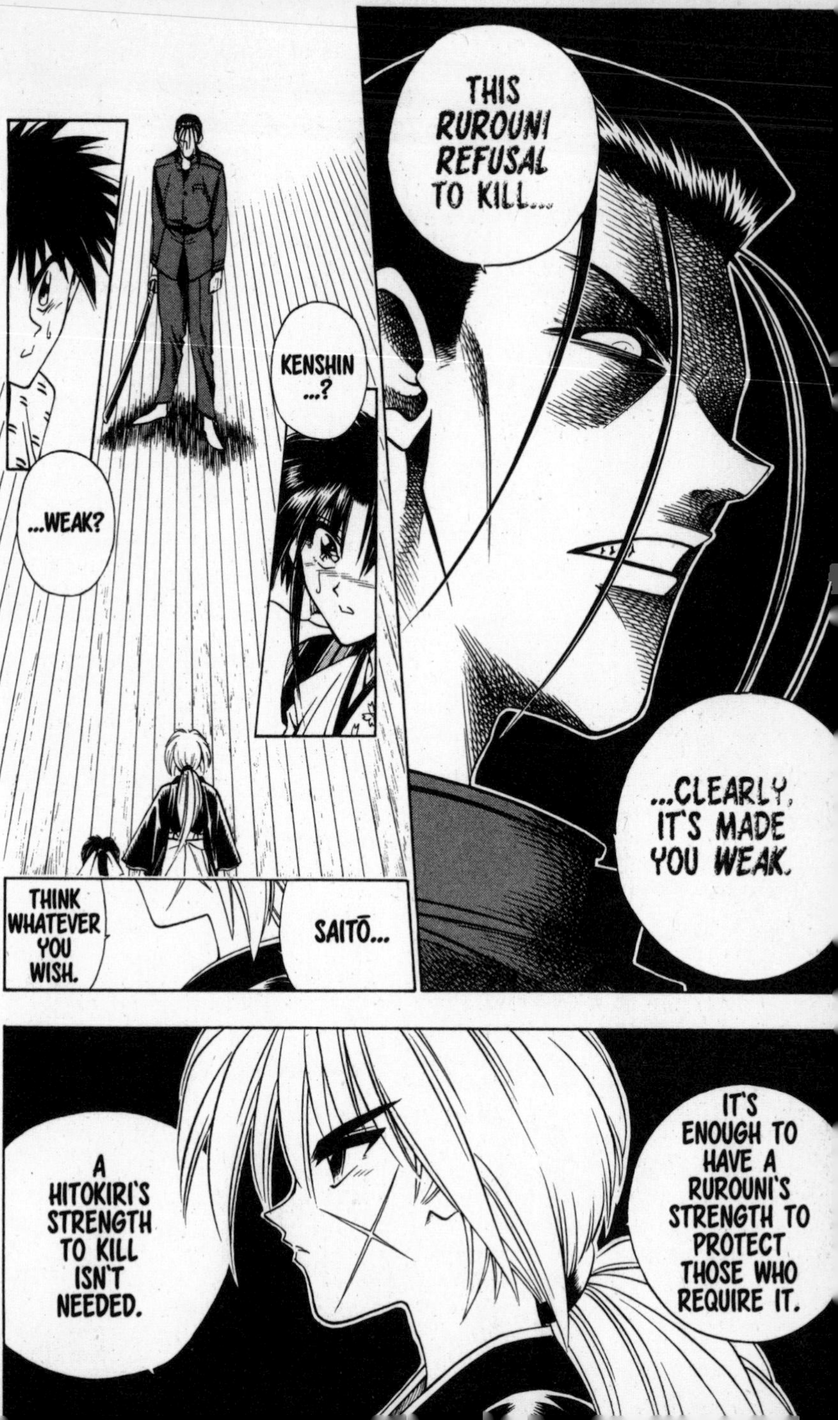
THIS RUROUNI REFUSAL TO KILL...
...CLEARLY, IT'S MADE YOU WEAK.
KENSHIN ...?
...WEAK?
SAITŌ...
THINK WHATEVER YOU WISH.
IT'S ENOUGH TO HAVE A RUROUNI'S STRENGTH TO PROTECT THOSE WHO REQUIRE IT.
A HITOKIRI'S STRENGTH TO KILL ISN'T NEEDED.

READ THIS WAY

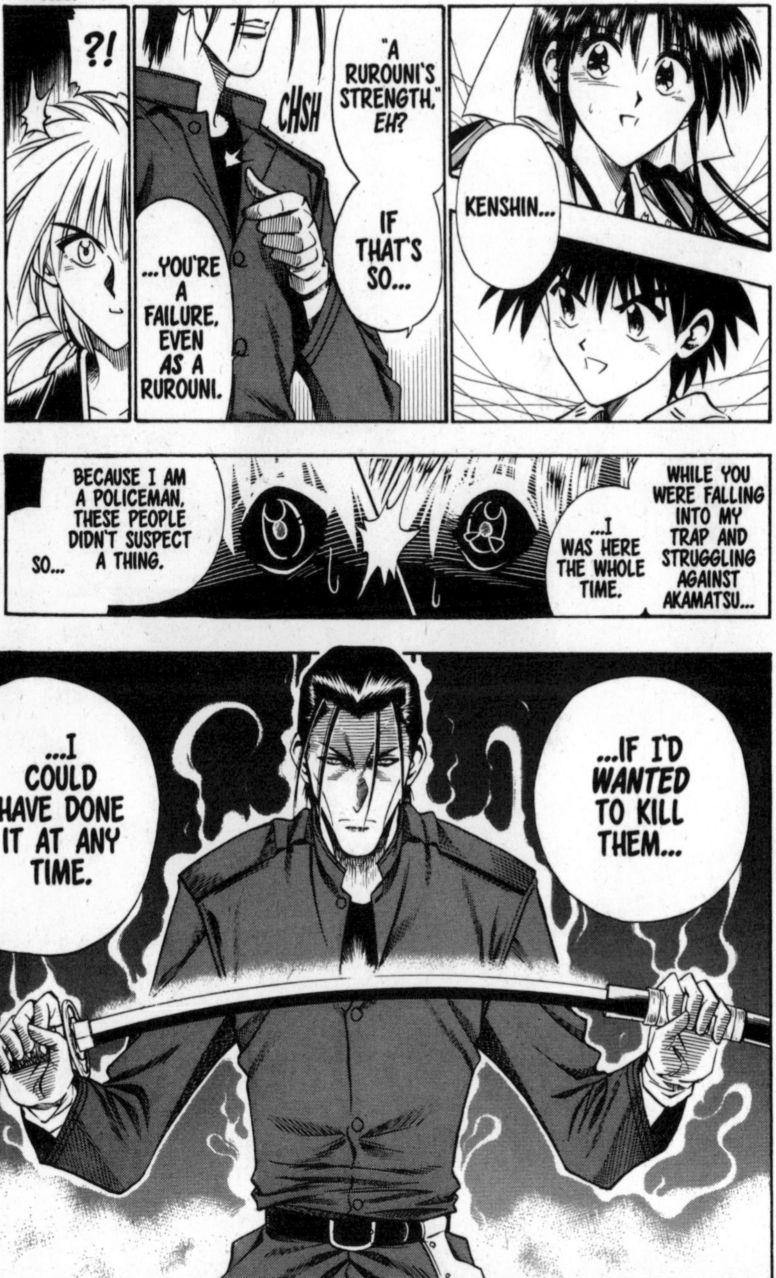
KENSHIN...
"A RUROUNI'S STRENGTH," EH?
CHSH
IF THAT'S SO...
...YOU'RE A FAILURE, EVEN AS A RUROUNI.
?!
WHILE YOU WERE FALLING INTO MY TRAP AND STRUGGLING AGAINST AKAMATSU...
...I WAS HERE THE WHOLE TIME.
BECAUSE I AM A POLICEMAN, THESE PEOPLE DIDN'T SUSPECT A THING.
SO...
...IF I'D *WANTED* TO KILL THEM...
...I COULD HAVE DONE IT AT ANY TIME.

READ THIS WAY

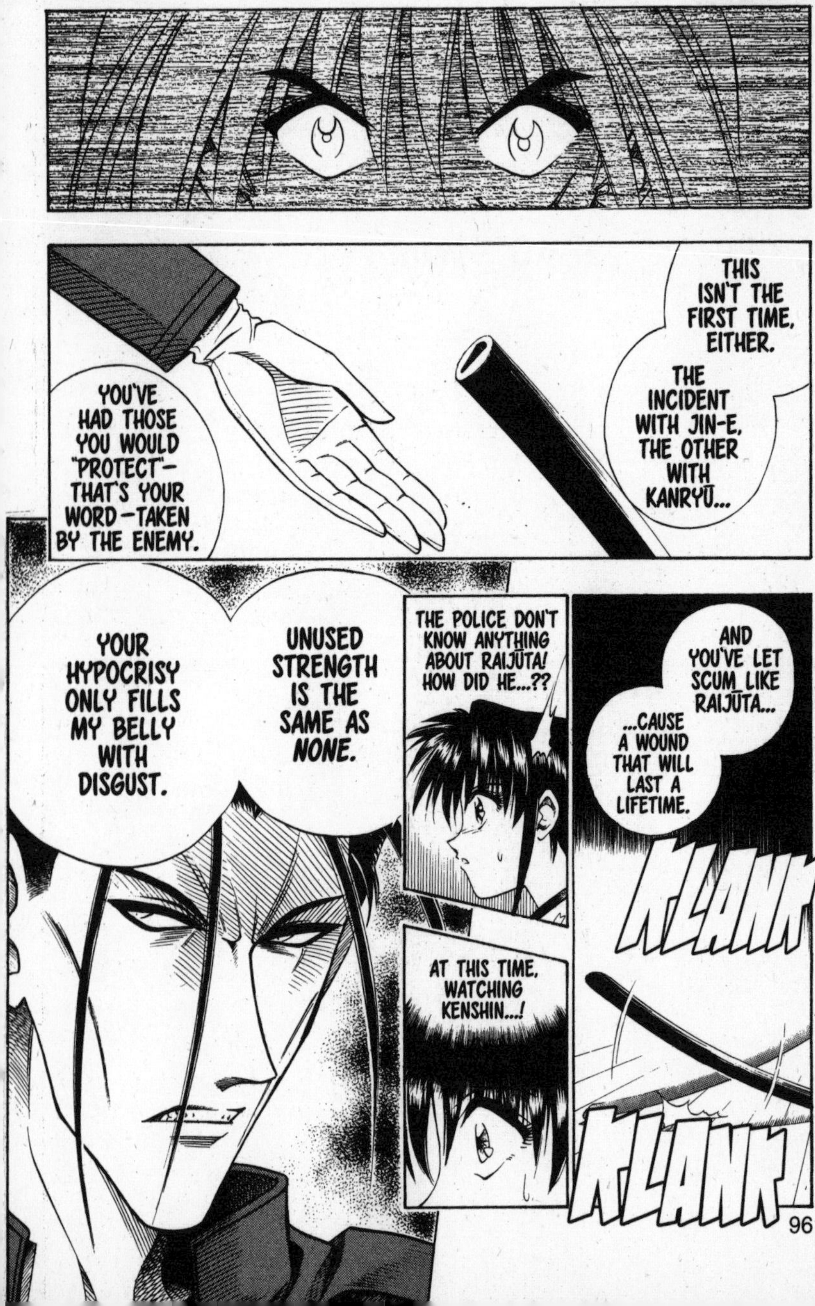
THIS ISN'T THE FIRST TIME, EITHER.
THE INCIDENT WITH JIN-E, THE OTHER WITH KANRYŪ...
YOU'VE HAD THOSE YOU WOULD "PROTECT"—THAT'S YOUR WORD—TAKEN BY THE ENEMY.
AND YOU'VE LET SCUM LIKE RAIJŪTA...
...CAUSE A WOUND THAT WILL LAST A LIFETIME.
KLANK
KLANK
THE POLICE DON'T KNOW ANYTHING ABOUT RAIJŪTA! HOW DID HE...??
AT THIS TIME, WATCHING KENSHIN...!
UNUSED STRENGTH IS THE SAME AS *NONE.*
YOUR HYPOCRISY ONLY FILLS MY BELLY WITH DISGUST.

READ THIS WAY

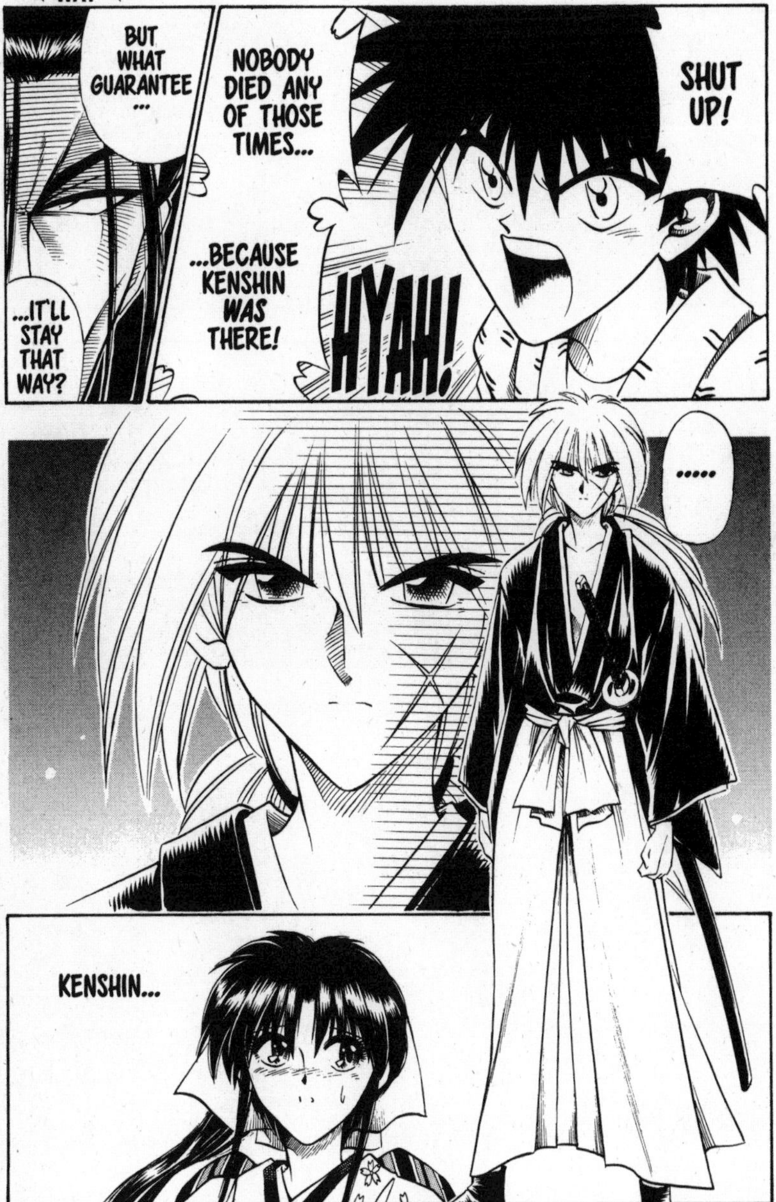
SHUT UP!
NOBODY DIED ANY OF THOSE TIMES...
HYAH!
...BECAUSE KENSHIN WAS THERE!
BUT WHAT GUARANTEE ...
...IT'LL STAY THAT WAY?
.....
KENSHIN...

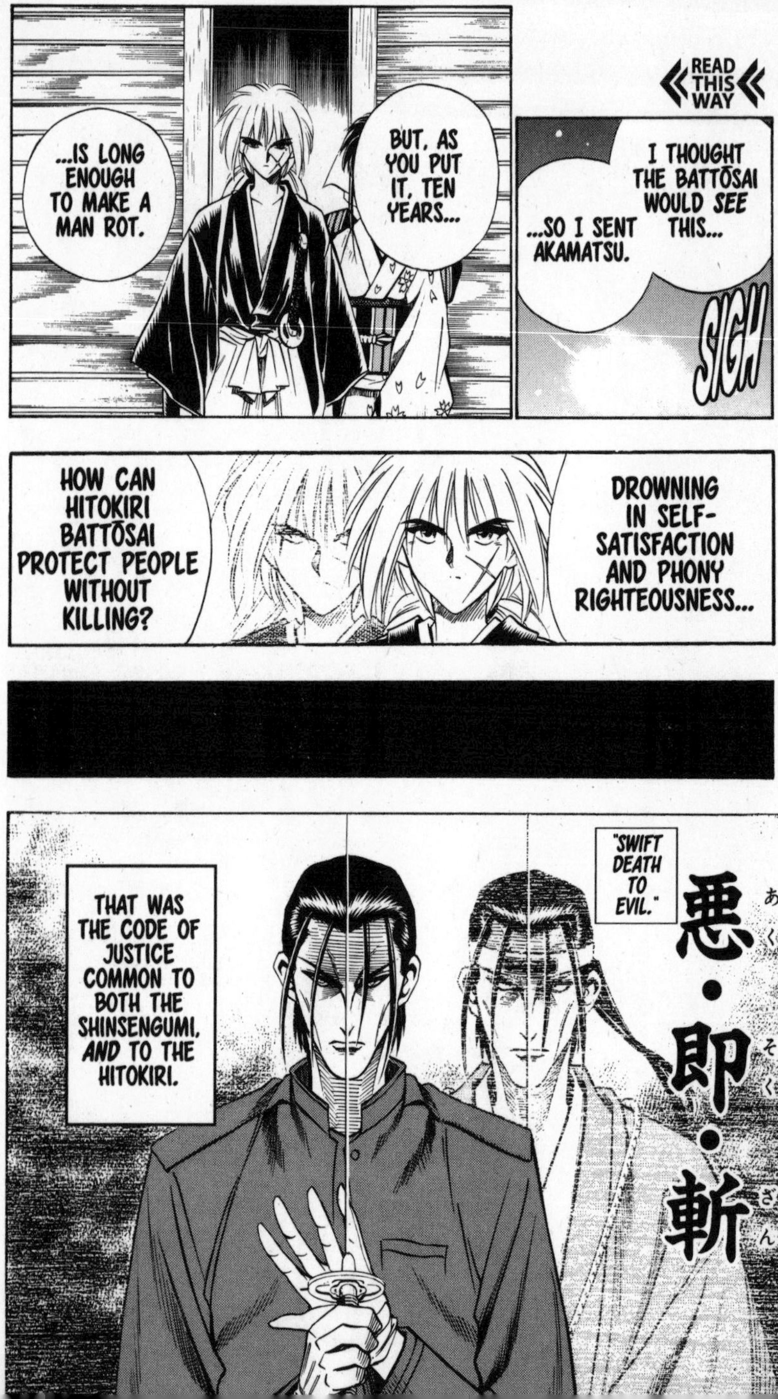
READ THIS WAY
I THOUGHT THE BATTŌSAI WOULD SEE THIS...
...SO I SENT AKAMATSU.
SIGH
BUT, AS YOU PUT IT, TEN YEARS...
...IS LONG ENOUGH TO MAKE A MAN ROT.
DROWNING IN SELF-SATISFACTION AND PHONY RIGHTEOUSNESS...
HOW CAN HITOKIRI BATTŌSAI PROTECT PEOPLE WITHOUT KILLING?
"SWIFT DEATH TO EVIL."
悪・即・斬
THAT WAS THE CODE OF JUSTICE COMMON TO BOTH THE SHINSENGUMI, AND TO THE HITOKIRI.

READ THIS WAY

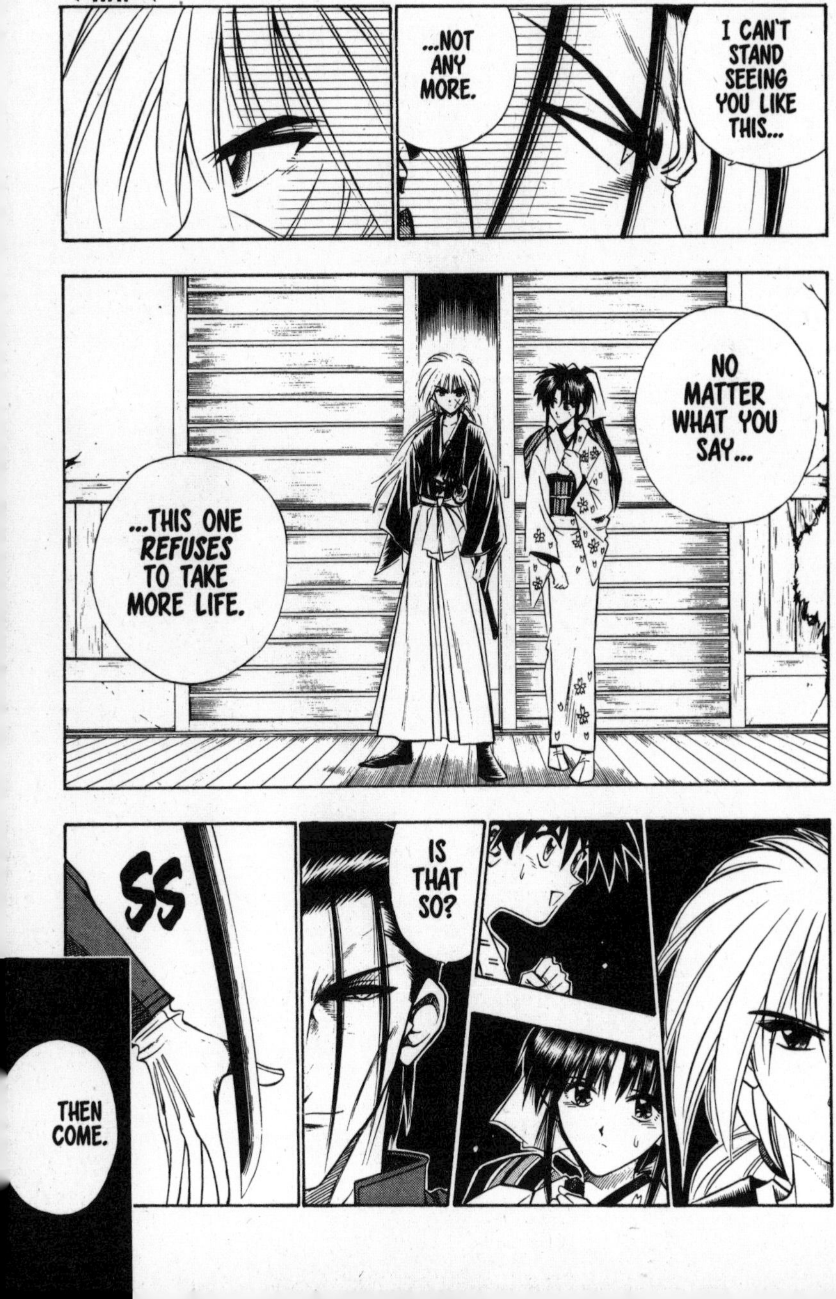
I CAN'T STAND SEEING YOU LIKE THIS...
...NOT ANY MORE.
NO MATTER WHAT YOU SAY...
...THIS ONE REFUSES TO TAKE MORE LIFE.
IS THAT SO?
SS
THEN COME.

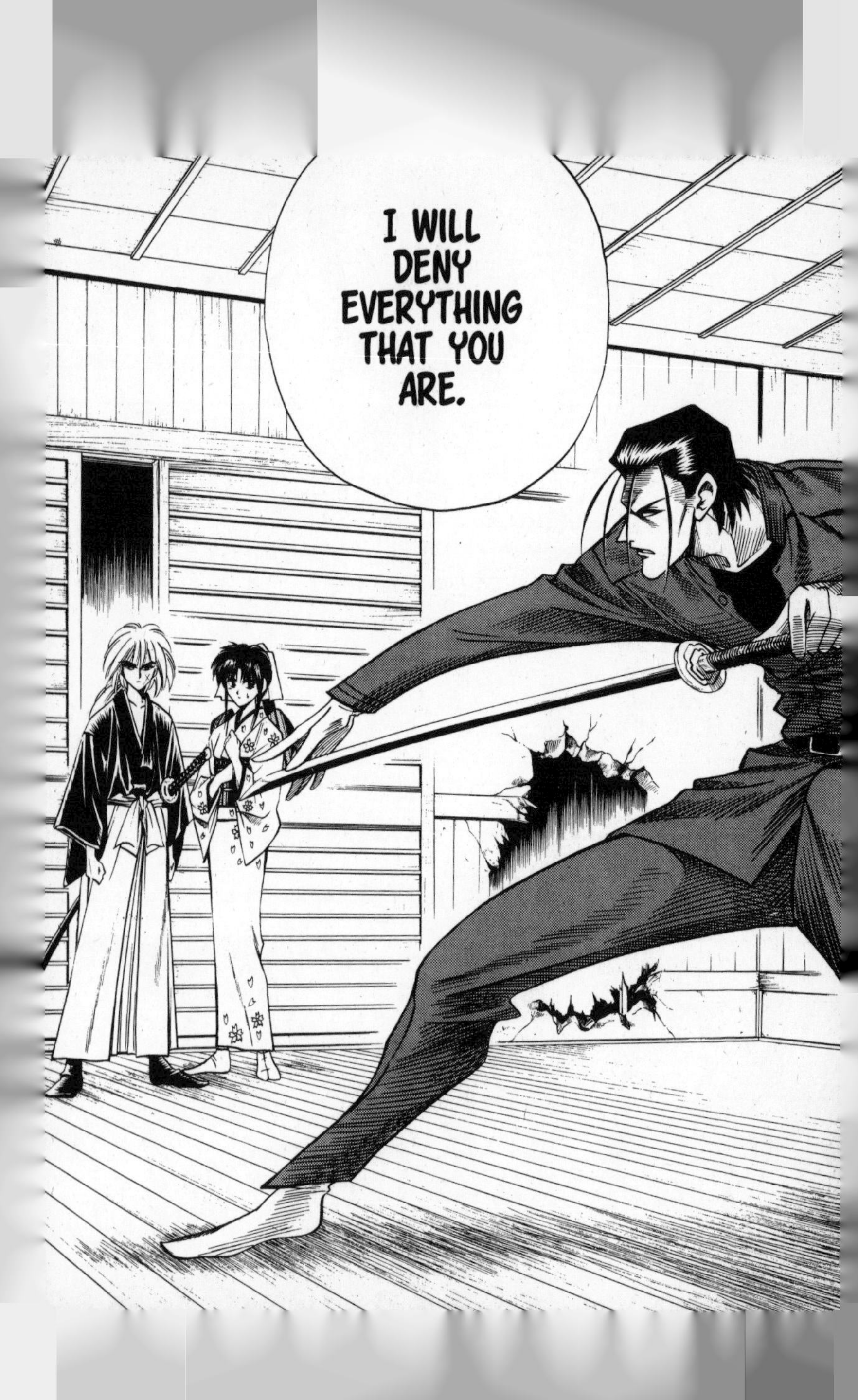
I WILL DENY EVERYTHING THAT YOU ARE.

READ THIS WAY

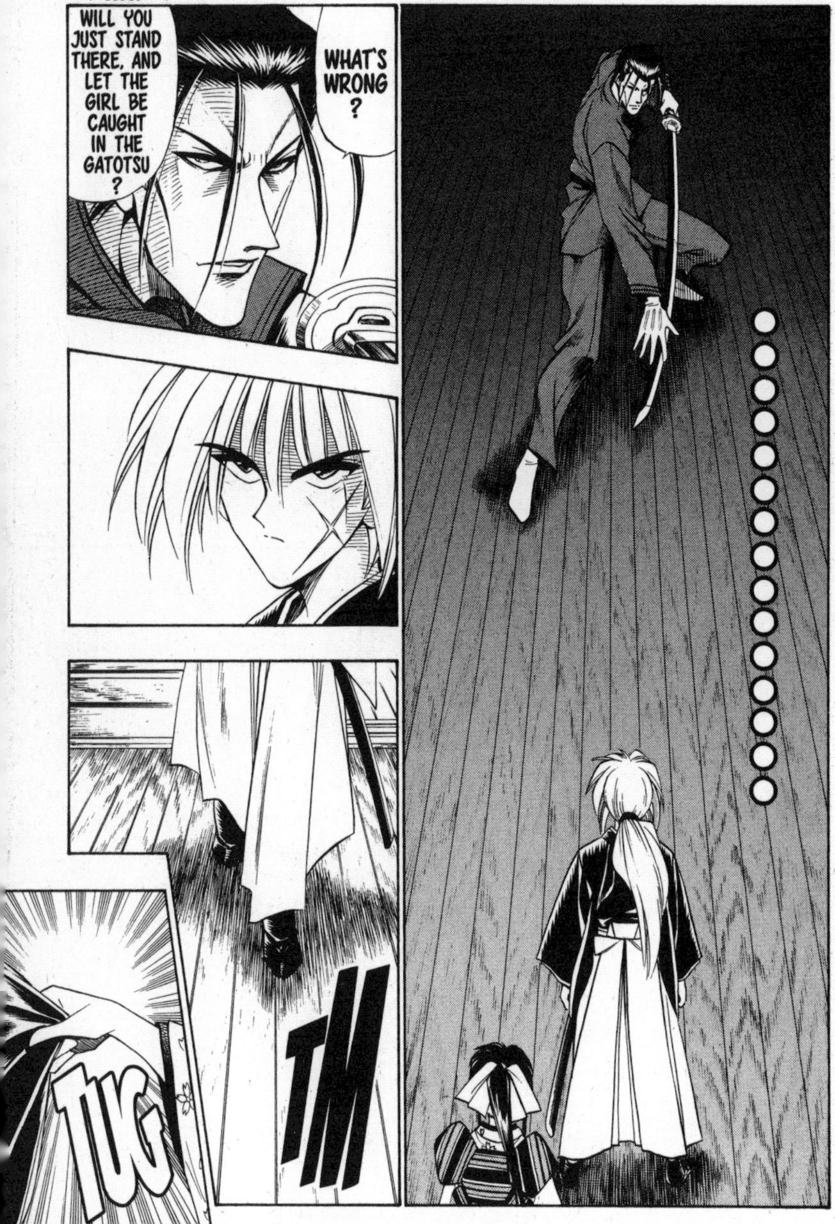
WHAT'S WRONG?
WILL YOU JUST STAND THERE, AND LET THE GIRL BE CAUGHT IN THE GATOTSU?
TM
TUG

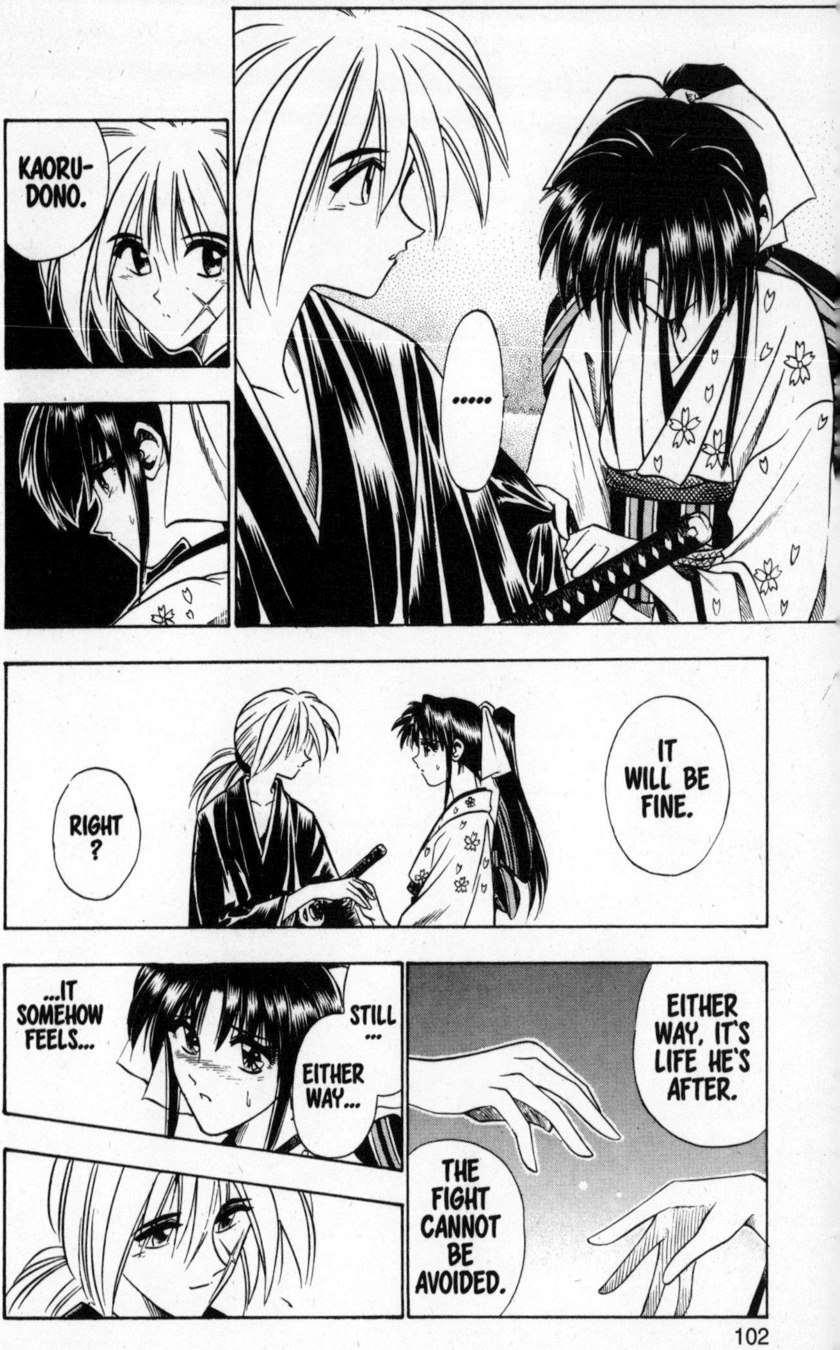
.....
KAORU-DONO.
IT WILL BE FINE.
RIGHT?
EITHER WAY, IT'S LIFE HE'S AFTER.
THE FIGHT CANNOT BE AVOIDED.
STILL...
EITHER WAY...
...IT SOMEHOW FEELS...

READ THIS WAY

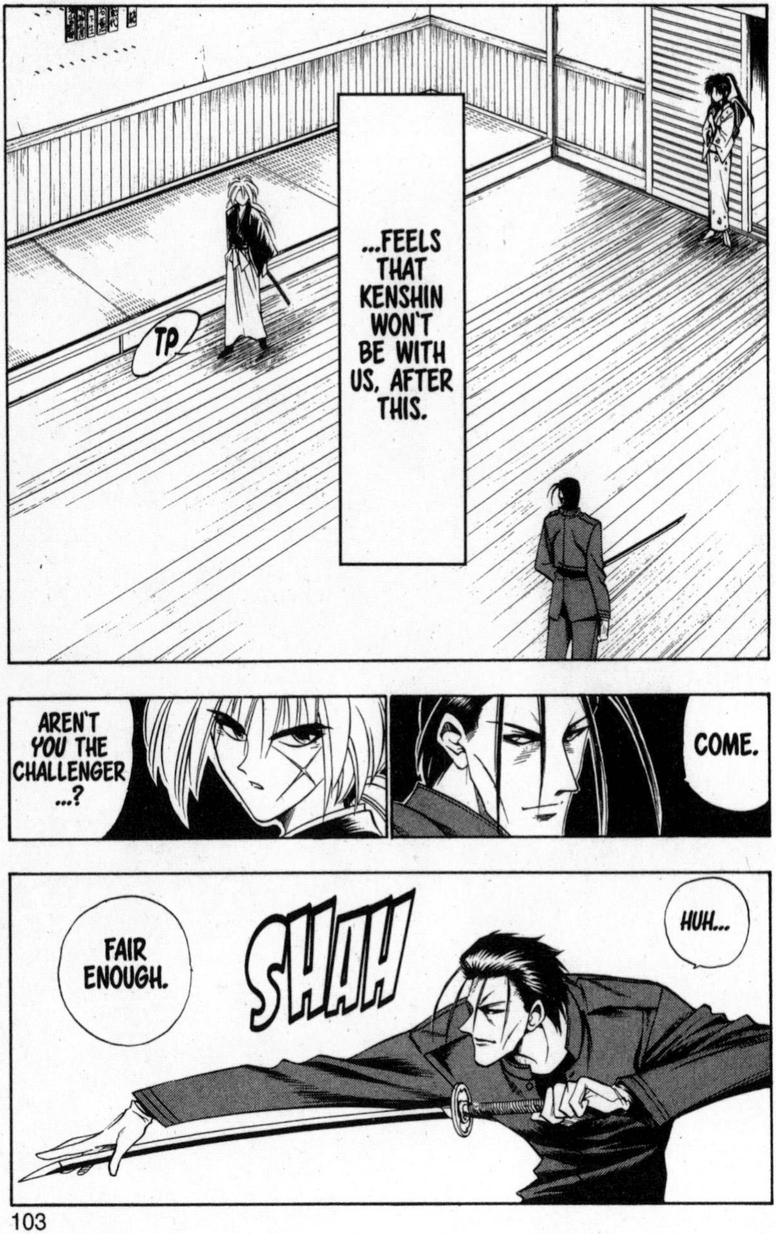

TP
...FEELS THAT KENSHIN WON'T BE WITH US, AFTER THIS.
COME.
AREN'T YOU THE CHALLENGER ...?
HUH...
SHAH
FAIR ENOUGH.

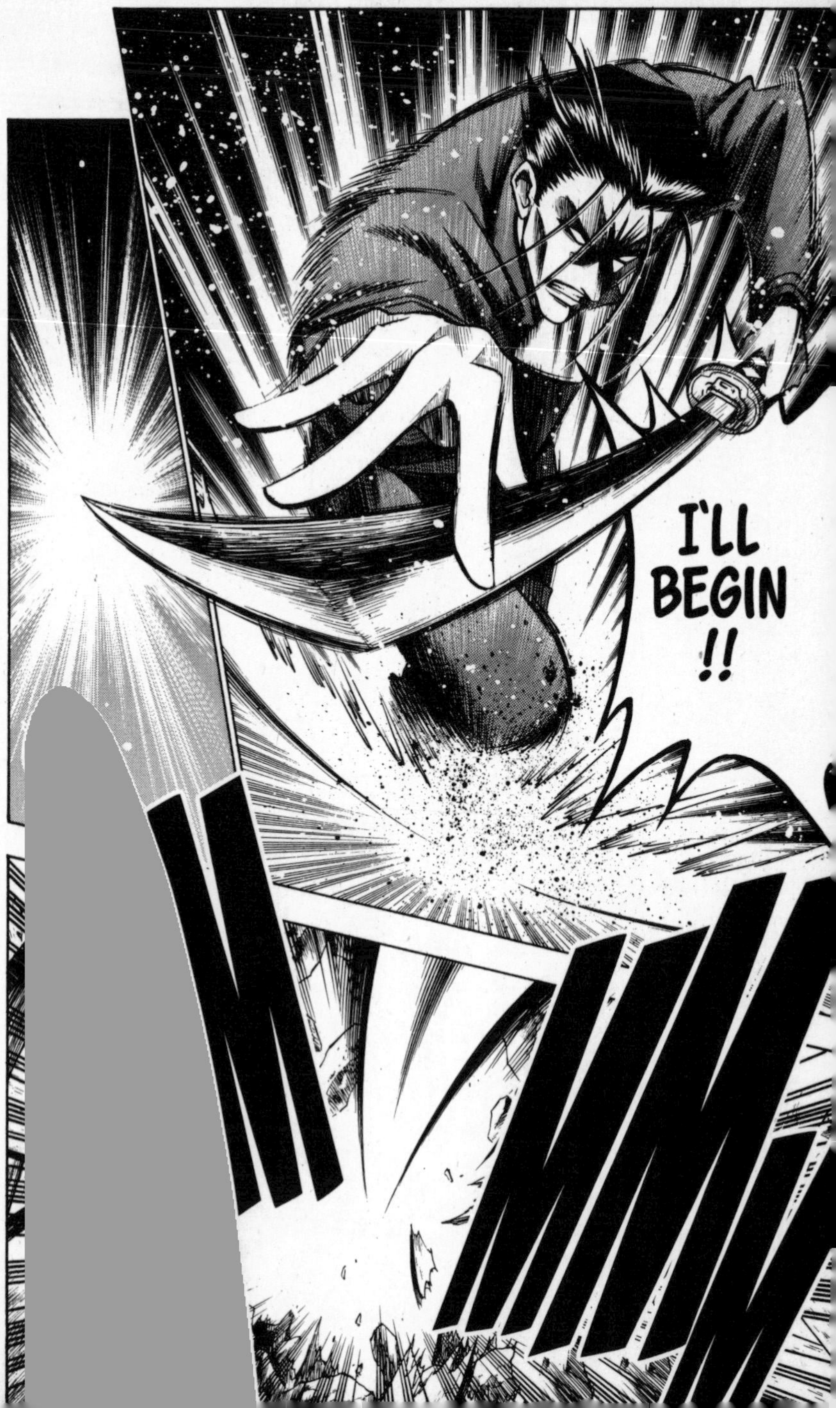
I'LL BEGIN !!

READ THIS WAY

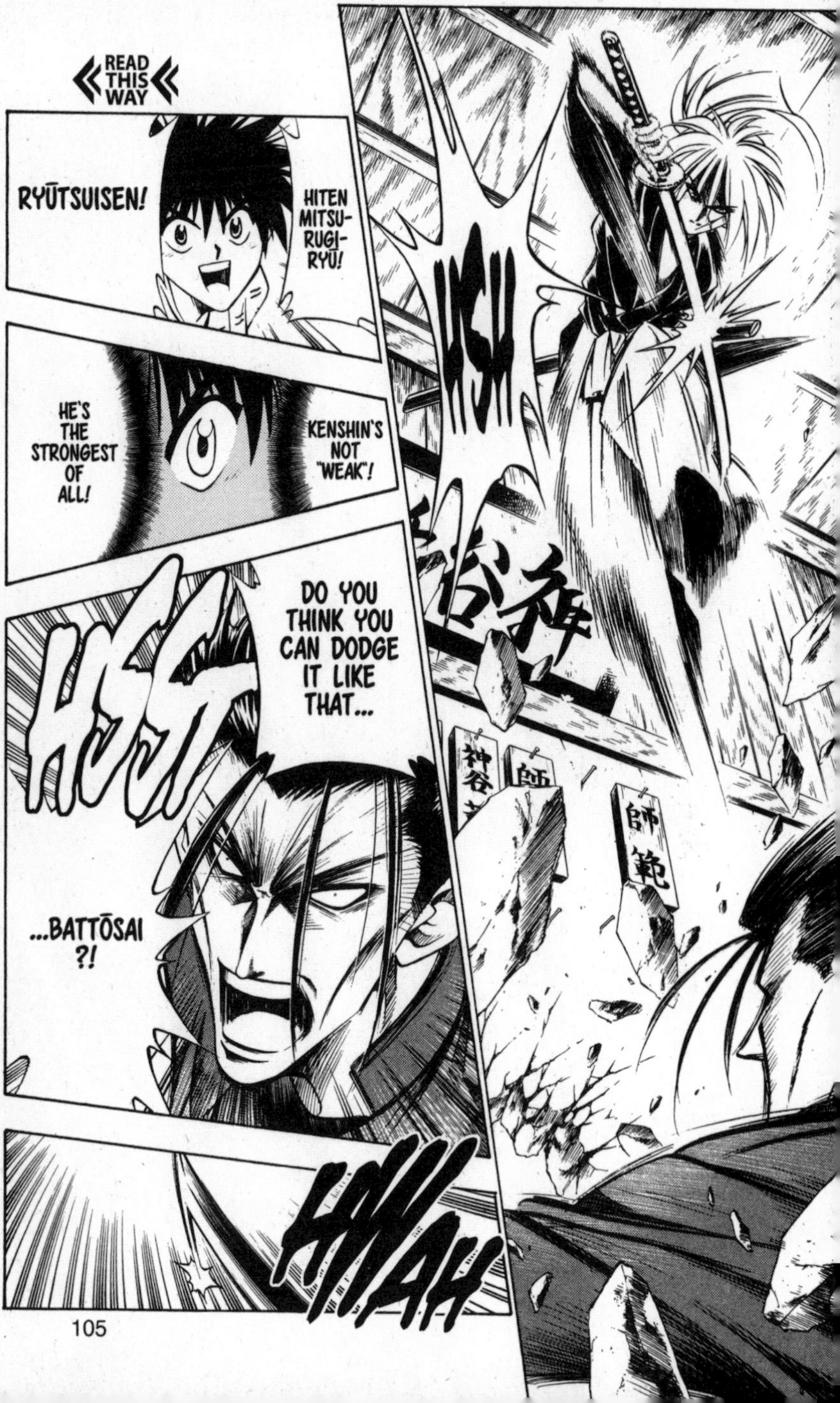
WHSH
師範
HITEN MITSURUGI-RYŪ!
RYŪTSUISEN!
KENSHIN'S NOT "WEAK"!
HE'S THE STRONGEST OF ALL!
DO YOU THINK YOU CAN DODGE IT LIKE THAT...
...BATTŌSAI?!
SWAH

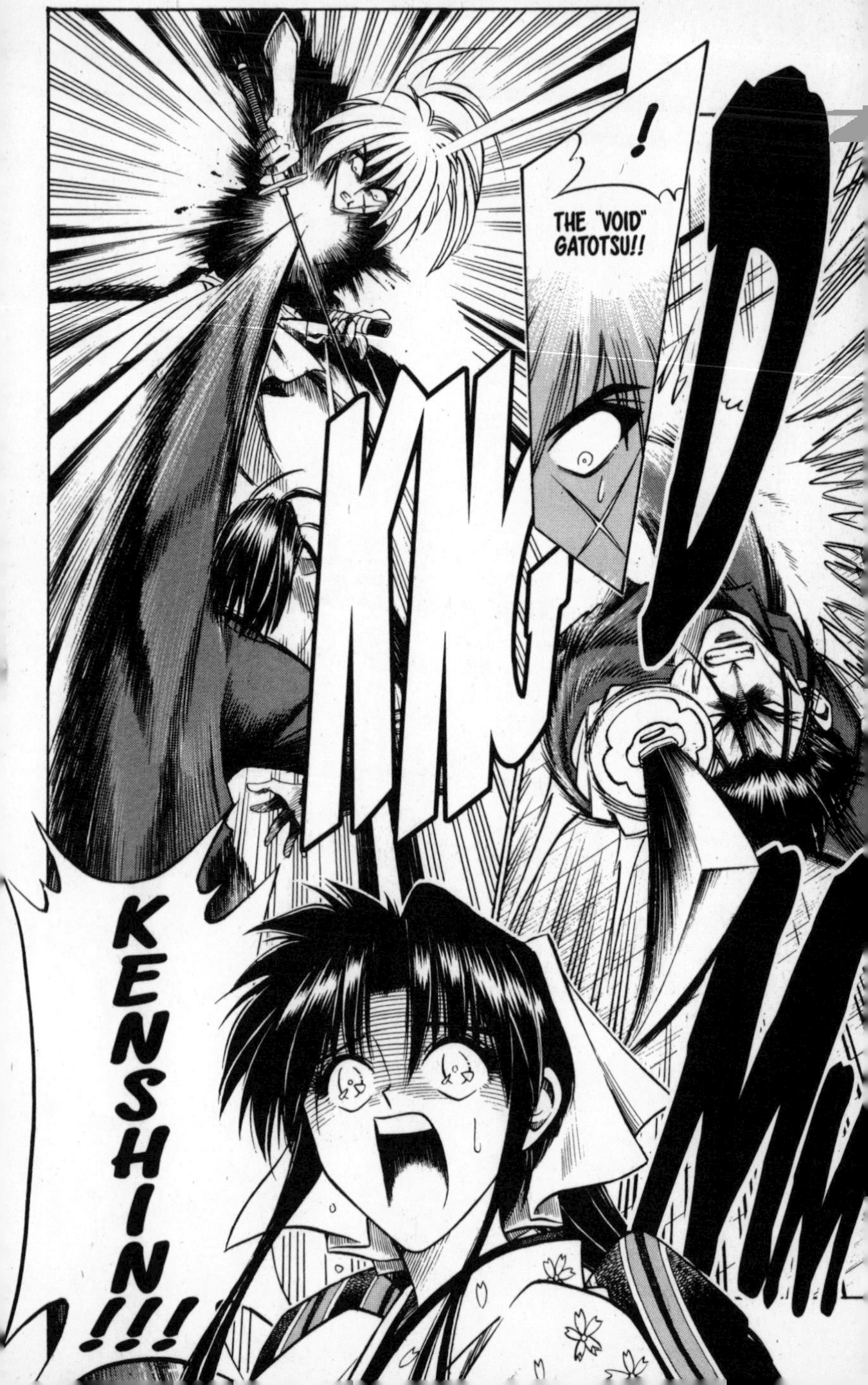
!
THE "VOID" GATOTSU!!
KENSHIN!!!

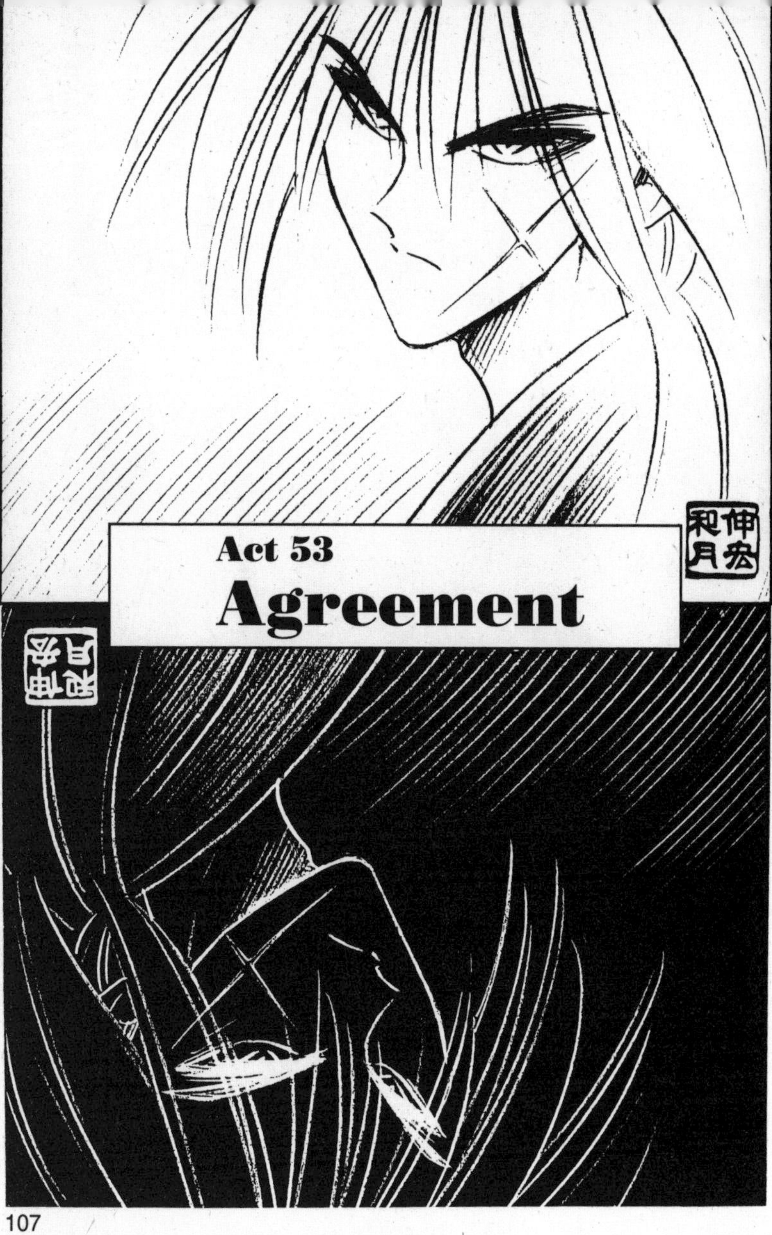
Act 53
Agreement

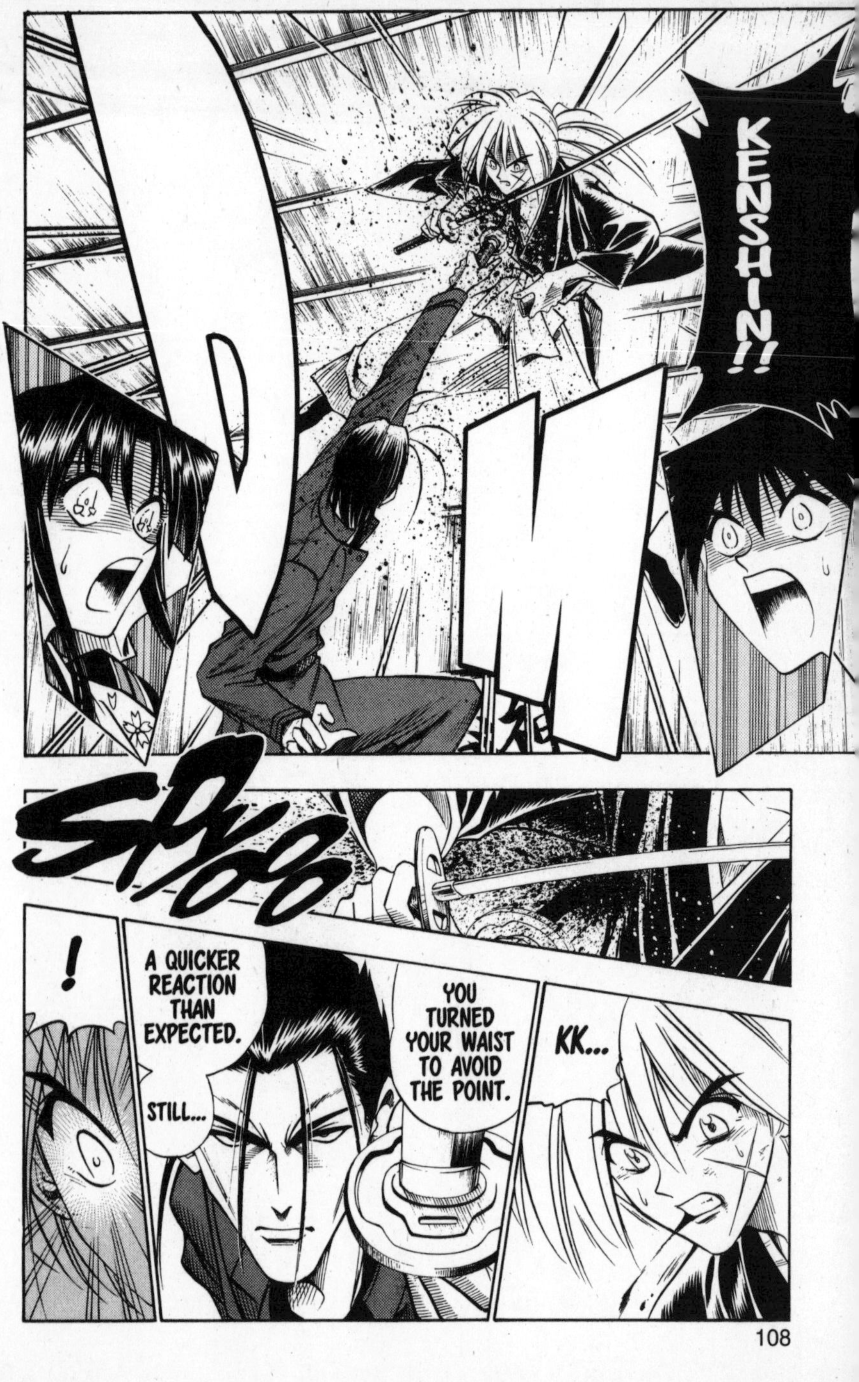
KENSHIN!!
KK...
YOU TURNED YOUR WAIST TO AVOID THE POINT.
A QUICKER REACTION THAN EXPECTED.
STILL...
!

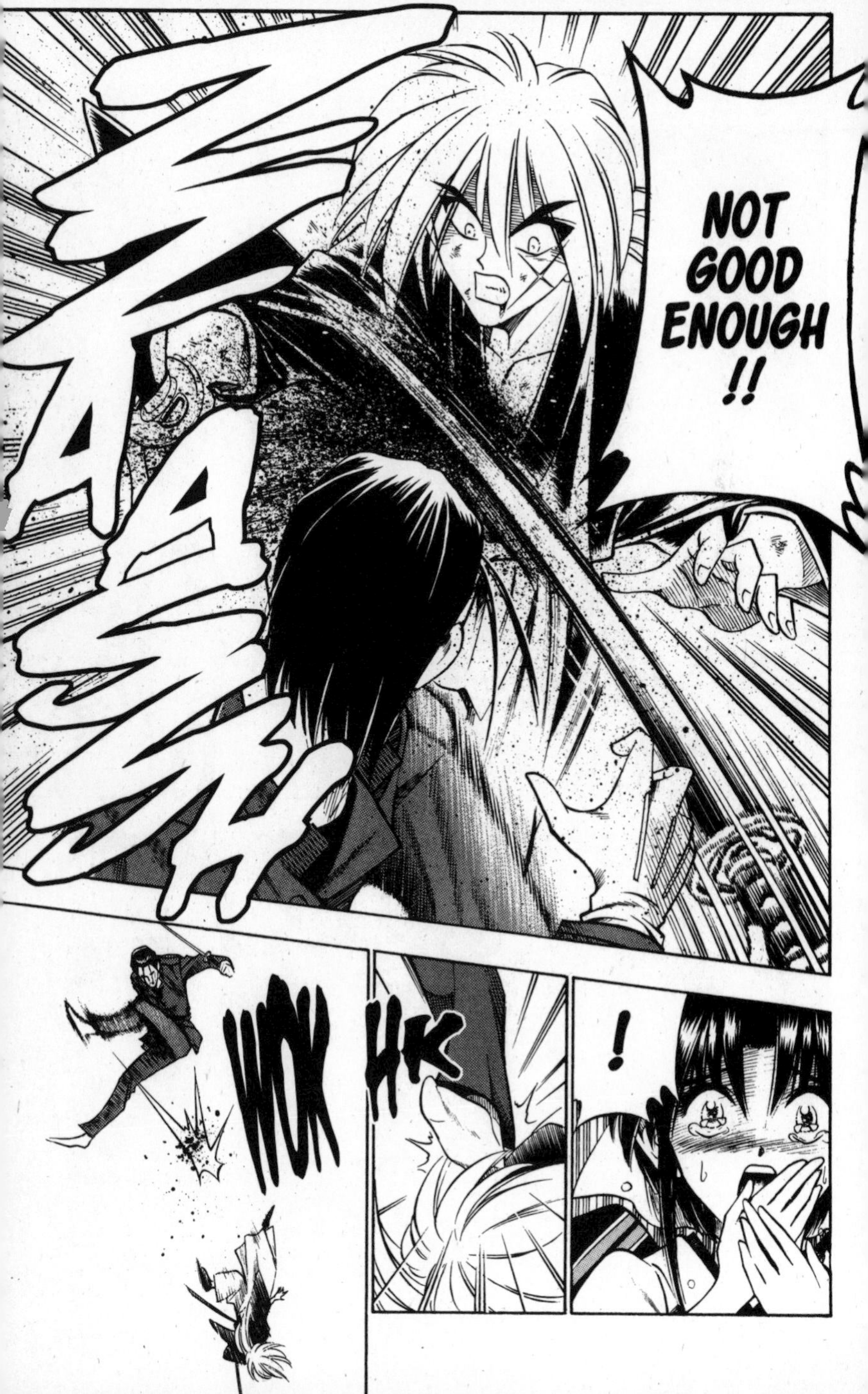
NOT GOOD ENOUGH !!
ZAASH
!
HK
WOK

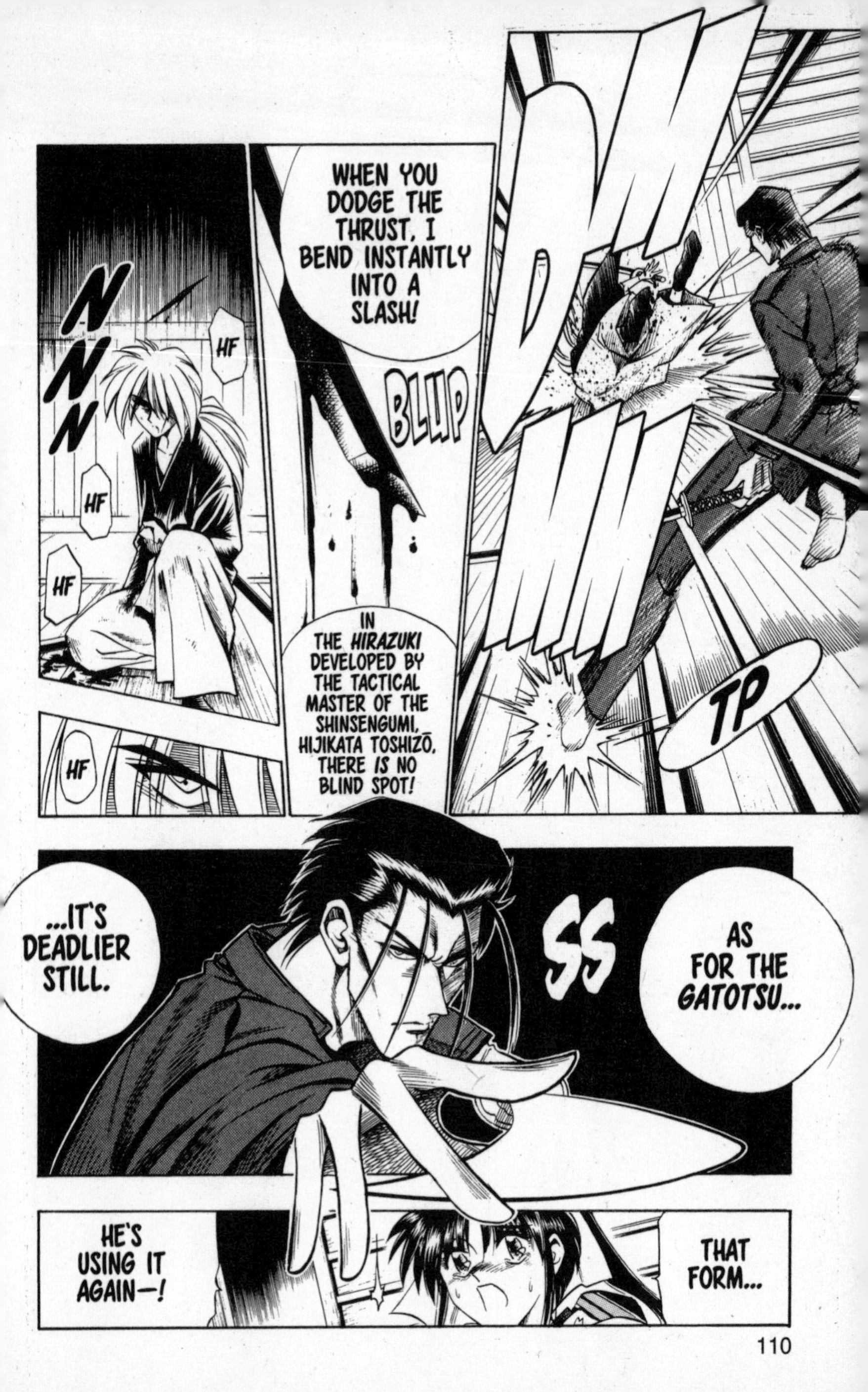
TP
WHEN YOU DODGE THE THRUST, I BEND INSTANTLY INTO A SLASH!
BLUP
IN THE *HIRAZUKI* DEVELOPED BY THE TACTICAL MASTER OF THE SHINSENGUMI, HIJIKATA TOSHIZŌ, THERE *IS* NO BLIND SPOT!
NNN
HF
HF
HF
HF
AS FOR THE GATOTSU...
SS
...IT'S DEADLIER STILL.
THAT FORM...
HE'S USING IT AGAIN—!

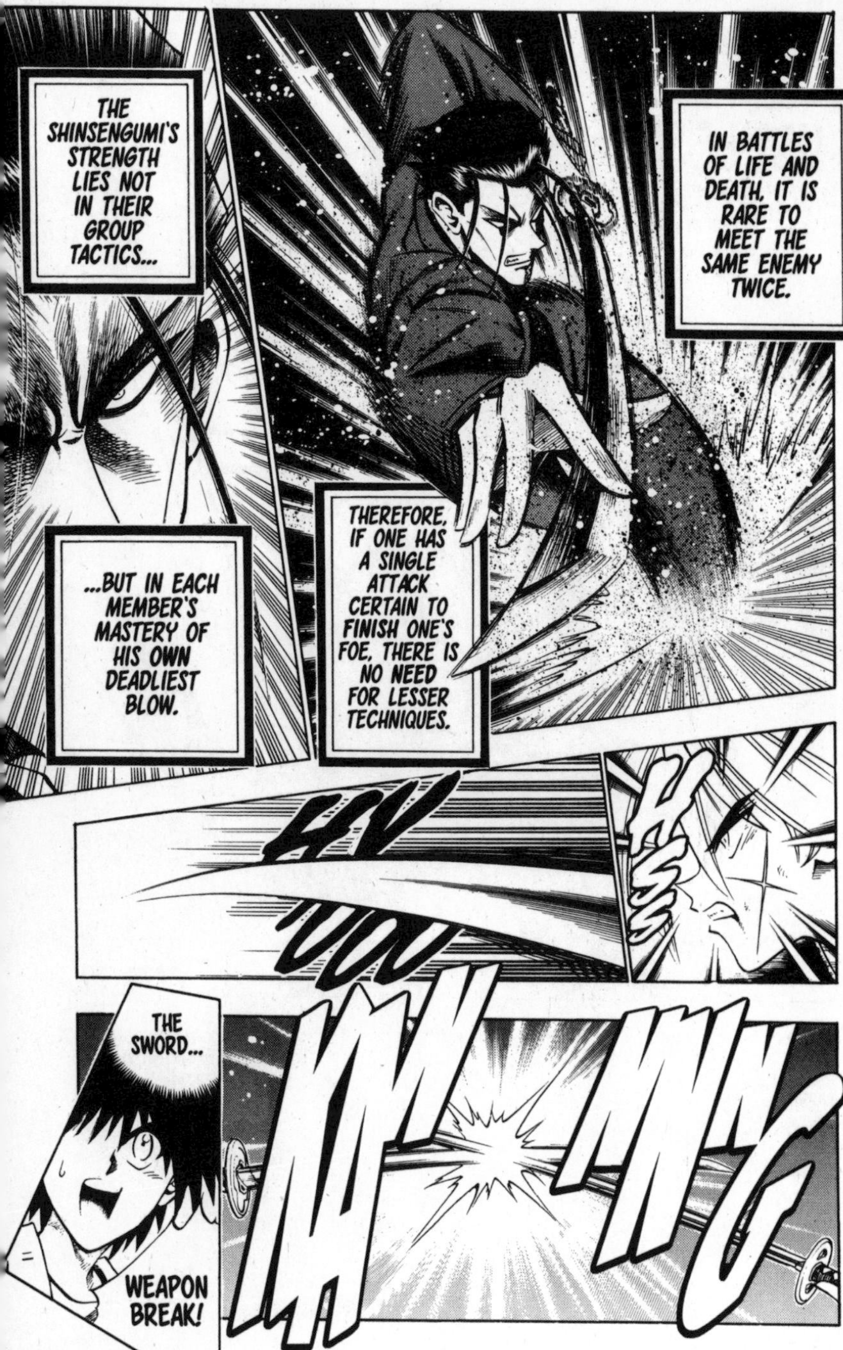
IN BATTLES OF LIFE AND DEATH, IT IS RARE TO MEET THE SAME ENEMY TWICE.
THEREFORE, IF ONE HAS A SINGLE ATTACK CERTAIN TO FINISH ONE'S FOE, THERE IS NO NEED FOR LESSER TECHNIQUES.
THE SHINSENGUMI'S STRENGTH LIES NOT IN THEIR GROUP TACTICS...
...BUT IN EACH MEMBER'S MASTERY OF HIS OWN DEADLIEST BLOW.
THE SWORD...
WEAPON BREAK!

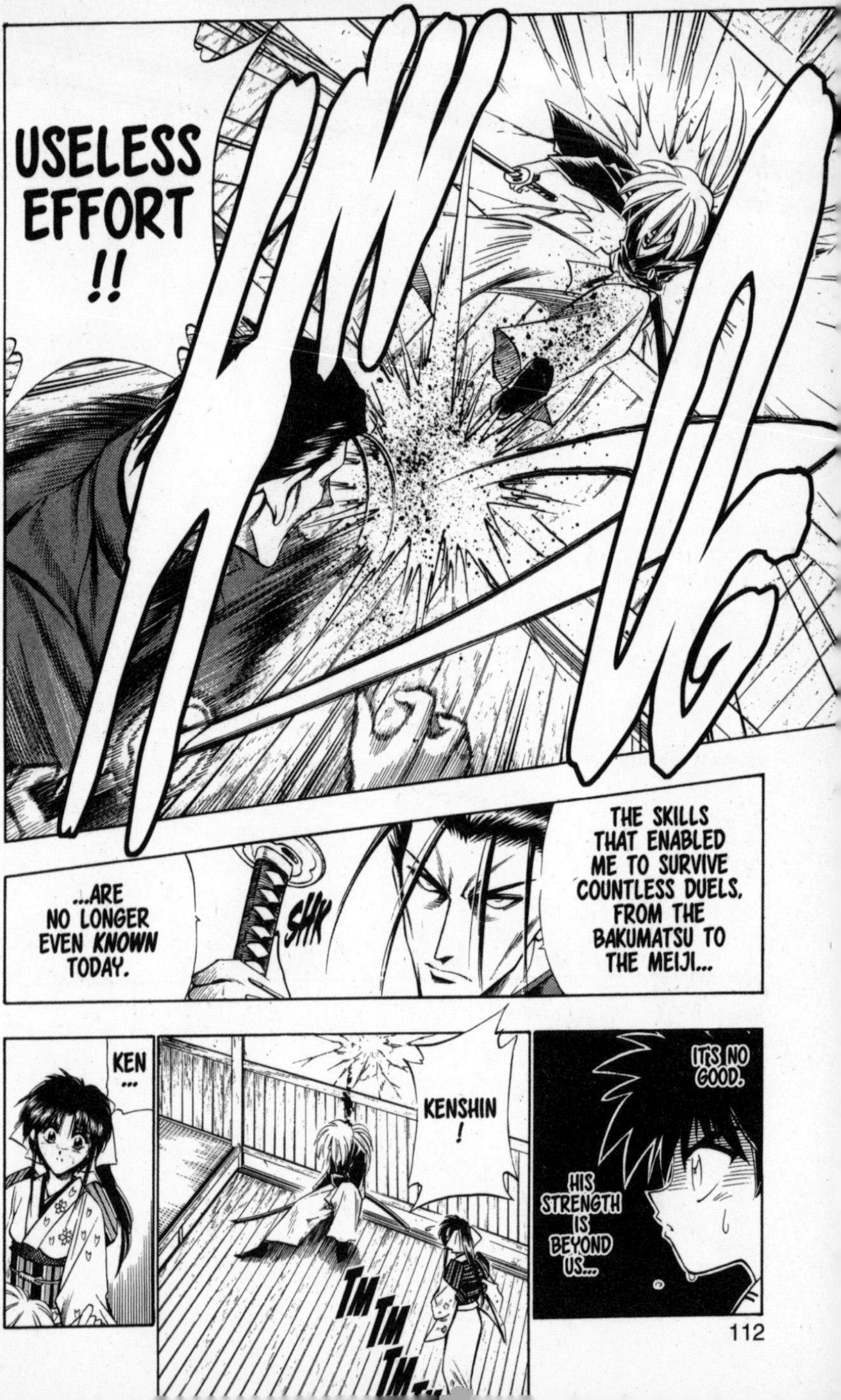
USELESS EFFORT!!
THE SKILLS THAT ENABLED ME TO SURVIVE COUNTLESS DUELS, FROM THE BAKUMATSU TO THE MEIJI...
SHK
...ARE NO LONGER EVEN KNOWN TODAY.
IT'S NO GOOD.
HIS STRENGTH IS BEYOND US...
KENSHIN!
TM TM TM...
KEN...

READ THIS WAY

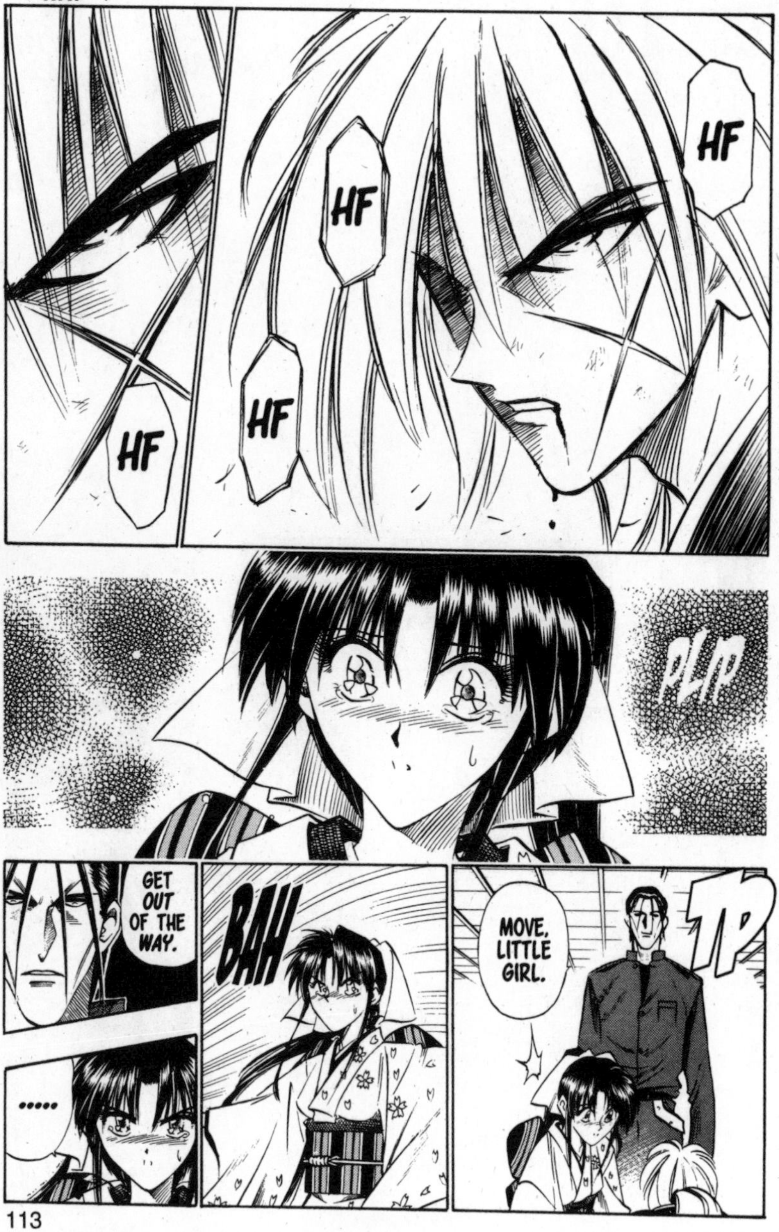
HF
HF
HF
HF
PLIP
TP
MOVE, LITTLE GIRL.
BAH
GET OUT OF THE WAY.
......

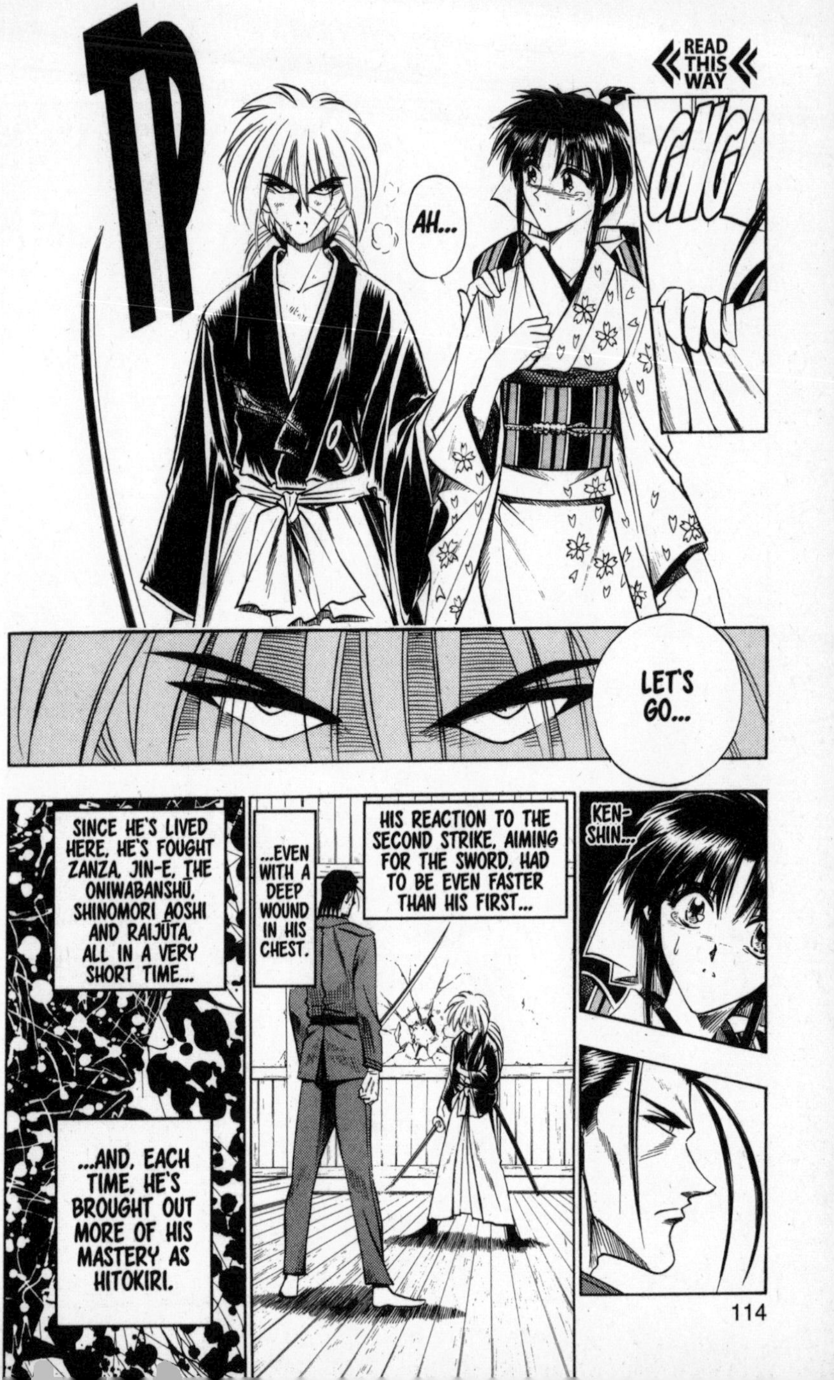
READ THIS WAY
GNG
TP
AH...
LET'S GO...
KEN-SHIN...
HIS REACTION TO THE SECOND STRIKE, AIMING FOR THE SWORD, HAD TO BE EVEN FASTER THAN HIS FIRST...
...EVEN WITH A DEEP WOUND IN HIS CHEST.
SINCE HE'S LIVED HERE, HE'S FOUGHT ZANZA, JIN-E, THE ONIWABANSHŪ, SHINOMORI AOSHI AND RAIJŪTA, ALL IN A VERY SHORT TIME...
...AND, EACH TIME, HE'S BROUGHT OUT MORE OF HIS MASTERY AS HITOKIRI.

READ THIS WAY

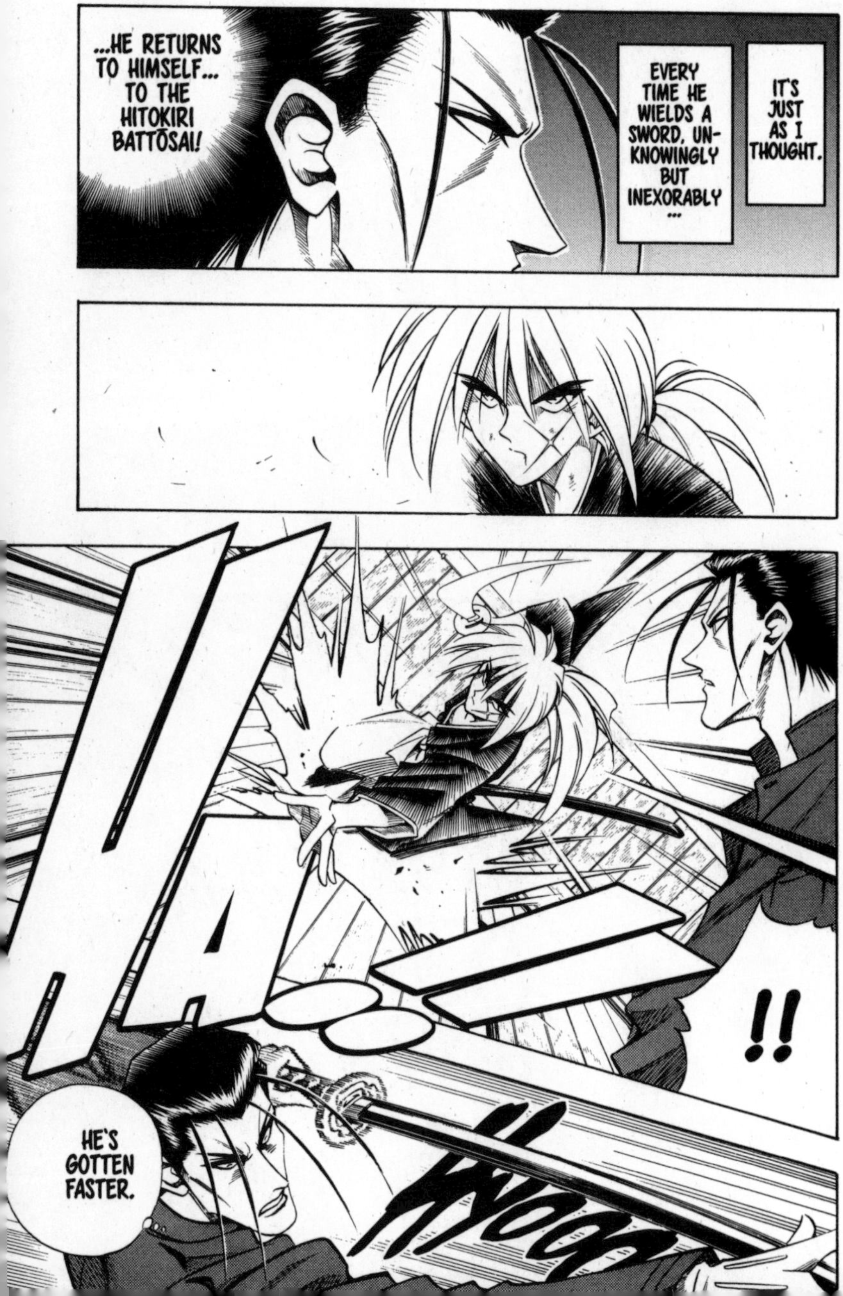
IT'S JUST AS I THOUGHT.
EVERY TIME HE WIELDS A SWORD, UN-KNOWINGLY BUT INEXORABLY...
...HE RETURNS TO HIMSELF... TO THE HITOKIRI BATTŌSAI!
HA...
!!
HE'S GOTTEN FASTER.

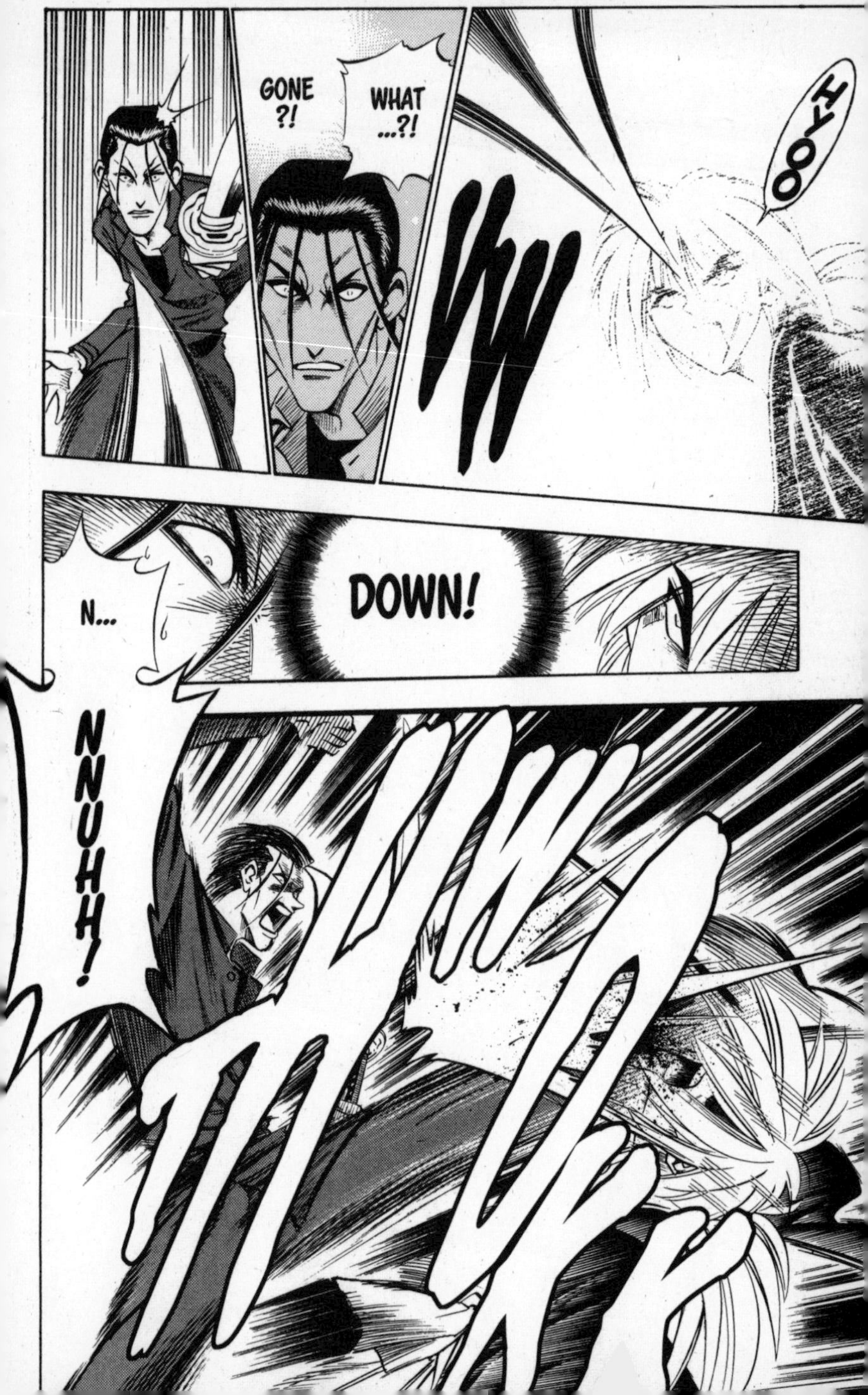
HYOO
WHAT ...?!
GONE ?!
DOWN!
N...
NNUHH!

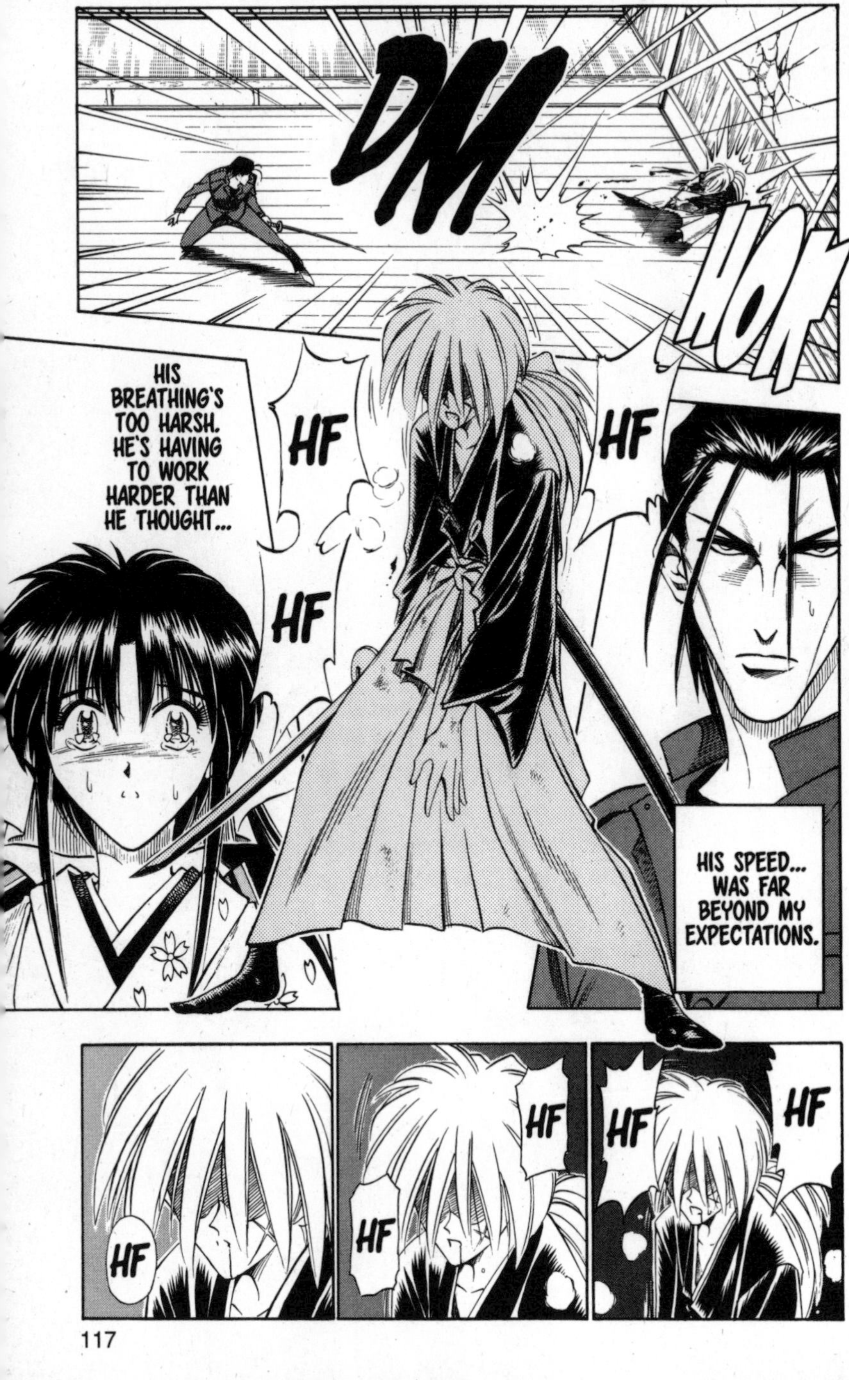
DM
HOK
HF
HIS SPEED... WAS FAR BEYOND MY EXPECTATIONS.
HIS BREATHING'S TOO HARSH. HE'S HAVING TO WORK HARDER THAN HE THOUGHT...
HF
HF
HF
HF
HF
HF
HF

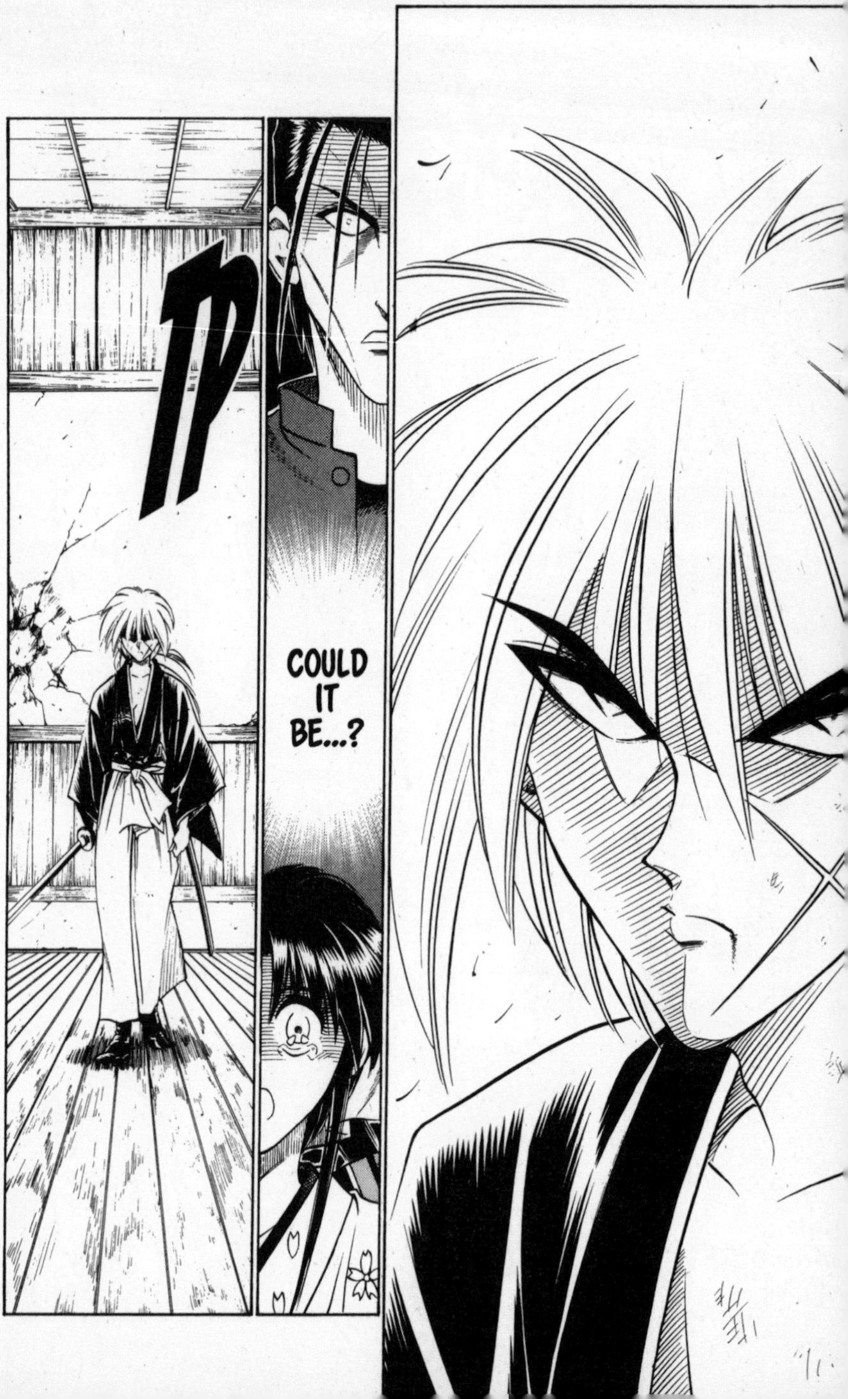
COULD IT BE...?
TP

READ THIS WAY

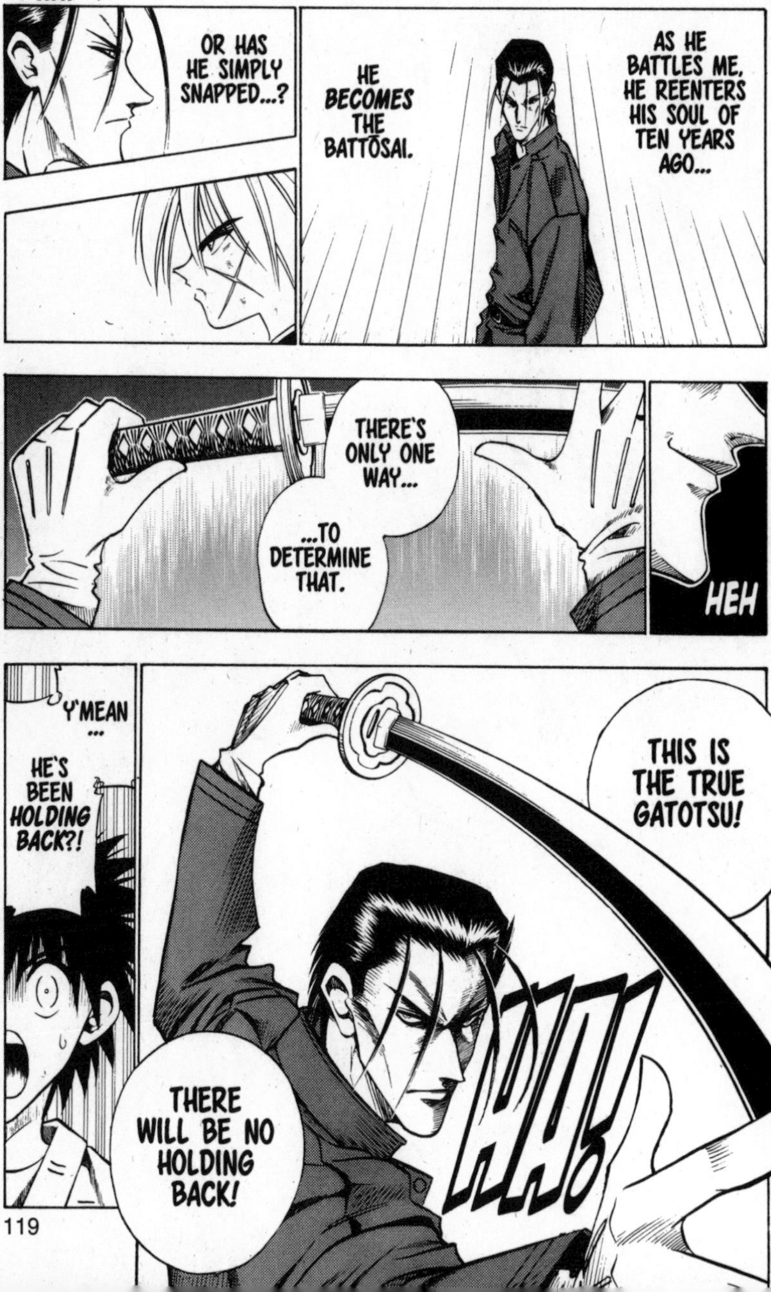
AS HE BATTLES ME, HE REENTERS HIS SOUL OF TEN YEARS AGO...
HE BECOMES THE BATTŌSAI.
OR HAS HE SIMPLY SNAPPED...?
HEH
THERE'S ONLY ONE WAY...
...TO DETERMINE THAT.
THIS IS THE TRUE GATOTSU!
THERE WILL BE NO HOLDING BACK!
Y'MEAN ...
HE'S BEEN HOLDING BACK?!

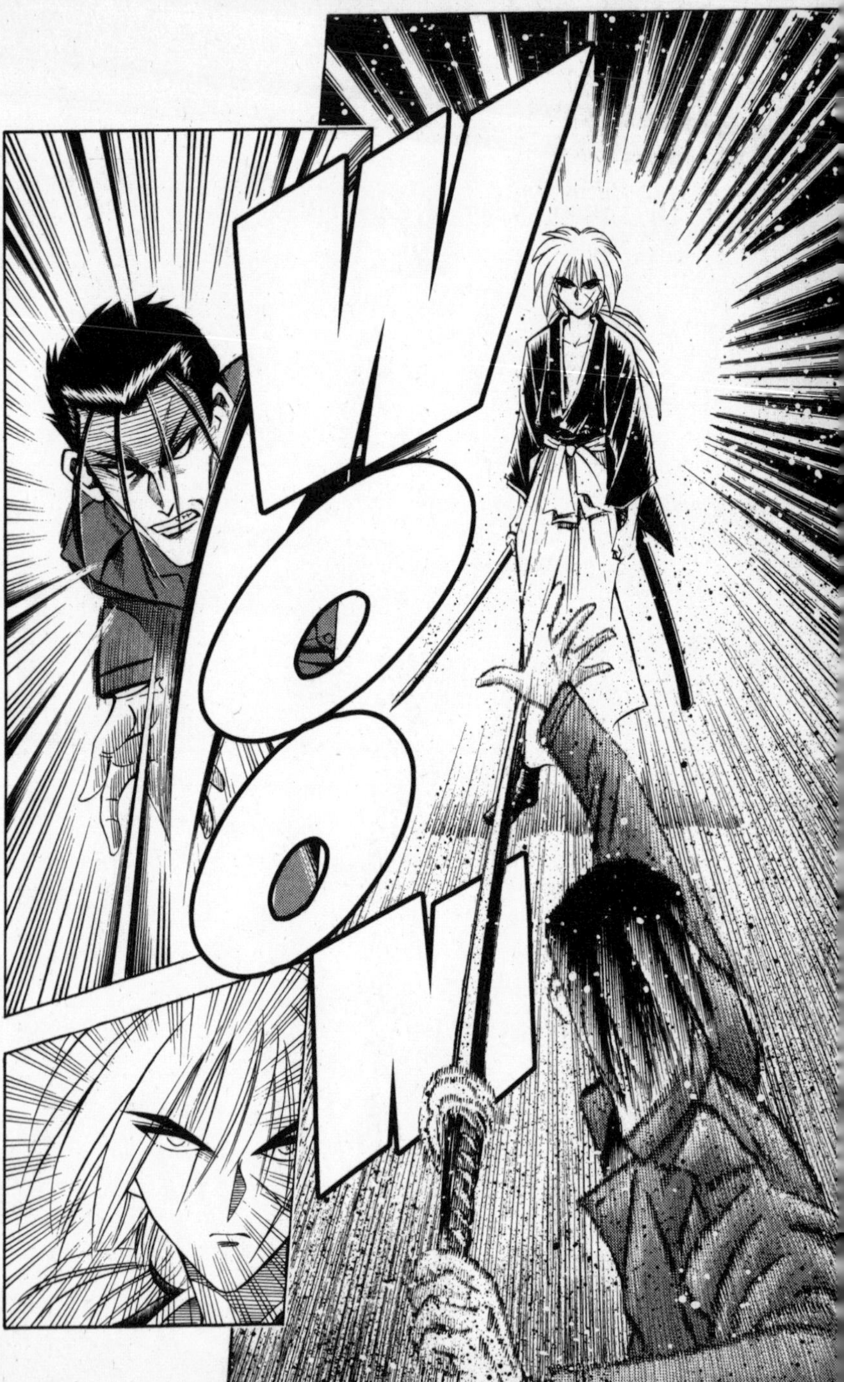
WHOOM!

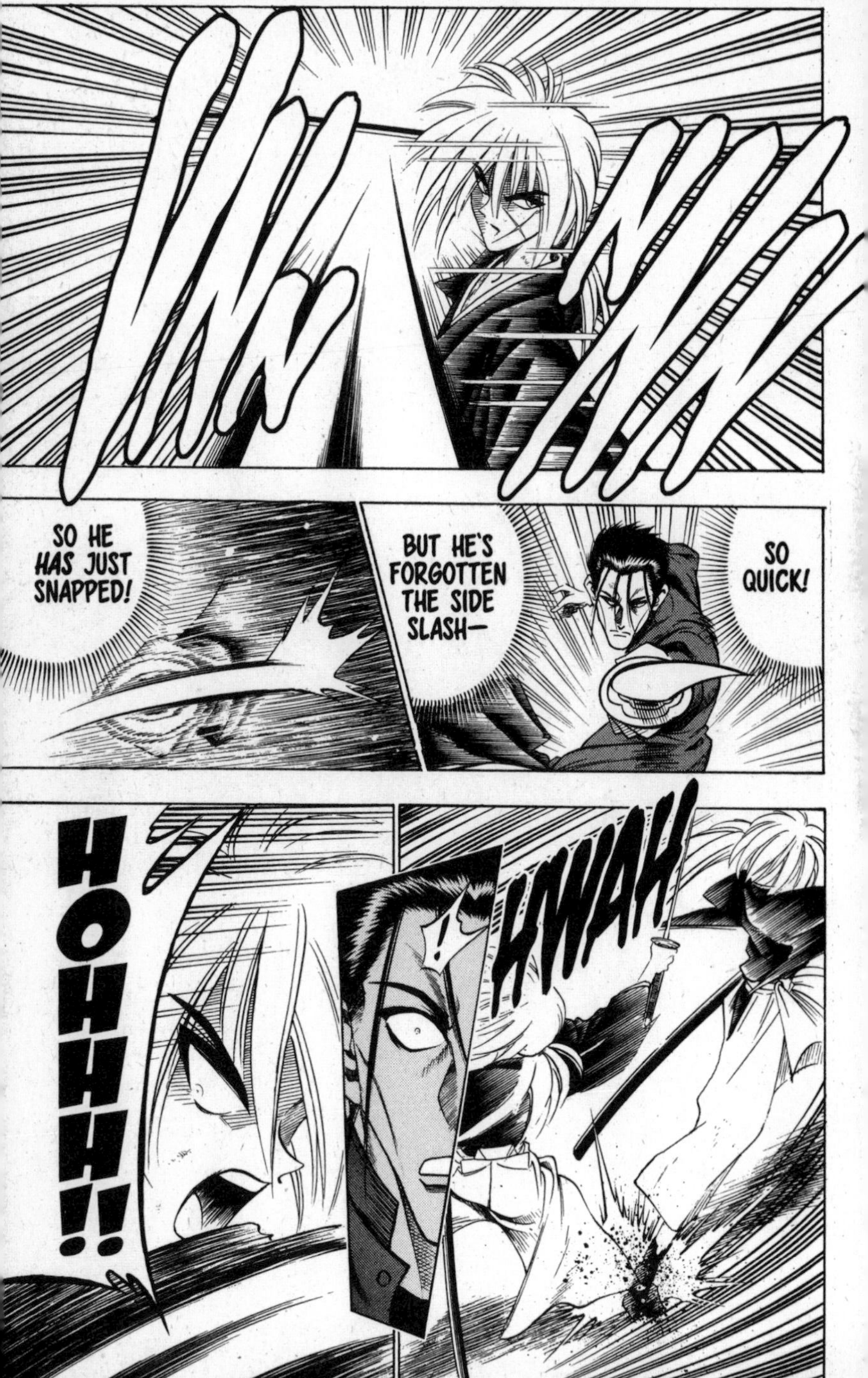
SO QUICK!
BUT HE'S FORGOTTEN THE SIDE SLASH—
SO HE HAS JUST SNAPPED!
HWAH!
!
HOHHHH!!

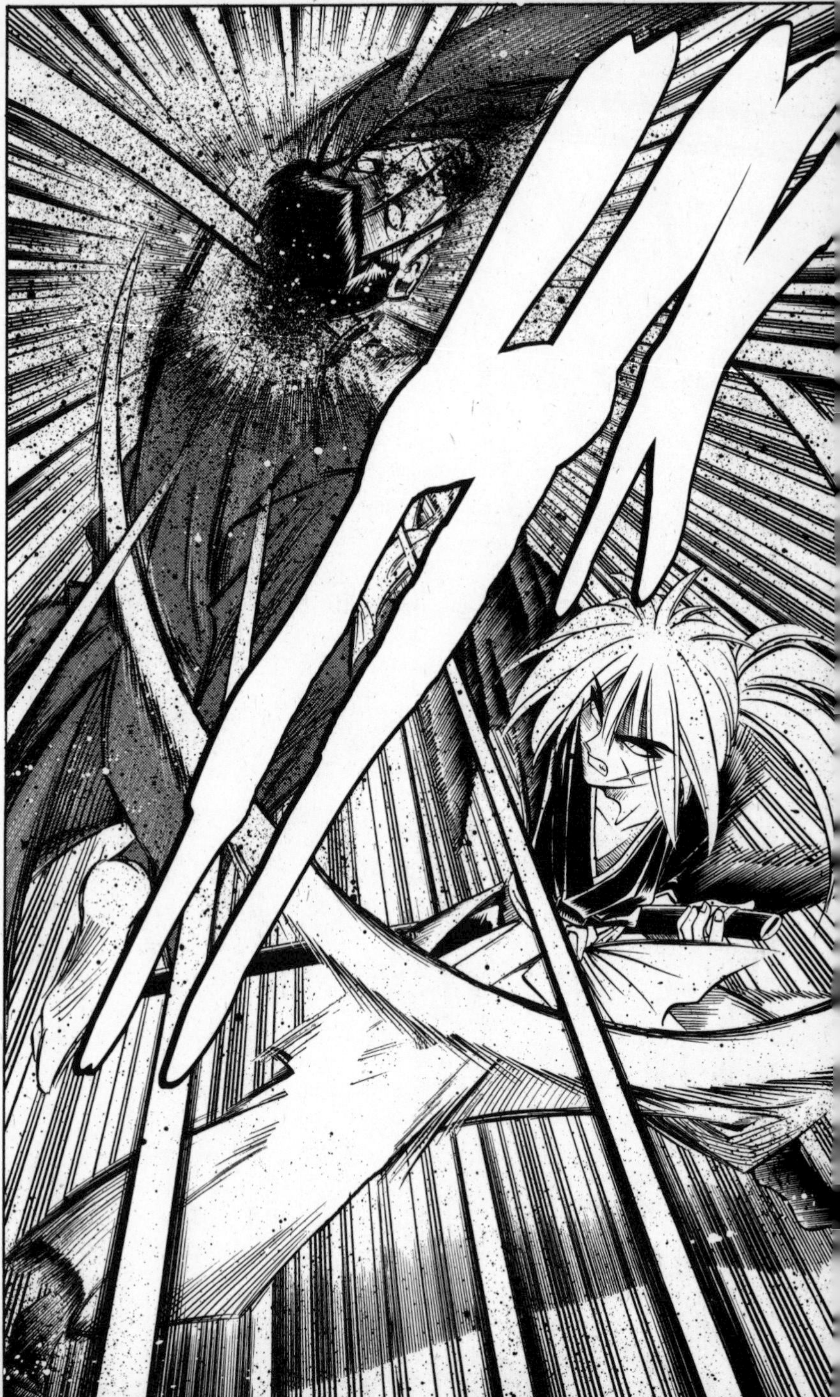

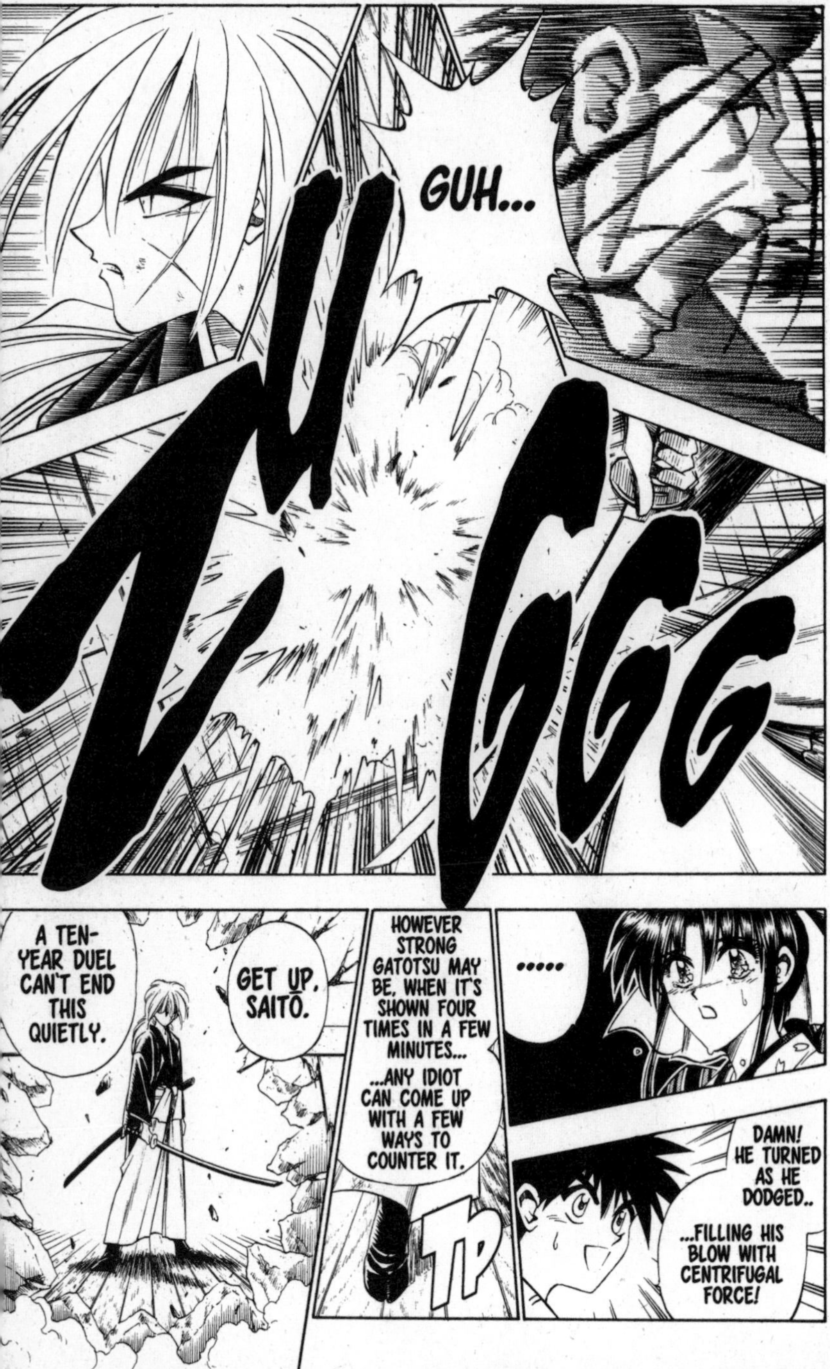
GUH...
.....
DAMN! HE TURNED AS HE DODGED..
...FILLING HIS BLOW WITH CENTRIFUGAL FORCE!
HOWEVER STRONG GATOTSU MAY BE, WHEN IT'S SHOWN FOUR TIMES IN A FEW MINUTES...
...ANY IDIOT CAN COME UP WITH A FEW WAYS TO COUNTER IT.
TP
GET UP, SAITŌ.
A TEN-YEAR DUEL CAN'T END THIS QUIETLY.

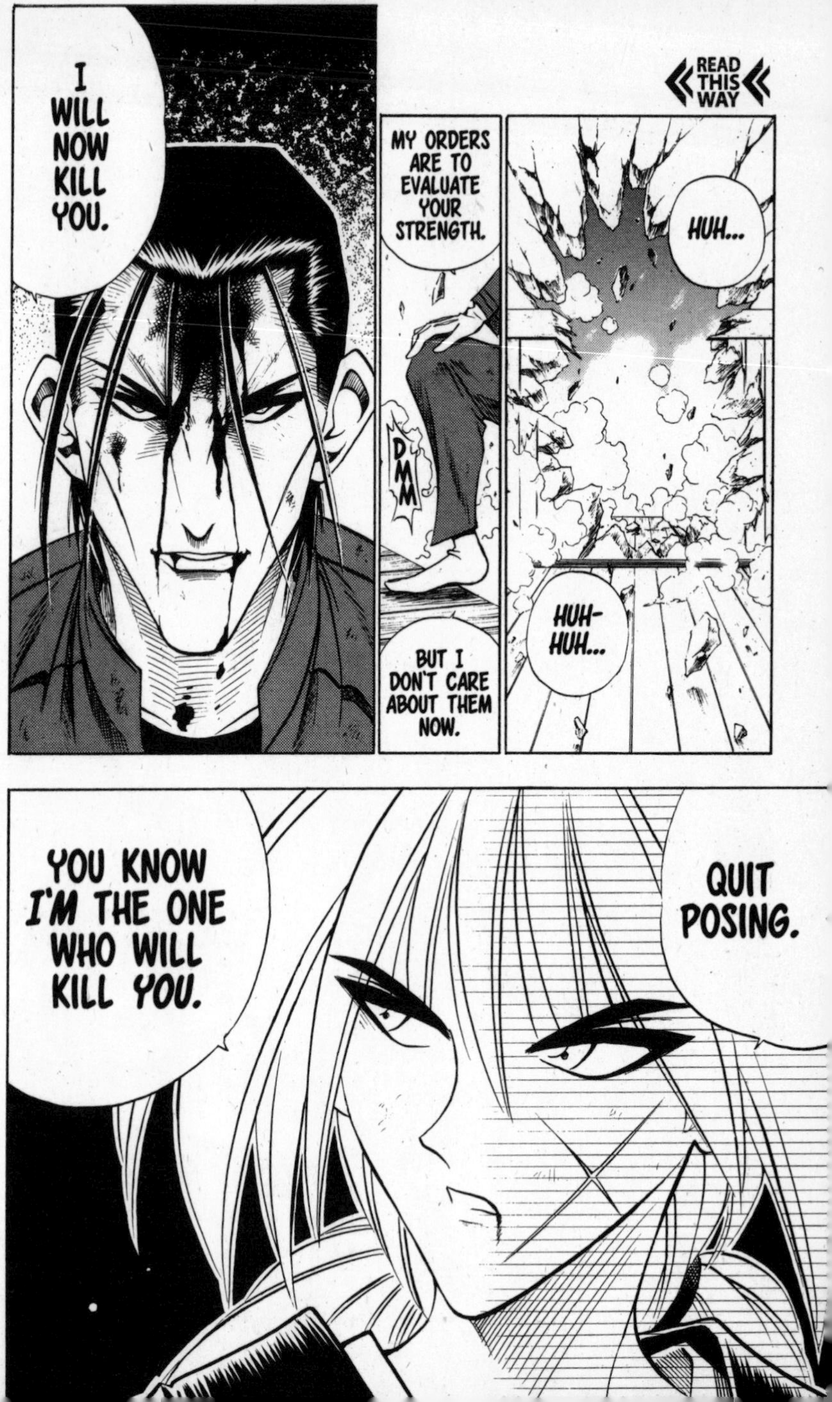
READ THIS WAY
HUH...
HUH-HUH...
MY ORDERS ARE TO EVALUATE YOUR STRENGTH.
DMM
BUT I DON'T CARE ABOUT THEM NOW.
I WILL NOW KILL YOU.
QUIT POSING.
YOU KNOW *I'M* THE ONE WHO WILL KILL *YOU*.

READ THIS WAY

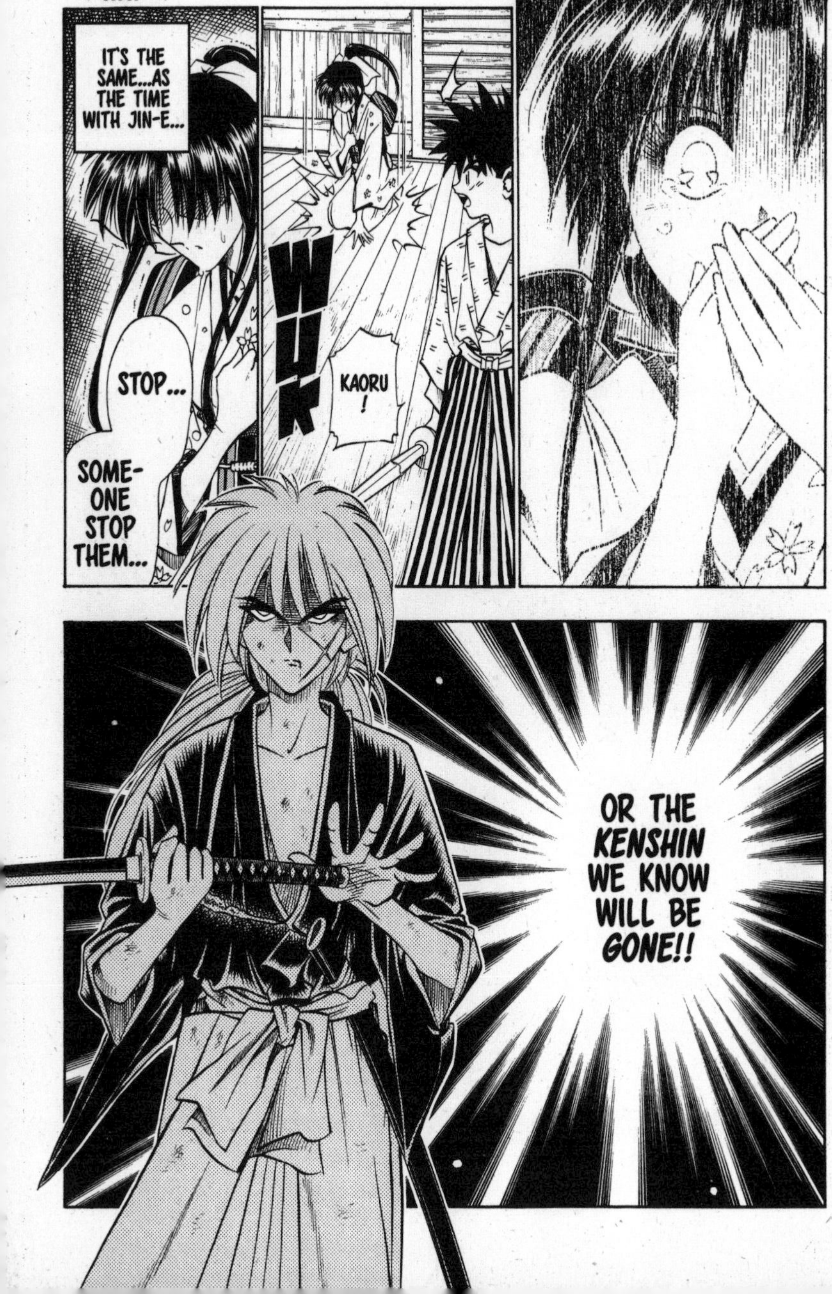
WUK
KAORU!
IT'S THE SAME...AS THE TIME WITH JIN-E...
STOP...
SOME-ONE STOP THEM...
OR THE KENSHIN WE KNOW WILL BE GONE!!

Rurouni Kenshin

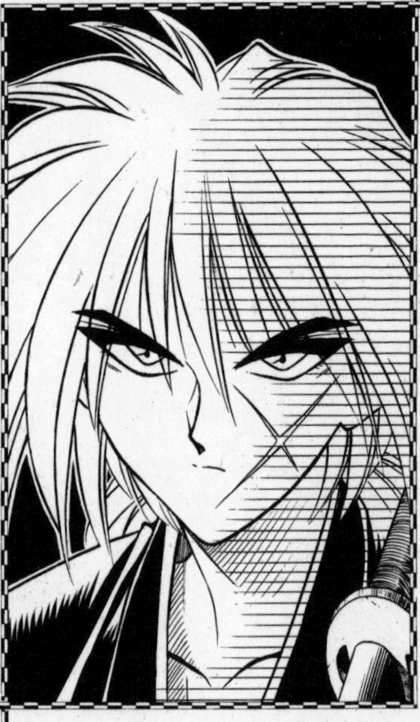

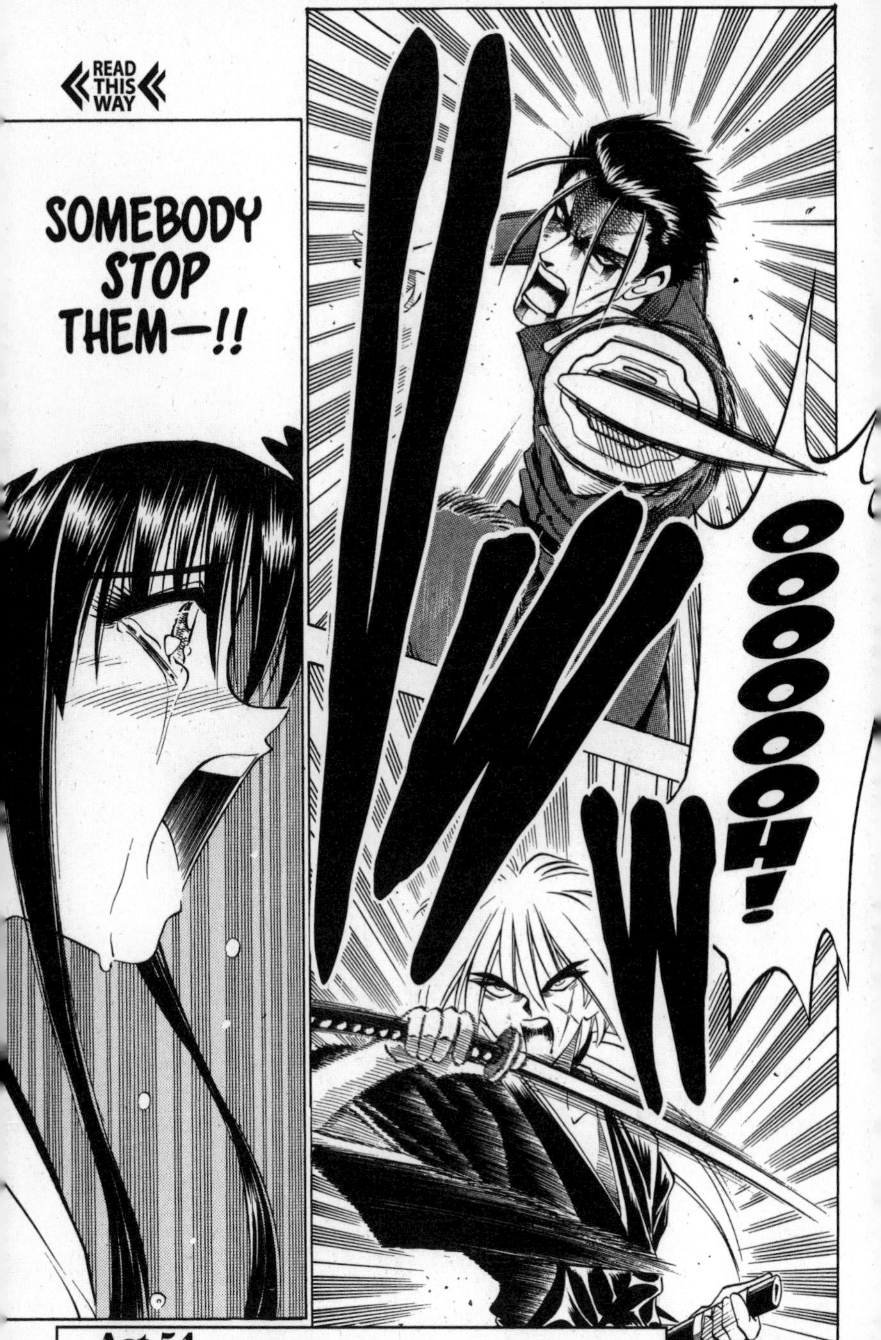
READ THIS WAY
OOOOOOH!
SOMEBODY STOP THEM—!!

Act 54
The One Who Stops the Two

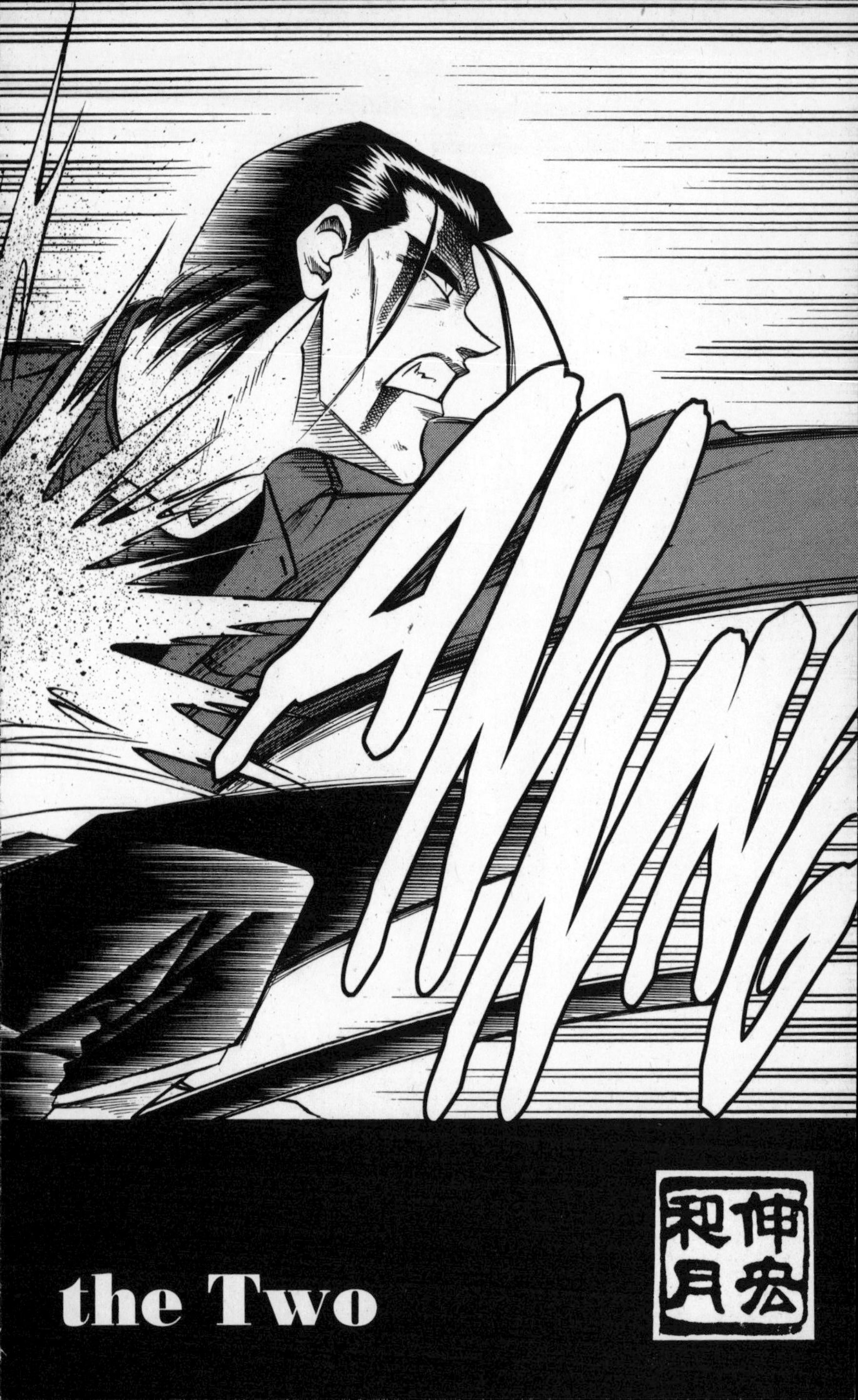
the Two
伸宏和月

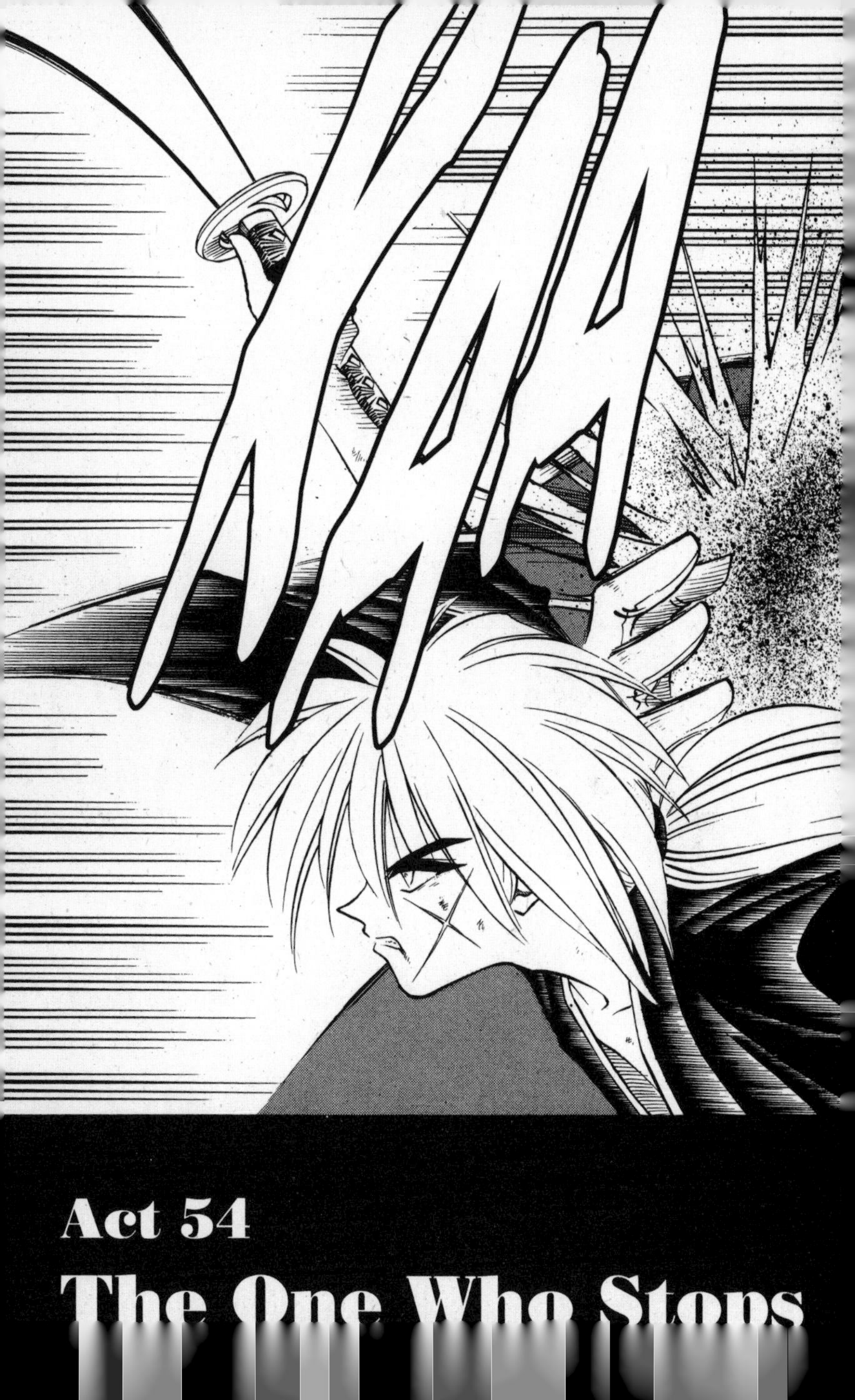

Act 54
The One Who Stops

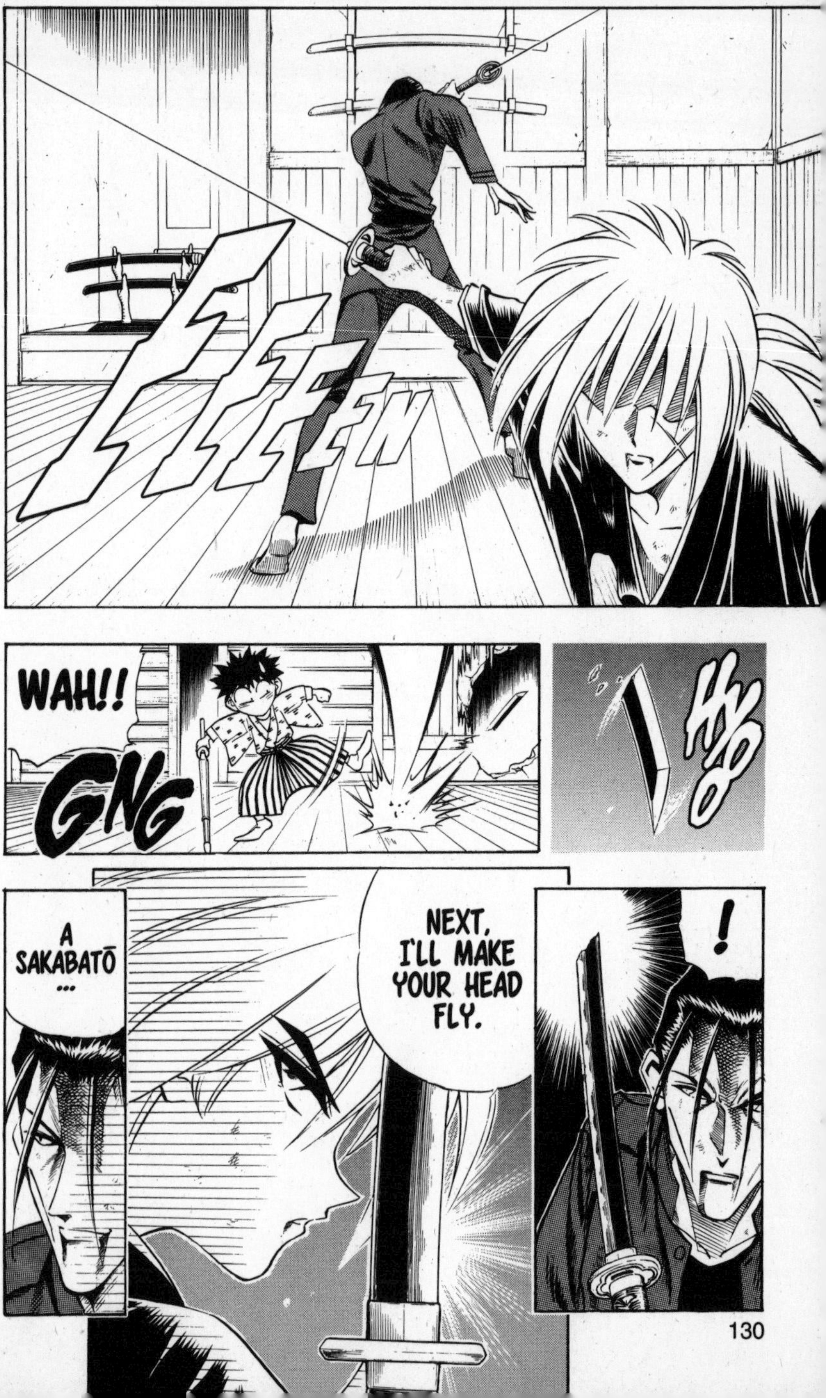
EEEEN
HYOO
WAH!!
GNG
!
NEXT, I'LL MAKE YOUR HEAD FLY.
A SAKABATŌ ...

READ THIS WAY

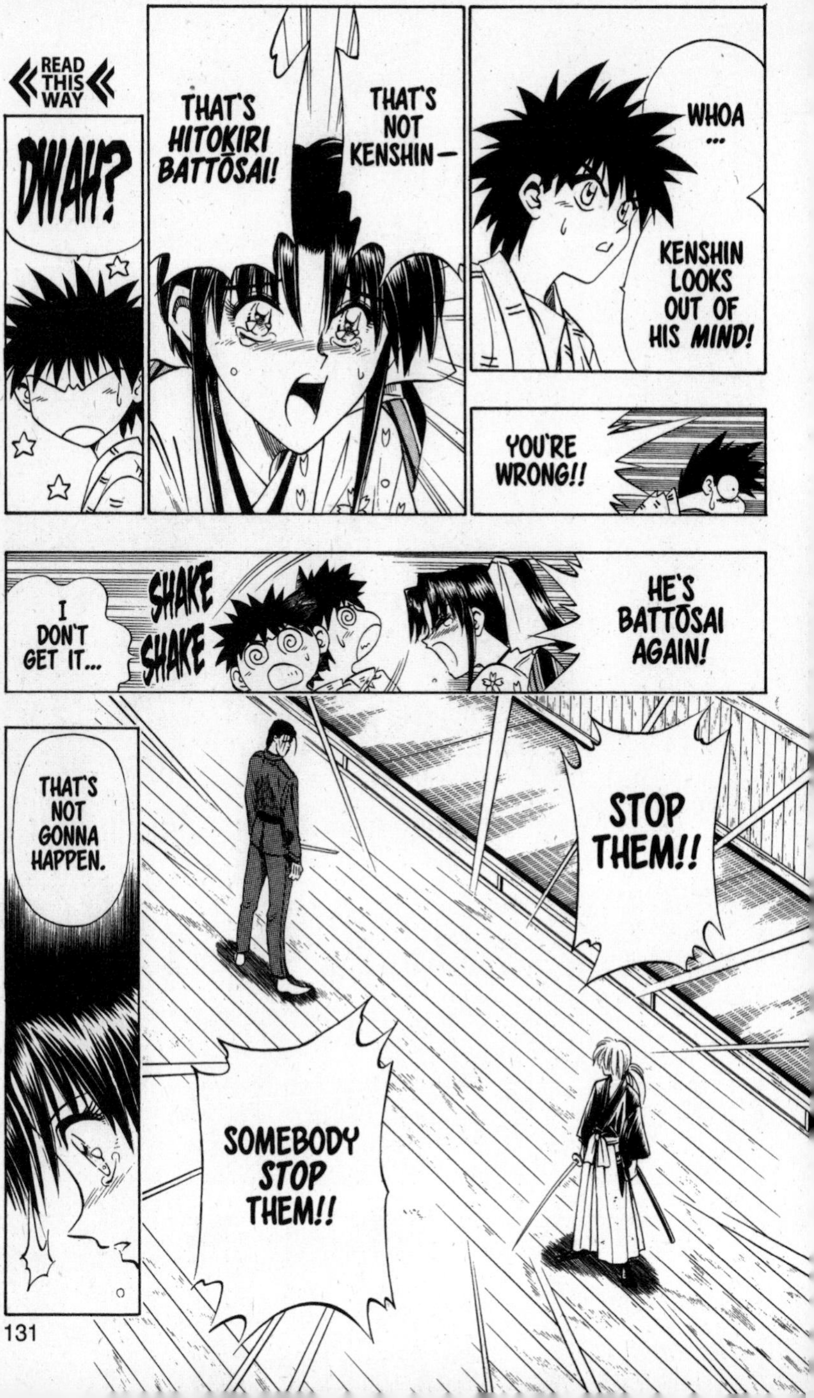

WHOA...
KENSHIN LOOKS OUT OF HIS MIND!
YOU'RE WRONG!!
THAT'S NOT KENSHIN—
THAT'S HITOKIRI BATTŌSAI!
DWAH?
HE'S BATTŌSAI AGAIN!
SHAKE SHAKE
I DON'T GET IT...
STOP THEM!!
SOMEBODY STOP THEM!!
THAT'S NOT GONNA HAPPEN.

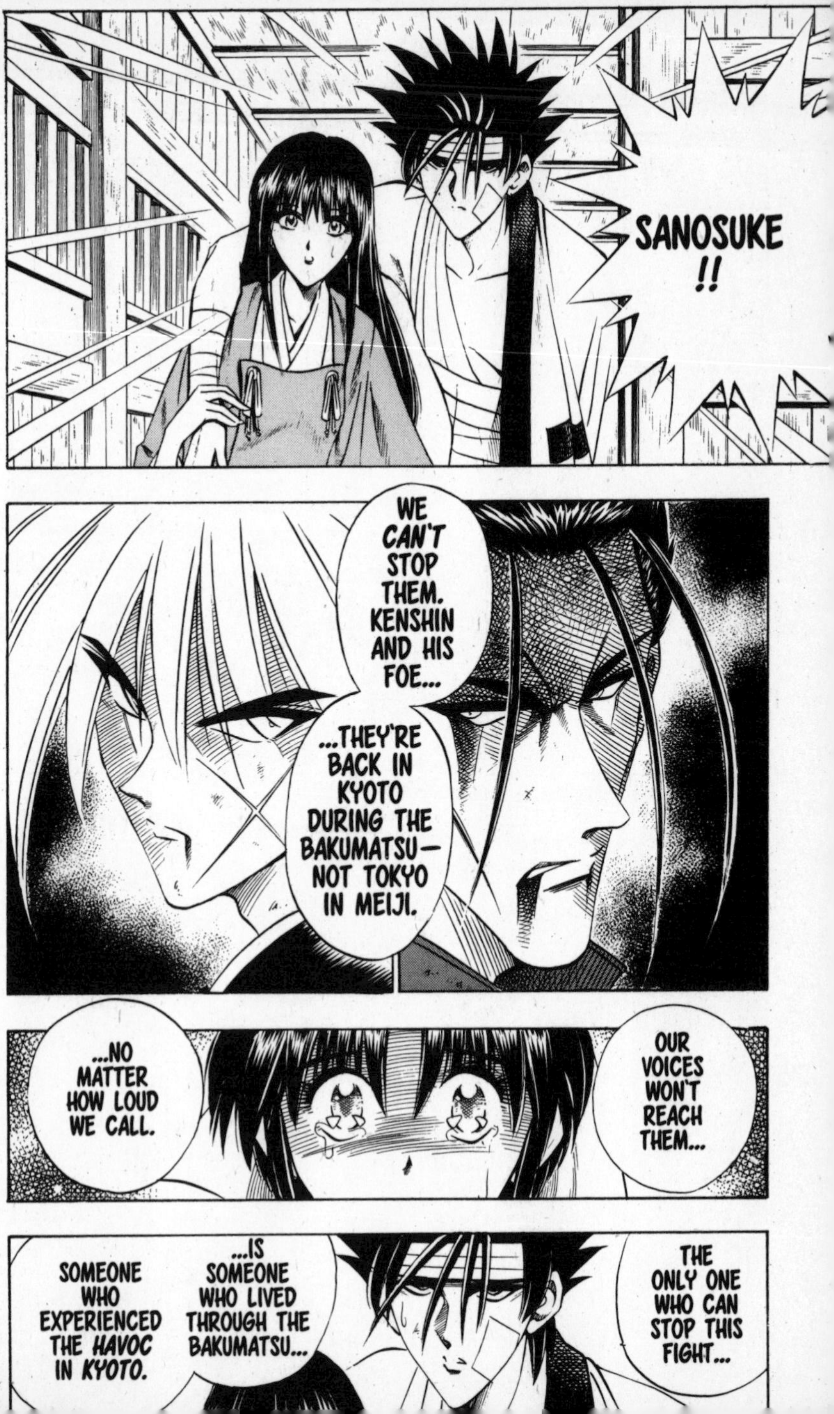
SANOSUKE !!
WE CAN'T STOP THEM. KENSHIN AND HIS FOE...
...THEY'RE BACK IN KYOTO DURING THE BAKUMATSU—NOT TOKYO IN MEIJI.
OUR VOICES WON'T REACH THEM...
...NO MATTER HOW LOUD WE CALL.
THE ONLY ONE WHO CAN STOP THIS FIGHT...
...IS SOMEONE WHO LIVED THROUGH THE BAKUMATSU...
SOMEONE WHO EXPERIENCED THE *HAVOC* IN *KYOTO*.

READ THIS WAY

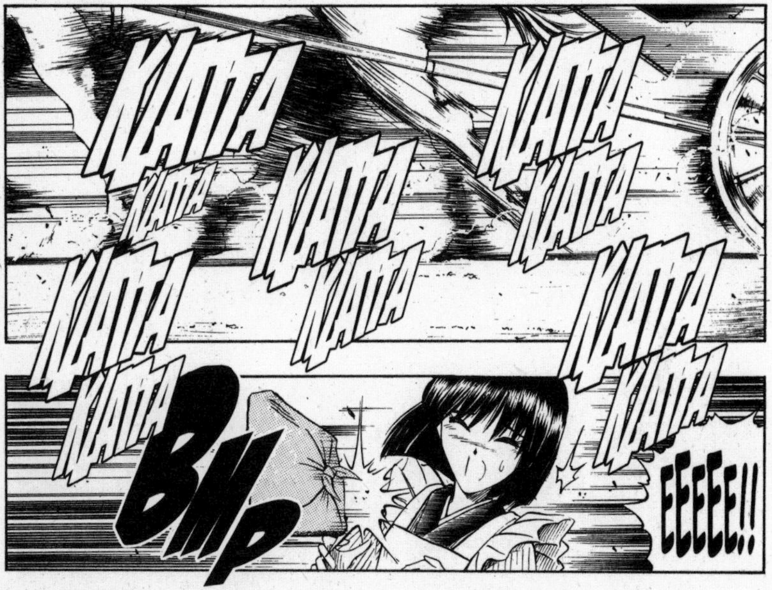
KATTA
KATTA
KATTA
KATTA
KATTA
KATTA
KATTA
KATTA
KATTA
KATTA
KATTA
EEEEE!!
BIIP

About the replies to your fan letters...recently they've started stacking up again. Sorry about that. Between getting the beginning of the volume colored, researching the Kyoto episode (this is a book requiring a lot of research to begin with, but these days, I'm about to lose it!) and, on top of that, moving our studio.... Anyway, let's just say, when I'm lucky, I get a half-day's worth of rest—but, if I use that half-day to reply to letters, I might do myself harm. Watsuki would like a LITTLE time to himself...truly, I'm very sorry, but please be patient.

As mentioned, we moved recently. The research materials that piled up, the fan letters that piled up, and the staff we had to hire to keep up with all the work made the old studio too small, so we bit the bullet and took the leap. Our new workplace is big and has a nice view, but it's also 20 years old. I guess maybe we should ready some emergency supplies, in case of an earthquake...

READ THIS WAY

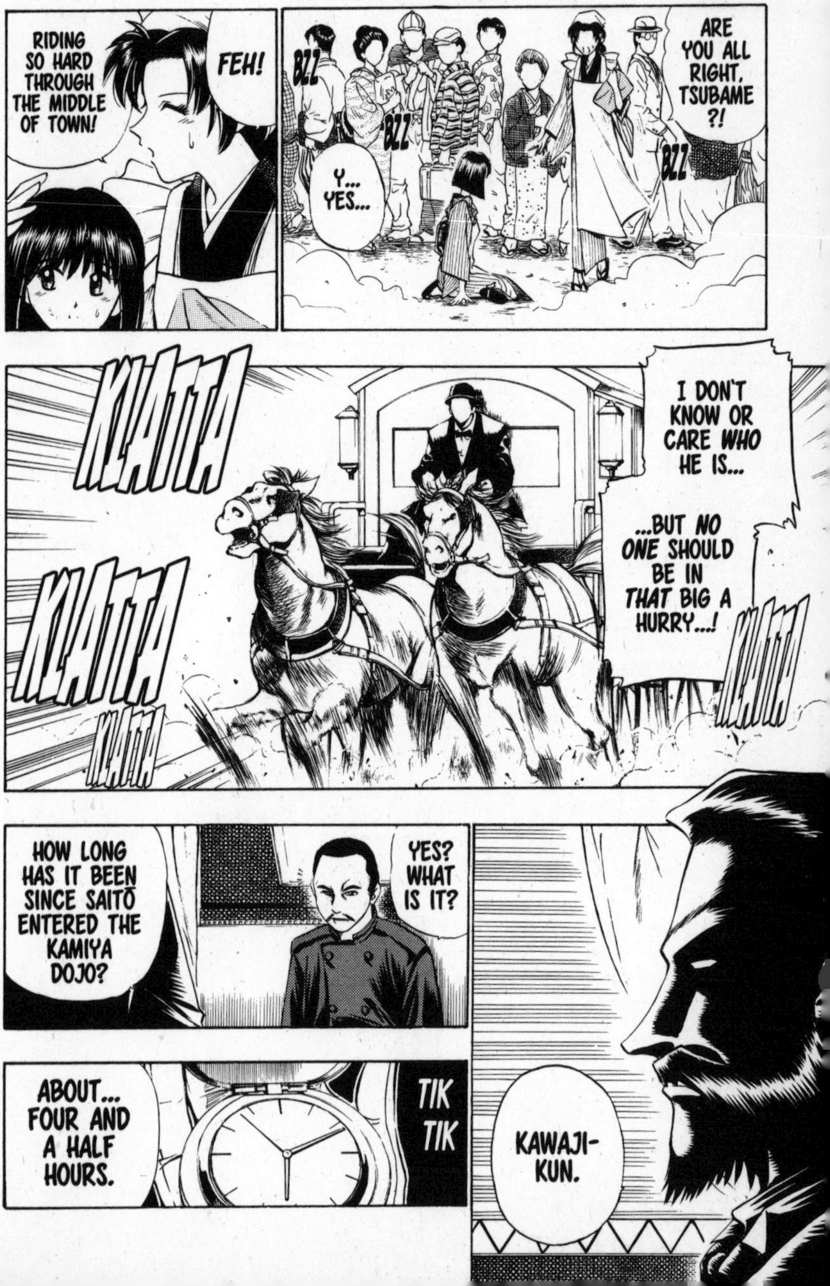
ARE YOU ALL RIGHT, TSUBAME?!
BZZ
BZZ
BZZ
Y... YES...
FEH!
RIDING SO HARD THROUGH THE MIDDLE OF TOWN!
I DON'T KNOW OR CARE WHO HE IS...
...BUT NO ONE SHOULD BE IN THAT BIG A HURRY...!
KLATTA
KLATTA
KLATTA
KLATTA
KAWAJI-KUN.
YES? WHAT IS IT?
HOW LONG HAS IT BEEN SINCE SAITŌ ENTERED THE KAMIYA DOJO?
TIK TIK
ABOUT... FOUR AND A HALF HOURS.

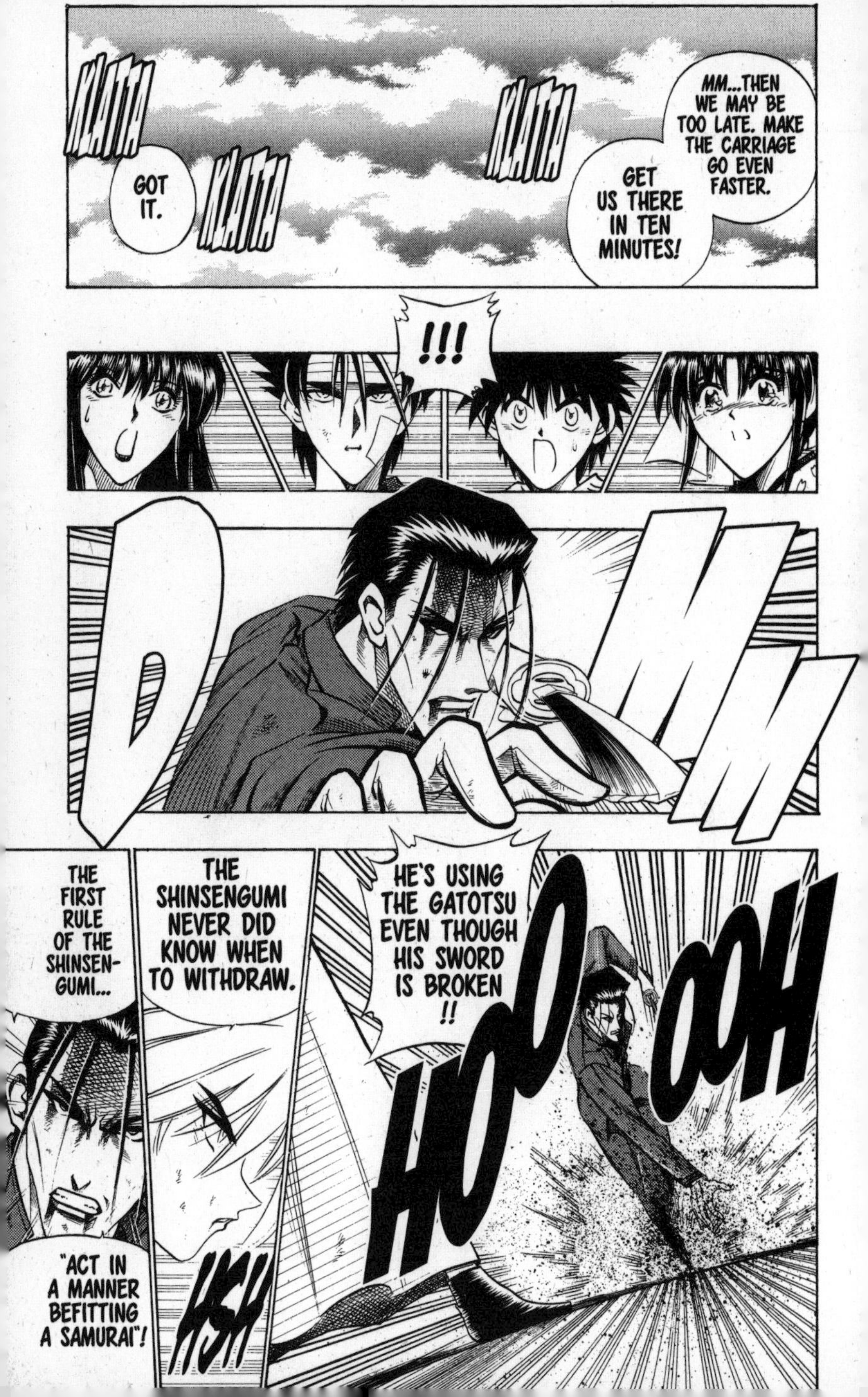
MM...THEN WE MAY BE TOO LATE. MAKE THE CARRIAGE GO EVEN FASTER.
GET US THERE IN TEN MINUTES!
KLATTA
KLATTA
GOT IT.
KLATTA
!!!
HE'S USING THE GATOTSU EVEN THOUGH HIS SWORD IS BROKEN!!
THE SHINSENGUMI NEVER DID KNOW WHEN TO WITHDRAW.
HSH
THE FIRST RULE OF THE SHINSEN-GUMI...
"ACT IN A MANNER BEFITTING A SAMURAI"!

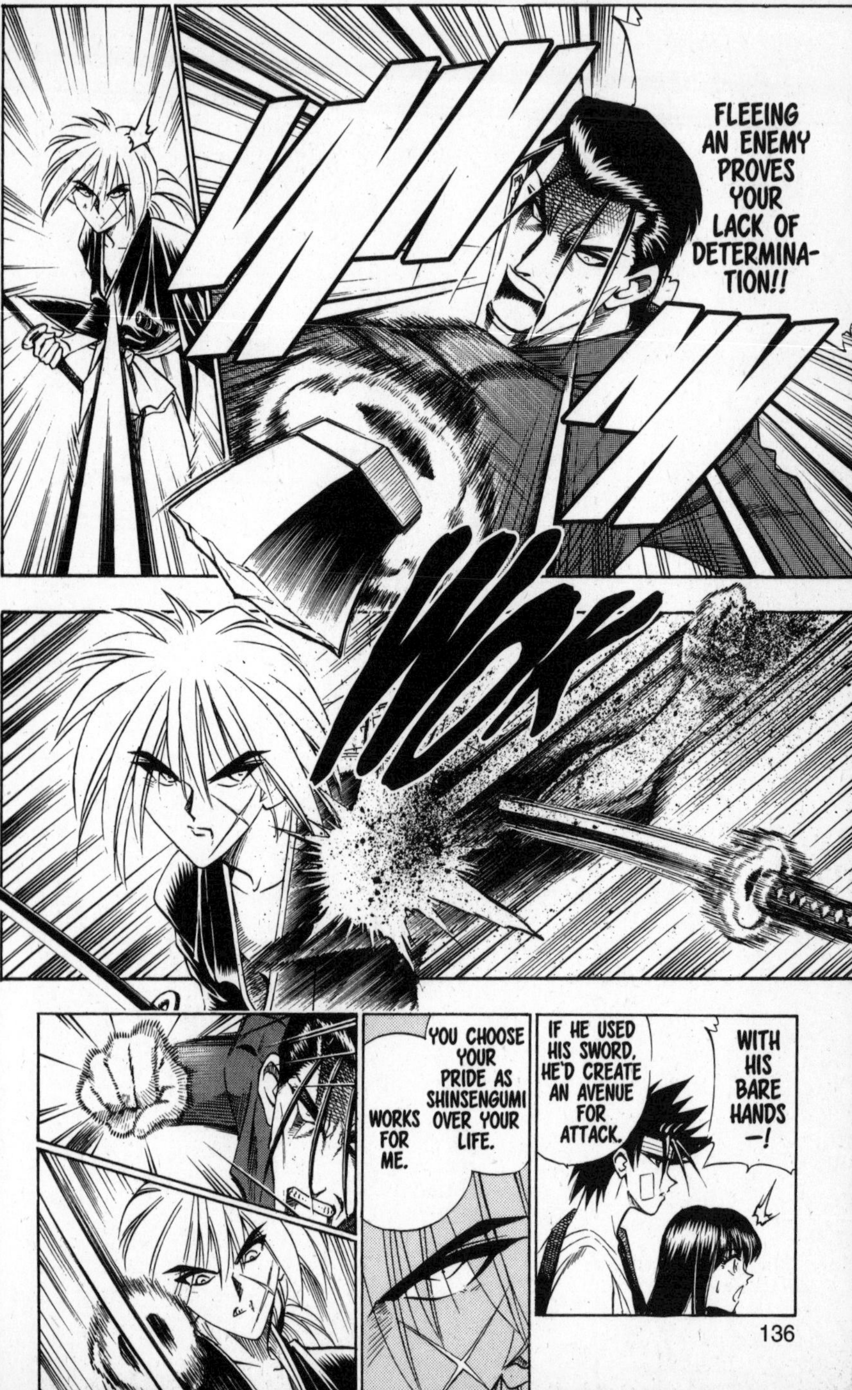
FLEEING AN ENEMY PROVES YOUR LACK OF DETERMINATION!!
WITH HIS BARE HANDS—!
IF HE USED HIS SWORD, HE'D CREATE AN AVENUE FOR ATTACK.
YOU CHOOSE YOUR PRIDE AS SHINSENGUMI OVER YOUR LIFE.
WORKS FOR ME.

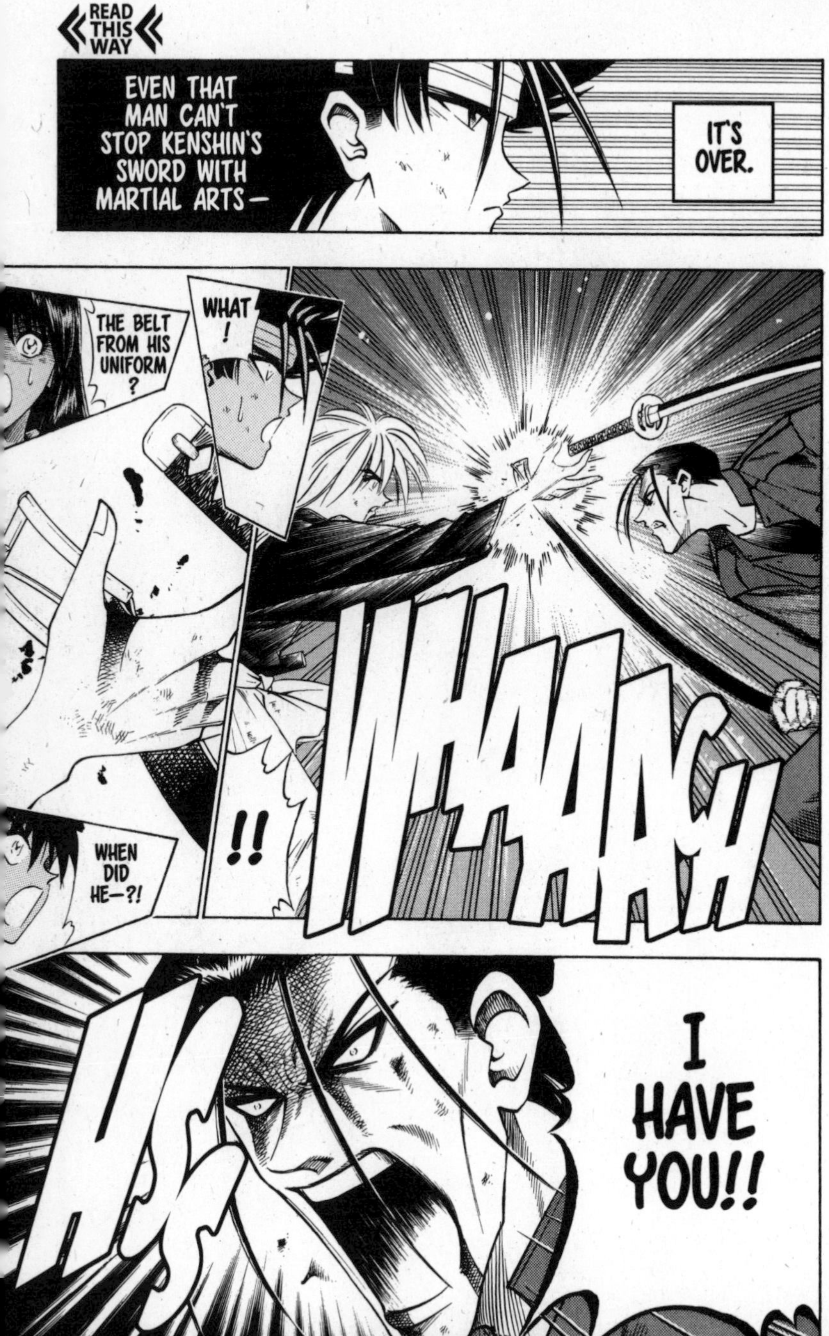
READ THIS WAY
IT'S OVER.
EVEN THAT MAN CAN'T STOP KENSHIN'S SWORD WITH MARTIAL ARTS—
WHAAACH
!!
WHAT!
THE BELT FROM HIS UNIFORM?
WHEN DID HE—?!
I HAVE YOU!!
HA

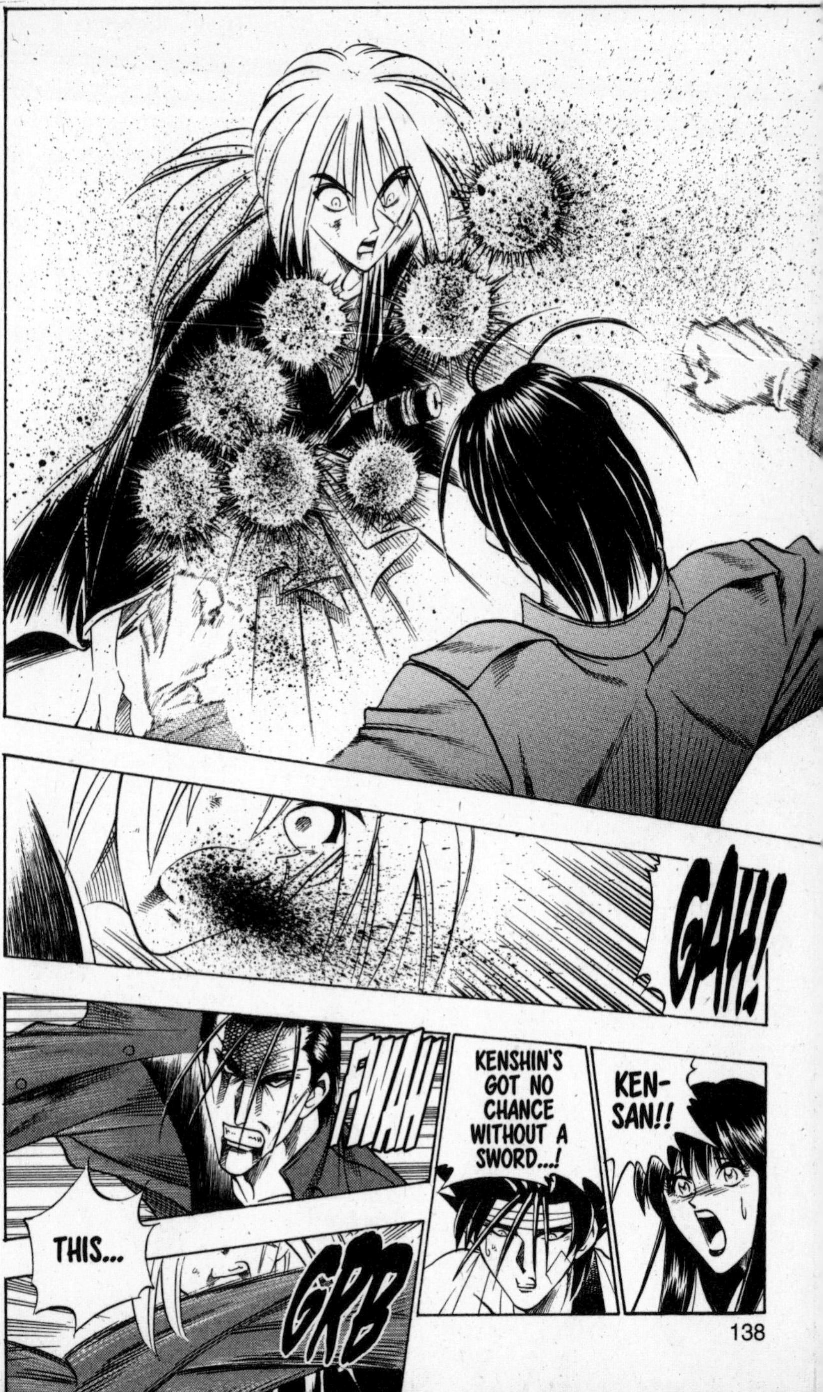
GAH!
KEN-SAN!!
KENSHIN'S GOT NO CHANCE WITHOUT A SWORD...!
PWAH
THIS...
GRB

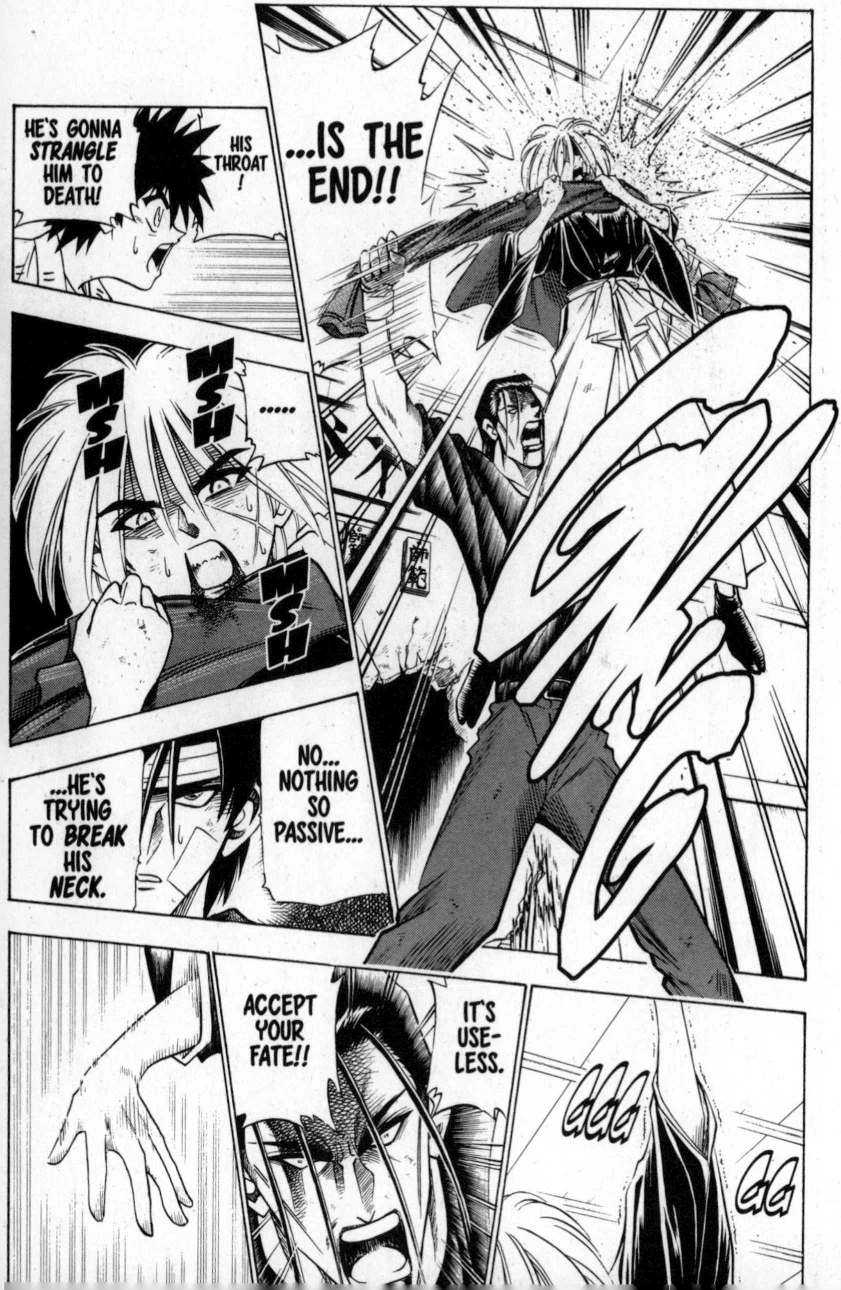
...IS THE END!!
HIS THROAT!
HE'S GONNA STRANGLE HIM TO DEATH!
.....
MSH
MSH
MSH
NO... NOTHING SO PASSIVE...
...HE'S TRYING TO BREAK HIS NECK.
GGG
GG
IT'S USE-LESS.
ACCEPT YOUR FATE!!

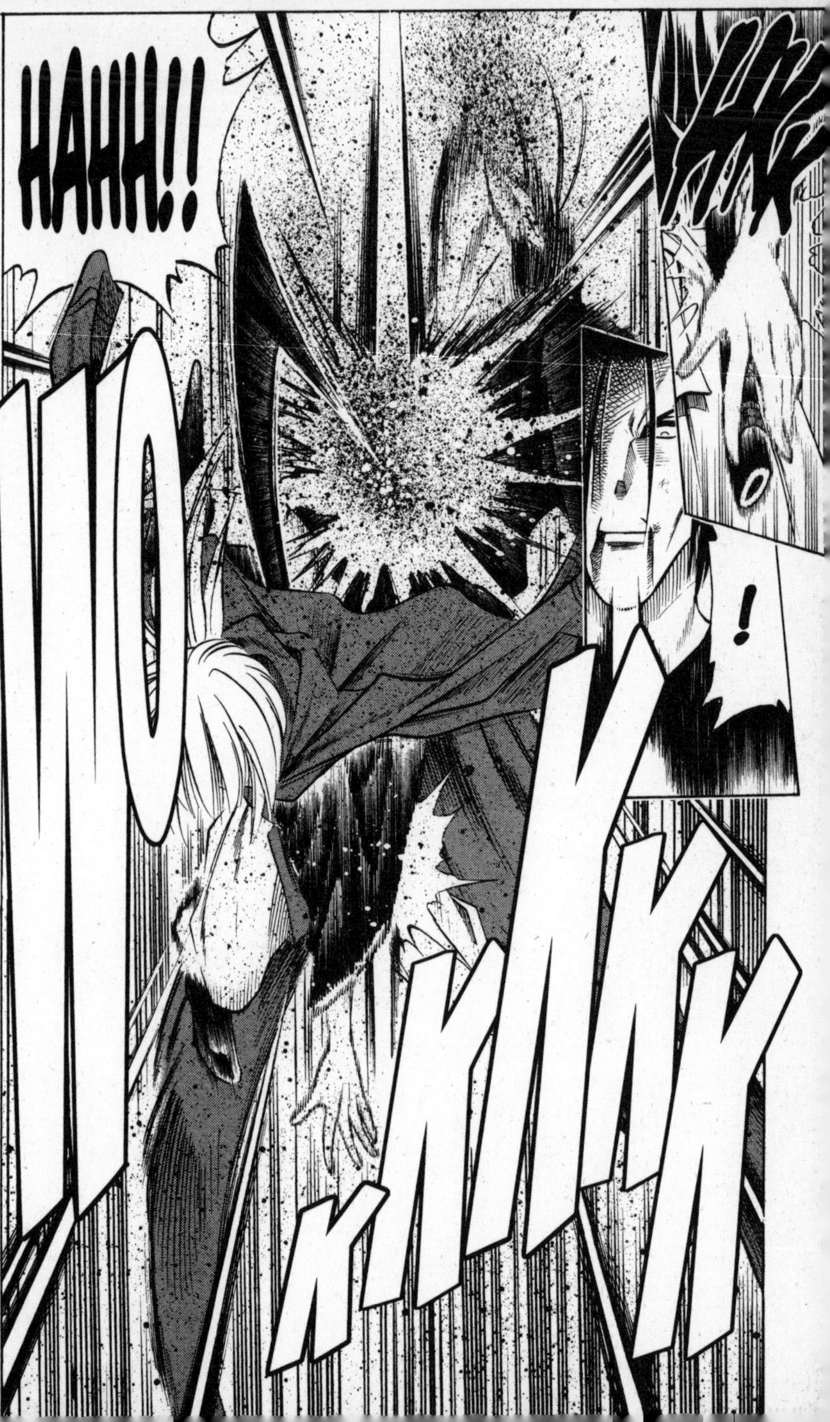

!
HAHH!!

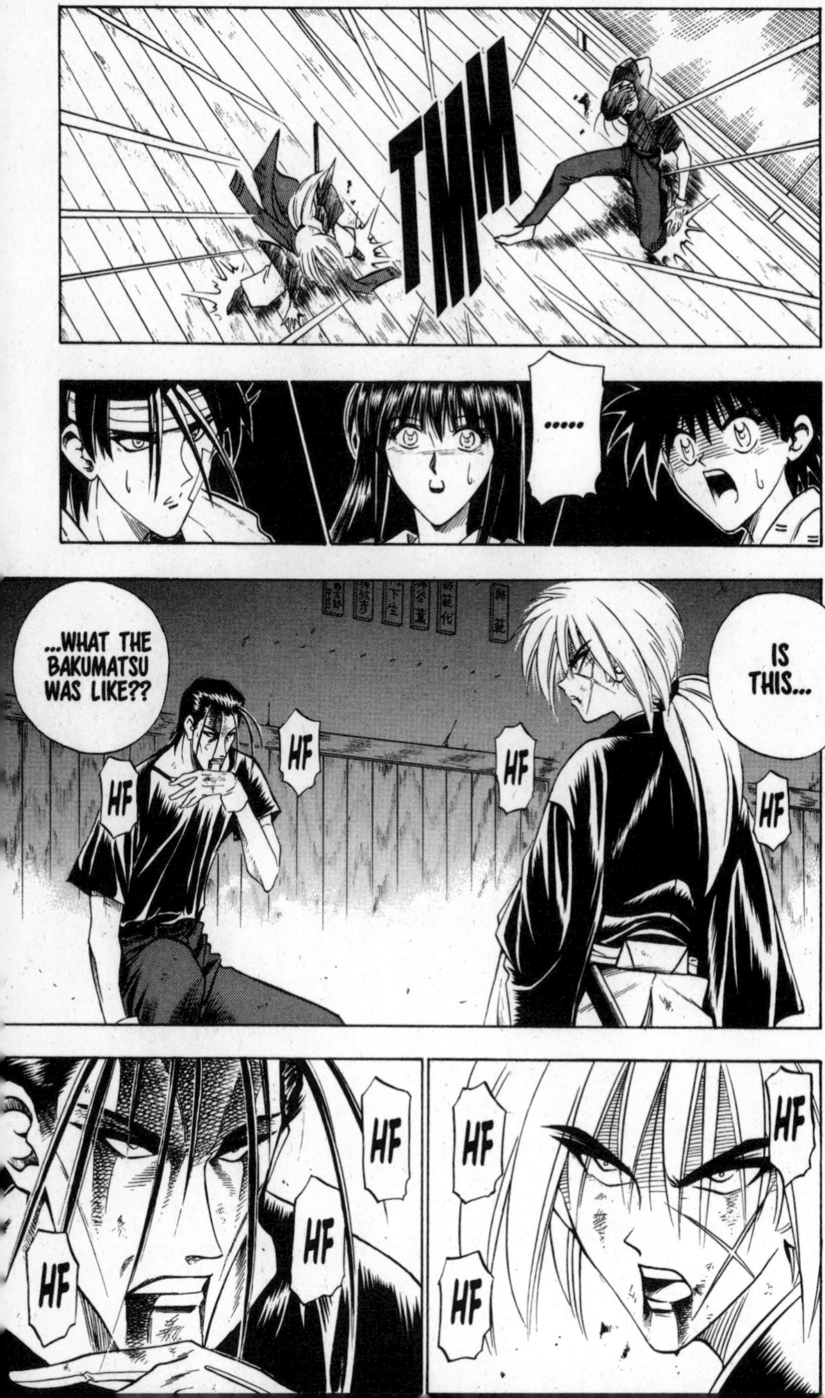
TMM
.....
IS THIS...
HF
HF
HF
HF
...WHAT THE BAKUMATSU WAS LIKE??
HF
HF
HF
HF
HF
HF

READ THIS WAY

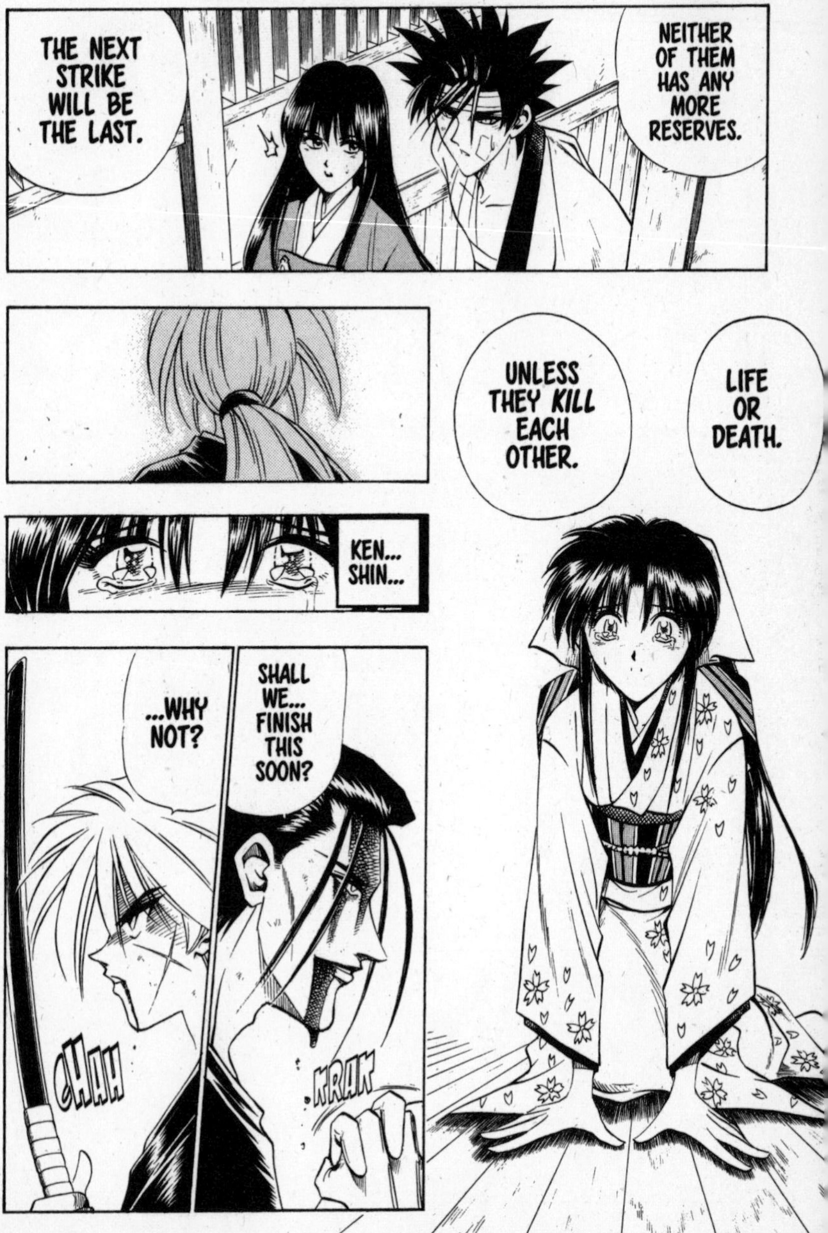
NEITHER OF THEM HAS ANY MORE RESERVES.
THE NEXT STRIKE WILL BE THE LAST.
LIFE OR DEATH.
UNLESS THEY *KILL* EACH OTHER.
KEN... SHIN...
SHALL WE... FINISH THIS SOON?
...WHY NOT?
KRAK
CHAH

READ THIS WAY

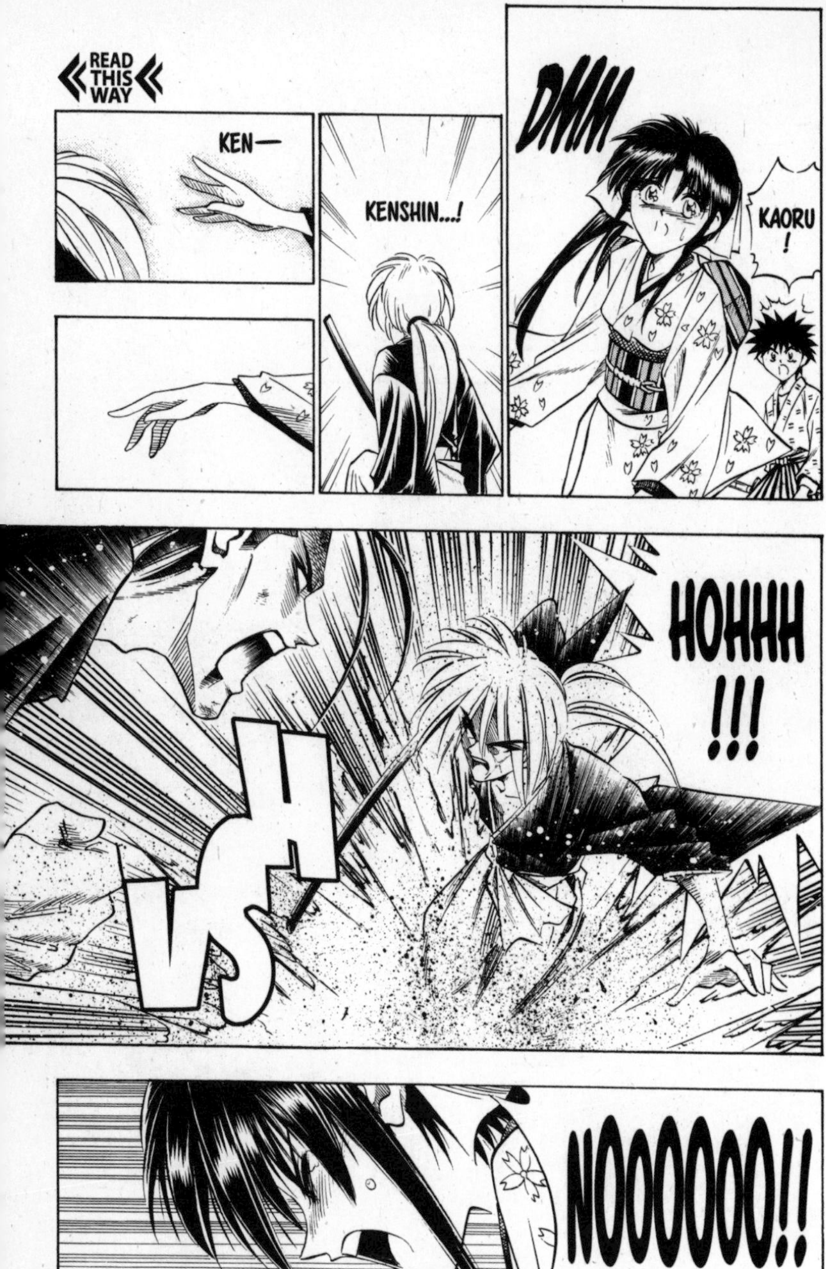
DMM
KAORU!
KENSHIN...!
KEN—
HOHHH!!!
VSH
NOOOOO!!

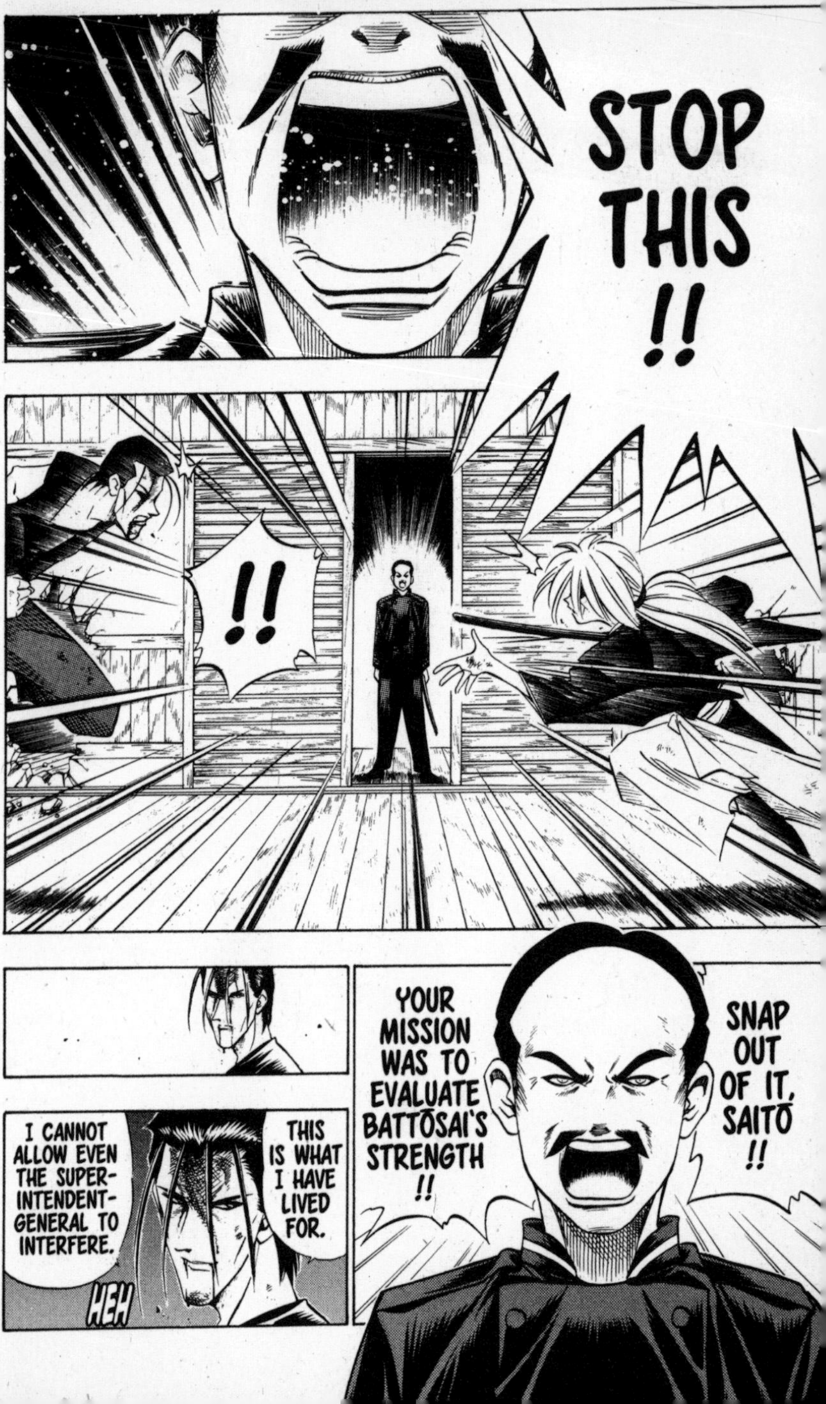
STOP THIS !!
!!
SNAP OUT OF IT, SAITŌ !!
YOUR MISSION WAS TO EVALUATE BATTŌSAI'S STRENGTH !!
. . .
THIS IS WHAT I HAVE LIVED FOR.
I CANNOT ALLOW EVEN THE SUPER-INTENDENT-GENERAL TO INTERFERE.
HEH

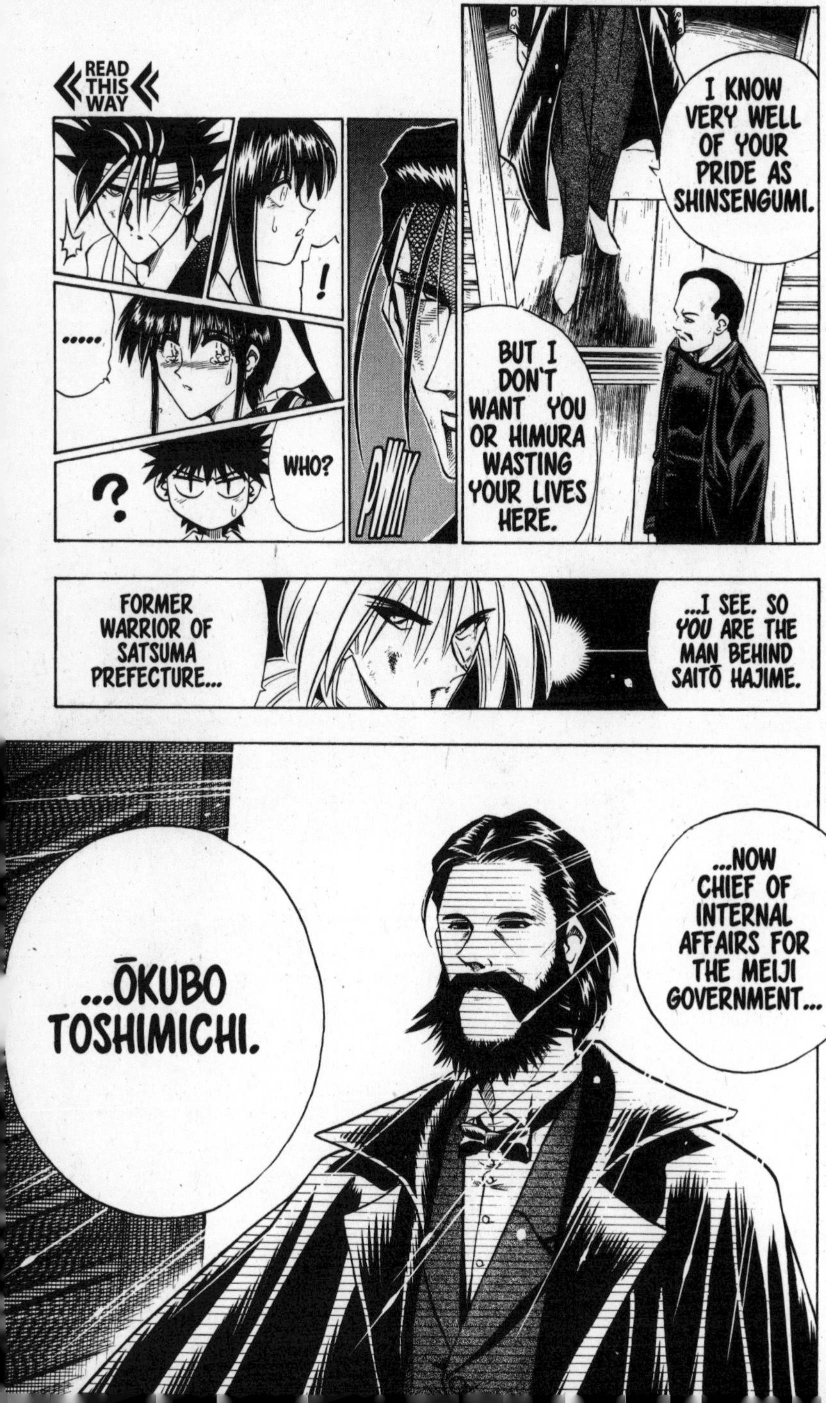
READ THIS WAY
I KNOW VERY WELL OF YOUR PRIDE AS SHINSENGUMI.
BUT I DON'T WANT YOU OR HIMURA WASTING YOUR LIVES HERE.
!
.....
WHO?
?
...I SEE. SO YOU ARE THE MAN BEHIND SAITŌ HAJIME.
FORMER WARRIOR OF SATSUMA PREFECTURE...
...NOW CHIEF OF INTERNAL AFFAIRS FOR THE MEIJI GOVERNMENT...
...ŌKUBO TOSHIMICHI.

Rurouni Kenshin

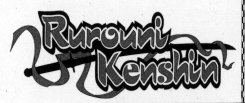

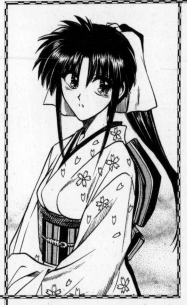

Act 55

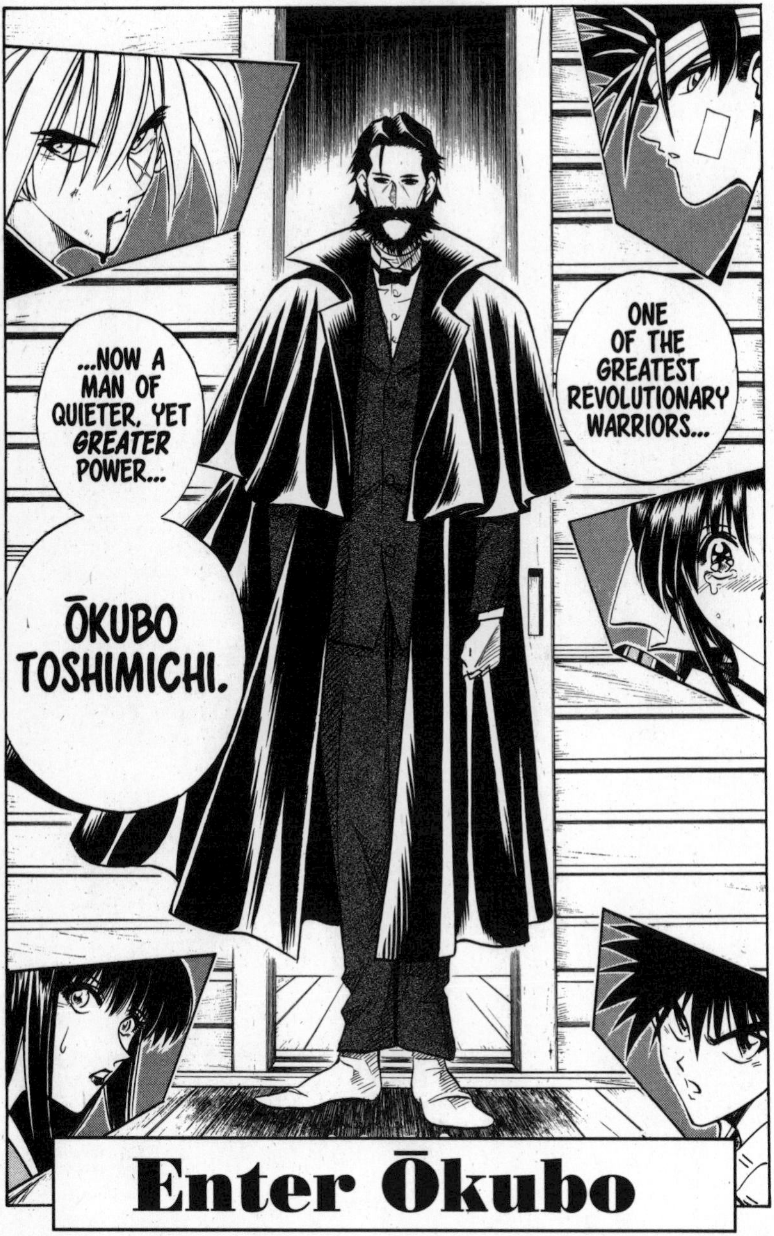
ONE OF THE GREATEST REVOLUTIONARY WARRIORS...
...NOW A MAN OF QUIETER, YET GREATER POWER...
ŌKUBO TOSHIMICHI.

Enter Ōkubo

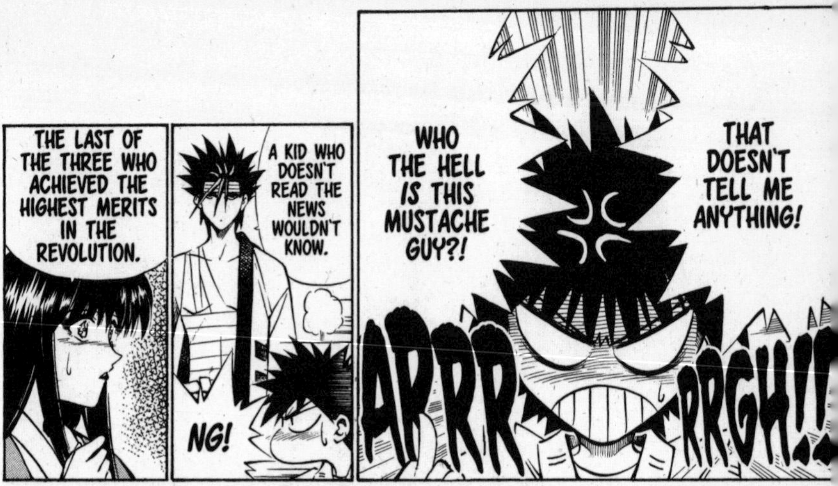
THAT DOESN'T TELL ME ANYTHING!
WHO THE HELL IS THIS MUSTACHE GUY?!
ARRRRRGH!!
A KID WHO DOESN'T READ THE NEWS WOULDN'T KNOW.
NG!
THE LAST OF THE THREE WHO ACHIEVED THE HIGHEST MERITS IN THE REVOLUTION.

*THE OTHER TWO (SAIGŌ TAKAMORI AND KATSURA KOGORŌ) BOTH HAVE DIED BY THE 11TH YEAR OF MEIJI.

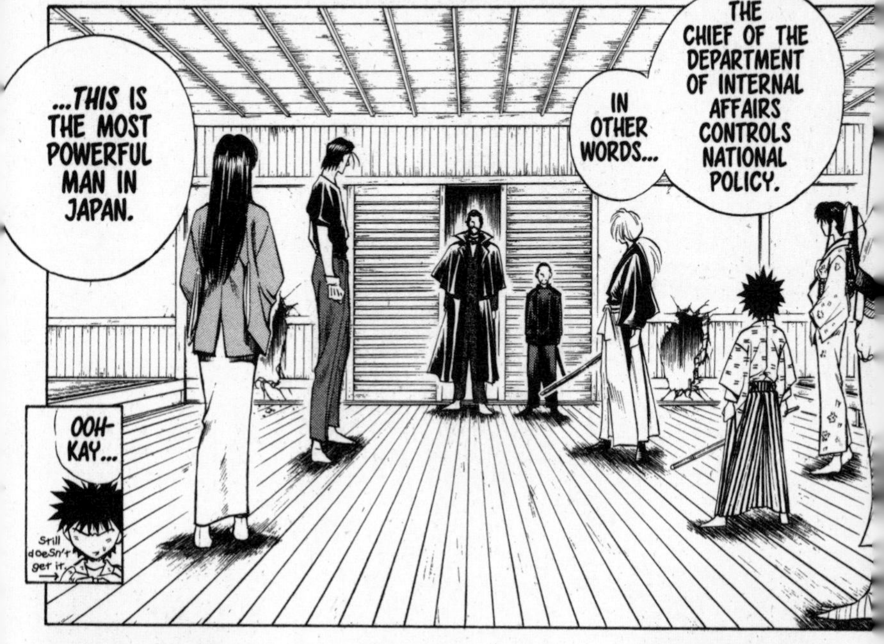
THE CHIEF OF THE DEPARTMENT OF INTERNAL AFFAIRS CONTROLS NATIONAL POLICY.
IN OTHER WORDS...
...THIS IS THE MOST POWERFUL MAN IN JAPAN.
OOH-KAY...
Still doesn't get it.

READ THIS WAY

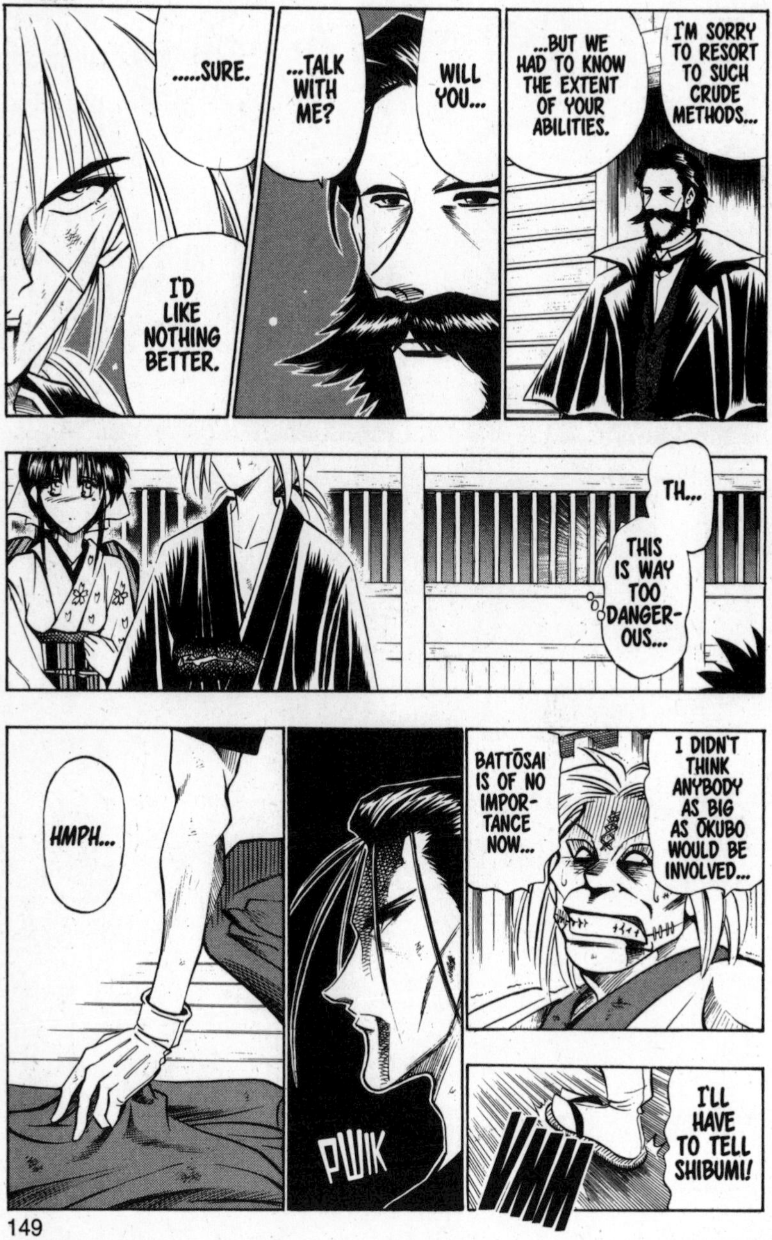

I'M SORRY TO RESORT TO SUCH CRUDE METHODS...
...BUT WE HAD TO KNOW THE EXTENT OF YOUR ABILITIES.
WILL YOU...
...TALK WITH ME?
......SURE.
I'D LIKE NOTHING BETTER.
TH...
THIS IS WAY TOO DANGER-OUS...
I DIDN'T THINK ANYBODY AS BIG AS ŌKUBO WOULD BE INVOLVED...
BATTŌSAI IS OF NO IMPOR-TANCE NOW...
I'LL HAVE TO TELL SHIBUMI!
VMM
PWIK
HMPH...

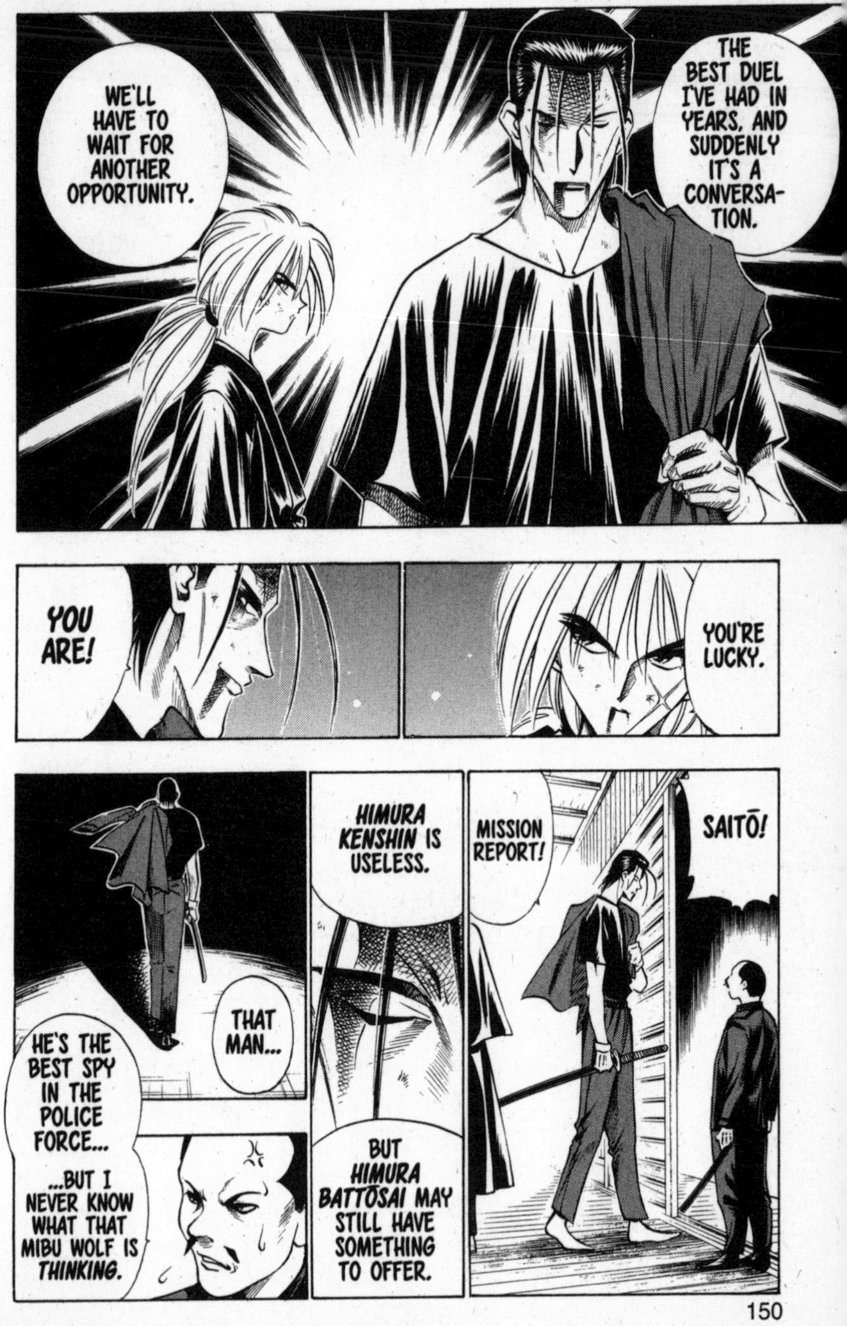
THE BEST DUEL I'VE HAD IN YEARS, AND SUDDENLY IT'S A CONVERSATION.
WE'LL HAVE TO WAIT FOR ANOTHER OPPORTUNITY.
YOU'RE LUCKY.
YOU ARE!
SAITŌ!
MISSION REPORT!
HIMURA KENSHIN IS USELESS.
BUT HIMURA BATTŌSAI MAY STILL HAVE SOMETHING TO OFFER.
THAT MAN...
HE'S THE BEST SPY IN THE POLICE FORCE...
...BUT I NEVER KNOW WHAT THAT MIBU WOLF IS THINKING.

READ THIS WAY

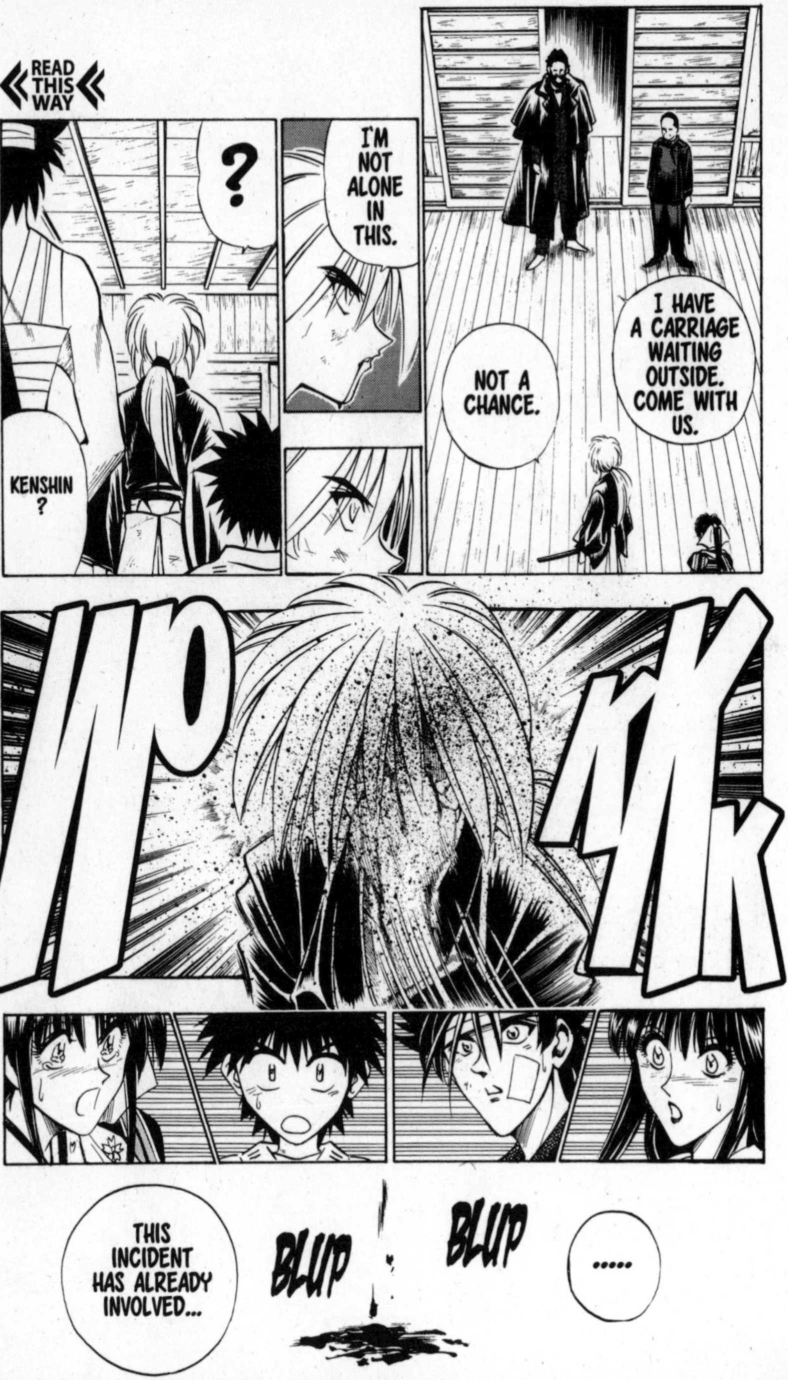

I HAVE A CARRIAGE WAITING OUTSIDE. COME WITH US.
NOT A CHANCE.
I'M NOT ALONE IN THIS.
?
KENSHIN ?
......
BLUP
BLUP
THIS INCIDENT HAS ALREADY INVOLVED...

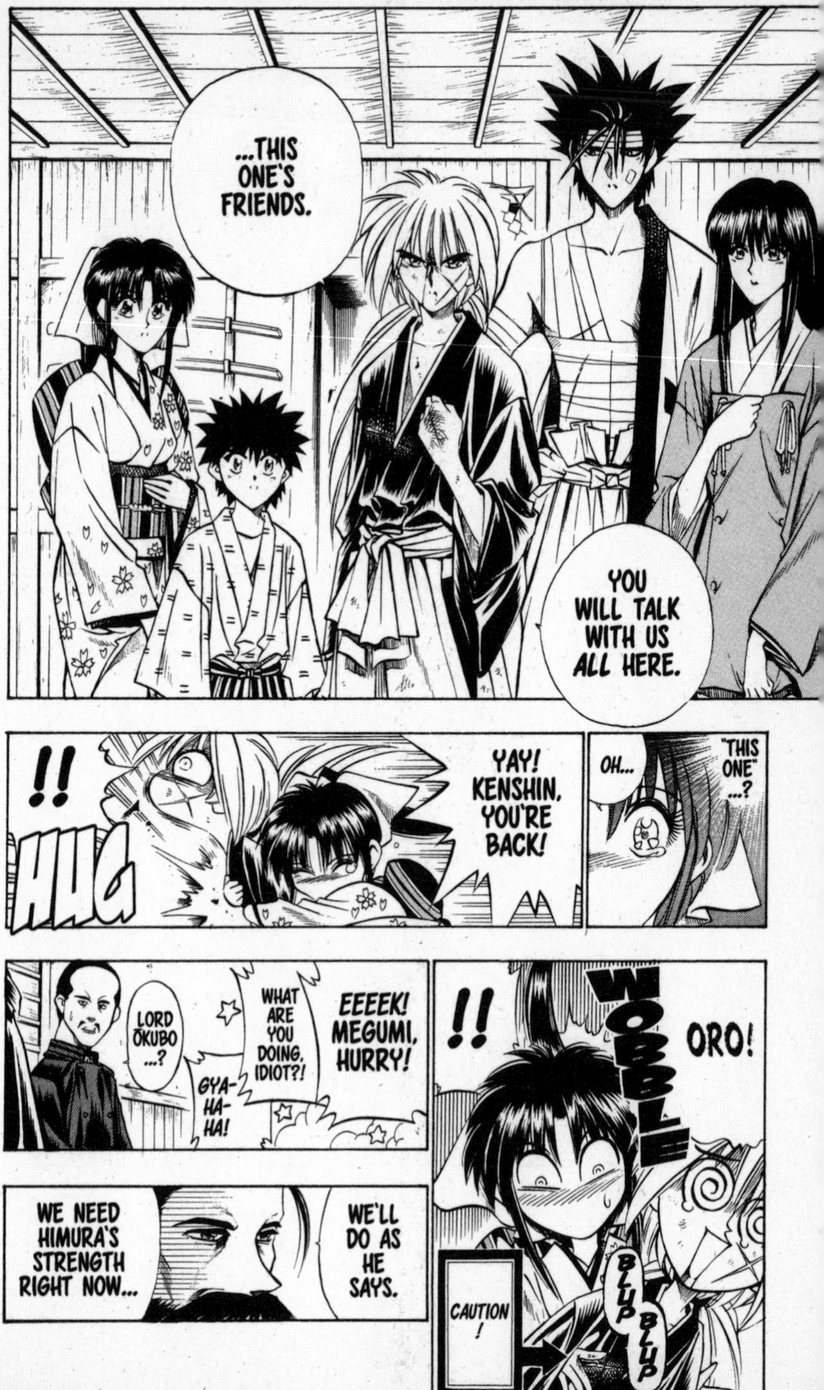
...THIS ONE'S FRIENDS.
YOU WILL TALK WITH US ALL HERE.
"THIS ONE" ...?
OH...
YAY! KENSHIN, YOU'RE BACK!
!!
HUG
ORO!
WOBBLE
!!
BLUP BLUP
CAUTION!
EEEEK! MEGUMI, HURRY!
WHAT ARE YOU DOING, IDIOT?!
GYA-HA-HA!
LORD ŌKUBO ...?
WE'LL DO AS HE SAYS.
WE NEED HIMURA'S STRENGTH RIGHT NOW...

READ THIS WAY

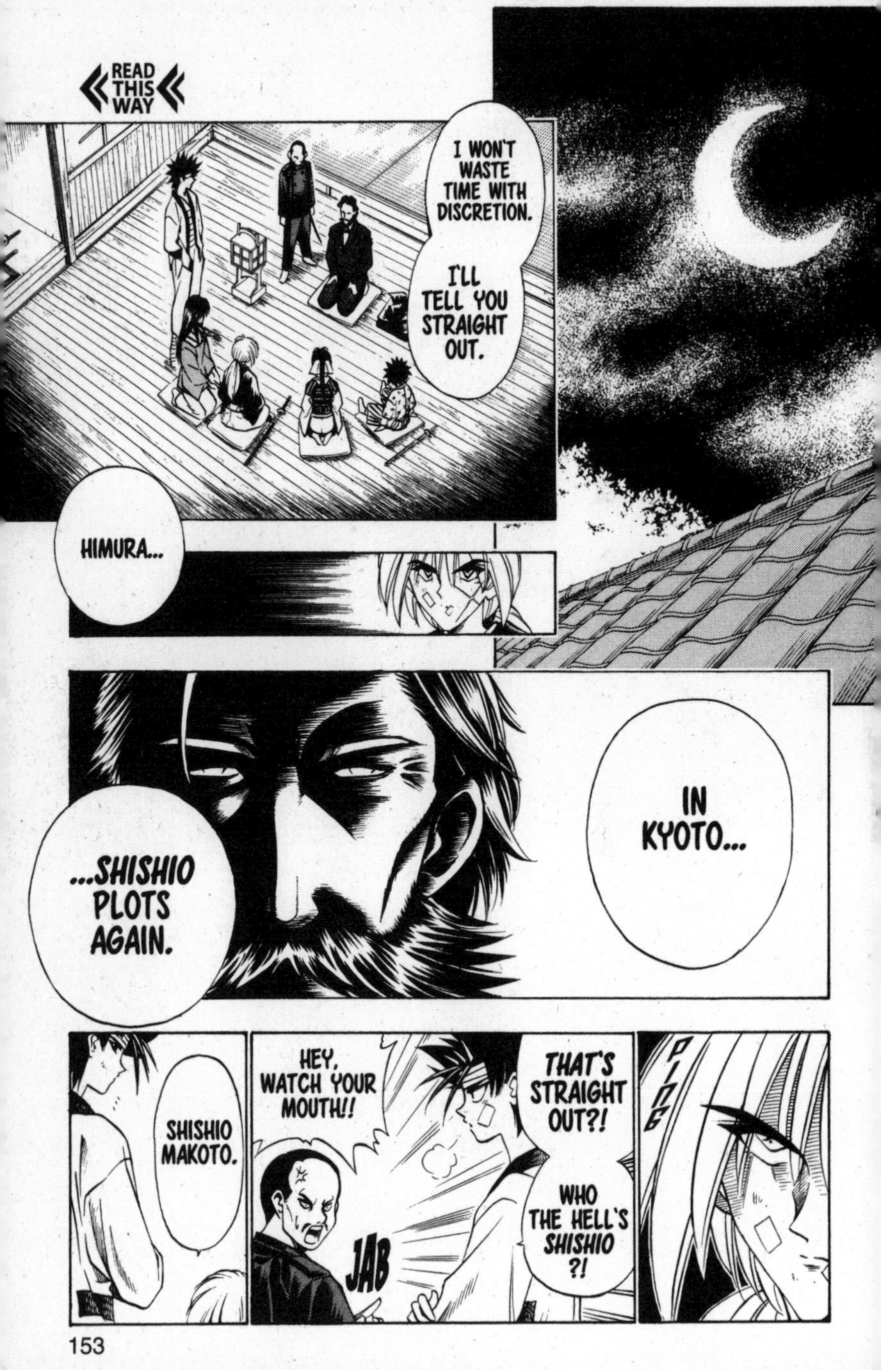

I WON'T WASTE TIME WITH DISCRETION.
I'LL TELL YOU STRAIGHT OUT.
HIMURA...
IN KYOTO...
...SHISHIO PLOTS AGAIN.
PING
THAT'S STRAIGHT OUT?!
WHO THE HELL'S SHISHIO?!
HEY, WATCH YOUR MOUTH!!
JAB
SHISHIO MAKOTO.

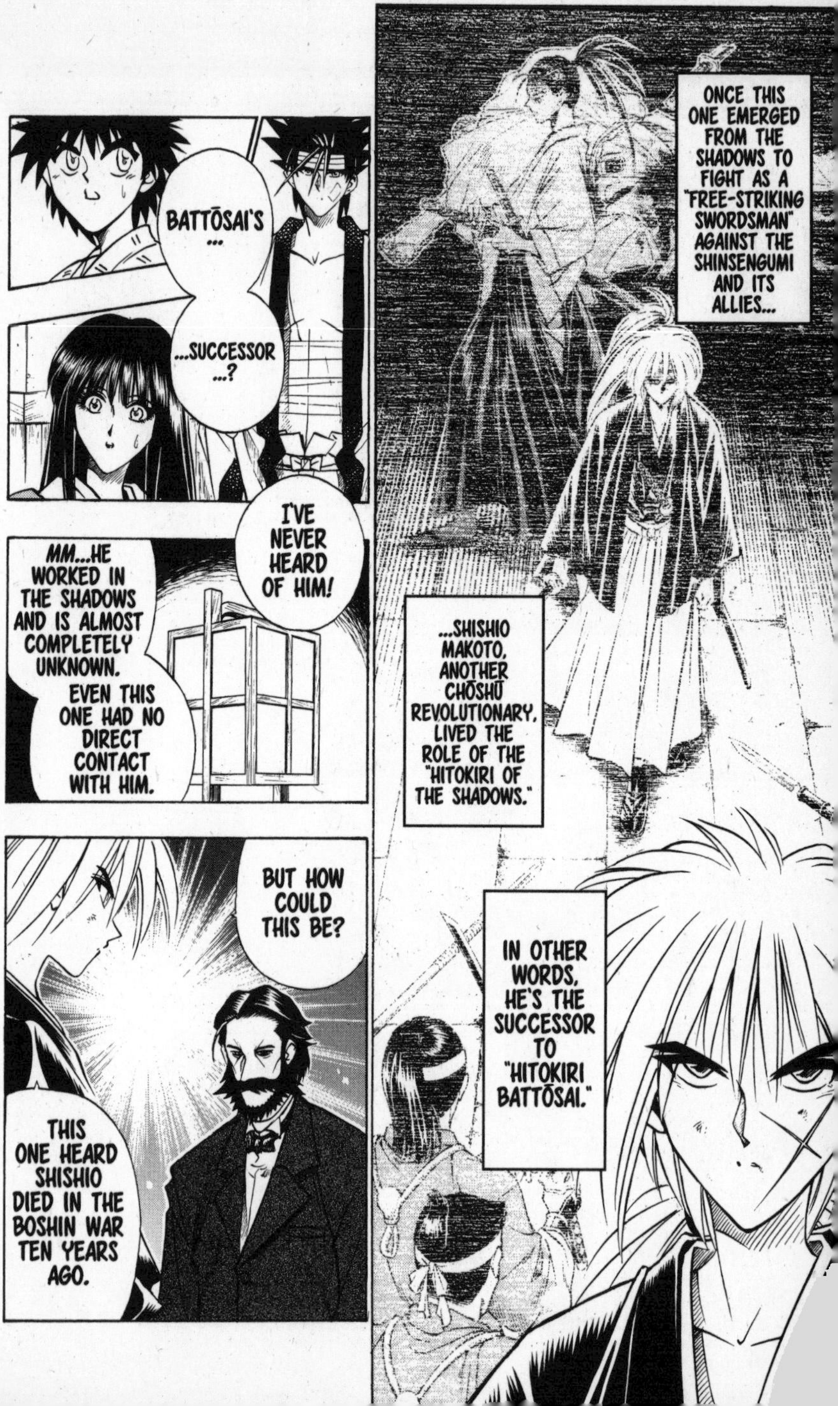
ONCE THIS ONE EMERGED FROM THE SHADOWS TO FIGHT AS A "FREE-STRIKING SWORDSMAN" AGAINST THE SHINSENGUMI AND ITS ALLIES...
...SHISHIO MAKOTO, ANOTHER CHŌSHŪ REVOLUTIONARY, LIVED THE ROLE OF THE "HITOKIRI OF THE SHADOWS."
IN OTHER WORDS, HE'S THE SUCCESSOR TO "HITOKIRI BATTŌSAI."
BATTŌSAI'S ...
...SUCCESSOR ...?
I'VE NEVER HEARD OF HIM!
MM...HE WORKED IN THE SHADOWS AND IS ALMOST COMPLETELY UNKNOWN.
EVEN THIS ONE HAD NO DIRECT CONTACT WITH HIM.
BUT HOW COULD THIS BE?
THIS ONE HEARD SHISHIO DIED IN THE BOSHIN WAR TEN YEARS AGO.

READ THIS WAY

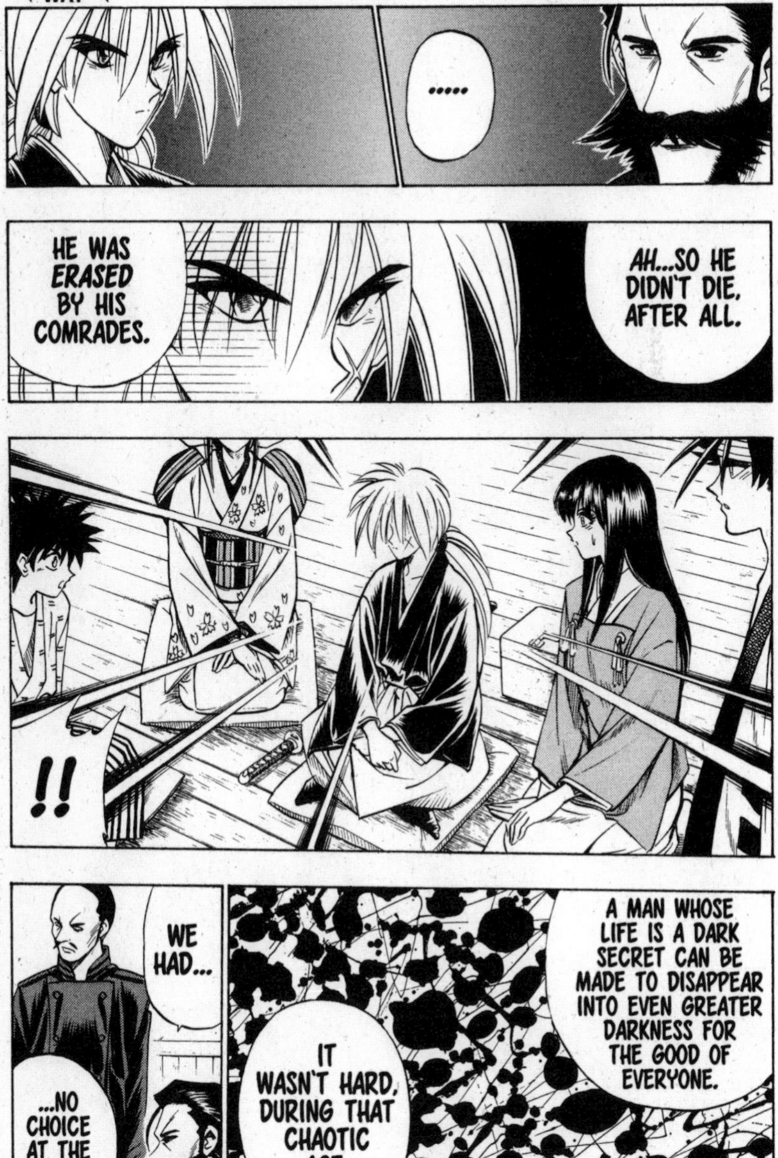
......
AH...SO HE DIDN'T DIE, AFTER ALL.
HE WAS ERASED BY HIS COMRADES.
!!
A MAN WHOSE LIFE IS A DARK SECRET CAN BE MADE TO DISAPPEAR INTO EVEN GREATER DARKNESS FOR THE GOOD OF EVERYONE.
IT WASN'T HARD, DURING THAT CHAOTIC AGE.
WE HAD...
...NO CHOICE AT THE TIME.

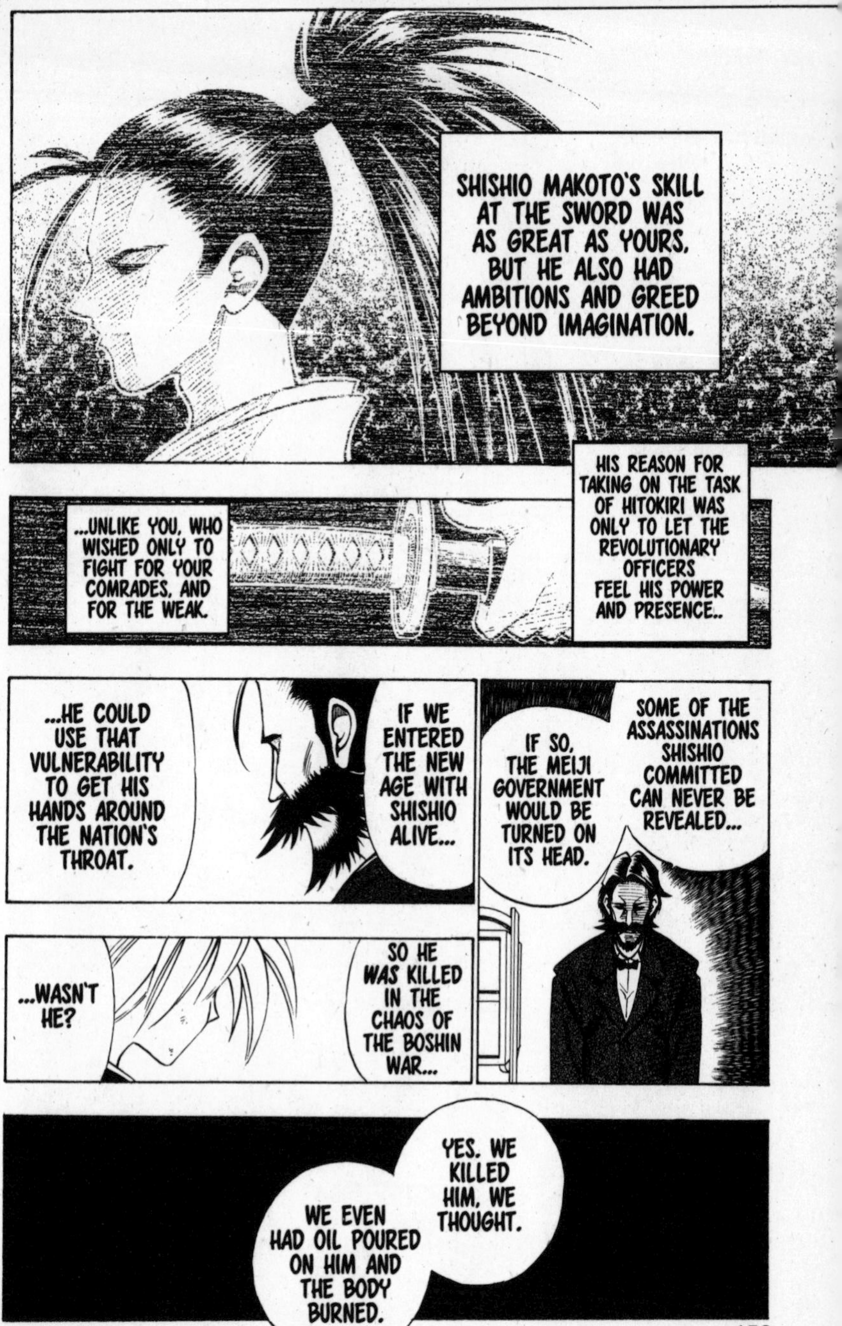
SHISHIO MAKOTO'S SKILL AT THE SWORD WAS AS GREAT AS YOURS, BUT HE ALSO HAD AMBITIONS AND GREED BEYOND IMAGINATION.
HIS REASON FOR TAKING ON THE TASK OF HITOKIRI WAS ONLY TO LET THE REVOLUTIONARY OFFICERS FEEL HIS POWER AND PRESENCE..
...UNLIKE YOU, WHO WISHED ONLY TO FIGHT FOR YOUR COMRADES, AND FOR THE WEAK.
SOME OF THE ASSASSINATIONS SHISHIO COMMITTED CAN NEVER BE REVEALED...
IF SO, THE MEIJI GOVERNMENT WOULD BE TURNED ON ITS HEAD.
IF WE ENTERED THE NEW AGE WITH SHISHIO ALIVE...
...HE COULD USE THAT VULNERABILITY TO GET HIS HANDS AROUND THE NATION'S THROAT.
SO HE WAS KILLED IN THE CHAOS OF THE BOSHIN WAR...
...WASN'T HE?
YES. WE KILLED HIM, WE THOUGHT.
WE EVEN HAD OIL POURED ON HIM AND THE BODY BURNED.

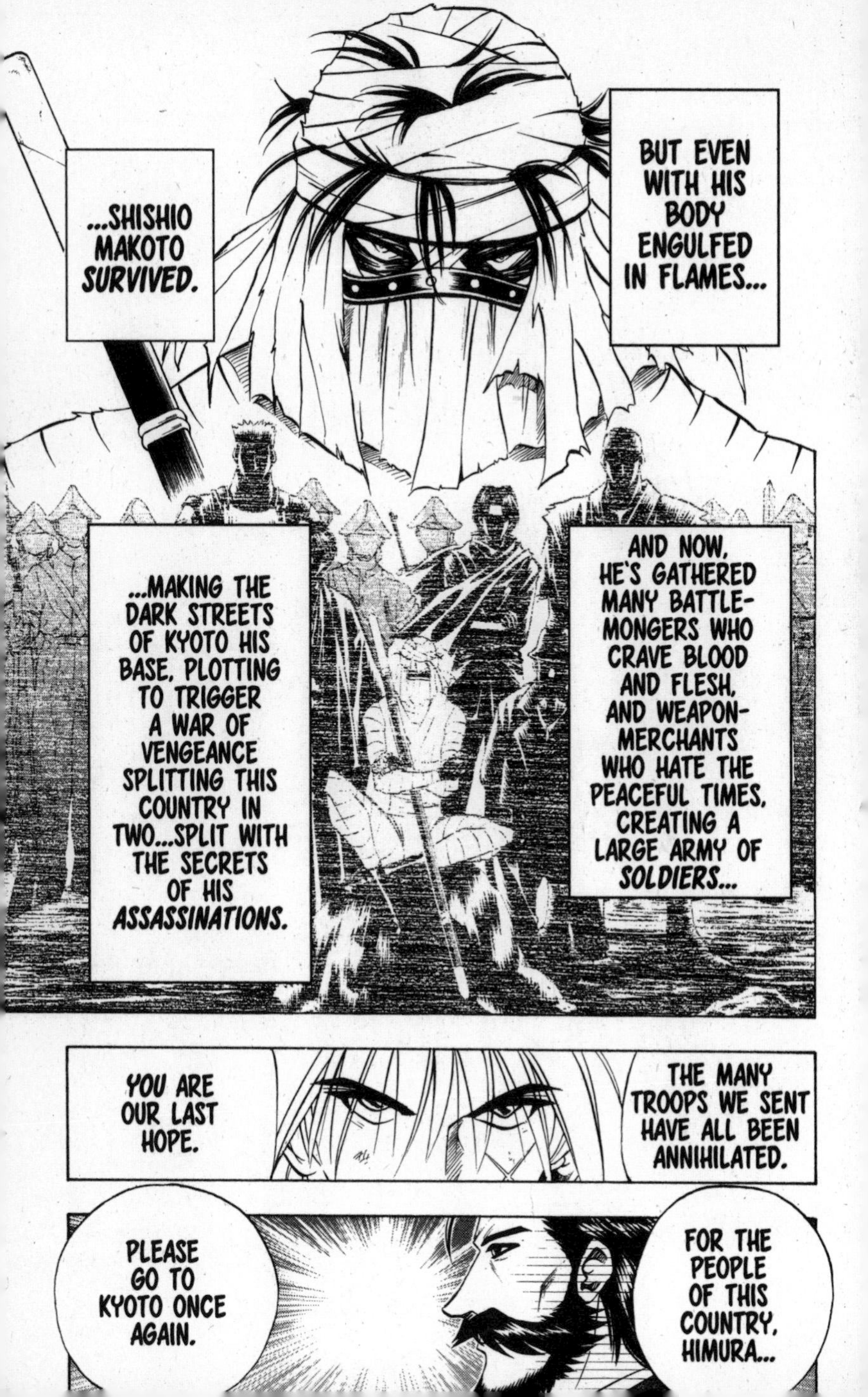
BUT EVEN WITH HIS BODY ENGULFED IN FLAMES...
...SHISHIO MAKOTO SURVIVED.
AND NOW, HE'S GATHERED MANY BATTLE-MONGERS WHO CRAVE BLOOD AND FLESH, AND WEAPON-MERCHANTS WHO HATE THE PEACEFUL TIMES, CREATING A LARGE ARMY OF SOLDIERS...
...MAKING THE DARK STREETS OF KYOTO HIS BASE, PLOTTING TO TRIGGER A WAR OF VENGEANCE SPLITTING THIS COUNTRY IN TWO...SPLIT WITH THE SECRETS OF HIS ASSASSINATIONS.
THE MANY TROOPS WE SENT HAVE ALL BEEN ANNIHILATED.
YOU ARE OUR LAST HOPE.
FOR THE PEOPLE OF THIS COUNTRY, HIMURA...
PLEASE GO TO KYOTO ONCE AGAIN.

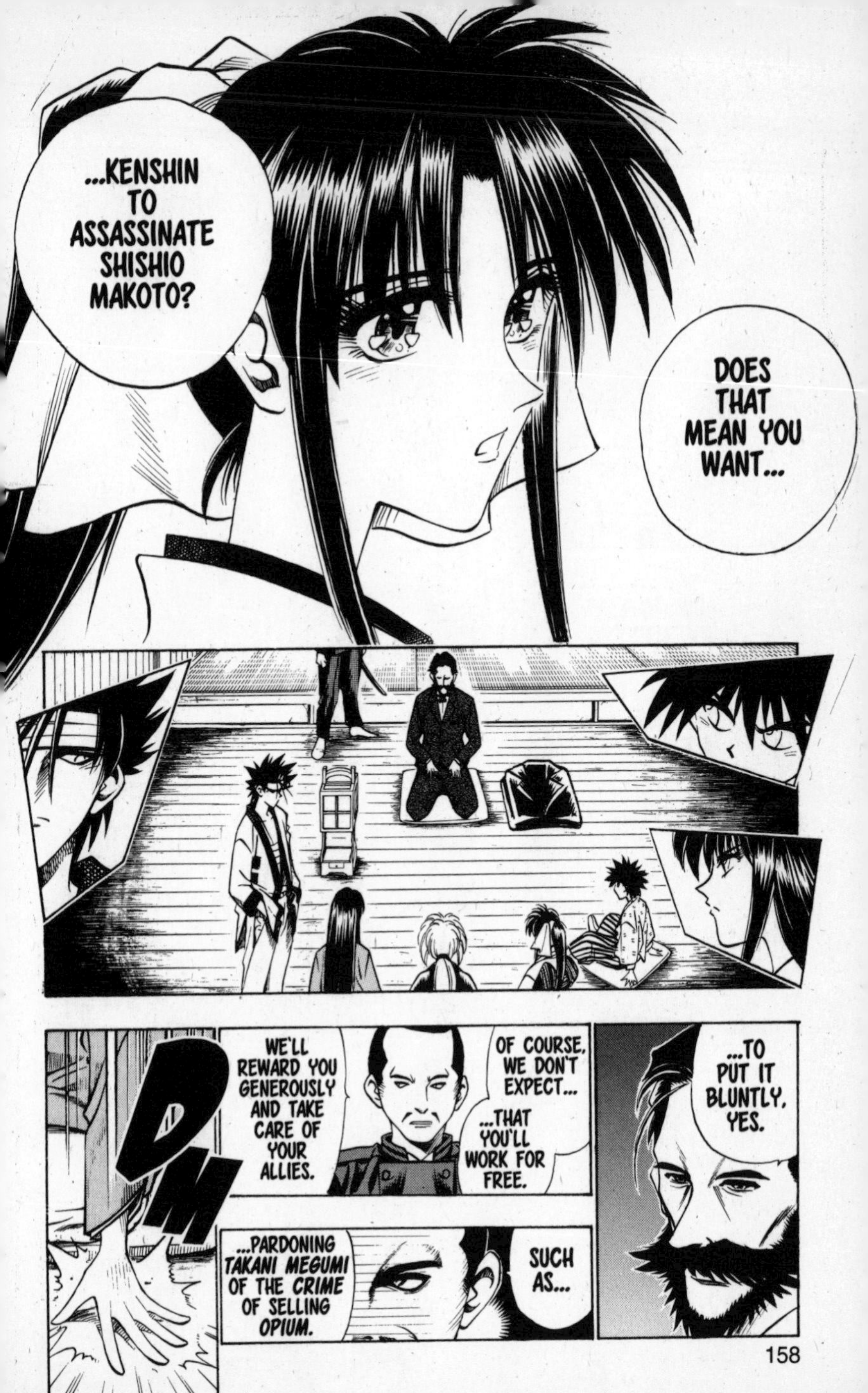
DOES THAT MEAN YOU WANT...
...KENSHIN TO ASSASSINATE SHISHIO MAKOTO?
...TO PUT IT BLUNTLY, YES.
OF COURSE, WE DON'T EXPECT...
...THAT YOU'LL WORK FOR FREE.
WE'LL REWARD YOU GENEROUSLY AND TAKE CARE OF YOUR ALLIES.
SUCH AS...
...PARDONING TAKANI MEGUMI OF THE CRIME OF SELLING OPIUM.
DM

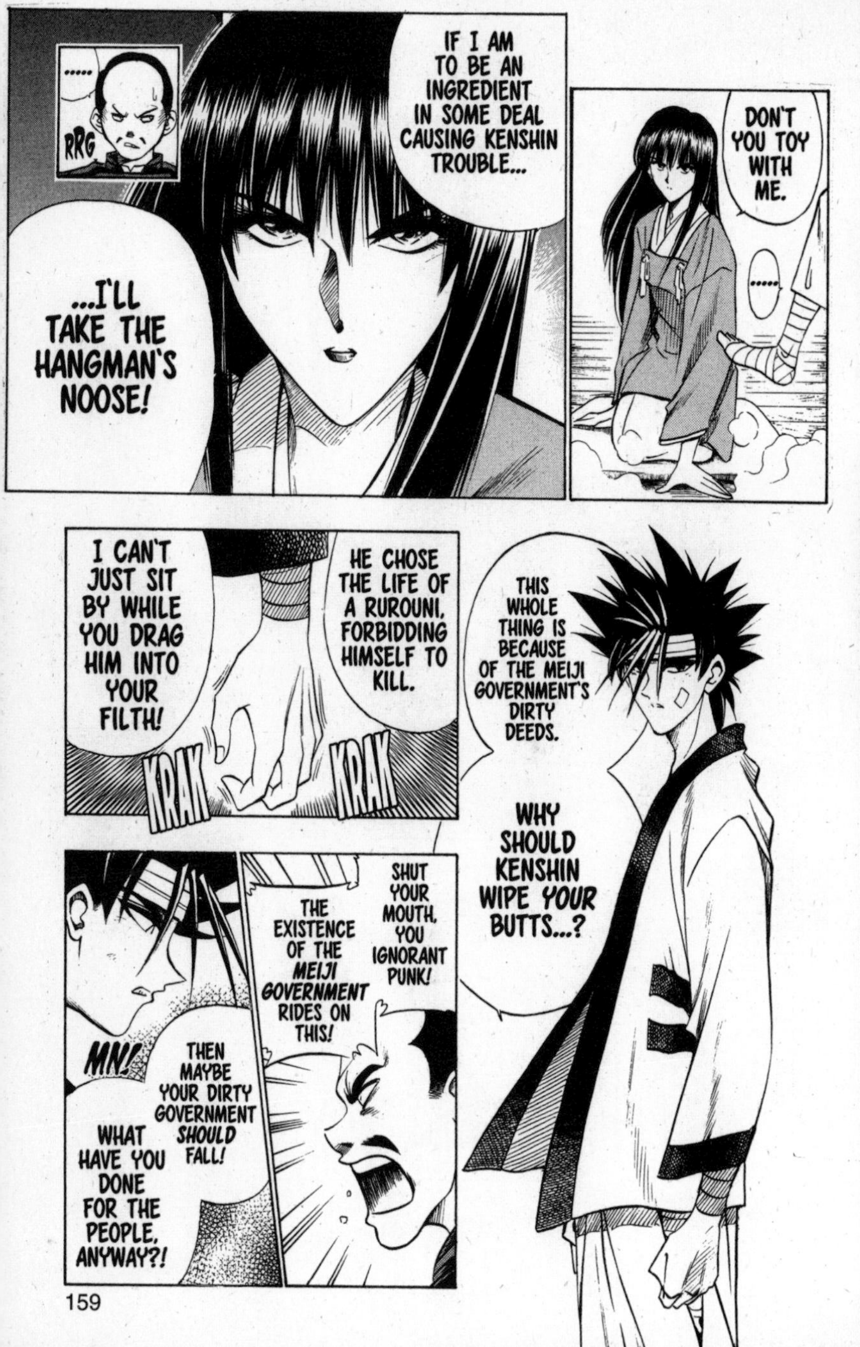
DON'T YOU TOY WITH ME.
......
IF I AM TO BE AN INGREDIENT IN SOME DEAL CAUSING KENSHIN TROUBLE...
......
RRG
...I'LL TAKE THE HANGMAN'S NOOSE!
THIS WHOLE THING IS BECAUSE OF THE MEIJI GOVERNMENT'S DIRTY DEEDS.
WHY SHOULD KENSHIN WIPE *YOUR* BUTTS...?
HE CHOSE THE LIFE OF A RUROUNI, FORBIDDING HIMSELF TO KILL.
I CAN'T JUST SIT BY WHILE YOU DRAG HIM INTO YOUR FILTH!
KRAK
KRAK
SHUT YOUR MOUTH, YOU IGNORANT PUNK!
THE EXISTENCE OF THE *MEIJI GOVERNMENT* RIDES ON THIS!
THEN MAYBE YOUR DIRTY GOVERNMENT *SHOULD* FALL!
MN!
WHAT HAVE YOU DONE FOR THE PEOPLE, ANYWAY?!

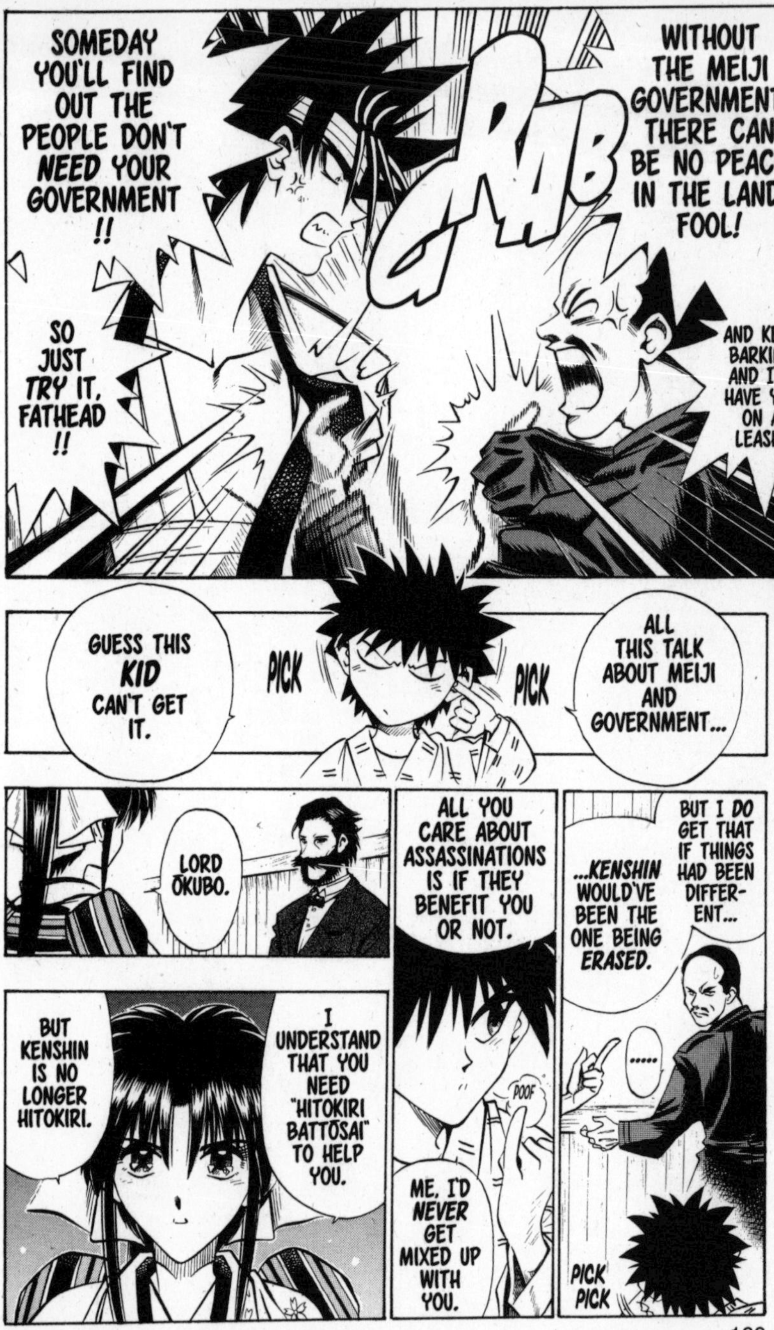
WITHOUT THE MEIJI GOVERNMENT, THERE CAN BE NO PEACE IN THE LAND, FOOL!
GRAB
AND KEEP BARKING AND I'LL HAVE YOU ON A LEASH!
SOMEDAY YOU'LL FIND OUT THE PEOPLE DON'T *NEED* YOUR GOVERNMENT !!
SO JUST *TRY* IT, FATHEAD !!
ALL THIS TALK ABOUT MEIJI AND GOVERNMENT...
PICK
PICK
GUESS THIS **KID** CAN'T GET IT.
BUT I *DO* GET THAT IF THINGS HAD BEEN DIFFER-ENT...
...KENSHIN WOULD'VE BEEN THE ONE BEING *ERASED*.
......
PICK PICK
ALL YOU CARE ABOUT ASSASSINATIONS IS IF THEY BENEFIT YOU OR NOT.
POOF
ME, I'D *NEVER* GET MIXED UP WITH YOU.
LORD ŌKUBO.
I UNDERSTAND THAT YOU NEED "HITOKIRI BATTŌSAI" TO HELP YOU.
BUT KENSHIN IS NO LONGER HITOKIRI.

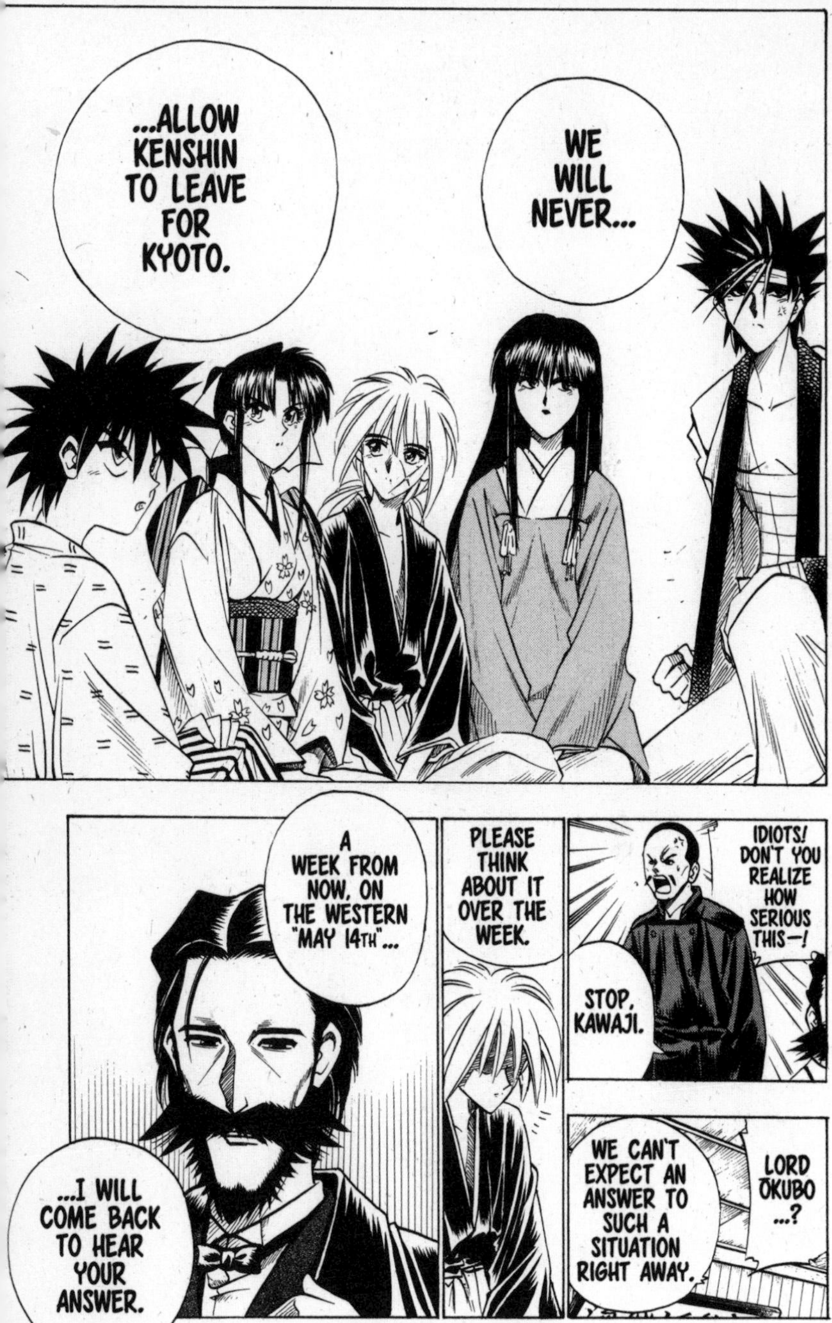
WE WILL NEVER...
...ALLOW KENSHIN TO LEAVE FOR KYOTO.
IDIOTS! DON'T YOU REALIZE HOW SERIOUS THIS—!
STOP, KAWAJI.
LORD ŌKUBO ...?
WE CAN'T EXPECT AN ANSWER TO SUCH A SITUATION RIGHT AWAY.
PLEASE THINK ABOUT IT OVER THE WEEK.
A WEEK FROM NOW, ON THE WESTERN "MAY 14TH"...
...I WILL COME BACK TO HEAR YOUR ANSWER.

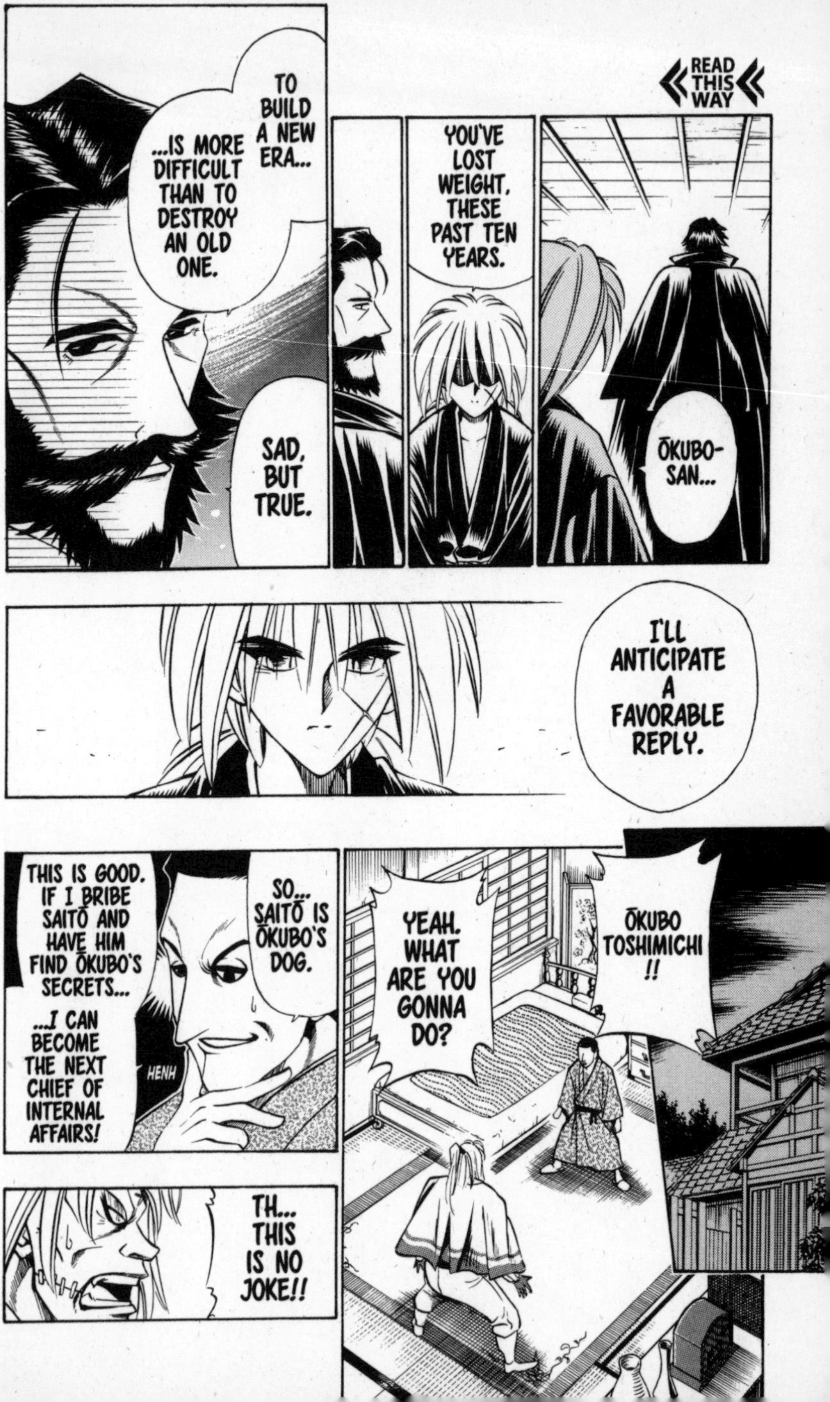
READ THIS WAY
ŌKUBO-SAN...
YOU'VE LOST WEIGHT, THESE PAST TEN YEARS.
TO BUILD A NEW ERA...
...IS MORE DIFFICULT THAN TO DESTROY AN OLD ONE.
SAD, BUT TRUE.
I'LL ANTICIPATE A FAVORABLE REPLY.
ŌKUBO TOSHIMICHI !!
YEAH. WHAT ARE YOU GONNA DO?
SO... SAITŌ IS ŌKUBO'S DOG.
THIS IS GOOD. IF I BRIBE SAITŌ AND HAVE HIM FIND ŌKUBO'S SECRETS...
...I CAN BECOME THE NEXT CHIEF OF INTERNAL AFFAIRS!
HENH
TH... THIS IS NO JOKE!!

READ THIS WAY

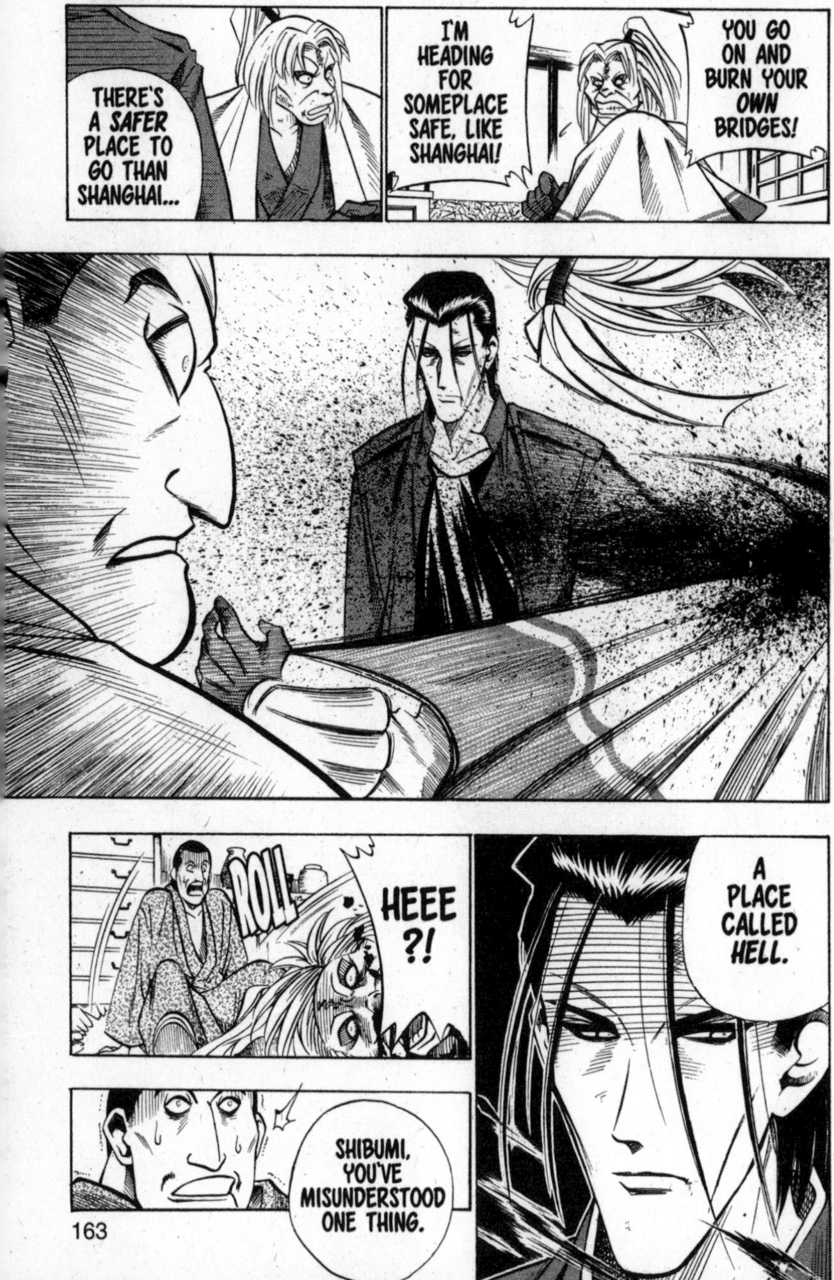
YOU GO ON AND BURN YOUR OWN BRIDGES!
I'M HEADING FOR SOMEPLACE SAFE, LIKE SHANGHAI!
THERE'S A SAFER PLACE TO GO THAN SHANGHAI...
A PLACE CALLED HELL.
HEEE?!
ROLL
SHIBUMI, YOU'VE MISUNDERSTOOD ONE THING.

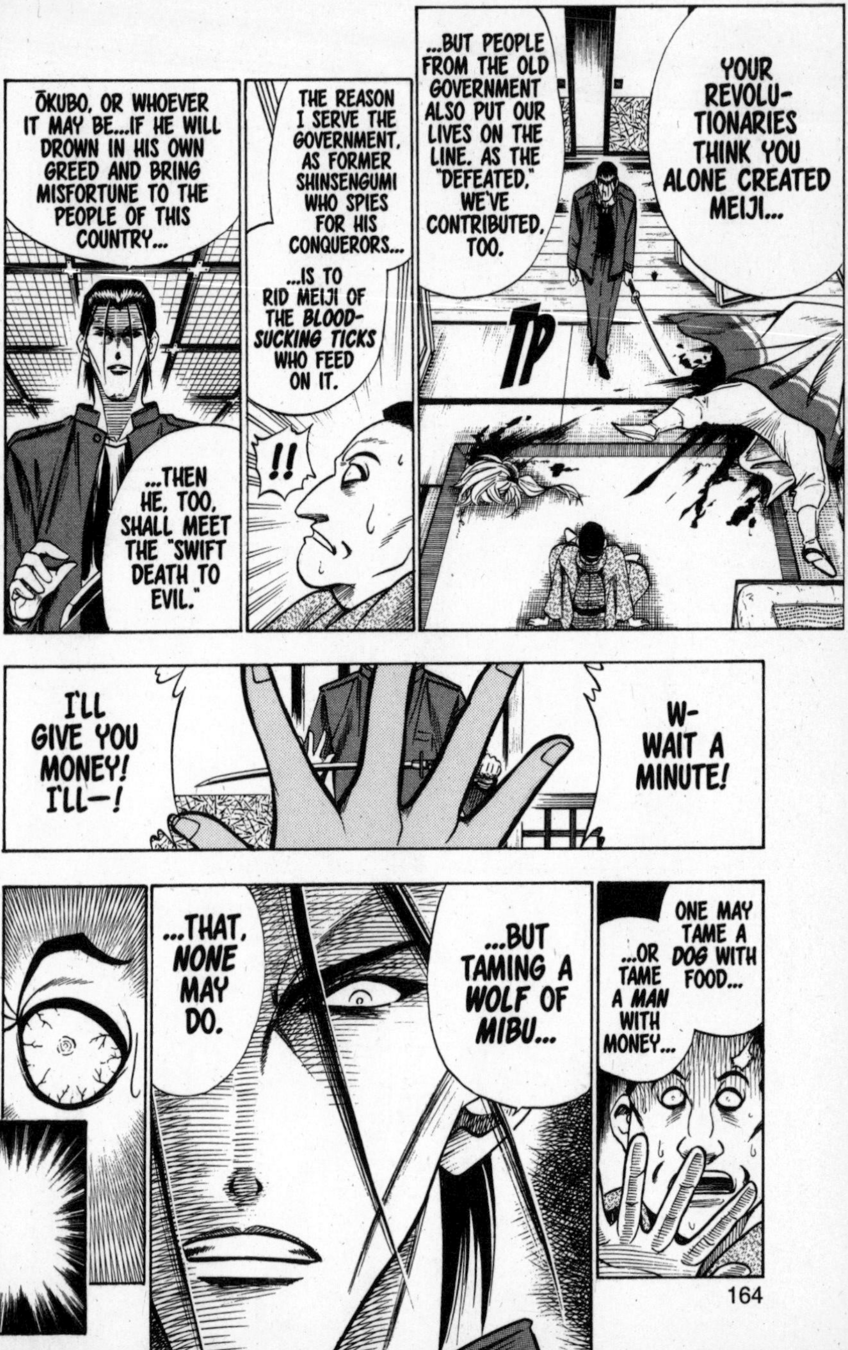
YOUR REVOLUTIONARIES THINK YOU ALONE CREATED MEIJI...
...BUT PEOPLE FROM THE OLD GOVERNMENT ALSO PUT OUR LIVES ON THE LINE. AS THE "DEFEATED," WE'VE CONTRIBUTED, TOO.
TP
THE REASON I SERVE THE GOVERNMENT, AS FORMER SHINSENGUMI WHO SPIES FOR HIS CONQUERORS...
...IS TO RID MEIJI OF THE *BLOOD-SUCKING TICKS* WHO FEED ON IT.
!!
ŌKUBO, OR WHOEVER IT MAY BE...IF HE WILL DROWN IN HIS OWN GREED AND BRING MISFORTUNE TO THE PEOPLE OF THIS COUNTRY...
...THEN HE, TOO, SHALL MEET THE "SWIFT DEATH TO EVIL."
W- WAIT A MINUTE!
I'LL GIVE YOU MONEY! I'LL—!
ONE MAY TAME A *DOG* WITH FOOD...
...OR TAME A *MAN* WITH MONEY...
...BUT TAMING A *WOLF* OF *MIBU*...
...THAT, *NONE* MAY DO.

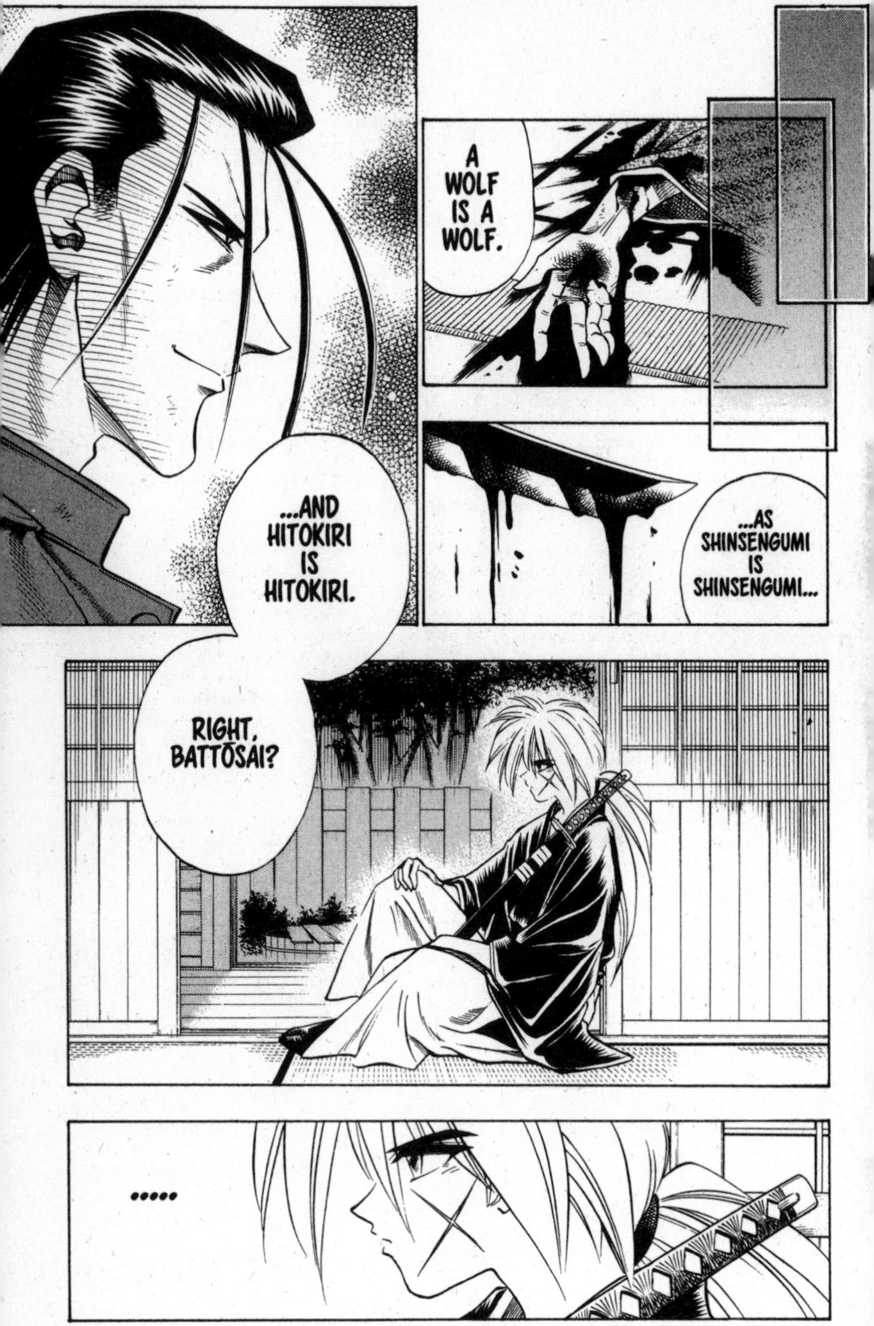
A WOLF IS A WOLF.
...AS SHINSENGUMI IS SHINSENGUMI...
...AND HITOKIRI IS HITOKIRI.
RIGHT, BATTŌSAI?
.....

The Secret Life of Characters (21)

—Saitō Hajime (Fujita Gorō)—

Model, schmodel.... Saitō's a real, historical figure. That being said—unlike Sagara Sōzō or Yamagata Aritomo—he'll have a *lot* to do with the storyline, so I've altered him to suit my own needs. I've altered him so much, in fact, that I've received letters of complaint from Shinsengumi fans. (I've had complaints before, sure, but never this many!) As the story's gone on, though, the popularity of the character has also increased, so I'm happy. Saitō's a character who's currently active, and I don't want to give too much away, but in the distant future, what I'd like is for him to become a "dirty" hero, sticking always with his "Swift Death to Evil" philosophy, never ever becoming a "nice guy" or becoming palsy-walsy with Kenshin and the gang.

No model in terms of design. Originally he appeared as an antagonist, so I made his face "villain-ish," but there were complaints. Shinsengumi fans, it seems, persist in thinking of Saitō as very handsome...despite the fact that not a single photo of him exists. (There *are* portraits, but if you think *that's* handsome...well, your mileage may vary, okay?) Speaking of complaints, there was one to the effect of, "Why is Saitō selling 'Ishida powdered medicine' made by the Hijikata family?" Fine, fine—that was just me, fooling around. I'll take the heat for some stuff (like Akamatsu), but when people start complaining about stuff like *that*...come on, now. Even a manga artist is human. Can't you Shinsengumi fans read this manga with a more open mind...? No...?

***Gatotsu* ("Fang Thrust") isn't a real move. Saitō Hajime's favorite move historically was the "left single-handed thrust," so I gave it the name "*gatotsu*" to better fit in with the whole action-manga thing. It is true, though, that the Shinsengumi used the *Hiratsuki* ("Parallel Thrust").**

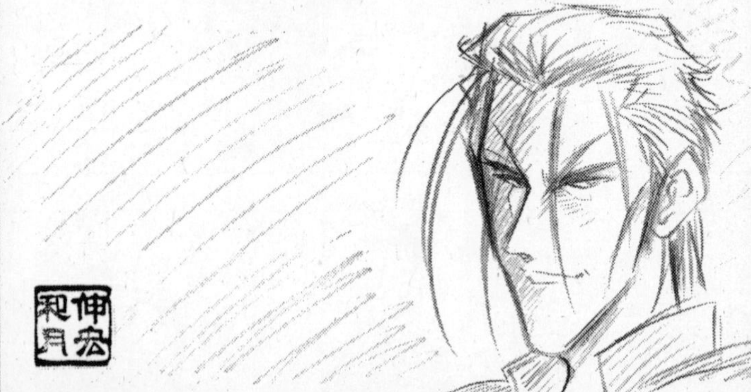
伸宏
和月

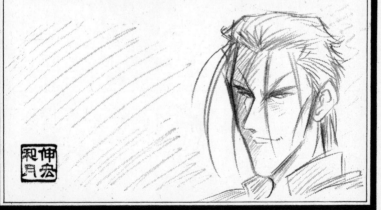

Act 56 Meiji 11, May 14th—Morning

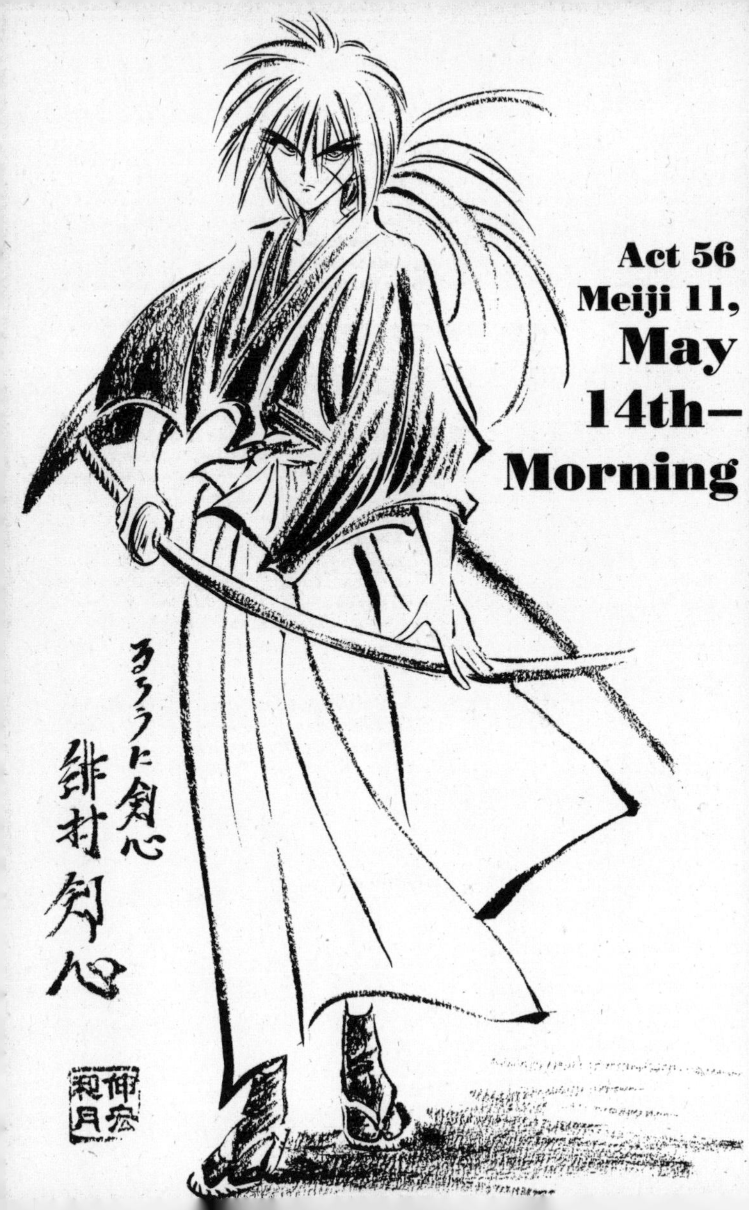
るろうに剣心
緋村剣心
和月伸宏

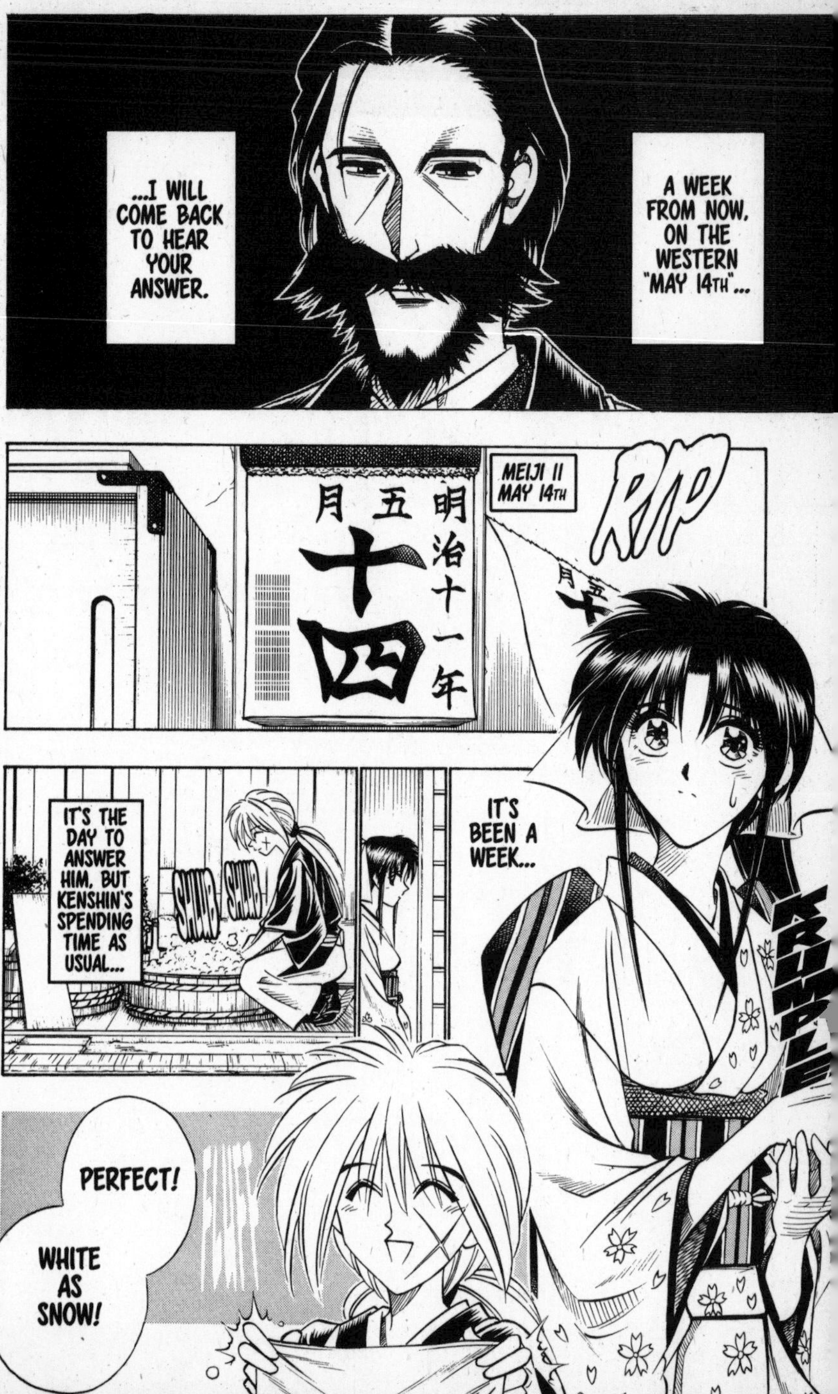
A WEEK FROM NOW, ON THE WESTERN "MAY 14TH"...
...I WILL COME BACK TO HEAR YOUR ANSWER.
RIP
MEIJI 11 MAY 14TH
明治十一年
五月
十四
IT'S BEEN A WEEK...
KRUMPLE
IT'S THE DAY TO ANSWER HIM, BUT KENSHIN'S SPENDING TIME AS USUAL...
PERFECT!
WHITE AS SNOW!

READ THIS WAY

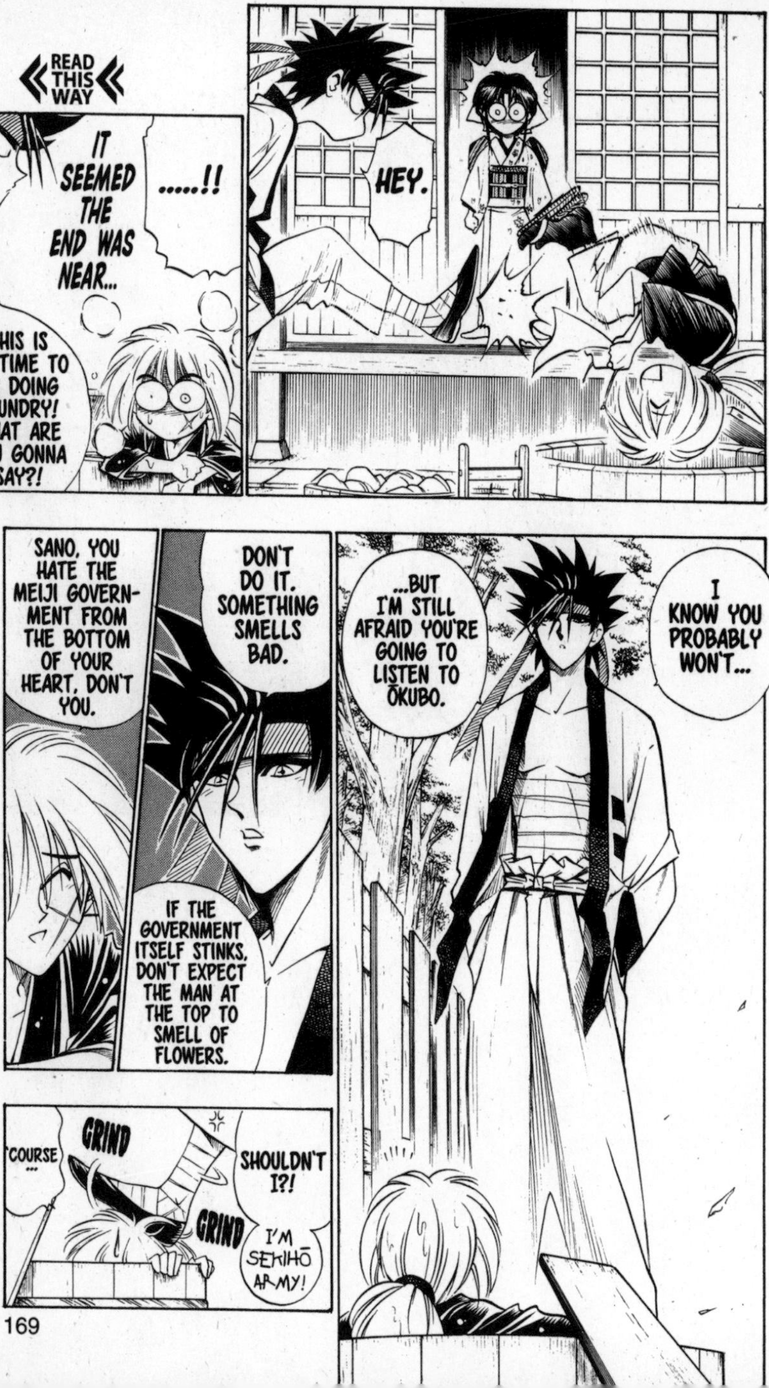
HEY.
.....!!
IT SEEMED THE END WAS NEAR...
THIS IS NO TIME TO BE DOING LAUNDRY! WHAT ARE YOU GONNA SAY?!
I KNOW YOU PROBABLY WON'T...
...BUT I'M STILL AFRAID YOU'RE GOING TO LISTEN TO ŌKUBO.
DON'T DO IT. SOMETHING SMELLS BAD.
IF THE GOVERNMENT ITSELF STINKS, DON'T EXPECT THE MAN AT THE TOP TO SMELL OF FLOWERS.
SANO, YOU HATE THE MEIJI GOVERN-MENT FROM THE BOTTOM OF YOUR HEART, DON'T YOU.
SHOULDN'T I?!
I'M SEKIHŌ ARMY!
GRIND
GRIND
'COURSE...

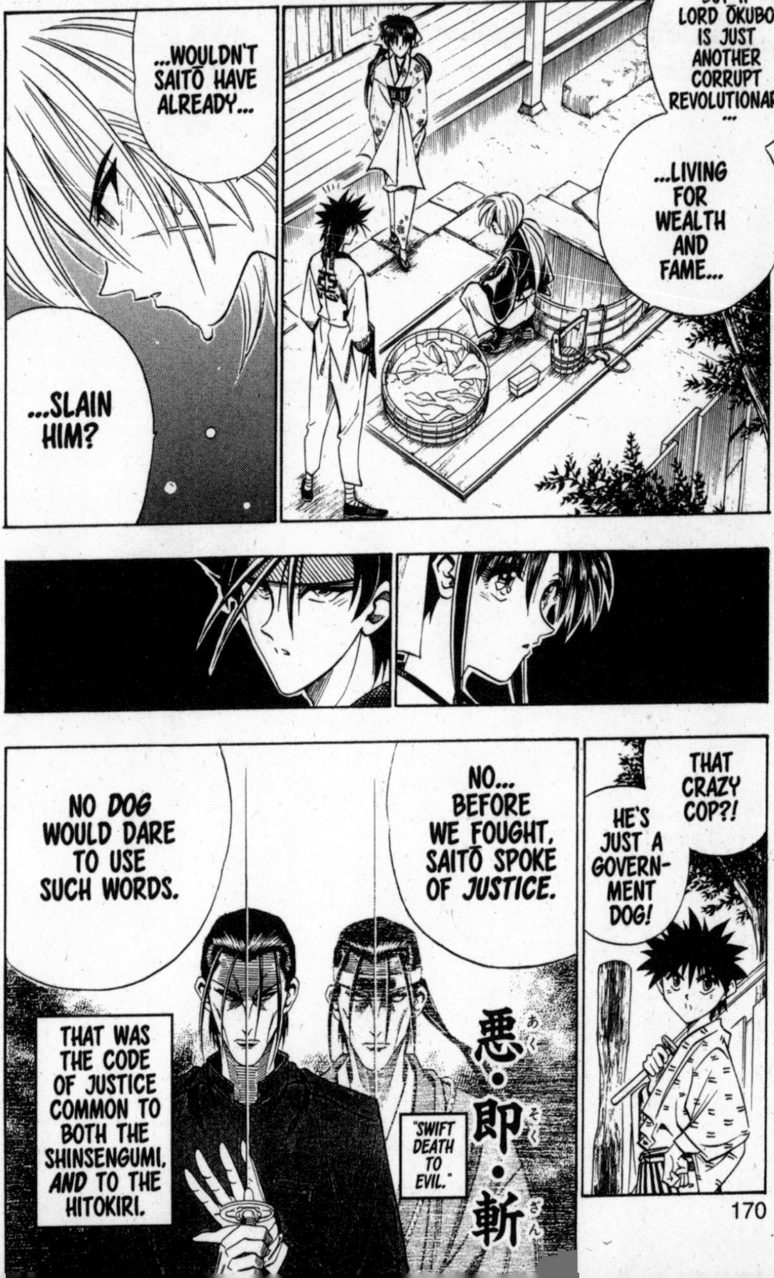
BUT IF LORD ŌKUBO IS JUST ANOTHER CORRUPT REVOLUTIONARY...
...LIVING FOR WEALTH AND FAME...
...WOULDN'T SAITŌ HAVE ALREADY...
...SLAIN HIM?
THAT CRAZY COP?!
HE'S JUST A GOVERNMENT DOG!
NO... BEFORE WE FOUGHT, SAITŌ SPOKE OF *JUSTICE*.
NO *DOG* WOULD DARE TO USE SUCH WORDS.
悪・即・斬
"SWIFT DEATH TO EVIL."
THAT WAS THE CODE OF JUSTICE COMMON TO BOTH THE SHINSENGUMI, *AND* TO THE HITOKIRI.

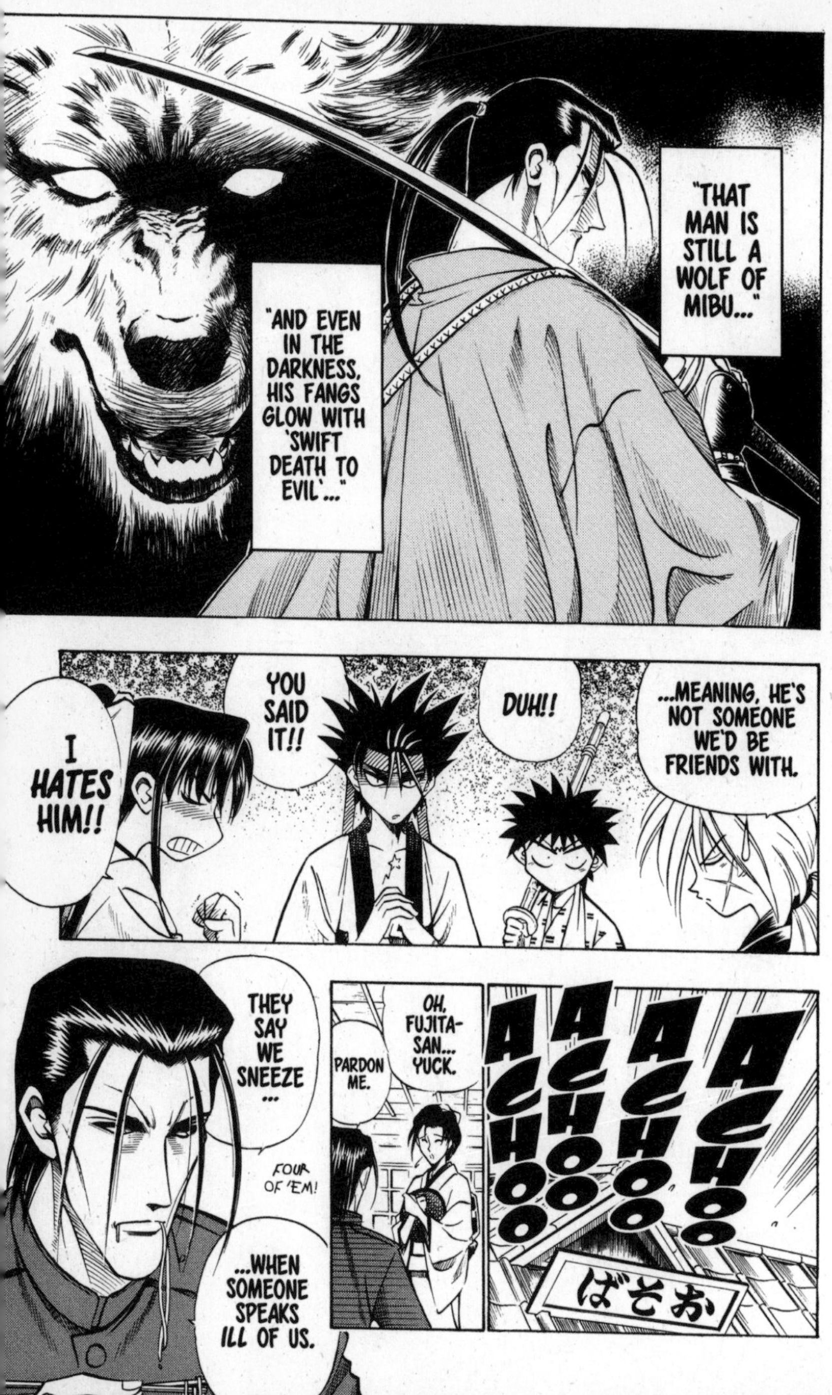
"THAT MAN IS STILL A WOLF OF MIBU..."
"AND EVEN IN THE DARKNESS, HIS FANGS GLOW WITH 'SWIFT DEATH TO EVIL'..."
...MEANING, HE'S NOT SOMEONE WE'D BE FRIENDS WITH.
DUH!!
YOU SAID IT!!
I HATES HIM!!
ACHOOO
ACHOOO
ACHOOO
ACHOOO
ばそお
OH, FUJITA-SAN... YUCK.
PARDON ME.
THEY SAY WE SNEEZE...
FOUR OF 'EM!
...WHEN SOMEONE SPEAKS ILL OF US.

READ THIS WAY

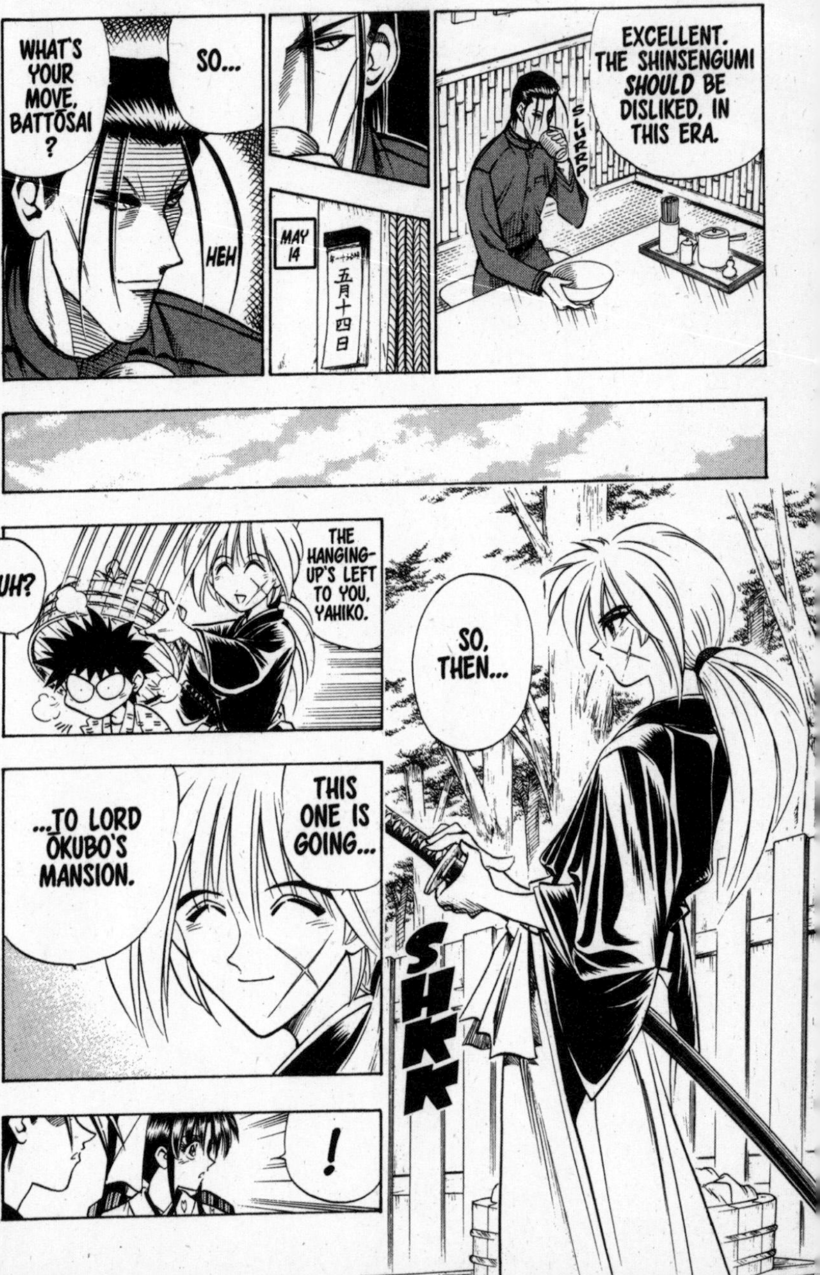
SLURRP
EXCELLENT. THE SHINSENGUMI *SHOULD* BE DISLIKED, IN THIS ERA.
MAY 14
五月十四日
SO...
WHAT'S YOUR MOVE, BATTŌSAI?
HEH
SO, THEN...
SHKK
THE HANGING-UP'S LEFT TO YOU, YAHIKO.
HUH?
THIS ONE IS GOING...
...TO LORD ŌKUBO'S MANSION.
!

READ THIS WAY

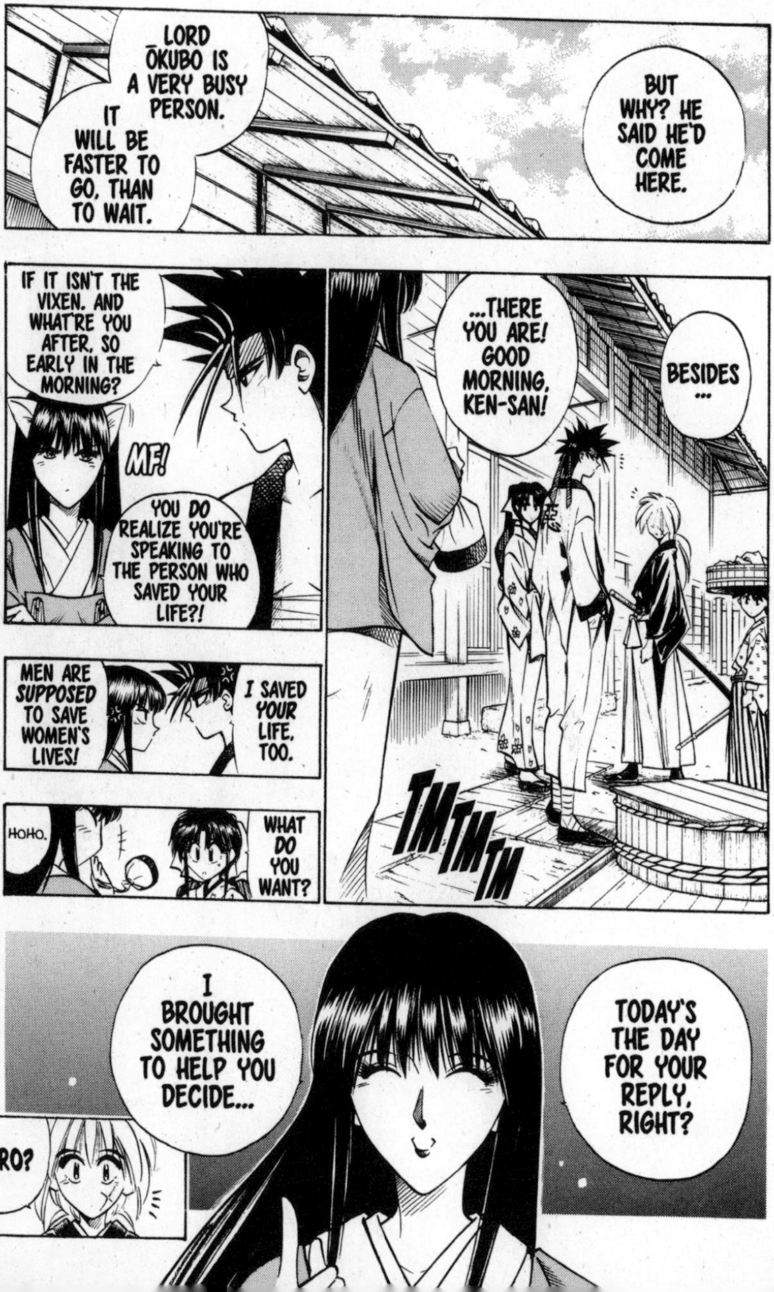
BUT WHY? HE SAID HE'D COME HERE.
LORD ŌKUBO IS A VERY BUSY PERSON.
IT WILL BE FASTER TO GO, THAN TO WAIT.
BESIDES...
...THERE YOU ARE! GOOD MORNING, KEN-SAN!
TM TM TM TM
IF IT ISN'T THE VIXEN. AND WHAT'RE YOU AFTER, SO EARLY IN THE MORNING?
MF!
YOU DO REALIZE YOU'RE SPEAKING TO THE PERSON WHO SAVED YOUR LIFE?!
I SAVED YOUR LIFE, TOO.
MEN ARE SUPPOSED TO SAVE WOMEN'S LIVES!
WHAT DO YOU WANT?
HOHO.
TODAY'S THE DAY FOR YOUR REPLY, RIGHT?
I BROUGHT SOMETHING TO HELP YOU DECIDE...
ORO?

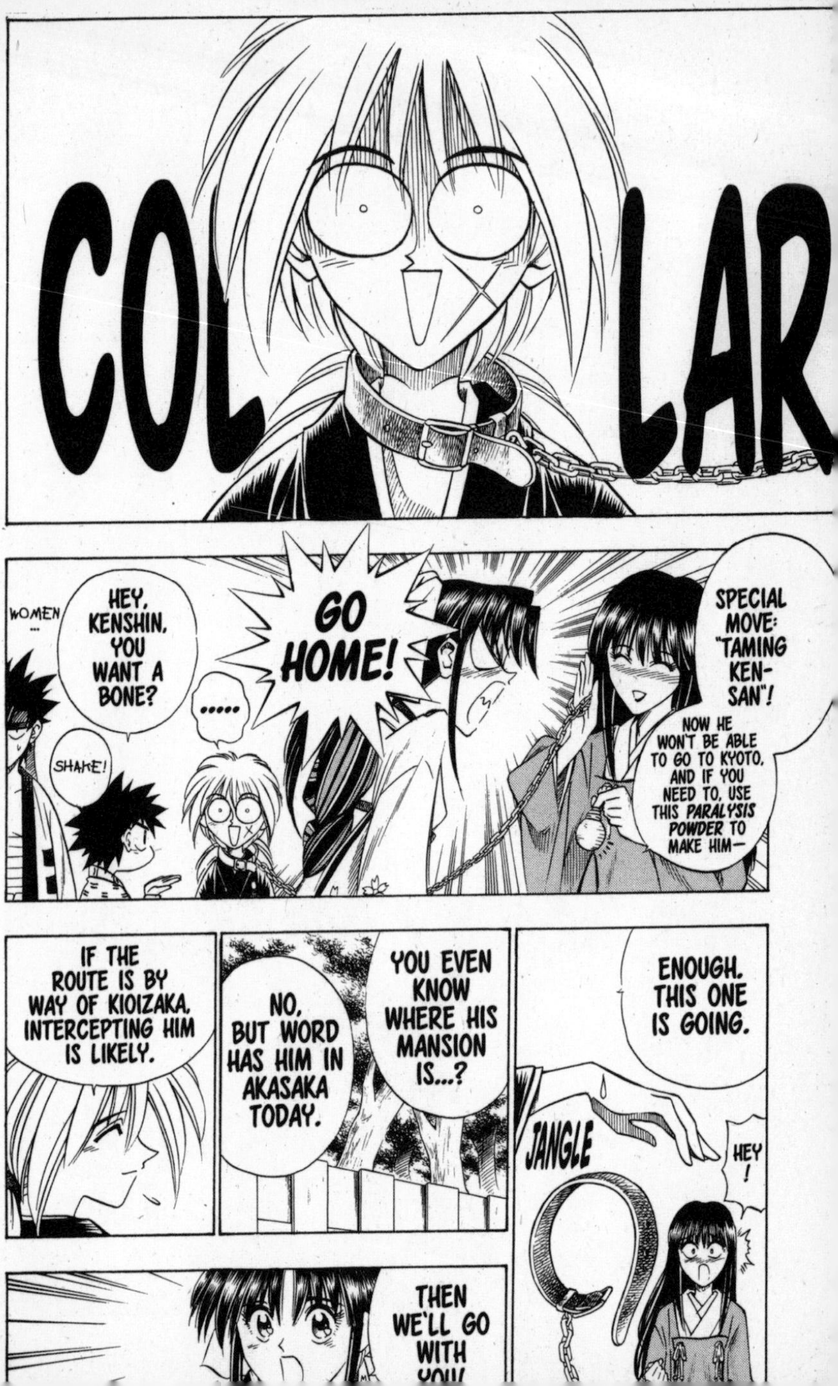
COLLAR
SPECIAL MOVE: "TAMING KEN-SAN"!
NOW HE WON'T BE ABLE TO GO TO KYOTO, AND IF YOU NEED TO, USE THIS *PARALYSIS POWDER* TO MAKE HIM—
GO HOME!
HEY, KENSHIN, YOU WANT A BONE?
......
SHAKE!
WOMEN...
ENOUGH. THIS ONE IS GOING.
JANGLE
HEY!
YOU EVEN KNOW WHERE HIS MANSION IS...?
NO, BUT WORD HAS HIM IN AKASAKA TODAY.
IF THE ROUTE IS BY WAY OF KIOIZAKA, INTERCEPTING HIM IS LIKELY.
THEN WE'LL GO WITH

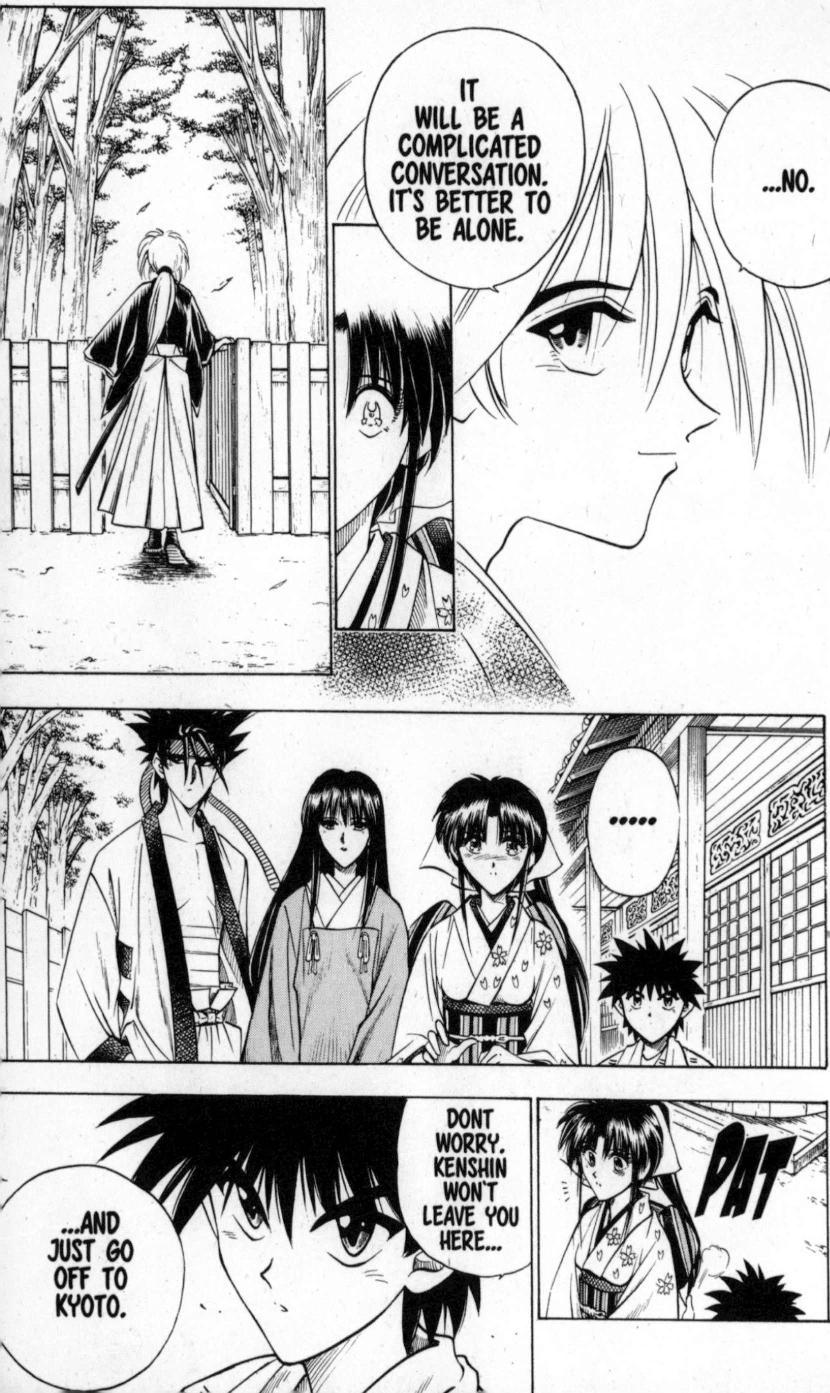

IT WILL BE A COMPLICATED CONVERSATION. IT'S BETTER TO BE ALONE.
...NO.
.....
PAT
DONT WORRY. KENSHIN WON'T LEAVE YOU HERE...
...AND JUST GO OFF TO KYOTO.

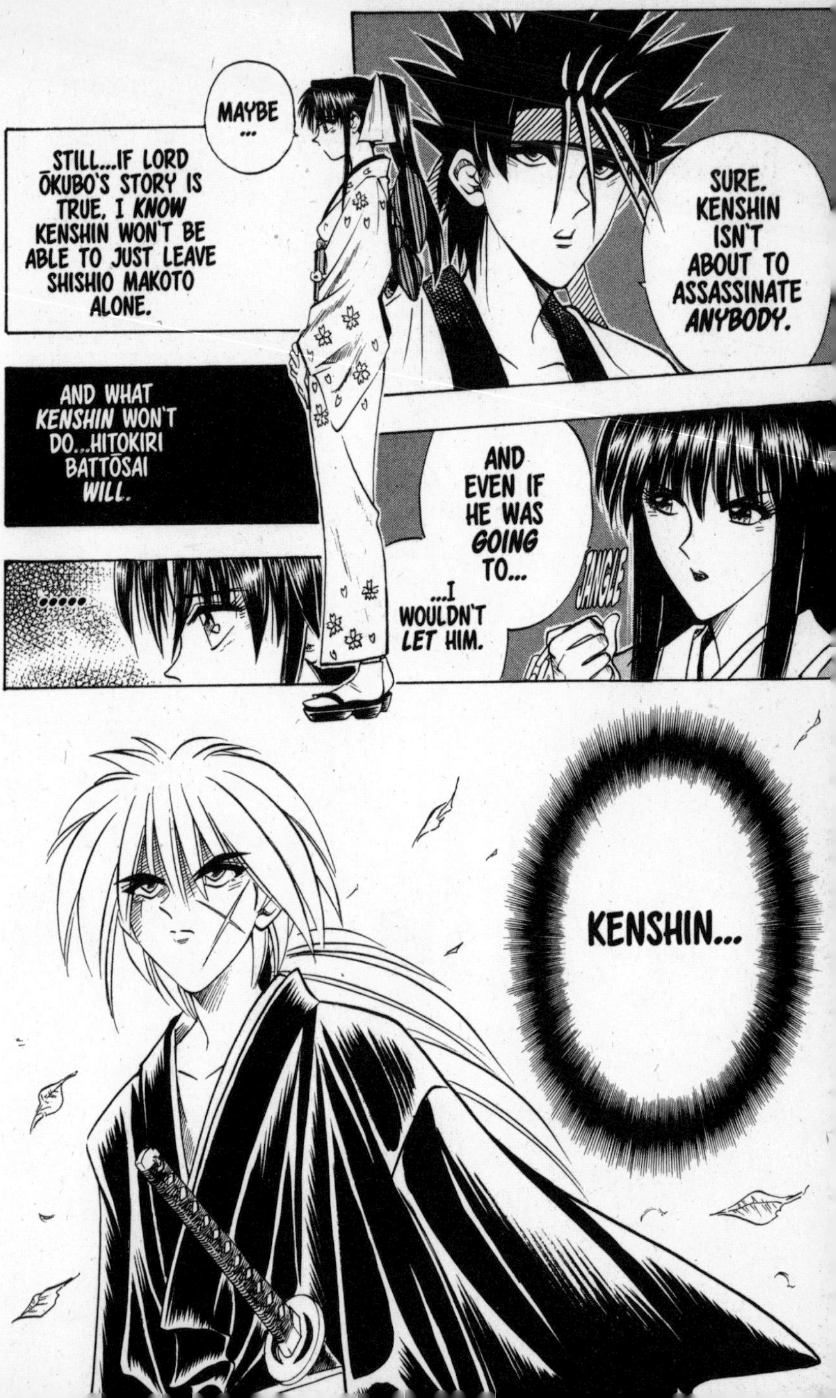
SURE. KENSHIN ISN'T ABOUT TO ASSASSINATE ANYBODY.
MAYBE...
STILL...IF LORD ŌKUBO'S STORY IS TRUE, I KNOW KENSHIN WON'T BE ABLE TO JUST LEAVE SHISHIO MAKOTO ALONE.
AND EVEN IF HE WAS GOING TO...
JANGLE
...I WOULDN'T LET HIM.
AND WHAT KENSHIN WON'T DO...HITOKIRI BATTŌSAI WILL.
......
KENSHIN...

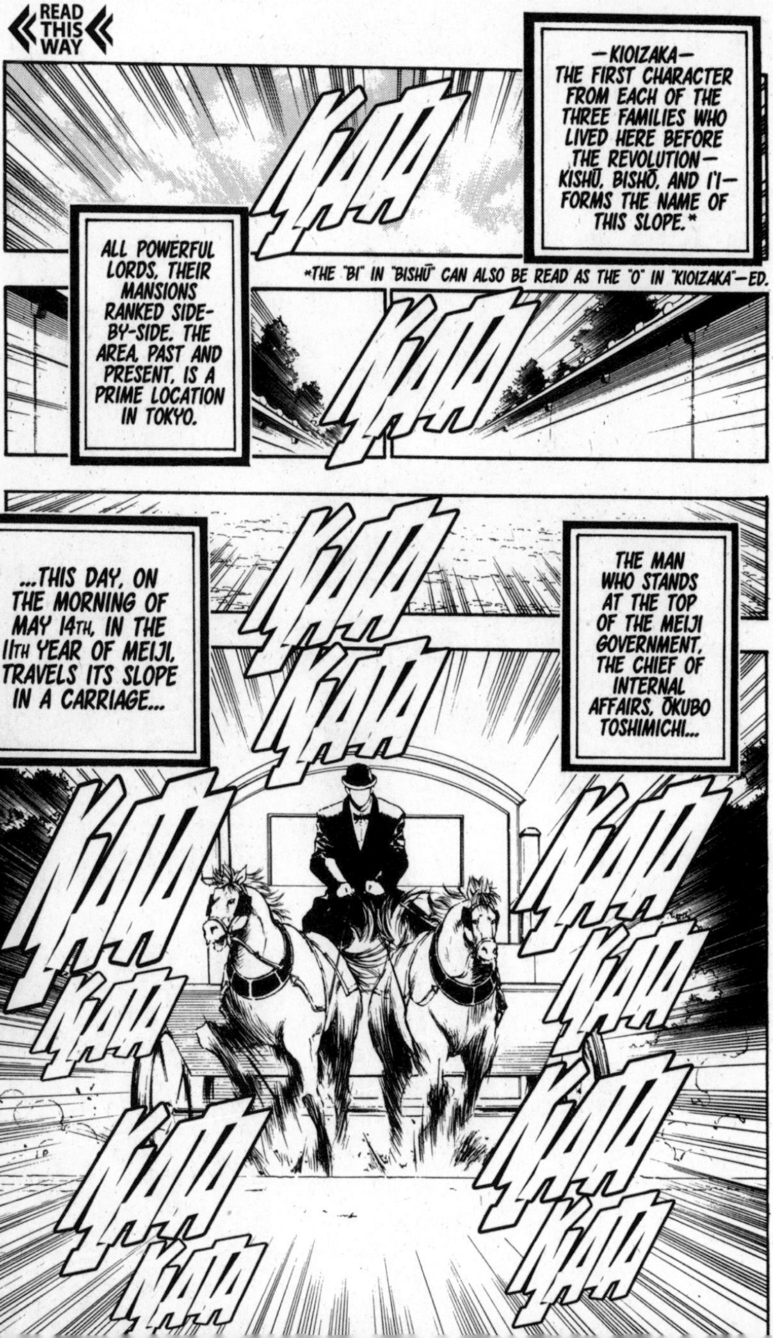
READ THIS WAY
—KIOIZAKA— THE FIRST CHARACTER FROM EACH OF THE THREE FAMILIES WHO LIVED HERE BEFORE THE REVOLUTION—KISHŪ, BISHŌ, AND I'I—FORMS THE NAME OF THIS SLOPE.*
*THE "BI" IN "BISHŪ" CAN ALSO BE READ AS THE "O" IN "KIOIZAKA"—ED.
KAPA
ALL POWERFUL LORDS, THEIR MANSIONS RANKED SIDE-BY-SIDE. THE AREA, PAST AND PRESENT, IS A PRIME LOCATION IN TOKYO.
KAPA
THE MAN WHO STANDS AT THE TOP OF THE MEIJI GOVERNMENT, THE CHIEF OF INTERNAL AFFAIRS, ŌKUBO TOSHIMICHI...
KAPA
KAPA
...THIS DAY, ON THE MORNING OF MAY 14TH, IN THE 11TH YEAR OF MEIJI, TRAVELS ITS SLOPE IN A CARRIAGE...
KAPA
KAPA
KAPA
KAPA
KAPA
KAPA
KAPA
KAPA
KAPA

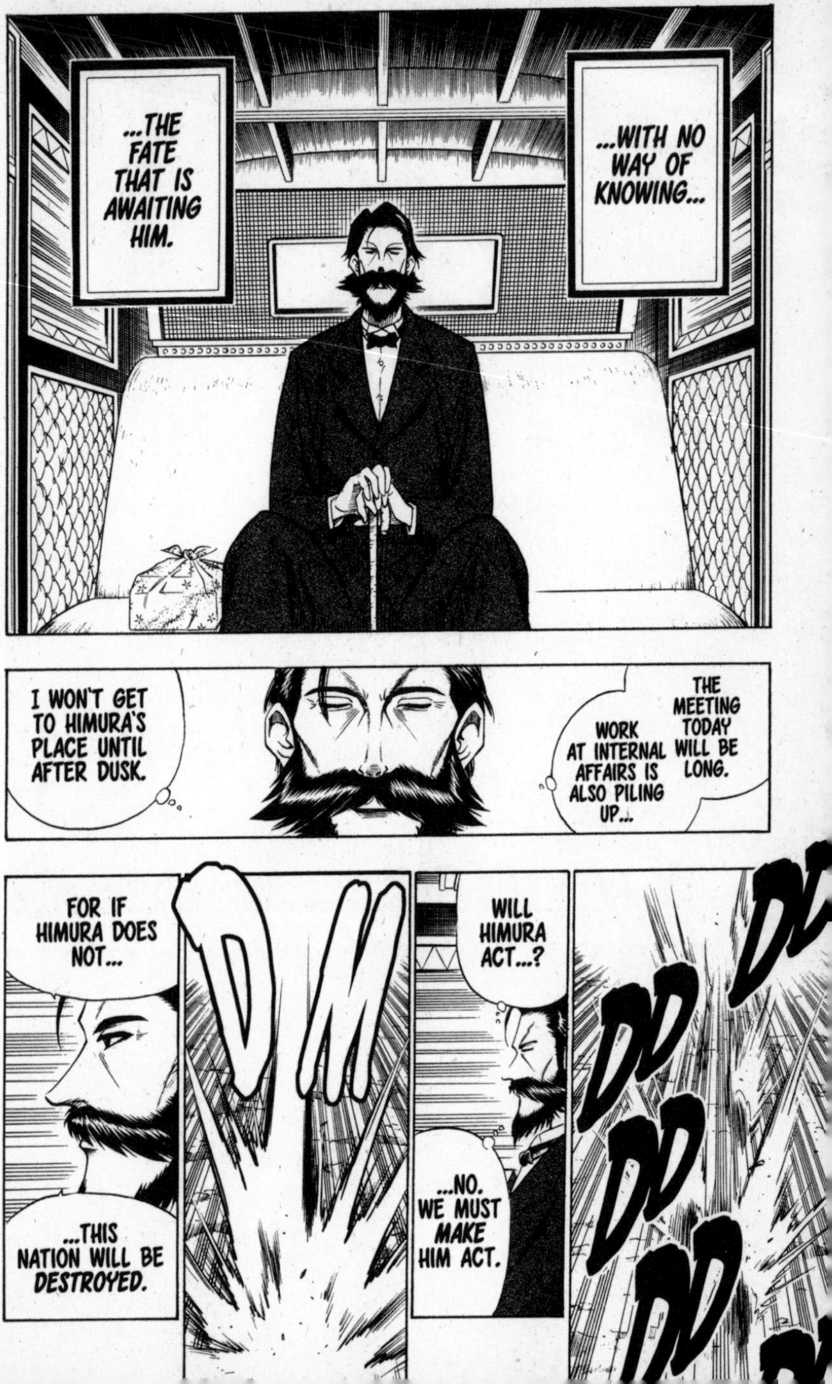

...WITH NO WAY OF KNOWING...
...THE FATE THAT IS AWAITING HIM.
THE MEETING TODAY WILL BE LONG.
WORK AT INTERNAL AFFAIRS IS ALSO PILING UP...
I WON'T GET TO HIMURA'S PLACE UNTIL AFTER DUSK.
DD DD DD DD DD
WILL HIMURA ACT...?
...NO. WE MUST MAKE HIM ACT.
DM
FOR IF HIMURA DOES NOT...
...THIS NATION WILL BE DESTROYED.

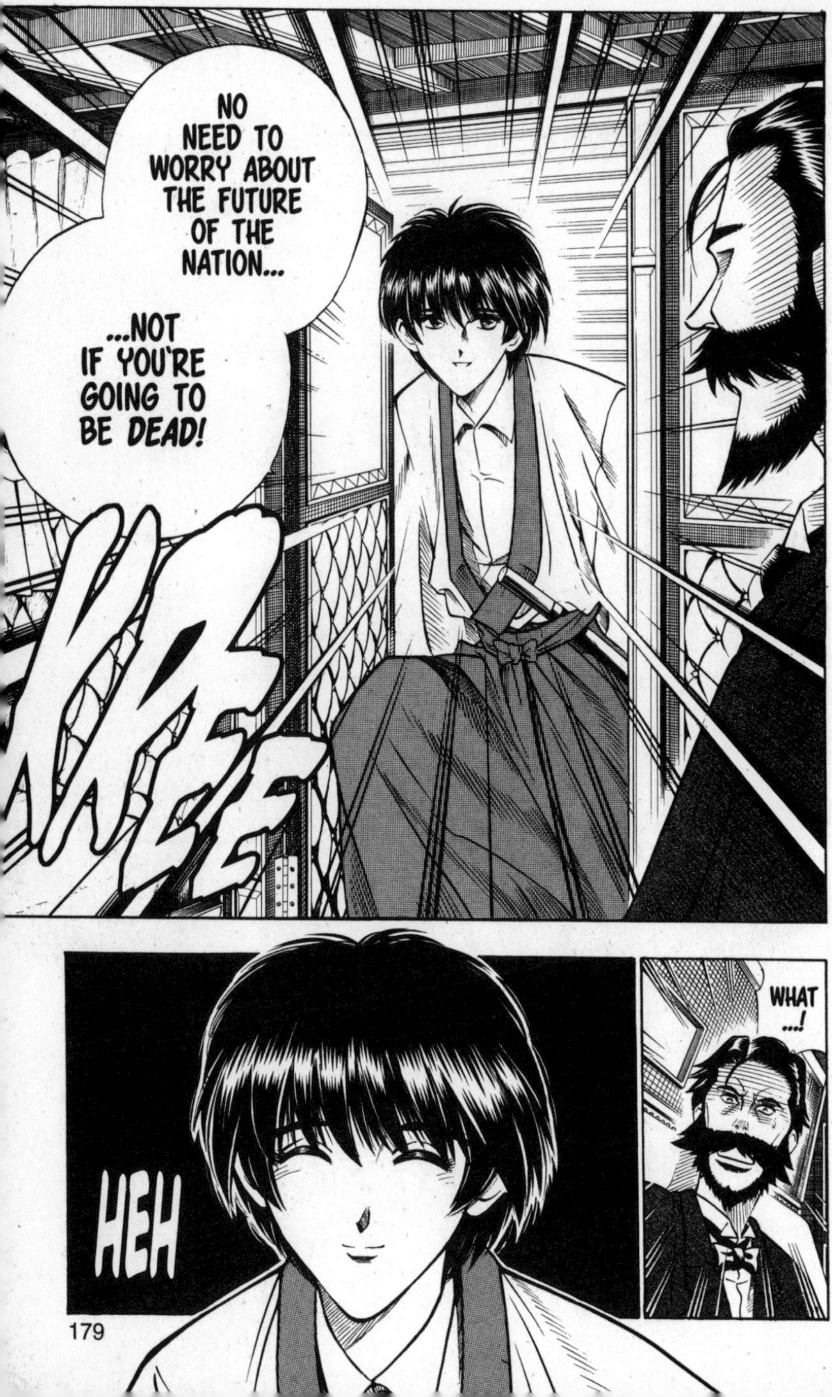
NO NEED TO WORRY ABOUT THE FUTURE OF THE NATION...
...NOT IF YOU'RE GOING TO BE DEAD!
WHAT ...!
HEH

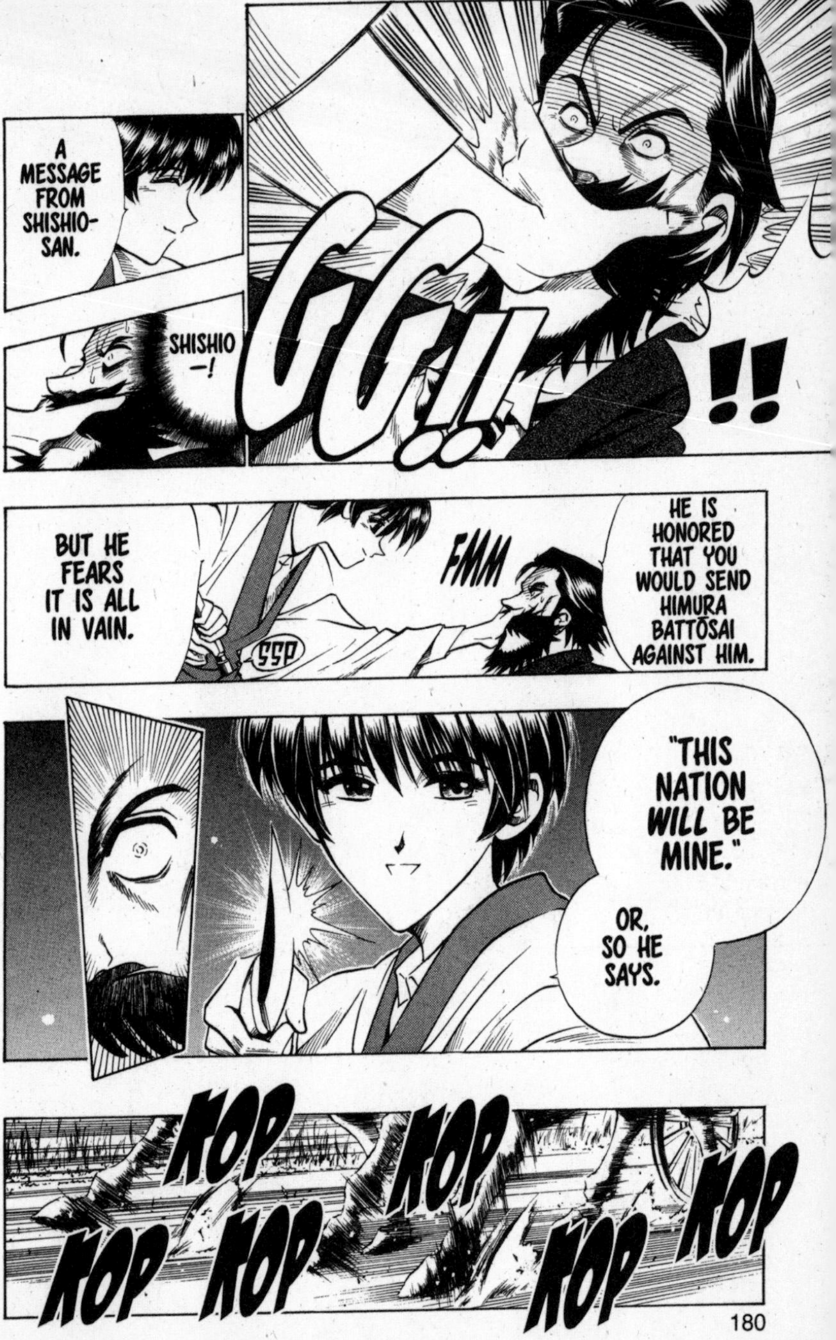
GGH..!!
A MESSAGE FROM SHISHIO-SAN.
SHISHIO—!
HE IS HONORED THAT YOU WOULD SEND HIMURA BATTŌSAI AGAINST HIM.
FMM
SSP
BUT HE FEARS IT IS ALL IN VAIN.
"THIS NATION *WILL* BE MINE."
OR, SO HE SAYS.
KOP KOP KOP KOP KOP KOP KOP KOP

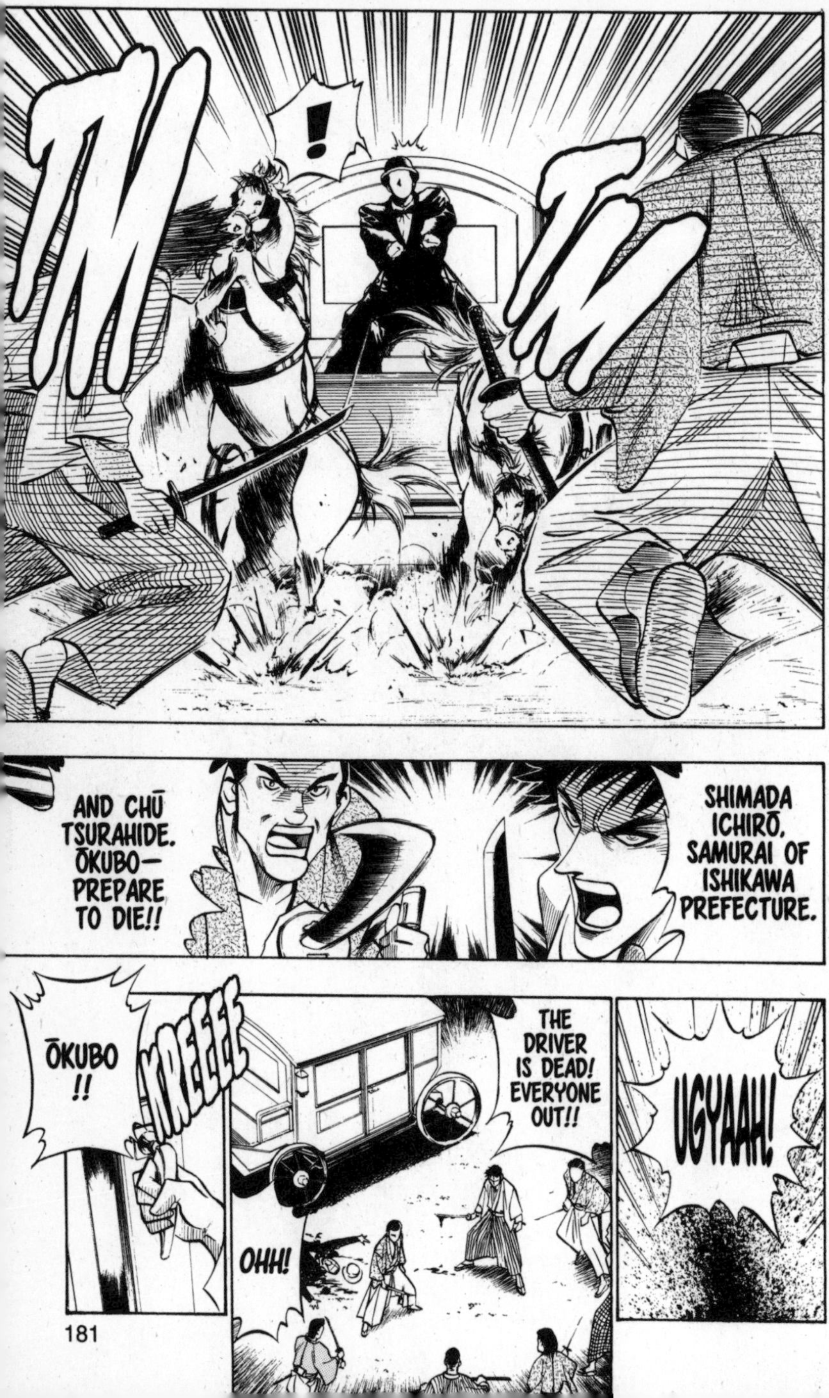
!
SHIMADA ICHIRŌ, SAMURAI OF ISHIKAWA PREFECTURE.
AND CHŪ TSURAHIDE. ŌKUBO— PREPARE TO DIE!!
UGYAAH!
THE DRIVER IS DEAD! EVERYONE OUT!!
OHH!
ŌKUBO !!

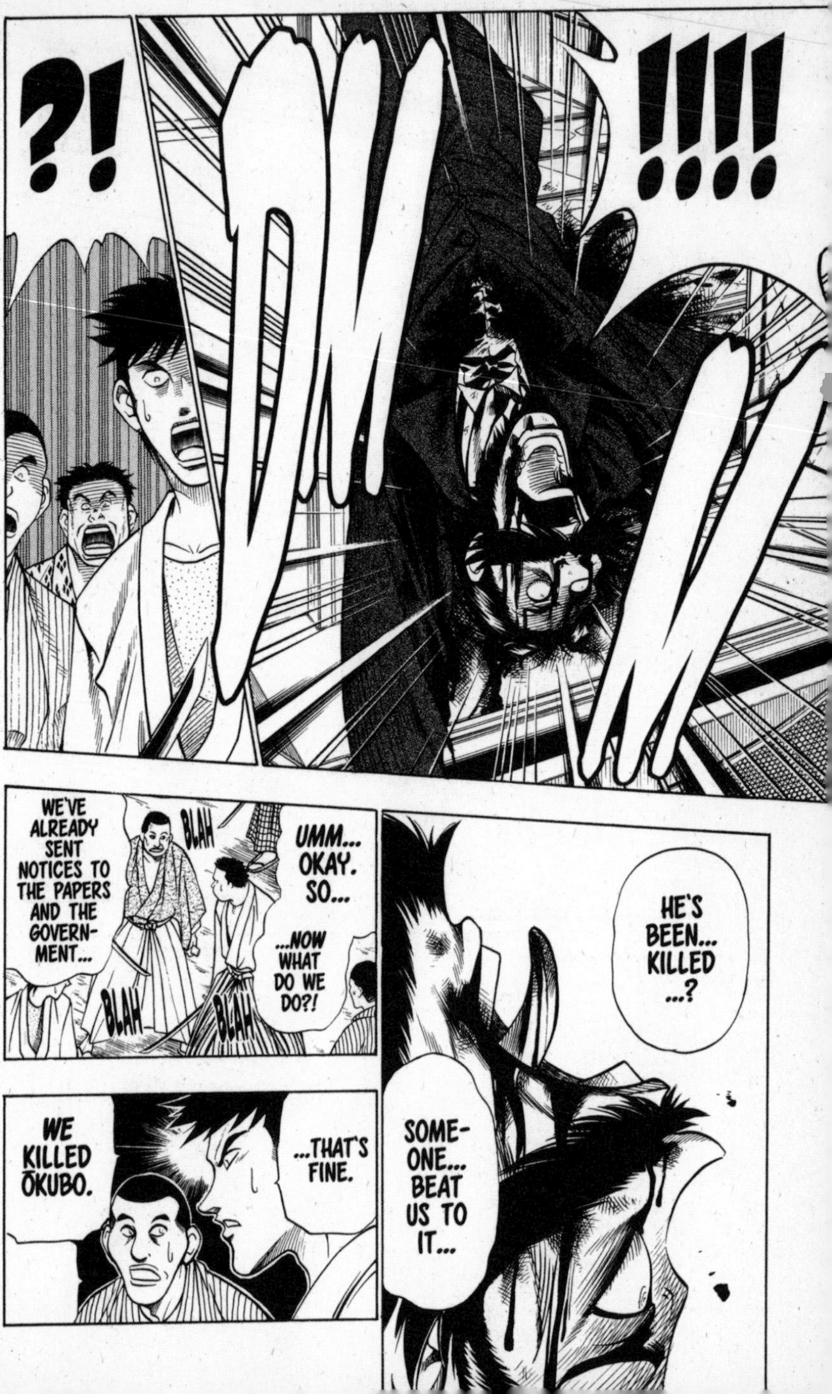
!!!!
?!
HE'S BEEN... KILLED ...?
SOME-ONE... BEAT US TO IT...
UMM... OKAY. SO...
...NOW WHAT DO WE DO?!
BLAH
WE'VE ALREADY SENT NOTICES TO THE PAPERS AND THE GOVERN-MENT...
BLAH
BLAH
...THAT'S FINE.
WE KILLED ŌKUBO.

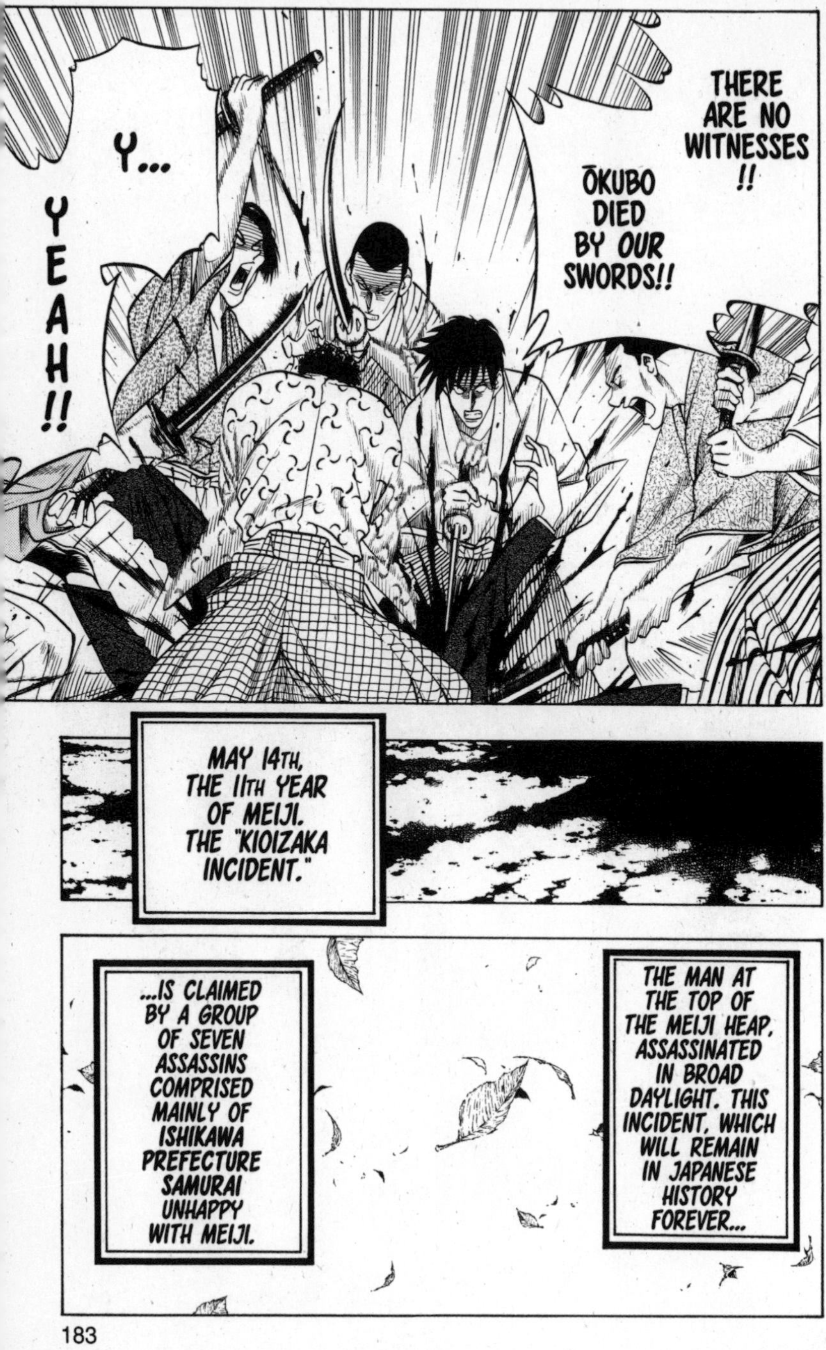
THERE ARE NO WITNESSES!!
ŌKUBO DIED BY OUR SWORDS!!
Y...
YEAH!!
MAY 14TH, THE 11TH YEAR OF MEIJI. THE "KIOIZAKA INCIDENT."
THE MAN AT THE TOP OF THE MEIJI HEAP, ASSASSINATED IN BROAD DAYLIGHT. THIS INCIDENT, WHICH WILL REMAIN IN JAPANESE HISTORY FOREVER...
...IS CLAIMED BY A GROUP OF SEVEN ASSASSINS COMPRISED MAINLY OF ISHIKAWA PREFECTURE SAMURAI UNHAPPY WITH MEIJI.

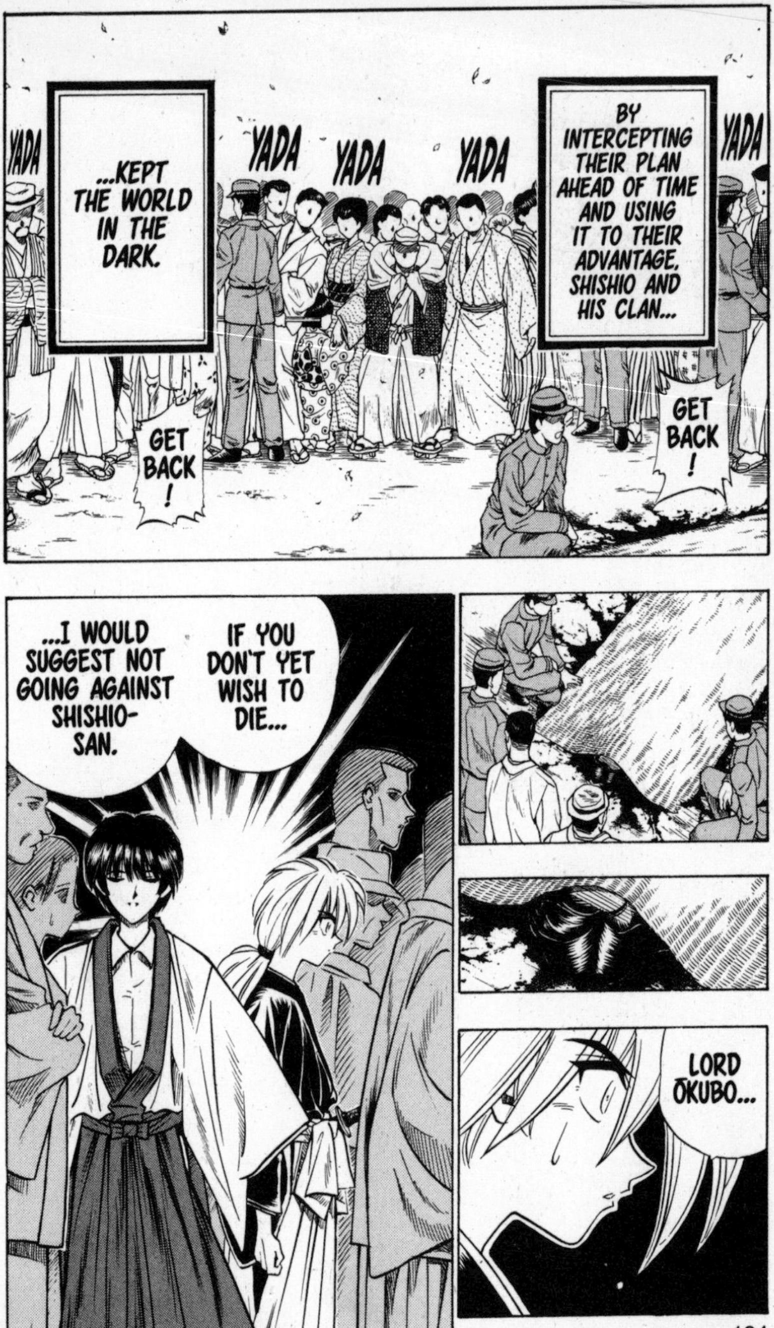
YADA
BY INTERCEPTING THEIR PLAN AHEAD OF TIME AND USING IT TO THEIR ADVANTAGE, SHISHIO AND HIS CLAN...
YADA
YADA
YADA
...KEPT THE WORLD IN THE DARK.
YADA
GET BACK!
GET BACK!
LORD ŌKUBO...
IF YOU DON'T YET WISH TO DIE...
...I WOULD SUGGEST NOT GOING AGAINST SHISHIO-SAN.

READ THIS WAY

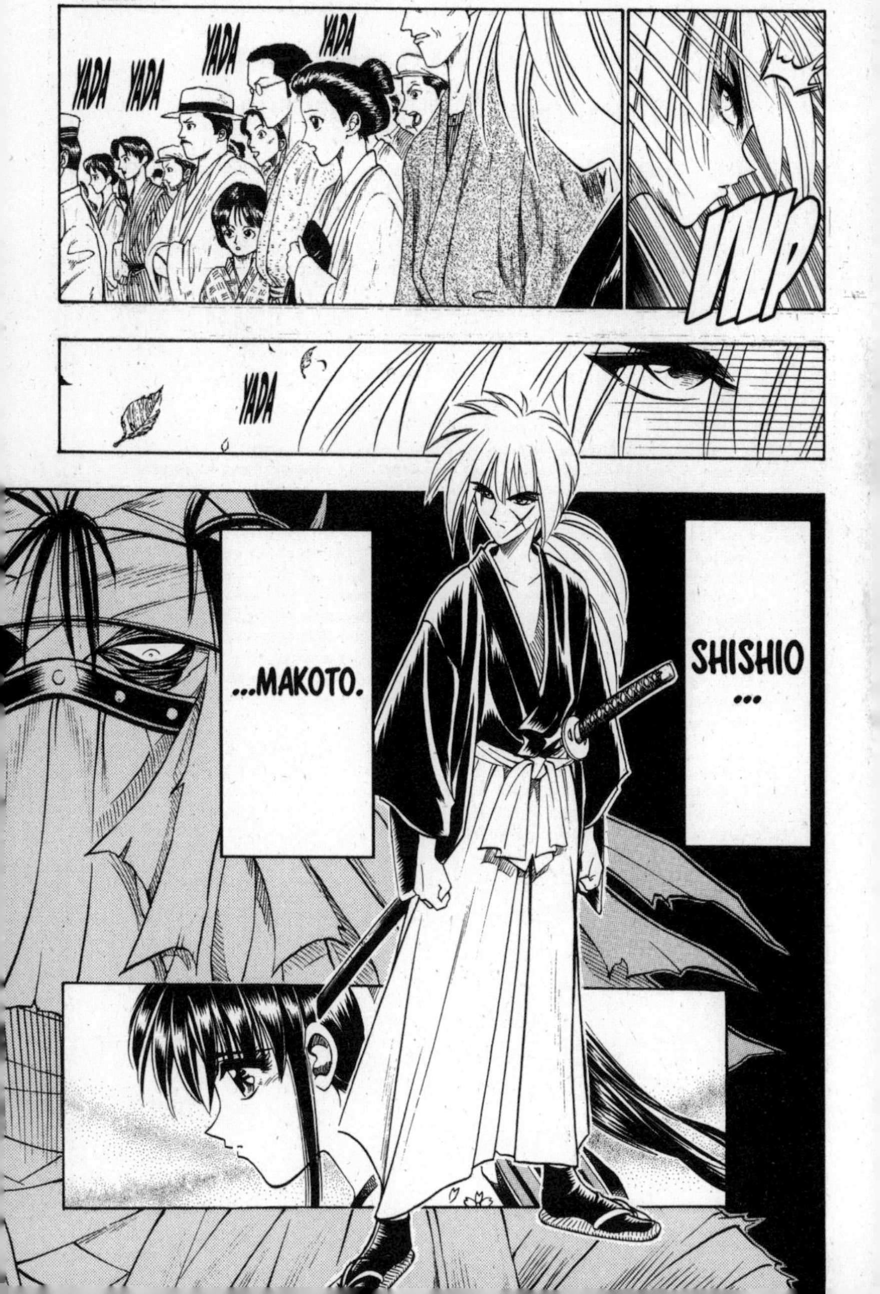
VMP
YADA
YADA
YADA
YADA
YADA
SHISHIO ...
...MAKOTO.

The Secret Life of Characters (22)

—Ōkubo Toshimichi—

Another historical personage—one of the three greatest revolutionaries. As with other real-life characters, I drew him to suit my own needs.

Ōkubo is well-known as a good friend of Saigō Takamori, but possibly because of the bias Japanese people have toward Saigō, Ōkubo is thought to be a sly, cunning man...and Watsuki finds himself disappointed by this. It is true that, during the Bakumatsu, Ōkubo had been the strategist but, after the revolution, he was very ethical, never enriching himself personally through politics (Saigō was sent off to his death because of it). Ōkubo is a great example of what a politician should be, if you ask Watsuki.

After his assassination at Kioizaka, Ōkubo's estate was audited and everyone was curious to know just *how* rich the richest man in Japan had been. As it turned out, he had only 500 yen in cash [in current terms, about $200,000] and, on top of that, was 6,000 yen in debt [about $2.4 million] because of loans taken out to cover government shortfalls. During a time when many politicians conspired with the wealthy to enrich their own personal fortunes, Ōkubo was probably the most honest of them all...and still he was dubbed "Saigō's murderer" and was hated by the people of his home prefecture, who refused to allow his remains to be interred there. It wasn't until the Heisei period that Ōkubo was even acknowledged by his people...that's right, the man who gave up everything in order to help Japan flourish wasn't allowed to go home for over 100 years. Ōkubo Toshimichi is definitely someone who deserves to be shown a little more love, if you ask me.

For a design, I'd originally wanted to look over his portrait photos, but was unable to find them. I drew him instead from the photo of a statue... but it turned out to be not similar at all. I notice when I look back now that he resembles President Lincoln (another man I like). That must have found its way in there, somehow...

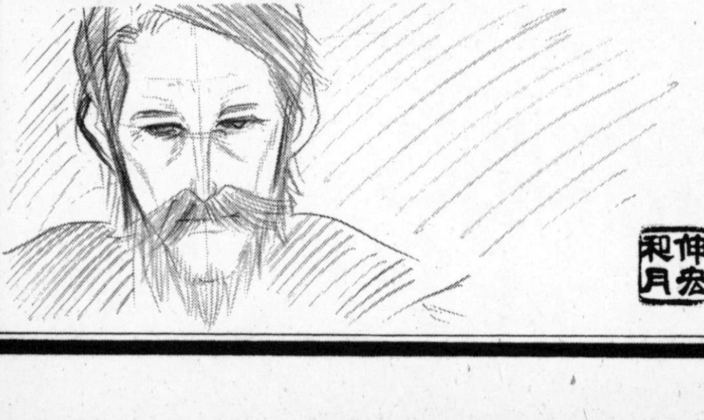

伸宏
和月

Act 57
Meiji 11, May 14th–Afternoon

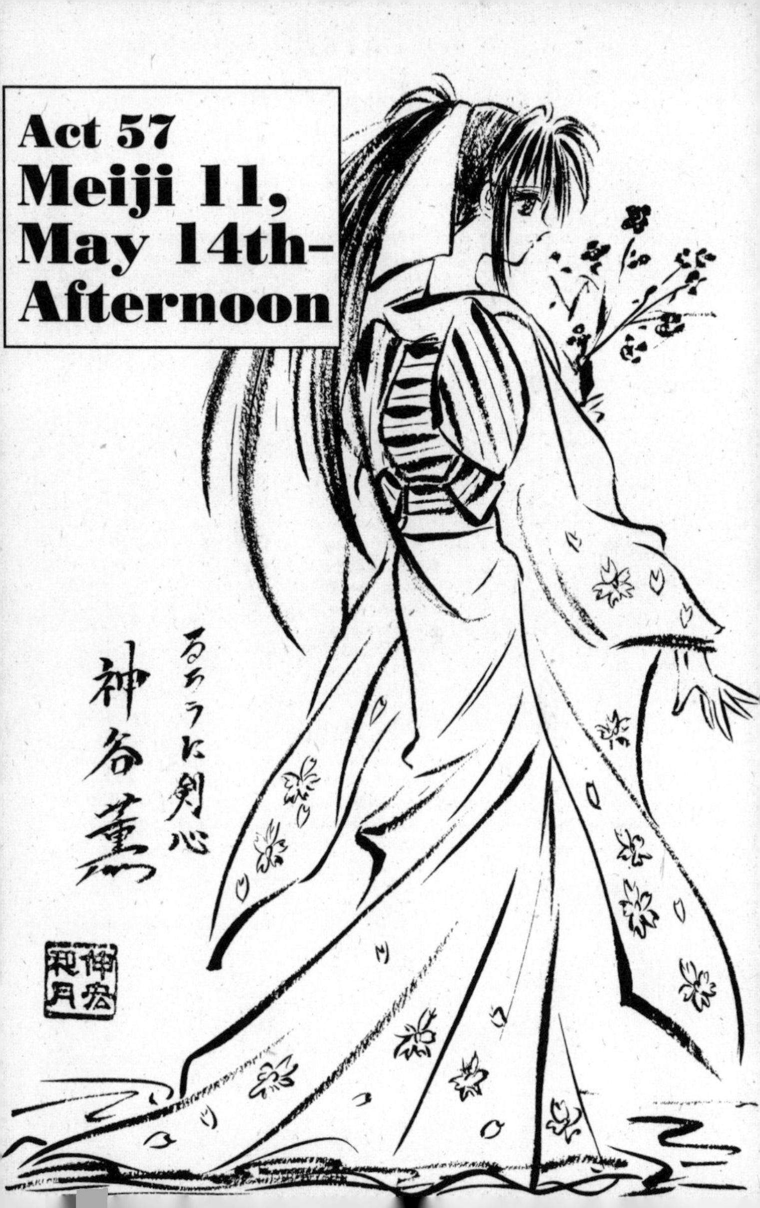
るろうに剣心
神谷薫
伸宏
和月

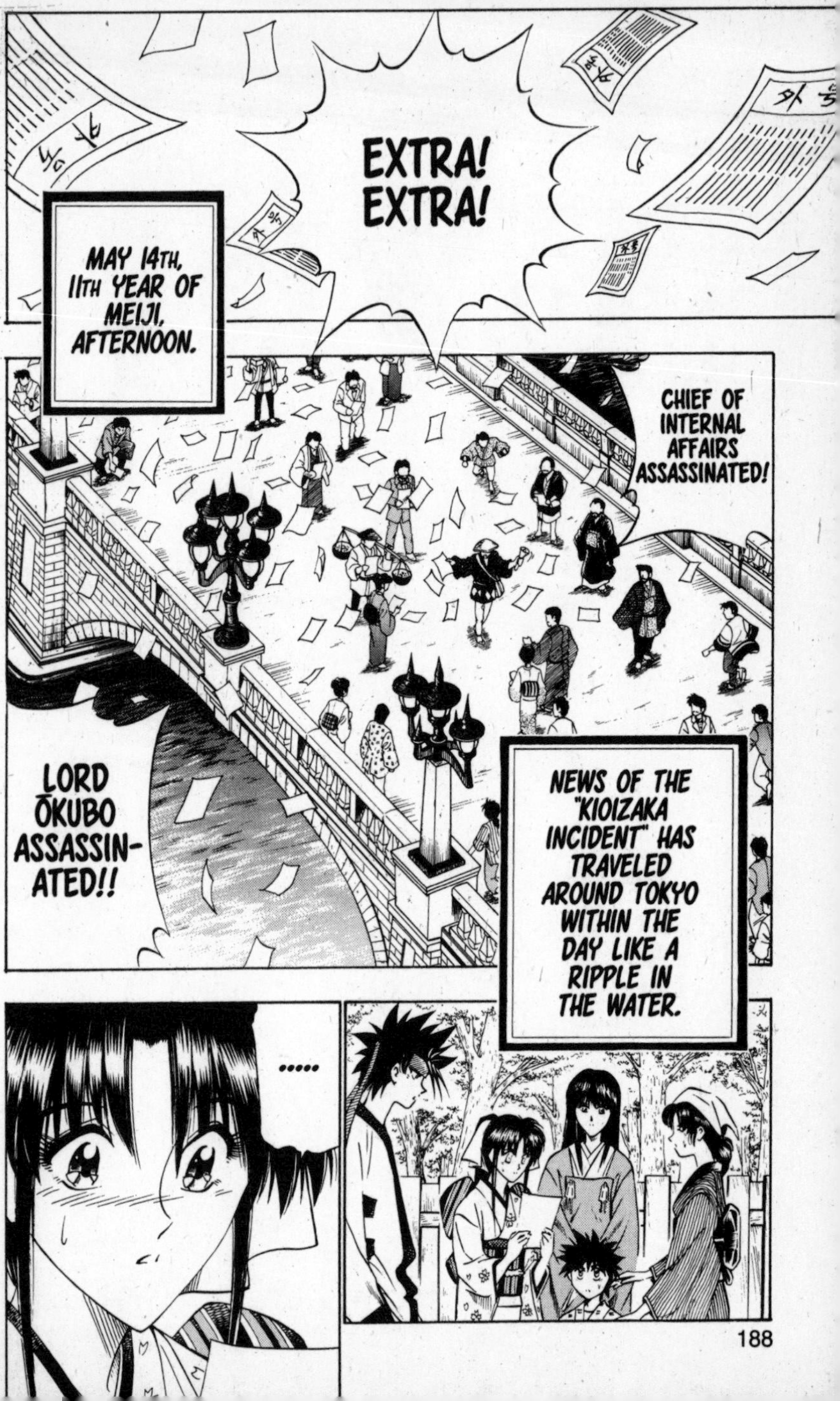
EXTRA! EXTRA!
MAY 14TH, 11TH YEAR OF MEIJI, AFTERNOON.
CHIEF OF INTERNAL AFFAIRS ASSASSINATED!
LORD ŌKUBO ASSASSIN-ATED!!
NEWS OF THE "KIOIZAKA INCIDENT" HAS TRAVELED AROUND TOKYO WITHIN THE DAY LIKE A RIPPLE IN THE WATER.
......

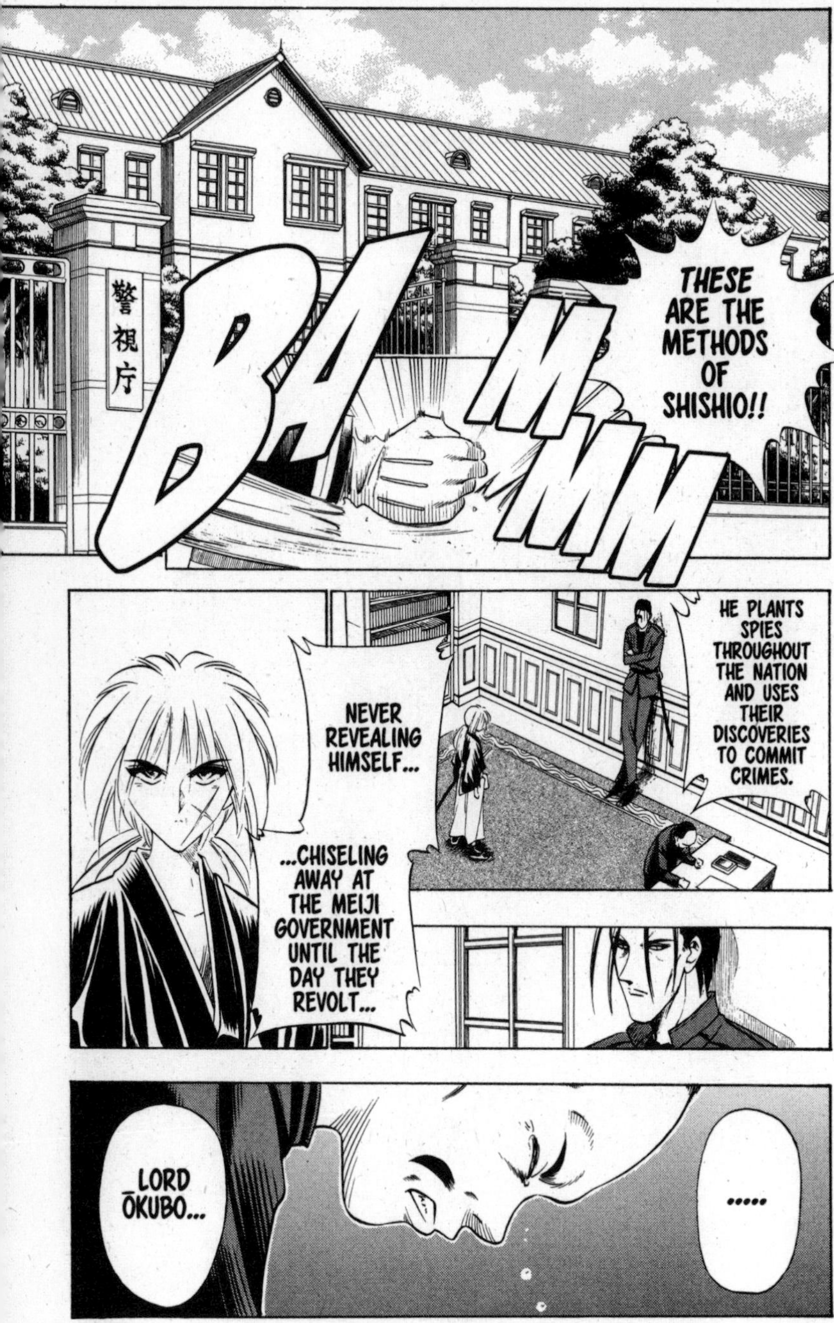

警視庁
THESE ARE THE METHODS OF SHISHIO!!
BAMMM
HE PLANTS SPIES THROUGHOUT THE NATION AND USES THEIR DISCOVERIES TO COMMIT CRIMES.
NEVER REVEALING HIMSELF...
...CHISELING AWAY AT THE MEIJI GOVERNMENT UNTIL THE DAY THEY REVOLT...
.....
LORD ŌKUBO...

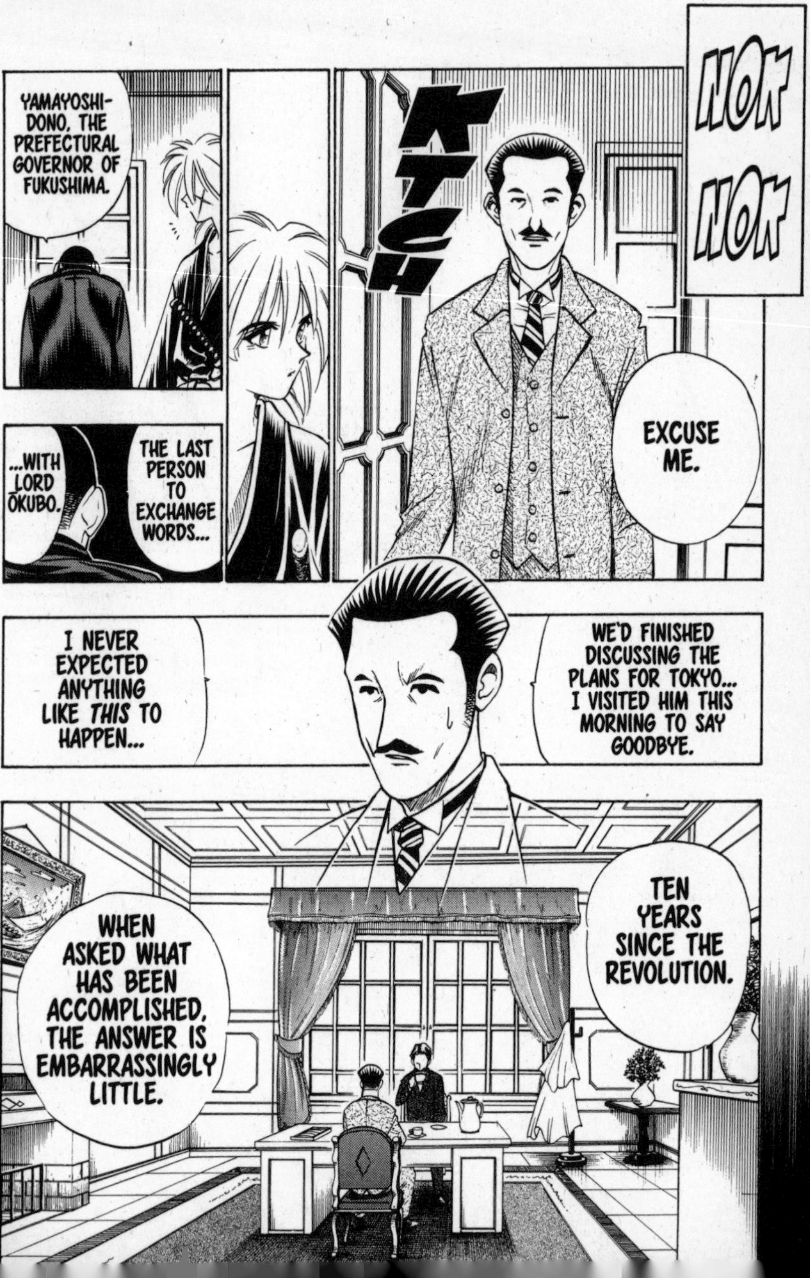
NOK NOK
KTCH
EXCUSE ME.
YAMAYOSHI-DONO, THE PREFECTURAL GOVERNOR OF FUKUSHIMA.
THE LAST PERSON TO EXCHANGE WORDS...
...WITH LORD ŌKUBO.
WE'D FINISHED DISCUSSING THE PLANS FOR TOKYO... I VISITED HIM THIS MORNING TO SAY GOODBYE.
I NEVER EXPECTED ANYTHING LIKE *THIS* TO HAPPEN...
TEN YEARS SINCE THE REVOLUTION.
WHEN ASKED WHAT HAS BEEN ACCOMPLISHED, THE ANSWER IS EMBARRASSINGLY LITTLE.

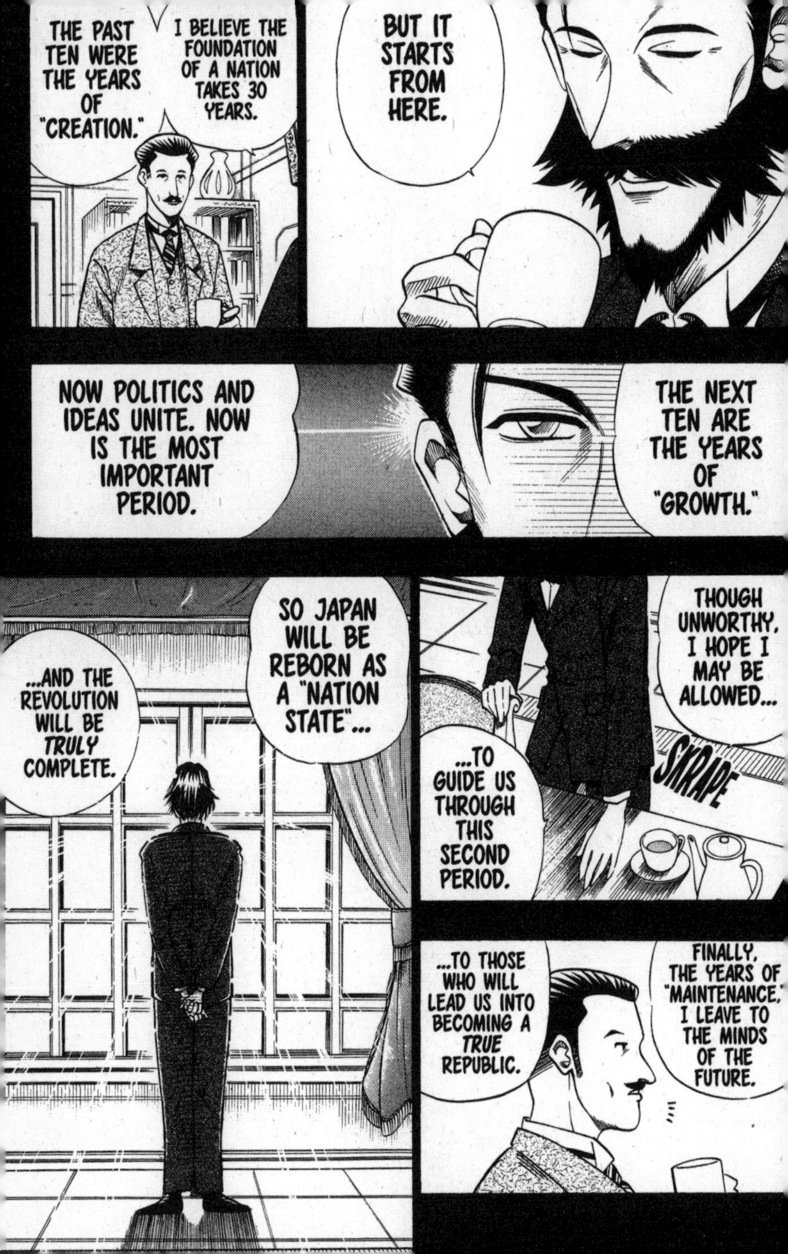
BUT IT STARTS FROM HERE.
I BELIEVE THE FOUNDATION OF A NATION TAKES 30 YEARS.
THE PAST TEN WERE THE YEARS OF "CREATION."
THE NEXT TEN ARE THE YEARS OF "GROWTH."
NOW POLITICS AND IDEAS UNITE. NOW IS THE MOST IMPORTANT PERIOD.
THOUGH UNWORTHY, I HOPE I MAY BE ALLOWED...
SKRAPE
...TO GUIDE US THROUGH THIS SECOND PERIOD.
FINALLY, THE YEARS OF "MAINTENANCE," I LEAVE TO THE MINDS OF THE FUTURE.
...TO THOSE WHO WILL LEAD US INTO BECOMING A *TRUE* REPUBLIC.
SO JAPAN WILL BE REBORN AS A "NATION STATE"...
...AND THE REVOLUTION WILL BE *TRULY* COMPLETE.

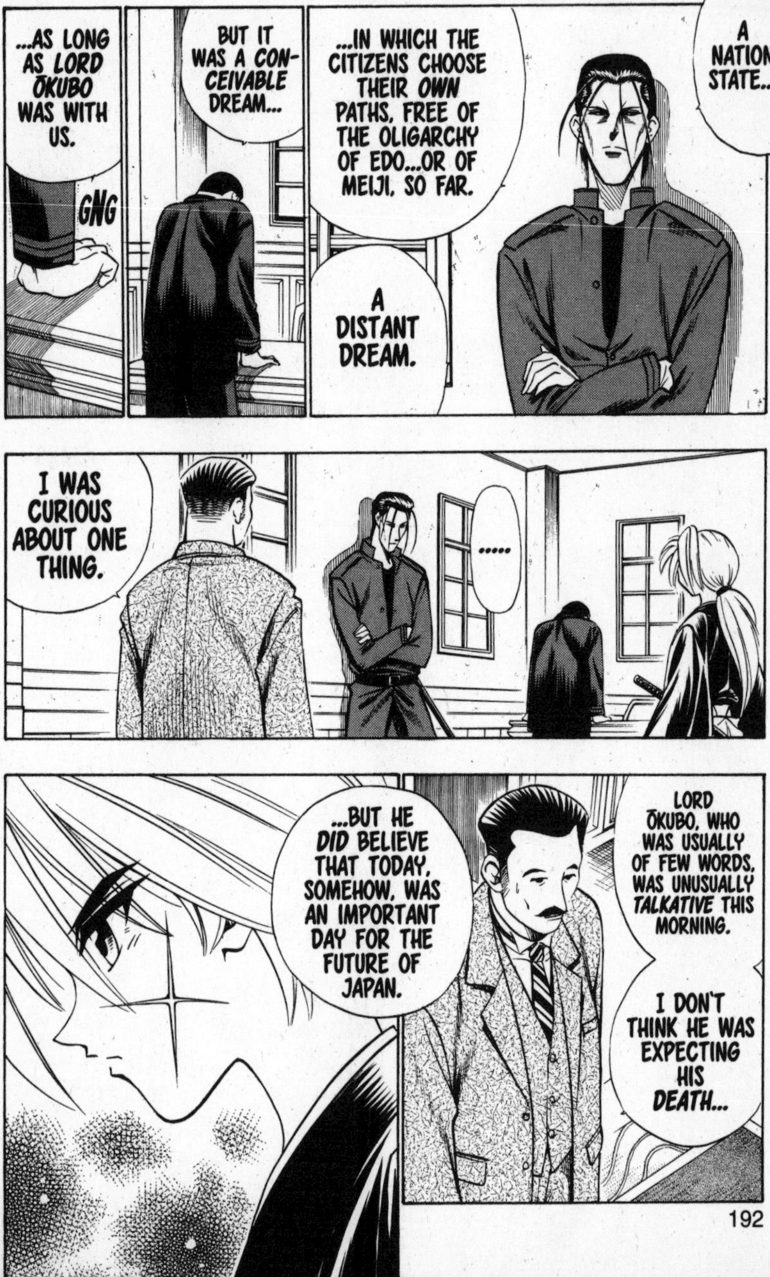
A NATION STATE...
...IN WHICH THE CITIZENS CHOOSE THEIR *OWN* PATHS, FREE OF THE OLIGARCHY OF EDO...OR OF MEIJI, SO FAR.
A DISTANT DREAM.
BUT IT WAS A *CONCEIVABLE* DREAM...
...AS LONG AS *LORD ŌKUBO* WAS WITH US.
GNG
.....
I WAS CURIOUS ABOUT ONE THING.
LORD ŌKUBO, WHO WAS USUALLY OF FEW WORDS, WAS UNUSUALLY *TALKATIVE* THIS MORNING.
I DON'T THINK HE WAS EXPECTING HIS *DEATH*...
...BUT HE *DID* BELIEVE THAT TODAY, SOMEHOW, WAS AN IMPORTANT DAY FOR THE FUTURE OF JAPAN.

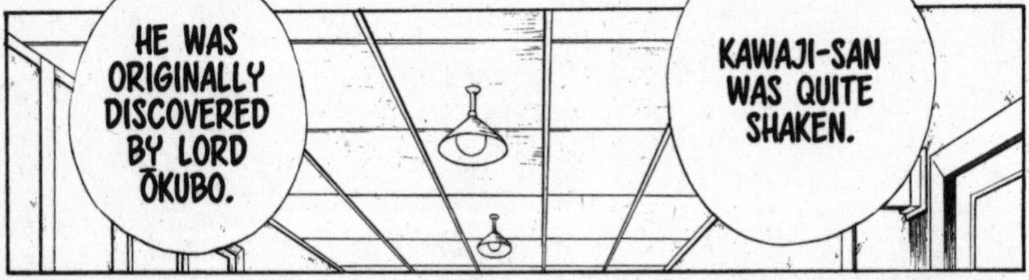
KAWAJI-SAN WAS QUITE SHAKEN.
HE WAS ORIGINALLY DISCOVERED BY LORD ŌKUBO.

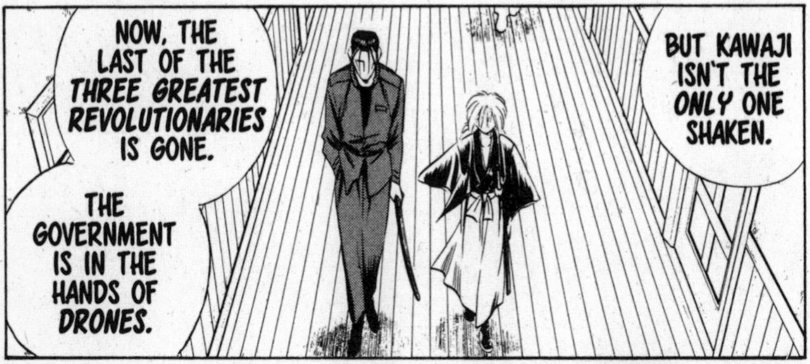
BUT KAWAJI ISN'T THE ONLY ONE SHAKEN.
NOW, THE LAST OF THE THREE GREATEST REVOLUTIONARIES IS GONE.
THE GOVERNMENT IS IN THE HANDS OF DRONES.

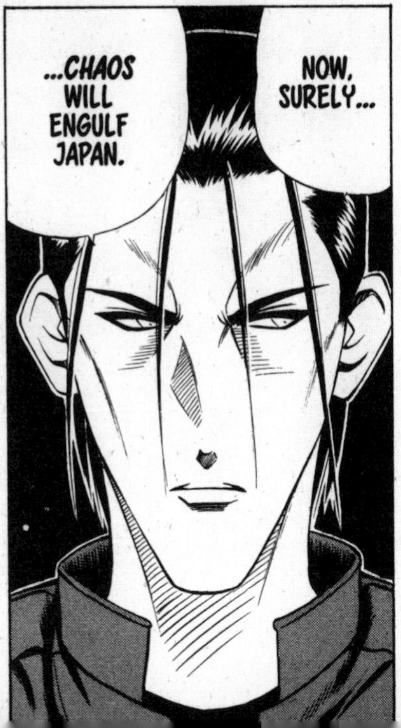
NOW, SURELY...
...CHAOS WILL ENGULF JAPAN.

Let's end this on a lighter note—and talk about games! Watsuki finally got his PlayStation. He also got a Sega Saturn. (N-san and friends, thank you for that! Please come and hang out again.) Sadly, though, I haven't been able to use either system—they've turned into the assistants' gaming machines! I haven't got the time.... (Dear, oh dear. So much for the "lighter note"!) I'm definitely going to play "Vampire" and "V.F 2," though!! I'm also going to master "(Shin) Samurai Spirits," even if I'm nowhere near there yet. (Only to the extent it won't affect "RuroKen," naturally.) See you next volume!

伸宏和月

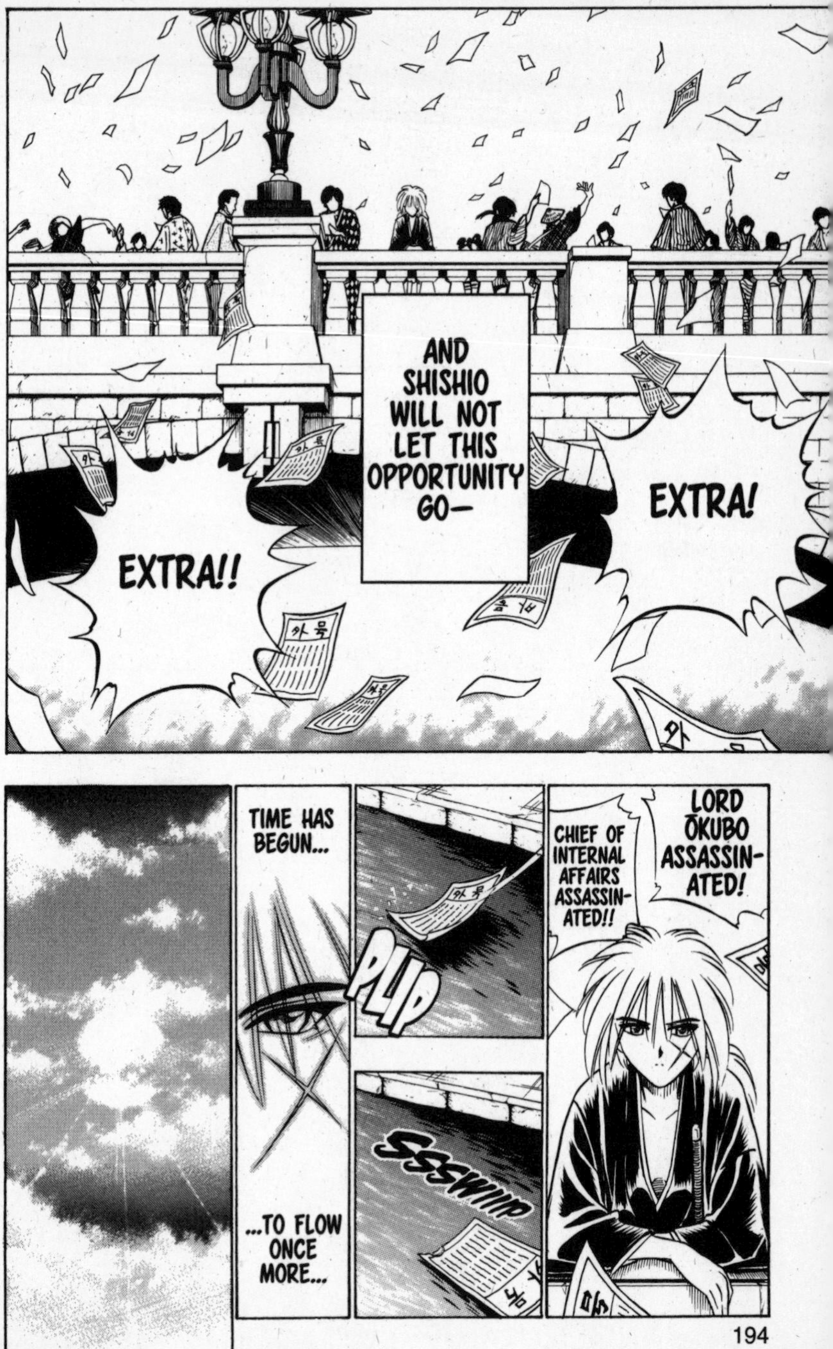
EXTRA!
AND SHISHIO WILL NOT LET THIS OPPORTUNITY GO—
EXTRA!!
LORD ŌKUBO ASSASSINATED!
CHIEF OF INTERNAL AFFAIRS ASSASSINATED!!
PLIP
SSSWIIIP
TIME HAS BEGUN...
...TO FLOW ONCE MORE...

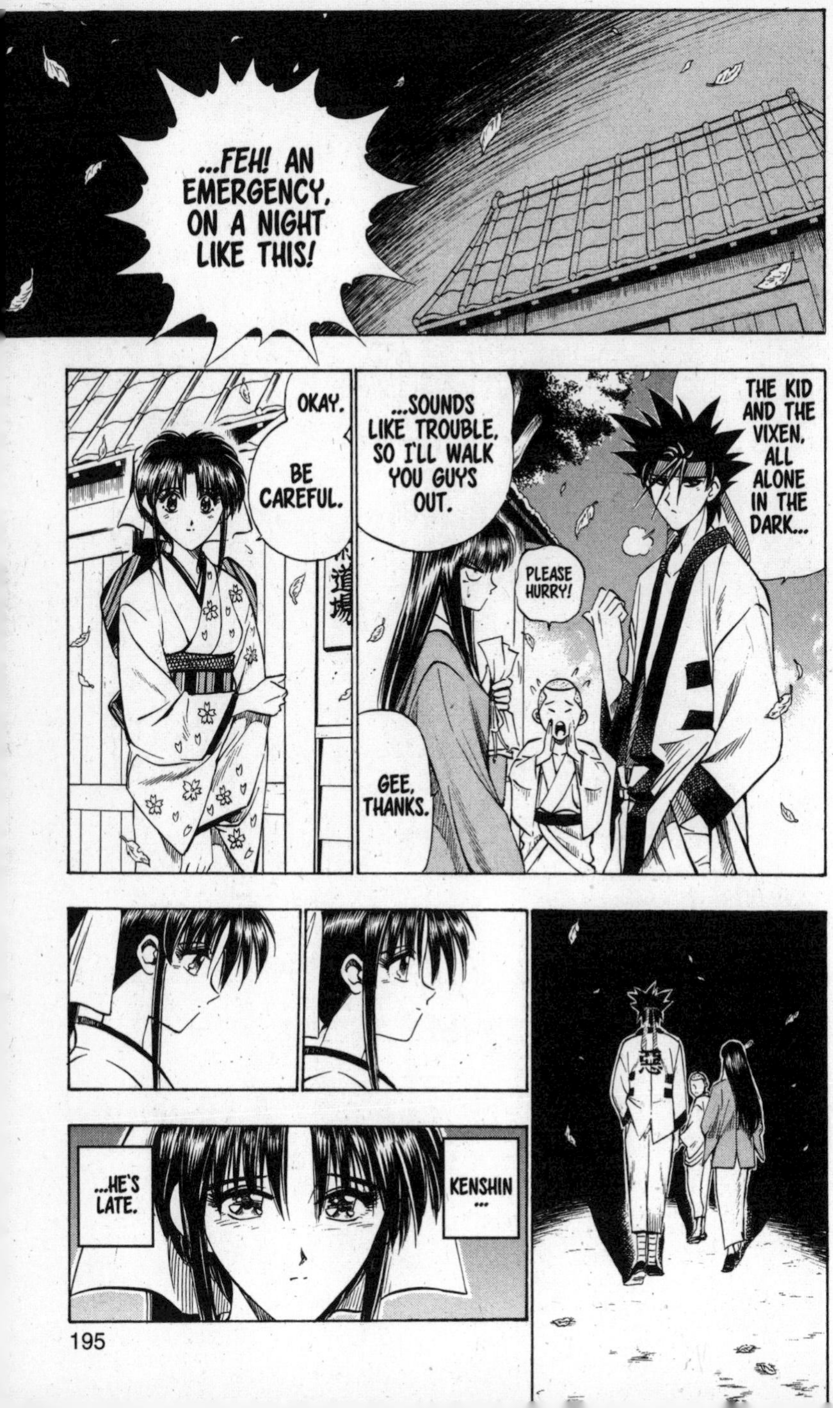
...FEH! AN EMERGENCY, ON A NIGHT LIKE THIS!
THE KID AND THE VIXEN, ALL ALONE IN THE DARK...
...SOUNDS LIKE TROUBLE, SO I'LL WALK YOU GUYS OUT.
PLEASE HURRY!
GEE, THANKS.
OKAY.
BE CAREFUL.
KENSHIN ...
...HE'S LATE.

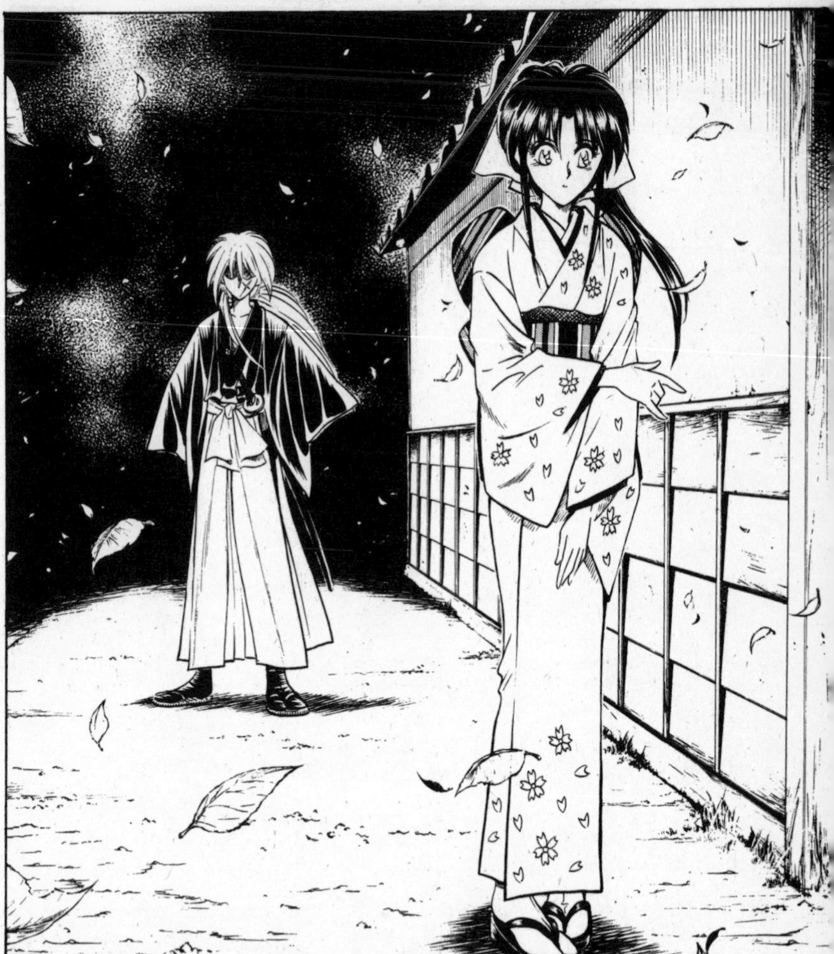

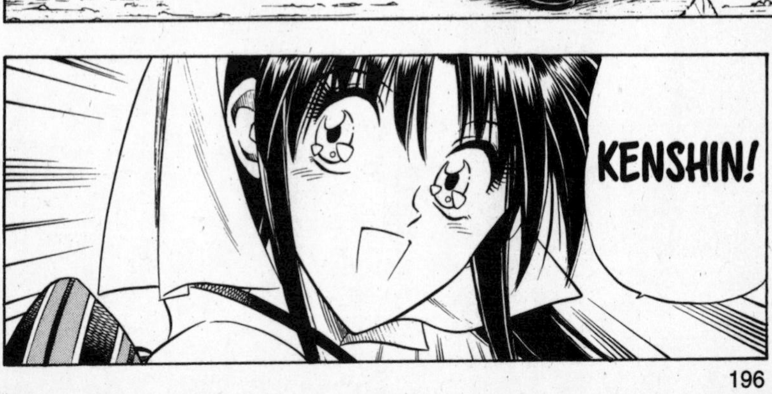
KENSHIN!

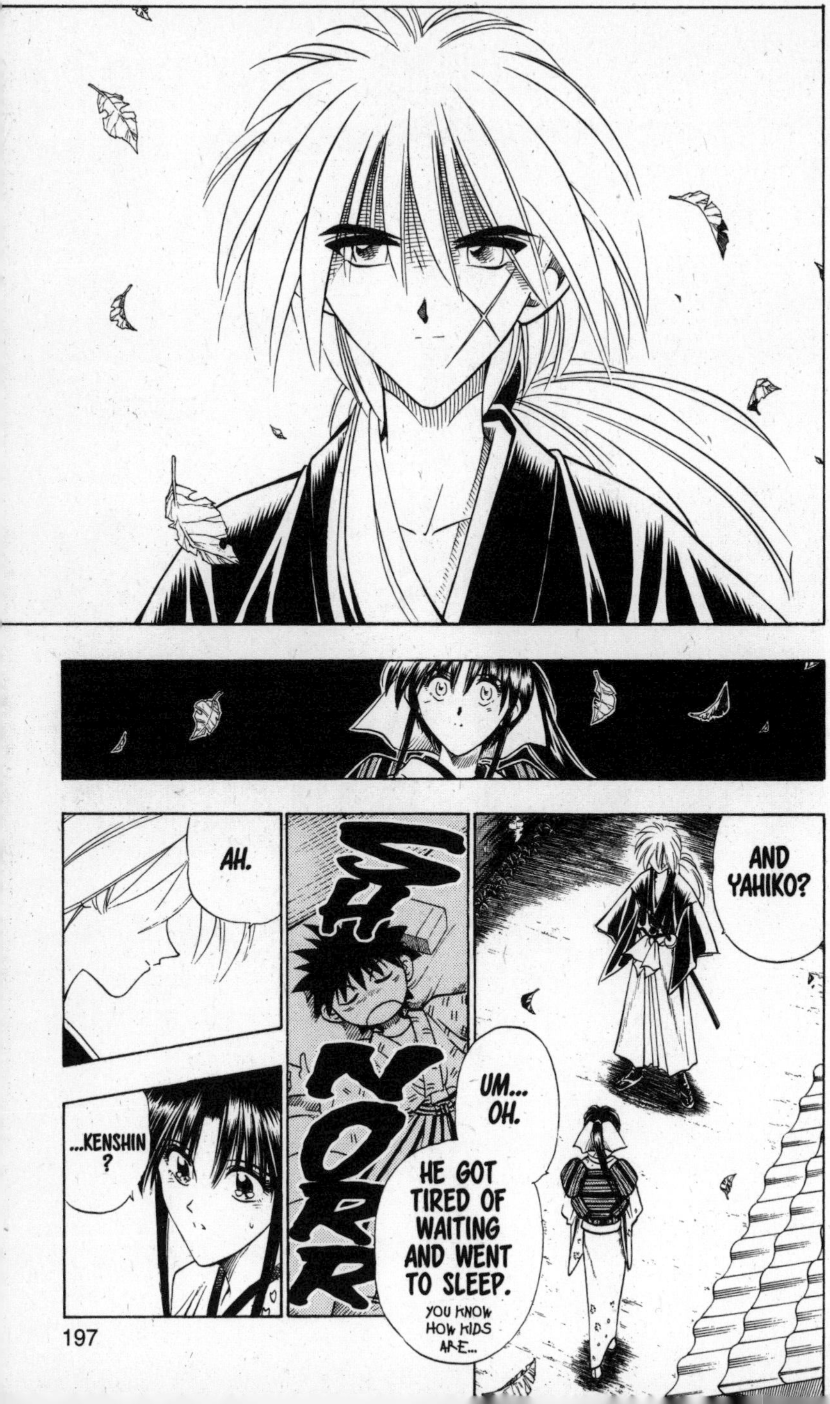
AND YAHIKO?
UM... OH.
HE GOT TIRED OF WAITING AND WENT TO SLEEP.
YOU KNOW HOW KIDS ARE...
AH.
...KENSHIN ?

READ THIS WAY

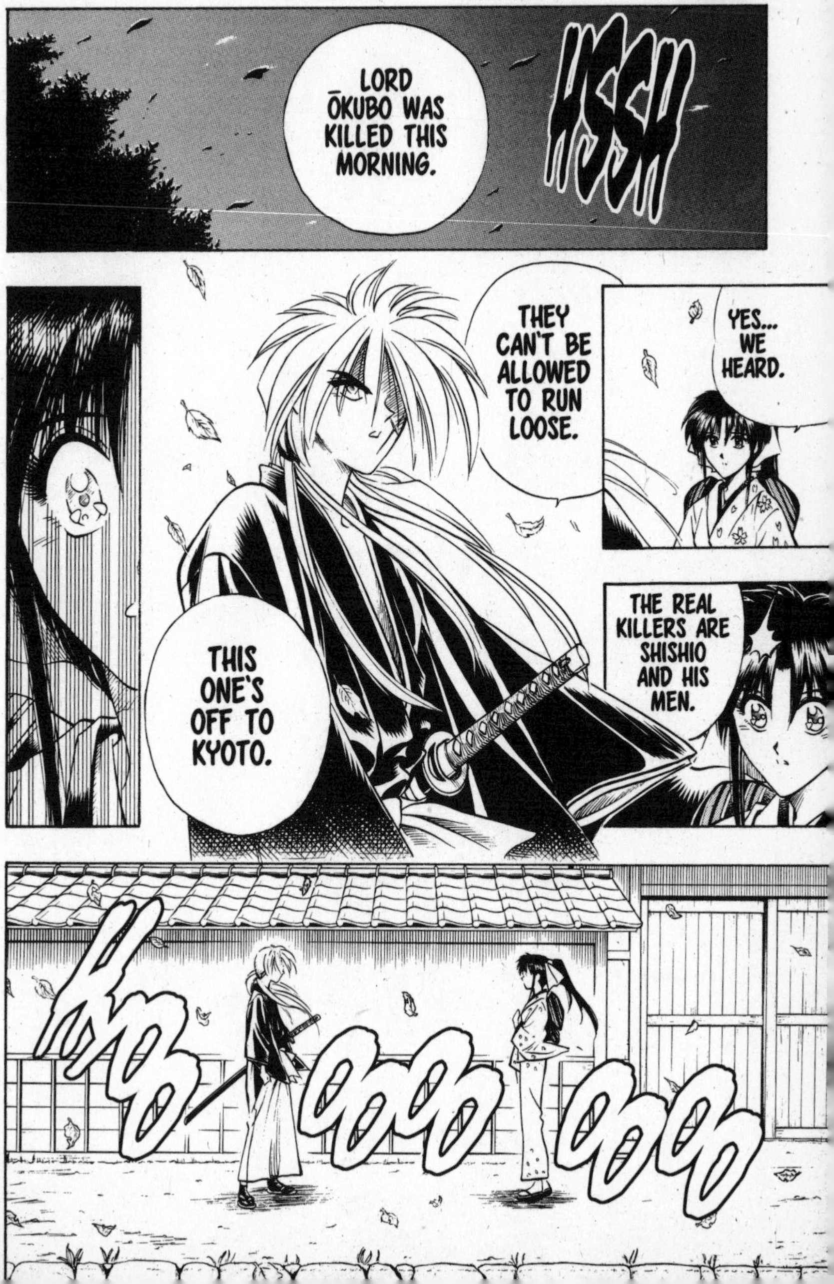
LORD ŌKUBO WAS KILLED THIS MORNING.
HSSH
YES... WE HEARD.
THE REAL KILLERS ARE SHISHIO AND HIS MEN.
THEY CAN'T BE ALLOWED TO RUN LOOSE.
THIS ONE'S OFF TO KYOTO.
HOOOOOOOOOOO

READ THIS WAY

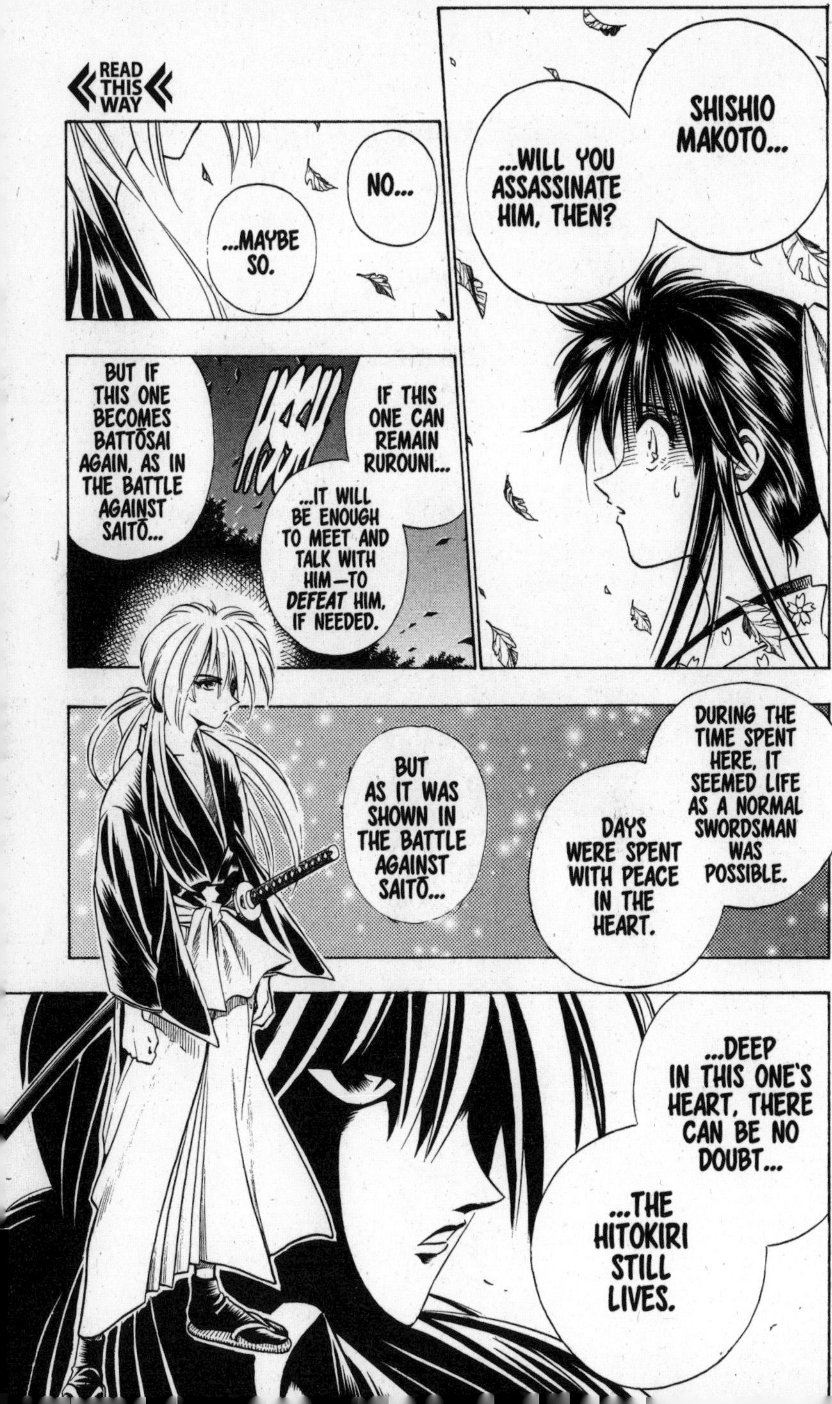
SHISHIO MAKOTO...
...WILL YOU ASSASSINATE HIM, THEN?
NO...
...MAYBE SO.
IF THIS ONE CAN REMAIN RUROUNI...
...IT WILL BE ENOUGH TO MEET AND TALK WITH HIM—TO *DEFEAT* HIM, IF NEEDED.
BUT IF THIS ONE BECOMES BATTŌSAI AGAIN, AS IN THE BATTLE AGAINST SAITŌ...
DURING THE TIME SPENT HERE, IT SEEMED LIFE AS A NORMAL SWORDSMAN WAS POSSIBLE.
DAYS WERE SPENT WITH PEACE IN THE HEART.
BUT AS IT WAS SHOWN IN THE BATTLE AGAINST SAITŌ...
...DEEP IN THIS ONE'S HEART, THERE CAN BE NO DOUBT...
...THE HITOKIRI STILL LIVES.

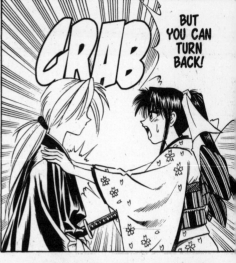

CRAB
BUT YOU CAN TURN BACK!
HOWEVER CLOSE YOU GET TO BATTŌSAI, KENSHIN IS STILL KENSHIN!
IT WAS THE SAME DURING THE TIME WITH JIN-E AND SAITŌ! YOU'LL BE FINE!
THIS IS DIFFERENT...
"WITH JIN-E, BATTŌSAI EMERGED FROM A DESIRE TO SAVE YOU, AND LEFT ONCE YOUR VOICE WAS HEARD.
AWNG
"BUT WITH SAITŌ, BATTŌSAI EMERGED JUST TO FIGHT *HIM*."
YOUR VOICE DIDN'T REACH.
SO, THIS IS DIFFERENT.

"TIME HAS BEGUN TO FLOW, ONCE MORE..."

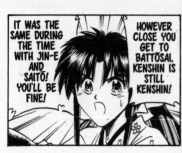

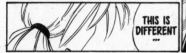

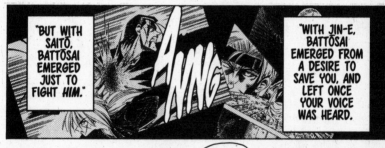

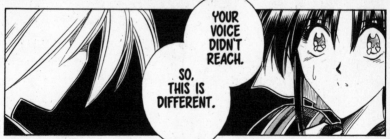

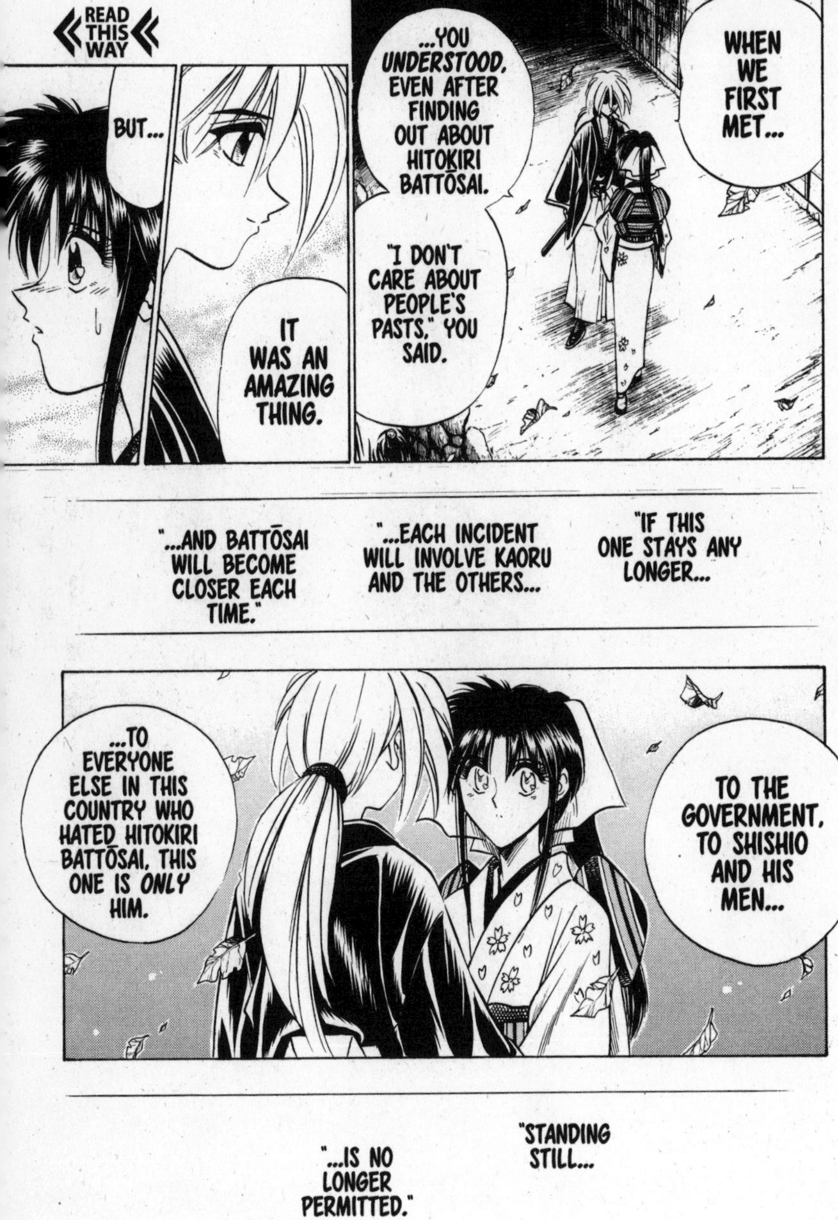
READ THIS WAY
WHEN WE FIRST MET...
...YOU UNDERSTOOD, EVEN AFTER FINDING OUT ABOUT HITOKIRI BATTŌSAI.
"I DON'T CARE ABOUT PEOPLE'S PASTS," YOU SAID.
IT WAS AN AMAZING THING.
BUT...
"IF THIS ONE STAYS ANY LONGER...
"...EACH INCIDENT WILL INVOLVE KAORU AND THE OTHERS...
"...AND BATTŌSAI WILL BECOME CLOSER EACH TIME."
TO THE GOVERNMENT, TO SHISHIO AND HIS MEN...
...TO EVERYONE ELSE IN THIS COUNTRY WHO HATED HITOKIRI BATTŌSAI, THIS ONE IS *ONLY* HIM.
"STANDING STILL...
"...IS NO LONGER PERMITTED."

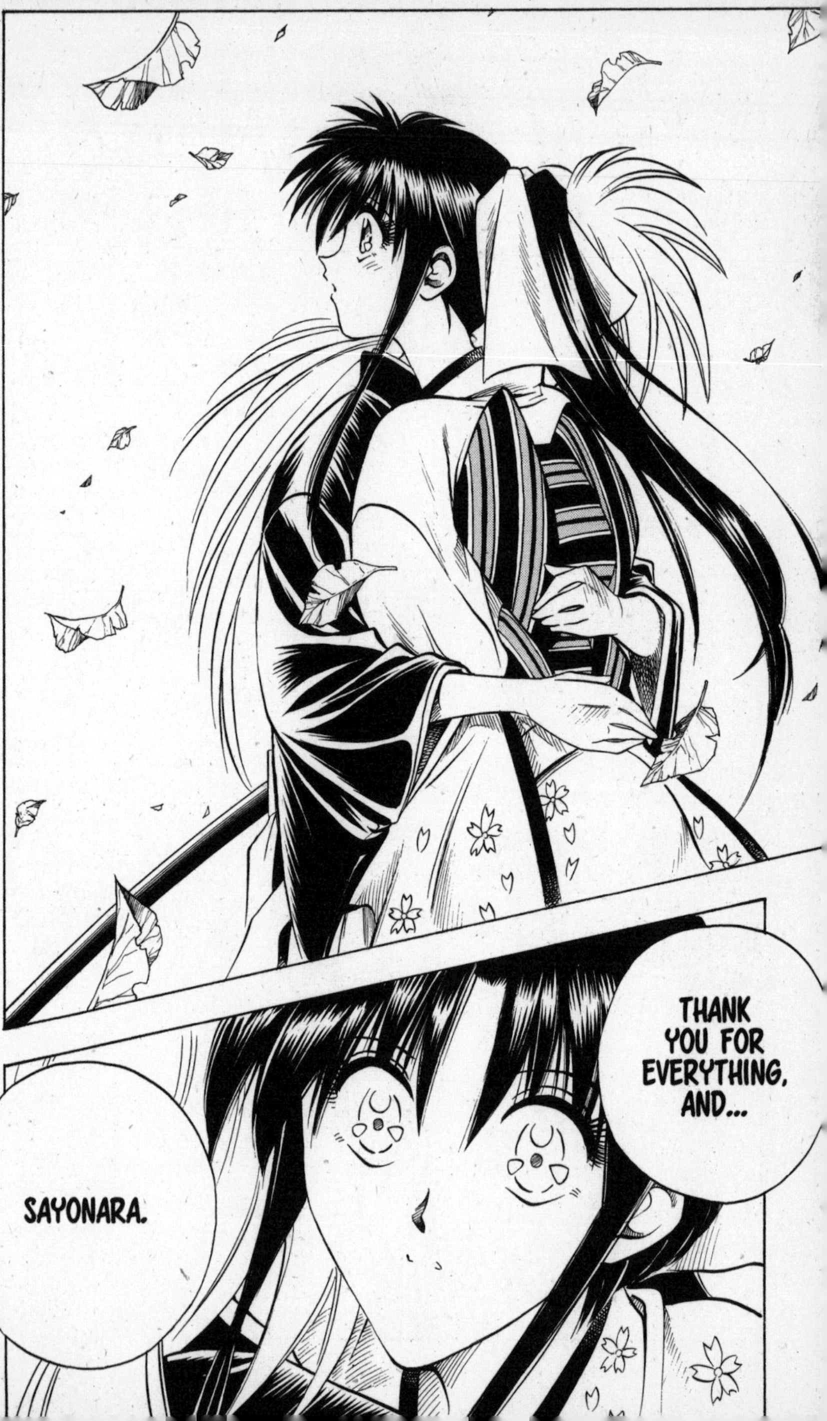
THANK YOU FOR EVERYTHING. AND...
SAYONARA.

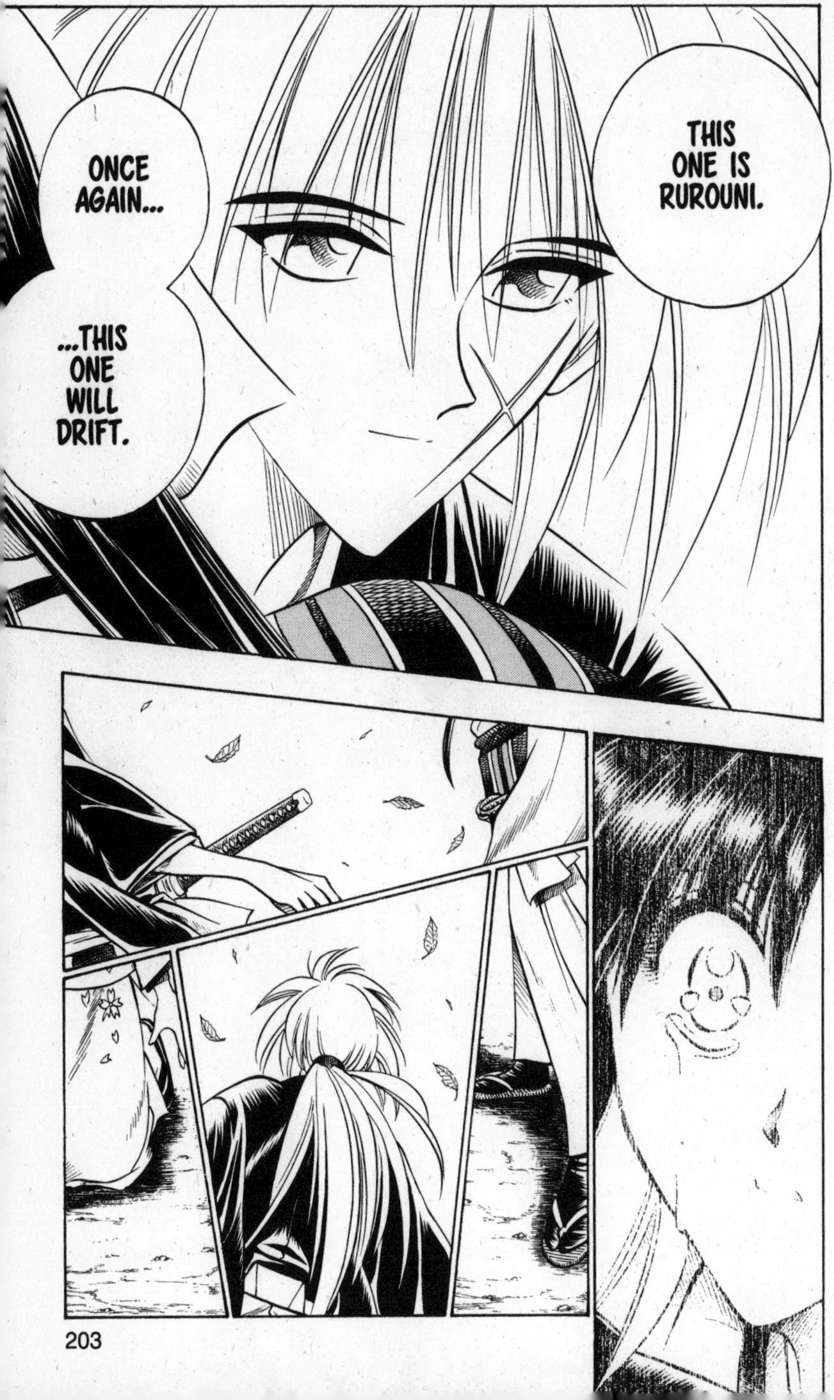
THIS ONE IS RUROUNI.
ONCE AGAIN...
...THIS ONE WILL DRIFT.

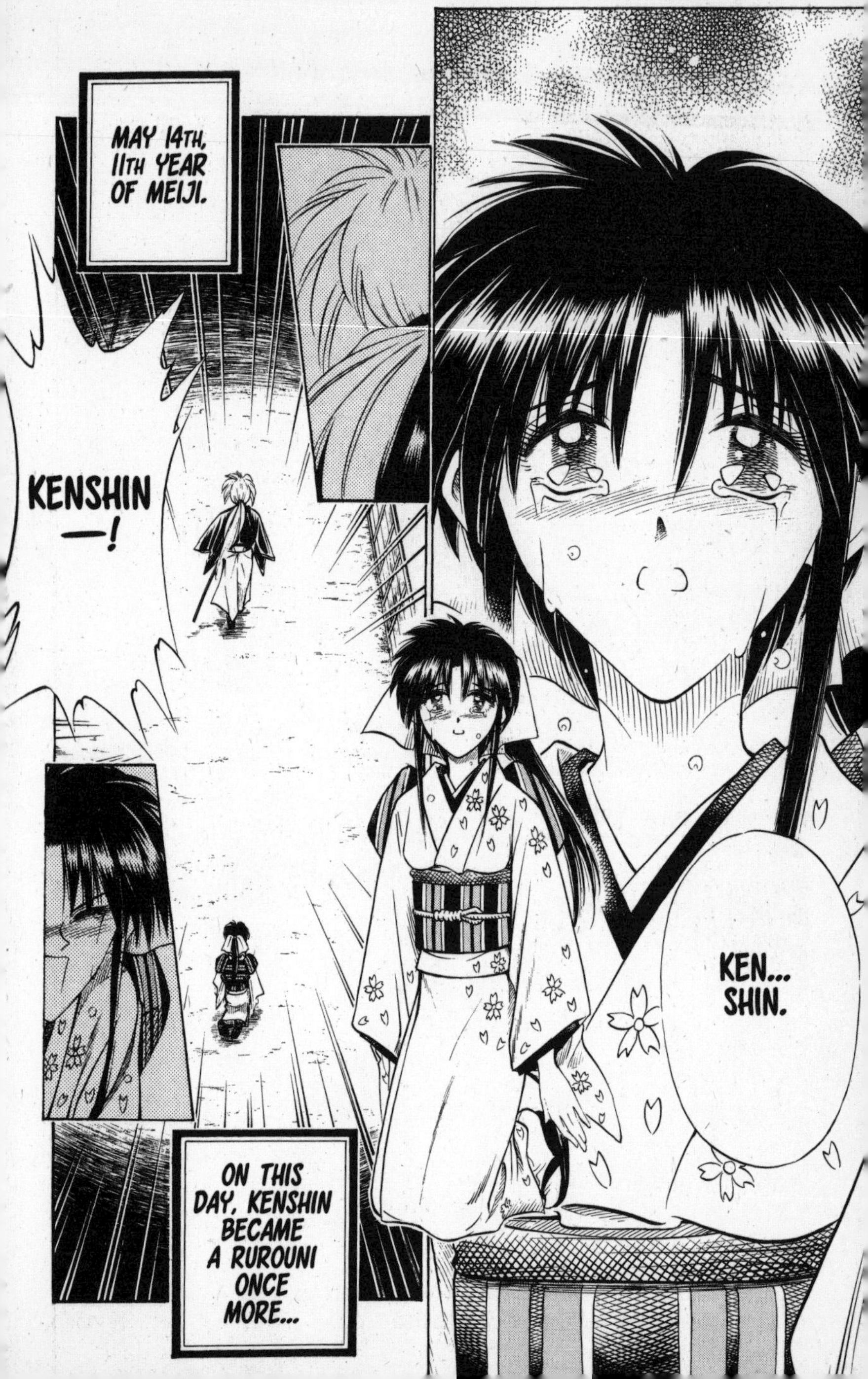
KEN... SHIN.
MAY 14TH, 11TH YEAR OF MEIJI.
KENSHIN—!
ON THIS DAY, KENSHIN BECAME A RUROUNI ONCE MORE...

READ THIS WAY

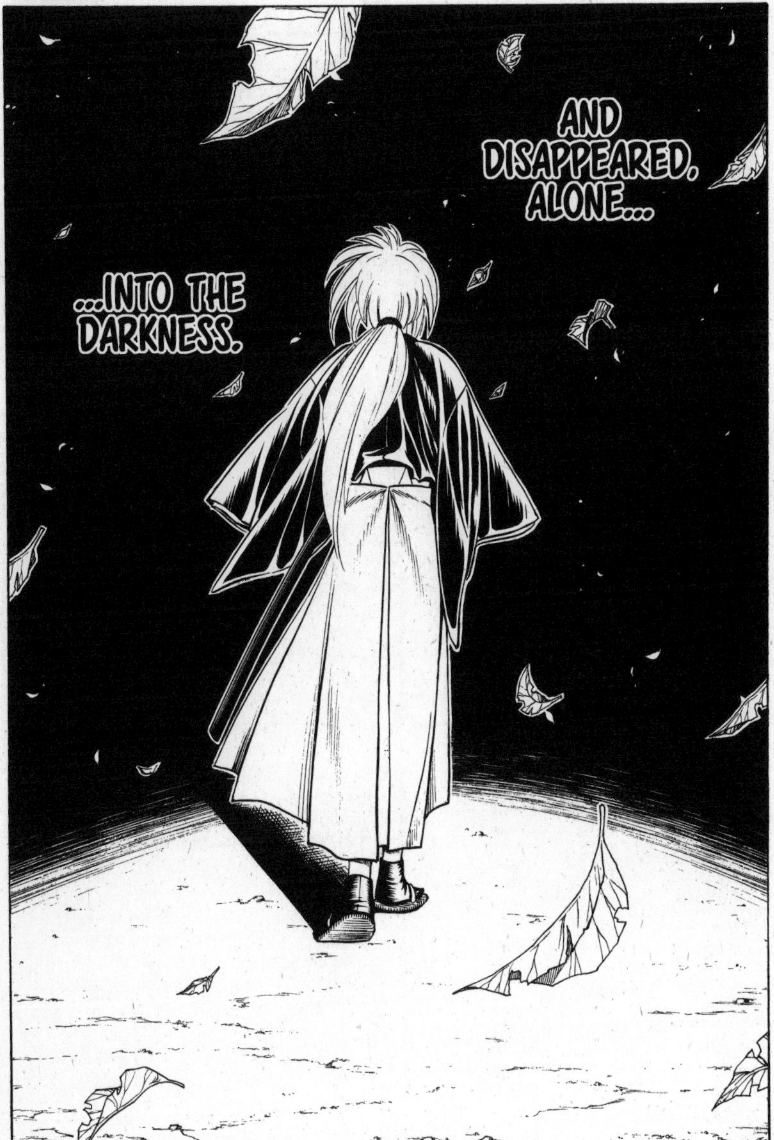
AND DISAPPEARED, ALONE...
...INTO THE DARKNESS.

 To be continued in Volume 8: On the East Sea Road

GLOSSARY of the RESTORATION

*A brief guide to select Japanese terms used in **Rurouni Kenshin**. Note that, both here and within the story itself, all names are Japanese style—i.e., last or "family" name first, with personal or "given" name following. This is both because **Kenshin** is a "period" story, as well as to decrease confusion—if we were to take the example of Kenshin's sakabatô and "reverse" the format of the historically established assassin-name "Hitokiri Battôsai," for example, it would make little sense to then call him "Battôsai Himura."*

Hirazuki
Said to be the original move upon which Saitô's *Gatotsu* is based, used mainly for thrusts, stabbing, and slashing downward.

Hiten Mitsurugi-ryû
Kenshin's sword technique, used more for defense than offense. An "ancient style that pits one against many," it requires exceptional speed and agility to master.

hitokiri
An assassin. Famous swordsmen of the period were sometimes thus known to adopt "professional" names—**Kawakami Gensai**, for example, was also known as "Hitokiri Gensai."

Ishin Shishi
Loyalist or pro-Imperialist *patriots* who fought to restore the Emperor to his ancient seat of power

Kamiya Kasshin-ryû
Sword-arts or *kenjutsu* school established by Kaoru's father, who rejected the ethics of *Satsujin-ken* for *Katsujin-ken*

katana
Traditional Japanese longsword (curved, single-edge, worn cutting-edge up) of the samurai. Used primarily for slashing; can be wielded either one- or two-handed.

Katsujin-ken
"Swords that give life"; the sword-arts style developed over ten years by Kaoru's father and founding principle of *Kamiya Kasshin-ryû*.

Bakumatsu
Final, chaotic days of the Tokugawa regime

-chan
Honorific. Can be used either as a diminutive (e.g., with a small child—"Little Hanako or Kentarô"), or with those who are grown, to indicate affection ("My dear...")

dojo
Martial arts training hall

-dono
Honorific. Even more respectful than *-san*; the effect in modern-day Japanese conversation would be along the lines of "Milord So-and-So." As used by Kenshin, it indicates both respect and humility.

Edo
Capital city of the *Tokugawa Bakufu*; renamed *Tokyo* ("Eastern Capital") after the Meiji Restoration

Gatotsu
The signature attack of Saitô Hajime, series creator Watsuki reportedly based his (fictional) version on an actual, historical, horizontal (or "flat") sword-technique.

Himura Battôsai
Swordsman of legendary skills and former assassin (*hitokiri*) of the *Ishin Shishi*

Himura Kenshin
Kenshin's "real" name, revealed to Kaoru only at her urging

Satsujin-ken
"Swords that give death"; a style of swordsmanship rejected by Kaoru's father

Shinsengumi
"True to the old ways and risking their lives to preserve the old shôgunate system," the popular view of the Shinsengumi ("newly elected group") was that of swordsmen as charismatic as they were skilled. Of note: Thanks to the popularity of the NHK drama of the same name, several historical sites in Japan are reportedly enjoying record attendance levels of late.

shôgun
Feudal military ruler of Japan

shôgunate
See *Tokugawa Bakufu*

soba
Noodles made usually of buckwheat, approximately as thick as spaghetti, served hot and/or cold. If there's a signifier, it's that their economy (simplicity) makes them a humble dish, eaten by humble folk (in the story, Saitô makes a point of mentioning that he's fond of them).

"Swift death to evil" (Aku • Soku • Zan)
Claimed within the story by Saitô to be a code of justice common not just to Shinsengumi, but also to hitokiri

Tokugawa Bakufu
Military feudal government which dominated Japan from 1603 to 1867

Tokyo
The renaming of "Edo" to "Tokyo" is a marker of the start of the Meiji Restoration

Kawakami Gensai
Real-life, historical inspiration for the character of *Himura Kenshin*

kenjutsu
The art of fencing; sword arts; kendô

-kun
Honorific. Used in the modern day among male students, or those who grew up together, but another usage—the one you're more likely to find in *Rurouni Kenshin*—is the "superior-to-inferior" form, intended as a way to emphasize a difference in status or rank, as well as to indicate familiarity or affection.

loyalists
Those who supported the return of the Emperor to power; *Ishin Shishi*

Meiji Restoration
1853-1868; culminated in the collapse of the *Tokugawa Bakufu* and the restoration of imperial rule. So called after Emperor Meiji, whose chosen name was written with the characters for "culture and enlightenment."

patriots
Another term for *Ishin Shishi*... and when used by Sano, not a flattering one

rurouni
Wanderer, vagabond

sakabatô
Reversed-edge sword (the dull edge on the side the sharp should be, and vice versa); carried by Kenshin as a symbol of his resolution never to kill again

-san
Honorific. Carries the meaning of "Mr.," "Ms.," "Miss," etc., but used more extensively in Japanese than its English equivalent (note that even an enemy may be addressed as "-san").

IN THE NEXT VOLUME...

Kyoto—once a paean to culture and enlightenment, now a scene of chaos and bloodshed. The shocking, midday murder of Department of Internal Affairs Chief Toshimichi Ôkubo a fait accompli, the obvious and inevitable can no longer be ignored or avoided, and Kenshin must leave Tokyo for Kyoto... against the wishes of everyone who knows him there as the gentle-eyed "*rurouni.*" Awaiting him is **Shishio Makoto**—burned over most of his body and quite insane—who replaced the cold-eyed assassin Himura Battôsai upon his forswearing of further killing and taking up of the reversed-blade *sakabatô*. But does Kenshin go to Kyoto for a duel... or for a death-match?!

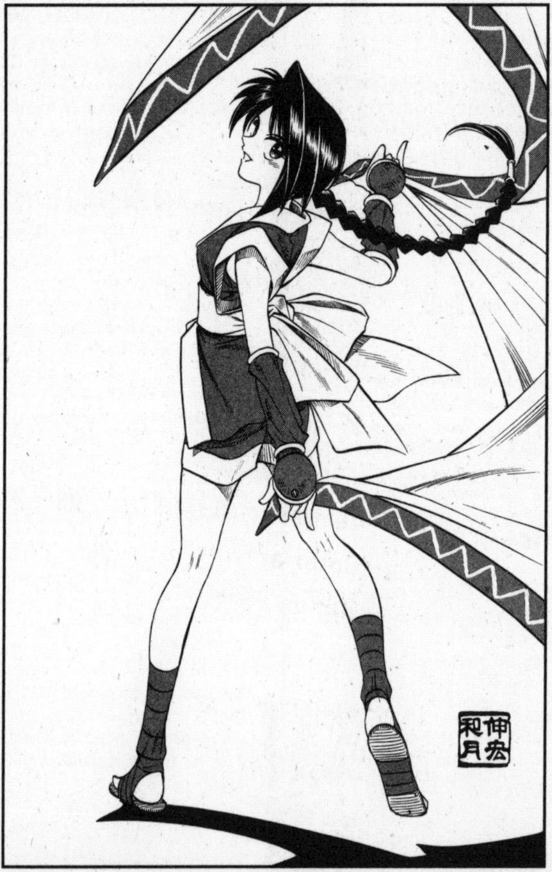
伸宏
和月

Available Now!

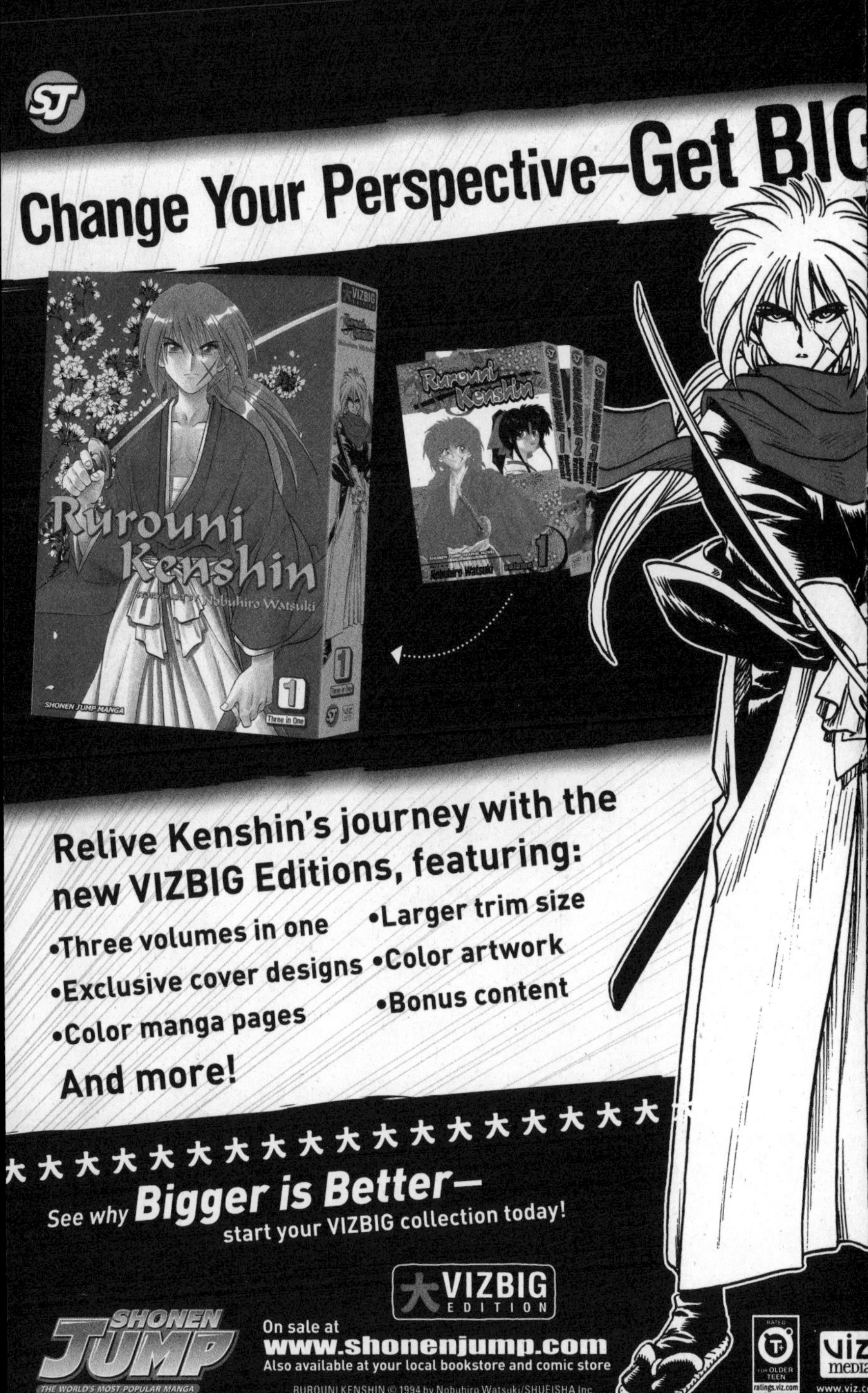
Change Your Perspective–Get BIG
Relive Kenshin's journey with the new VIZBIG Editions, featuring:
•Three volumes in one
•Larger trim size
•Exclusive cover designs
•Color artwork
•Color manga pages
•Bonus content
And more!
See why Bigger is Better— start your VIZBIG collection today!
VIZBIG EDITION
SHONEN JUMP
THE WORLD'S MOST POPULAR MANGA
On sale at
www.shonenjump.com
Also available at your local bookstore and comic store
RUROUNI KENSHIN © 1994 by Nobuhiro Watsuki/SHUEISHA Inc.
RATED T+ FOR OLDER TEEN
ratings.viz.com

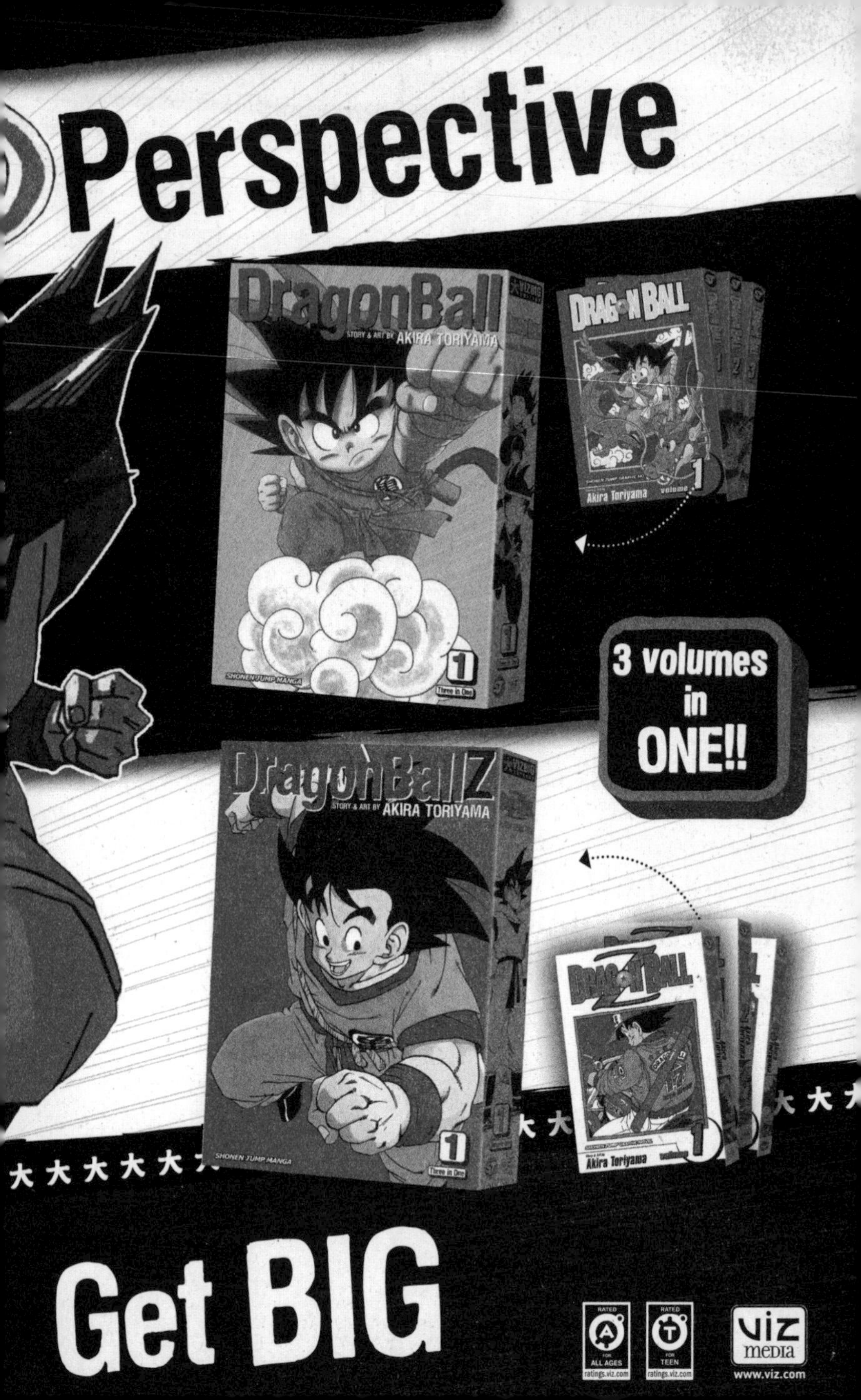
Perspective
DragonBall
STORY & ART BY AKIRA TORIYAMA
SHONEN JUMP MANGA
1
Three in One
DRAGON BALL
Akira Toriyama
volume 1
3 volumes in ONE!!
DragonBall Z
STORY & ART BY AKIRA TORIYAMA
SHONEN JUMP MANGA
1
Three in One
DRAGON BALL Z
Akira Toriyama
Get BIG
RATED A FOR ALL AGES ratings.viz.com
RATED T FOR TEEN ratings.viz.com
VIZ media
www.viz.com

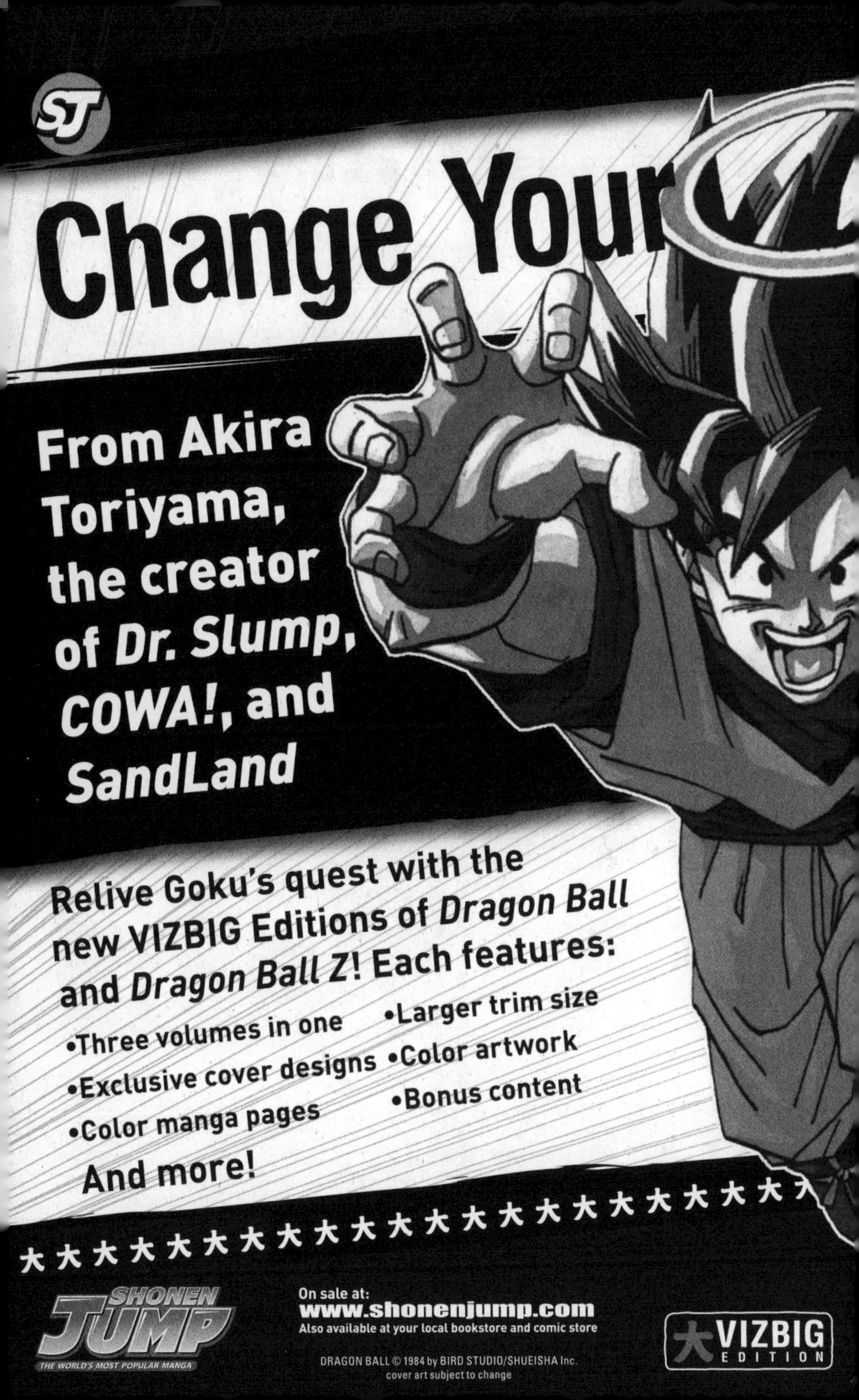
SJ
Change Your
From Akira Toriyama, the creator of *Dr. Slump*, *COWA!*, and *SandLand*
Relive Goku's quest with the new VIZBIG Editions of *Dragon Ball* and *Dragon Ball Z*! Each features:
•Three volumes in one
•Larger trim size
•Exclusive cover designs
•Color artwork
•Color manga pages
•Bonus content
And more!
SHONEN JUMP
THE WORLD'S MOST POPULAR MANGA
On sale at:
www.shonenjump.com
Also available at your local bookstore and comic store
VIZBIG EDITION
DRAGON BALL © 1984 by BIRD STUDIO/SHUEISHA Inc.
cover art subject to change

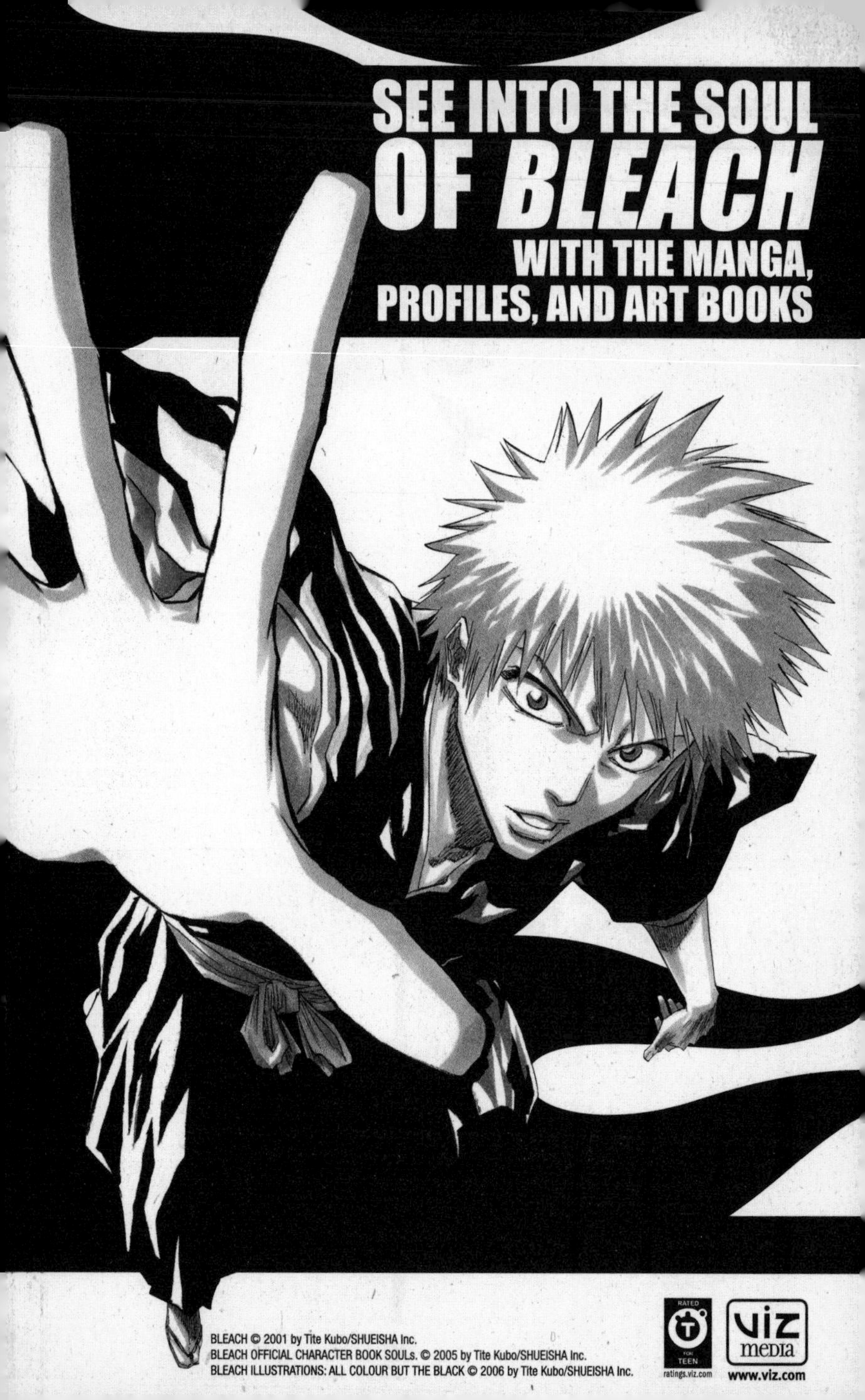
SEE INTO THE SOUL
OF *BLEACH*
WITH THE MANGA,
PROFILES, AND ART BOOKS
RATED T FOR TEEN
ratings.viz.com
viz media
www.viz.com
BLEACH © 2001 by Tite Kubo/SHUEISHA Inc.
BLEACH OFFICIAL CHARACTER BOOK SOULs. © 2005 by Tite Kubo/SHUEISHA Inc.
BLEACH ILLUSTRATIONS: ALL COLOUR BUT THE BLACK © 2006 by Tite Kubo/SHUEISHA Inc.